ROOT OF BITTERNESS

ROOT OF BITTERNESS

Documents of the Social History of American Women

Edited, with an introduction
and a new foreword, by Nancy F. Cott

Northeastern University Press • *Boston*

Northeastern University Press edition 1986
Copyright © 1972 by Nancy F. Cott
Reprinted 1986 by permission of Nancy F. Cott

Library of Congress Cataloging in Publication Data
Root of bitterness.

  Originally published: New York : Dutton, c1972.
  Bibliography: p.
  1. Women—United States—History—Sources.
2. Women—United States—Social conditions—Sources.
I. Cott, Nancy F.
HQ1410.C68   1986   305.4'0973   86-12628
ISBN 1-55553-002-8 (alk. paper)
ISBN 0-930350-95-2 (pbk. : alk paper)

Printed and bound by Edwards Brothers, Inc., Ann Arbor, Michigan. The paper is Glatfelter Offset, an acid-free sheet.

MANUFACTURED IN THE UNITED STATES OF AMERICA
91 90   5   4   3

That there is a root of bitterness continually springing up
in families and troubling the repose of both men and women,
must be manifest to even a superficial observer, and I believe
it is the mistaken notion of the inequality of the sexes.

—Sarah Grimké,
*Letters on the Equality of the Sexes and
the Condition of Women*, 1838.

Acknowledgments

Without the resources of the Arthur and Elizabeth Schlesinger Library on the History of Women in America (at Radcliffe College), and the support of the Library's staff, my work of selection for this volume would have been much more laborious. I am particularly grateful to Jeannette Cheek, the Director, to Barbara Haber, Librarian, and to Diane Dorsey, Archivist, for their consistent amiability and helpfulness as I mined the Library's holdings for the majority of the documents collected here.

I also wish to express my thanks to John Demos, for his encouragement and advice in all phases of this project; to Doug Jones and Elizabeth Pleck for their comments on my introduction; and to Anita Rutman for her permission to use her typescript of the trial of Mistress Hibbens. I am no less indebted to my students at Wheaton College, who got excited about women's history.

Contents

Foreword to the 1986 Edition

I began to select and arrange these documents in 1970 and 1971, to use in teaching women's history to college undergraduates. At the time, I admit, I distrusted most available accounts of women's lives in history books. Those did not adequately convey to me the richness and variety and change that I was sure inhered in women's social experience and consciousness over time. Most of the existing scholarship on women's history with which I was familiar seemed faulty in one way or another: too narrowly conceived, or merely antiquarian, or too exclusively focused on exceptional women, or far too redolent of conventional stereotypes of women; too dismissive of women's range, or even too celebratory of women's traditional virtues—all in all, too wedded to an outlook in which the male was the norm, the female another and lesser case. Flush with the energies of the women's movement and the aim to resurrect women's history, I probably too cavalierly dismissed the efforts of previous historians, on which young scholars and activists had to build. The same motivation, however, led me to research documents of women's lives in the past. Rather than present students with inadequate historical treatments I resorted to women's own words and words addressed to them, for use as texts.

Root of Bitterness itself has become a historical document of sorts, indicative of a certain time and intent in the generation of the "new women's history." The assumption in the Introduction that women share a "general condition," the emphases on sex roles, socialization, consciousness and self-consciousness, and the subtextual positing of woman's individuality against the mold of family demands and sexual ideology—all these bear the earmarks of the intellectual tide of 1970 and 1971. In those years major texts by radical and socialist feminists, including Kate Millett's *Sexual Politics*, Juliet Mitchell's *Woman's Estate*, Jill Johnston's *Lesbian Nation*, Robin Morgan's *Sisterhood is Powerful*, Shulamith Firestone's *The Dialectic of Sex*, and Germaine Greer's *The Female Eunuch*, were published. I spoke of "differentiated women" and "women's group consciousness as a subculture uniquely divided against itself by ties to the dominant culture" in 1971, but I would now feel compelled to stress more systematically the ways in which women's putative solidarity fragments not only because of women's socialization in a system of gender hierarchy and individual women's ties to individual men, but also because of our willed and unwilled rootedness in specific kin, culture, and community in which gender identity is realized. In the Introduction, the historical formation of gender identity by the impress of region and class and economic structure is recognized, though not sufficiently to highlight how far the "general condition" of women is inferred there from the condition of women who were white, Protestant, middle-class or upper middle-class, and urban. The theme absent in the Introduction (though subversively present in the documents) is that of conflict among women themselves—among subgroups of women—complicating their sharing in a "general condition." Such conflicts of interest and identity are evident, for instance, between enslaved black women and free white women of the planter class, between domestic servants and their mistresses, between industrial wage-earners and "respectable ladies."

The growth in the "new women's history" in the fifteen years since I planned *Root of Bitterness* surely proves that although the past cannot change, the telling of history can and does. This is a new era in women's history. Rediscovery and analysis of women's past have taken root and sprouted in schools and colleges, community organizations and women's centers, museums and historical societies. Academic enterprise has nourished a vigorous growth of books and articles, bringing to light diverse women of every region, race, class, and age. We are still far from the day when changes in housework patterns, or availability of birth control methods, may be taken as epochal markers as wars or rulers' reigns have been; yet it can truthfully be said that inclusion of women's lives and points of view in what is seen as constituting the past has made a quantum leap from the state of things fifteen years ago. An updated "Suggestions for Further Reading," reflecting the current state of the historical literature, has been appended to this volume.

This growth in the writing of the new women's history, marvelous as it is, cannot replace the appeal or immediacy of documentary sources as an introduction to—or confrontation with—women's historical experiences. What we gain in breadth, in measured judgment, and in efficacy from a good historian's treatment that takes into consideration many and diverse sources, we may nonetheless sacrifice in telling detail and emotional specificity: that is one of the ironies of the historian's craft. To admit the particular superiority of historical quality in documentary sources does not of course answer the question—*which* documentary sources? *Root of Bitterness* originally proposed to be "demonstrative, if not representative," while surveying several centuries, and that intent holds. Encouraging the modern reader to hold intimate conversation with voices from women's past, the selections herein have lost none of their power to reveal and astonish; retaining their own integrity, the documents provide the field for modern interpretation and reinterpretation.

April 1986   N.F.C.

ROOT OF BITTERNESS

Introduction

This volume is an invitation to examine the range and depth of American women's past experience. In materials written, spoken, or read by women, the collection brings together a variety of particular instances and particular individuals in order to clarify women's general condition. It proposes to be demonstrative, if not representative; and by using primary-source documents, to emphasize the interaction of personal lives with cultural norms. Although conventional myths, expectations, and prescriptions for women are being increasingly exposed, we need to look further to comprehend women's private experience, and the self-image created by that experience. The choice of documents in this collection has been in response to the general questions: What roles have women been compelled to take, and which ones have they chosen? How have they seen their circumstances and opportunities? How have they operated within the constraints placed upon them? Historical scrutiny of women not only as they act out their roles, but as they name them and reconsider them, leads to some understanding of women's consciousness and self-image. This perspective does not produce a history of the feminist movement, though the documents contain some feminist arguments and support feminist interpretation; it does not produce a history of women's progress through institutional barriers, though it views women in the context of institutions.[1] The documents here (if a single character can be given them) deal with the consciousness and self-consciousness of American women.

Women in America have been united by their common assigned interests—caring for men and children—and divided by those same interests, because of the insularity of the private home. We can view women's group consciousness as a subculture uniquely divided against itself by ties to the dominant culture. While the ties to the dominant culture are the informing and restricting ones, they provoke within the

[1] For other collections of documents, see Aileen Kraditor (ed.), *Up from the Pedestal* (Chicago: Quadrangle Books, 1968), which details the thought of the women's rights movement, and William O'Neill, *The Woman Movement* (London: George Allen & Unwin, 1969), which includes documents on the suffrage movement and "social feminism."

subculture certain strengths as well as weaknesses, enduring values as well as accommodation. By evading the abstract "woman," and looking at particular women as members of a group of differentiated women, we are more likely to discover the substance of this subculture, and its change over time. We may also avoid historical tokenism—acceptance of past tokens as past reality.

Studying women's history makes the complex interdependence between historical continuity and change readily apparent; for example, during periods of economic or political change women's status in a particular social group may be a constant, or, some aspects of women's condition may be made to seem eternal while others undergo rapid alteration. The examination of women's experience over more than two centuries in America forces the question of how sex-stereotyped roles interact with social change. Factors that induce social change—such as industrialization, urbanization, new forms of politics, increased wealth or productivity—can also effect changes in sex roles. We note observable change in sex roles as an index of social change. Yet little historical data have been turned to expose the varying and reciprocal relations of material change to changes or persistences in the ascribed functions, values, and self-definition of American women.[2] Because the family is the major vehicle of socialization, and since the "domestic sphere" has defined the activities of most American women in the past, any study of women's history will be at least in part a study of family life and of the functions the family performs internally (for its members) and externally (in the larger social grouping). These questions about family life, sex roles, and social change need to be asked, not only to reveal the specific experience of women in America, but to elucidate American social history. Without understanding the half of society that women comprise, without cognizance of women's modes of participation in and contribution to the social order, our view of history is partial—that is, both fragmentary and tendentious.

The raw materials of a social history which would incorporate the experience and consciousness of women include not only women's

---

[2] For an excellent review of the historiography on American women, and projection of the direction further work in American women's history should take, see Mari Jo Buhle, Anne G. Gordon, and Nancy Schrom, "Women in American Society: An Historical Contribution," *Radical America,* V:4 (July–August, 1971).

autobiographical narratives, diaries, and letters, but also court transcripts, industrial and institutional reports, purposive tracts, sermons, stories, genealogies, domestic artifacts, and vital statistics. This volume contains some of these materials, demonstrating aspects and qualities of women's circumstances. Characterizing these documents as exemplary or typical would understate the range and intensity of centuries of women's experience. Each document has an integrity, and each should provide ground for probing some of the larger questions in smaller compass. Some of the documents might be called informers of consciousness: prescriptive voices such as those of the Puritan elders or the nineteenth-century gynecological advisors. The larger number are reflections of consciousness: women writing or talking about their expectations, their work, their roles. Whether individual women associate their destinies or complaints with their sex roles, or rather with their economic condition, race, or state of soul, prompts immediate inquiry and provides the first basis for interpretation.

To these documents we can address some specific questions about American women—not only about women's role in family life, but about women's part in the transmission of culture, about the relation of women's domestic work to the capitalist economy, about distinctions of age, marital status, class, and race among women. Women have been compelled to be subordinate to men throughout American history, but this constancy should not blind us to the shifting formulations of this secondary status. The internal modulations, additions and subtractions that definitions of "woman" have undergone describe significant currents in American society. When women's past is incoherent, women's nature and women's roles seem synonymous; this not only identifies "woman's place," but makes it timeless. Instead, past perceptions of women's capabilities and deficiencies should be understood as related to the demands of particular historical periods.

I. THE EARLY COLONIAL MILIEU:
GOODWIVES, SHREWS, AND WITCHES

The history of the early colonial period lets us view women in America in a preindustrial society, a society primarily English in its customs, but affected in vital ways by the shock of entry into a wilderness. Any attempt to deal with this period as the beginnings of "American" history should be prefaced with a caveat—to avoid gratuitously reading back into seventeenth-century history the seeds of late eighteenth- or nineteenth-century phenomena. The colonists of the seventeenth century must be approached on their own terms, which derived from the past and were conditioned by their struggling present, but were far from projecting to a future United States of America.

To approach the seventeenth-century colonists on their own terms means to recognize the primacy of religious awareness in their lives—in Virginia as well as New England, although the government in New England gave more weight to religious conformity. If on the one hand seventeenth-century Protestant religion gave women the benefit of having immortal souls as precious as those of men, on the other hand it also enforced biblical (particularly Pauline) injunctions that wives must be subject to husbands. The question in practice was which one of these emphases shaped women's lives more thoroughly. It seems particularly useful to apply this query to New England, where Puritan religious tenets gave the condition of the soul higher priority than earthly loyalties, and where the establishment of *families* was a more distinct premise of colonial settlement than in Virginia. Personal and court records, sermons and speeches from New England give the impression that Puritan ideology respected women's immortal spirits; yet it failed to be "no respecter of persons" as true Christianity, following God's example, would demand. That women's souls were capable of being chosen by God, and their earthly roles were necessary to a community of saints, did not diminish the assumption that they were secondary. And yet, the necessary and good aspect of women's creation—necessary not just for convenience, but in God's plan—gave their position a substantial strength.

Besides the religious integrity that women were able to preserve as souls in God's sight, preindustrial society allotted positive work roles to women. In a farming economy in which the family, rather than the individual, was the functioning unit—and in which the home (farm) was the place of work—both women's and men's tasks were seen as complementary parts of one whole. Women's accomplishments in domestic crafts commanded the esteem that was due to all necessary functions. Those nonagricultural, nondomestic occupations (such as trades, shopkeeping, innkeeping), which were part of town life, were also frequently carried on by the members of a family working together. A woman's participation in agricultural, commercial, or mercantile pursuits while part of a family could become her own endeavor, if she were widowed. Most often, however, the lone woman's commercial occupations were those that related to women's traditional domestic or nurturing functions. More widows appeared operating taverns to dispense victuals and drink than running shipyards. The healing arts and the practice of midwifery were also in women's province. (The good repute that Ann Hutchinson's skills in medicine and midwifery established for her, it is evident, played a part in her ability to acquire a ready following for her theological opinions.)

The *fact* of women's activities often superseded their theoretical station. Though women were "dead in law" and were denied the ability to make contracts alone, the importance of property transactions in marriage, remarriage, bequests, and wills resulted in women's making prenuptial contracts, acting as executrixes of husbands' estates, bargaining for remarriage on the basis of property holdings. In a property-conscious society, which the colonial communities certainly were, a woman's power over property was at least as compelling as the possibility of her soul's election to grace.

The very centrality of women's activities in community life in seventeenth-century America did not prevent—in fact may have promoted—men's psychological objectification of women's "otherness," in Simone de Beauvoir's usage. The cast of mind of the New England Puritan was closer to the medieval than to the modern, and in that medieval cast the potential of women to appear evil, shrewish, treacherous, or witchlike was latent. New England children began to learn their ABCs with "In Adam's Fall, We Sinned All," and the supposed treachery of Eve, in Adam's sin, was never far from mind. The Old and New Testaments supplied a variety of female models—sufficient to fuel debates with chapter, verse, and interpretation to support opposing contentions—but the strong female character was usually dangerous as well. In the early colonial settlements women were needed to be strong, but feared to be dangerous. It is worth noting that when sociologist Kai Erikson sought to apply the theoretical apparatus of the sociology of deviance historically, to seventeenth-century Puritan New England, the three episodes of "deviant" behavior that impressed him all derived from the activities of women: the Antinomian crisis surrounding Ann

Hutchinson; the scare set off by the appearance of Quaker women; and the witch trials at Salem.[3]

The seventeenth-century documents which are included here present evidence from extraordinary rather than ordinary events. Church examinations such as those of Ann Hibbens and Ann Hutchinson, or the process and accusation of witchcraft, were not common occurrences (though the other court transactions were). New England is over-represented in comparison to the southern Colonies, because of the availability of documents. The justification for using these extraordinary documents is that they are extraordinarily interesting, and reveal by inference the attitudes, anxieties, and expectations that shaped day-to-day life for ordinary women. Clergymen's questioning, testimony from men in the community, women's replies, unroll before us the literal give-and-take between men and women in the society formed by English colonial settlement. Any conclusions about women's status or roles in the preindustrial Protestant communities of early America must, then, take this kind of evidence into account.

II. AN ACHIEVING SOCIETY: THE EIGHTEENTH CENTURY

The eighteenth century in America encompassed a great variety of life-styles. While some Colonies were just being founded, their first inhabitants settling raw land, in other areas English society was a century old. The experience of founding a community was being repeated again and again, farther south, north, and west, the parceling out of new land to new settlers being accomplished—while in cities such as Boston and Philadelphia a polite society was developing, whose arbiters' tastes were decided by English or European culture rather than by the struggle against a wilderness. Besides the divergent experience offered by different parts of the American continent at any one time (a phenomenon that continues through American history), the advances in scientific knowledge, technology, communications, and political organization of the eighteenth century make its end notably different from its beginning. Thus women's experience in America in "the eighteenth century" is an area too broad to admit of more than a sampling here. The documents collected in this section can only suggest some

[3] Kai Erikson, *Wayward Puritans* (New York: Wiley Press, 1966).

varieties of female experience, and leading tendencies in the development from the initial colonial setting.

The secularization of life during the eighteenth century implied a reliance on other than strictly religious norms for female behavior. Searching out the attitudes which shaped women's consciousness, one must acknowledge the extent to which the American Colonies were part of a transatlantic culture. For those in the seaboard centers of population, the source of books and higher education was England. American printing of books did not begin to compete with importation of British books until after the Revolution. In the southern Colonies in particular, the wealthy inhabitants looked to British models of female decorum. An example of the means of transmission of guiding precepts is the little volume called The Lady's New Year's Gift, or *Advice to a Daughter*, excerpts of which are included here. Written in 1688 by George Savile, 1st Marquis of Halifax, it had run through fifteen editions in England by 1765. As it was frequently advertised in colonial newspapers, and recommended as indispensable for ladies' libraries, its audience among literate upper-class women was apparently assured.[4] The repute of such books indicates how early women's "proper" duties and obligations were considered, by the upper class, a matter for appraisal by men and attention by women.

In newspaper articles, cartoons, and pamphlets in the second half of the eighteenth century, the subject of women's proper roles was one of great interest. A process of schematic, secular definition of woman's nature and capacities was taking place. The main subjects and audience of this definition were women who were removed from the exigencies of farm or frontier life, in whose society servants performed the manual labor and men carried on the business. Eliza Southgate, the young American girl whose letters from the very end of the eighteenth century appear in this section, had the time, interest, and education to consider women's place abstractly. Earlier formulations of appropriate female conduct (such as the one by George Savile) underlay her assessment of herself and her defense of her integrity, but she had read a

[4] On the circulation of British books of female decorum among southern colonial women, see Julia Spruill, *Women's Life and Work in the Southern Colonies* (Chapel Hill, N.C.: University of North Carolina Press, 1938), pp. 215–216.

more recent importation from England—Mary Wollstonecraft's *Vindication of the Rights of Women* (1792), the first feminist document to have an important effect on women in America. Although unable to support the whole of Wollstonecraft's position, Eliza Southgate voiced a contemporary restiveness about the attribution of sex roles. Comparable opportunities probably occurred in the lives of Ann Warder and Sally Wister, though their documents show no comparable discontent. The widening distance between social classes in eighteenth-century America, the increasing range of social and economic inequality, appears in the imposition of requirements on this "privileged" class of women that were quite divergent from the determinants of the lives of the servant Elizabeth Sprigs, or the religious teacher Sarah Osborn.

The image of the ideal woman adapted as wealth and influence became concentrated in the upper classes in eastern cities. In a society whose prototype was Benjamin Franklin—in his character as the enterprising young man on the make—the desirable role for women became an enhancing, rather than a sustaining one. One element in the process of emergence of a ladylike ideal was the appearance and advocacy of education for women. The proper lady would be educated, in order to carry on conversation to charm a beau, to reflect creditably on her father or husband, to act as a profitable mentor to her children. Her assets were decorative and supportive ones: preserving a cultivated gentility and a respectable piety, making her company and her home a place of refreshment and harmony. As Eliza Southgate rather unconvincingly argued, an educated woman should be more intelligently aware of her "place." Ladies were allotted matters of "taste," "delicacy," "sentiment"— a division of emotional response furthered by the idealization in literature of the chaste, demure, innocent maiden. American acceptance of this sentimental theme in the new form of the novel was signified in the popularity of one of the first, and longest-lasting, best sellers, Susanna Rowson's *Charlotte Temple*. Aside from influencing female audiences with her novels, Mrs. Rowson also educated young girls, and among the pupils in her school in Medford, Massachusetts, in the 1790s was Eliza Southgate. An appropriate sphere of conduct for women was thus cultivated, by education and example, among the upper classes in eighteenth-century cities—although its most inclusive elaboration, and most vigorous defense, did not appear until the middle decades of the nineteenth century.

III. THE CULT OF DOMESTICITY VERSUS SOCIAL CHANGE

To all appearances, the first half of the nineteenth century saw the emergence of an American "cult" whose goddess was the woman at her household hearth. "The cult of true womanhood," as Barbara Welter has described it from the evidence of ladies' magazines, dictated the ideal feminine characteristics as piety, purity, submissiveness, and domesticity.[5] In sermons, prescriptive etiquette books, child-rearing manuals, and domestic novels, as well as in ladies' magazines, this stereotype was widely propounded to the reading public. Although delineation of a lady's decorous conduct, incorporating the sentimental ideal of the inspiring, chaste maiden, had influence in the late eighteenth century, the "cult" of true womanhood in the nineteenth century was a much more inclusive ideology with wider effect. The expansion of American printing and advances in transportation, as well as the actual movement of population westward, meant that an ideal propagated in eastern cities had its impact in rural towns and pioneer settlements as well.

The cult of true womanhood had such wide range and effect because it concerned not only women's ideal characteristics but also the nature and functions of family life. Its focus of attention was not the virtuous maid versus the false coquette (a favorite theme of the eighteenth century), but the virtuous wife and mother, whose role had everything to do with harmony in the home. What was, in the eighteenth century, called the "sphere" of women's proper conduct—i.e., admissible behavior—developed in the early nineteenth century the fuller meaning of the "domestic sphere" as woman's proper realm.

Concern about stabilizing the "domestic sphere" was only one evidence that the demands on the family were changing. In cities and towns the unity of workplace with home, which existed on the farm or in colonial crafts and trades, dissolved; getting "a living" meant becoming part of an exclusively money economy. A much wider range of choice and concomitant uncertainty appeared with the growth of urban populations, new technological processes, more accessible national communication and transportation networks, and the beginning

[5] Barbara Welter, "The Cult of True Womanhood, 1820–1860," *American Quarterly*, XVIII (1966), 151–174.

of industrial production of essential commodities. (And always, the underlying choice existed to forgo the city, to move west, to try one's hand in a boom town, or stake out new land.) This wide range of choice was implicitly open to males only, because the female role in supporting expansive entrepreneurship was to be displayed at home. The family, losing its functions as an economic unit, had severed many of the links which opened the home to the community; home and family became increasingly self-contained, the refuge where the lone battler for economic advancement could find serenity and inspiration.

The wife's role in the home—not only maintaining her own virtue and gentility, but insuring her husband's comfort and her children's decency—became a crucial part of the rhetoric that championed the economic adventurer at the same time that it demanded social stability. Woman's stationary "place" supplied an element of anticompetitiveness and fixed morality, relieving the opportunism, greed, uncertainty, and impersonality that marked the dark side of the coin of Jacksonian "individualism." Under woman's reigning presence, the domestic realm was made the source of personal virtue and social adjustment, the preserve of Christian morality. "The Home," and the beatific rituals and emotions supposed to take place within it, attracted an almost fetishistic concern. Shedding the functions that it performed as a unit in the community, the family was the more staunchly cultivated for the functions it was to perform internally, for its members. For many women, including opinion-makers such as Sarah J. Hale and Catharine Beecher, this restructured understanding of the family provided a positive concept of womanhood, and a means of elaborating woman's responsibility to society without diverging from her "sphere." Woman's thorough fulfillment of her responsibility to the members of her family —imbuing them with her own morality, self-sacrifice, and Christian love—became her contribution to society. This formulation so often had a defensive cast because it reflected anxieties about the family's capacity to assure social adjustment, about the aims of child-rearing in a world of variable norms, and about the lure of new possibilities that would draw women, like men before them, out of the home to new places of work.

The era in which "home" and woman's place in it were most loudly championed also saw the first large-scale use of female labor in the American factory—more than an ironic coincidence. As Gerda Lerner has pointed out in her article on "The Lady and the Mill-girl," in this period, ". . . role expectations were adaptable provided the inferior status group filled a social need."[6] While the upwardly mobile middle class cultivated the inspirational domestic role of the female as synonymous with "the lady," early factories in the Northeast found female industrial labor available, cheap, and malleable.

When the mills at Lowell, Massachusetts, first sought out farm girls as their main source of employees, two contradictory views of woman's purpose were briefly held in tenuous balance. The factory girls left their homes, left domestic employments, worked long hours at machines and received money wages, but their motives kept them rooted to the homes they left behind. Aiming to earn enough to support ailing fathers or widowed mothers, or to send younger brothers to college, they hoped that their work would be temporary—to be ended by creation of their own homes. But despite their thorough indoctrination with the ideology of the sacredness of the home—reinforced by the paternalistic system of mill boardinghouses—employment of the female operatives did mean that women's labor outside the home had, for the first time in any considerable way in the United States, a money value. The potential impact of the new opportunity is hinted at in an anonymous Lowell mill girl's defense of the "Dignity of Labor":

> From whence originated the idea, that it was derogatory to a lady's dignity, or a blot upon the female character, to labor? and who was the first to say sneeringly, "Oh, she *works* for a living?" Surely, such ideas and expressions ought not to grow on republican soil. . . . To be able to earn one's own living by laboring with the hands should be reckoned among female accomplishments; and I hope the time is not far distant when none of my countrywomen will be ashamed to have it known that they are better versed in useful than they are in ornamental accomplishments.[7]

The new demand of factories for female labor offered women a livelihood, and women's entry into the realm of paid labor pointed a way out of women's economic dependence on men. On the other hand, since the morality of female employment was clearly linked to economic necessity, it accentuated status distinctions between women in

[6] Gerda Lerner, "The Lady and the Mill-girl: Changes in the Status of Women in the Age of Jackson," *Mid-Continent American Studies Journal*, X (1969), 10.

[7] Signed C. B., in *Mind among the Spindles: A Miscellany wholly composed by the factory girls* (Boston, 1845), p. 187.

paid employment and women serving their station in the home. As the benign atmosphere of the first Lowell years faded, and wages dropped, the employment of women in industry became more clearly a form of exploitation of women's dependence. The potential of early industrial labor for women as an avenue for female self-awareness and possible self-fulfillment seems hazy; yet it had that potential for some—witness Lucy Larcom—simply by giving women an alternative to the home.

The documents in this section are voices engaged in contemporary definition and debate, in an era when "women's work" absorbed new meanings and "women's sphere" became fighting words. They allow us to explore the concerns that a society characterized by social and geographical mobility engendered in its women.

IV. SLAVERY AND SEX

The organized women's rights movement in America began in the midst of, and among proponents of, the antislavery crusade. Angelina Grimké, southern by birth, abolitionist by "calling," and feminist by perception, proclaimed in 1838 that "the discussion of the rights of the slave has opened the way for the discussion of *other* rights, and the ultimate result will most certainly be, 'the breaking of every yoke,' . . . an introduction into that 'liberty wherewith Christ hath made his people free.' "[8] Joining in the campaign to abolish slavery gave many women a sense of their own enforced disabilities, and an argument against them: for, as the Grimké sisters said, the abolitionist cause was the school of *human* rights, and many of its female participants applied its lessons to themselves.

The conjunction of women's antislavery sentiments with the first significant evocation of feminist sentiment is evidence that the system of slavery and the customs of sexism were not only in some ways analogous, but mutually reinforcing. Mary Boykin Chesnut, wife of a Confederate general, did not hesitate to admit that "there is no slave, after all, like a wife." The analogy between white women, and black slaves, vis-à-vis their white masters—their common treatment as property rather than human beings, their dependent status, etc.—has been noted by critical observers in America since the late eighteenth century.

[8] Angelina Grimké, *Letters to Catharine E. Beecher* (Boston, 1838), p. 126.

This analogy sheds light on the status of women, though it somewhat obscures the larger ramifications of slave status and racism. It is also germane to recognize that the status of white women in the antebellum South was *counterpoint* to the system of black slavery.

The myth of southern womanhood in the antebellum South was an exaggerated version of the romantic, inspirational aspects of the cult of true womanhood—conceding to women command of worshipful attention but no real responsibility. William Taylor has described the South's exaggerated chivalry to white women as a means of buying them off, an offer of "half the loaf in the hope they would not demand more"—"the deference ordinarily shown to an honored but distrusted servant."[9] To demand more, as Angelina and Sarah Grimké did when they undertook voluntary exile from the South and achieved notoriety in the North as abolitionists and feminists, meant to reject the kind of deference offered to women and assume individual responsibility for oneself instead. Angelina Grimké felt that any woman who understood "her dignity as a moral, intellectual, and accountable being" would loathe the palliative of chivalry: "Her noble nature is insulted by such paltry, sickening adulation, and she will not stoop to drink the foul waters of so turbid a stream."[10] The false elevation of the white woman matched the degradation of the slave—both conditions far from the conception of moral and spiritual equality on which the Grimké sisters based their reasoning. With consistent logic the Grimkés acted out feminist principles in their adoption of the antislavery standard.

In contrast to the Grimkés, Mary Boykin Chesnut remained essentially loyal to the life-style of the southern slaveholding class. Though indignant at many manifestations of male dominance and the system of slaveholding—particularly its burdens upon the wives of slaveholders—Chesnut had no Christian premise, or any other, on which she could support a thorough reprobation of either chivalry or slavery. Despite her recurring resentment of the double standard, she could not act effectively against the hierarchical order that put woman in her place, just as she accepted the hierarchical order that put blacks in their place. Instead she saw the southern white woman's life as a model of righteous

[9] William Taylor, *Cavalier and Yankee* (New York: Anchor Books, 1963), p. 146.
[10] Angelina Grimké, *op. cit.*, pp. 119, 107.

self-abnegation, because her duties—such as caring for home, family, and slaves, and catering to a husband's will—precluded any possibility for self-definition.

As Edmund Wilson and others have noted, not only the rule of gallantry toward the southern white woman, but also her own exacting sense of self-control, occurred partly in reaction to the sexual exploitation of female slaves by their masters.[11] The enforcement of sexual license on black women left southern white women to assert a prudish self-control in defense of their own status. The impact of sexual exploitation on black women was less important to someone like Mary Chesnut than its effect on her white friends and relatives. As a foil to white women's lives of self-sacrifice she portrayed black women's lives as paths of licentious self-expression, never appreciating that the latter definition was also forced on black women by slaveholding society.

The plight of the female slave naturally drew the attention of antislavery women, black and white. Slavery not only deprived black women of their dignity and humanity by means of chains, whippings, and hard labor; it also made them the "brood mares," as abolitionist indignation phrased it, of their masters. The nonrecognition of slave marriages, the separation of slave children from their mothers by the vagaries of a master's will, and the necessary submission of the slave to her master's lust, all figured prominently in antislavery literature. *Uncle Tom's Cabin* amply demonstrates how the antislavery feelings of northern women gathered force from the image of slavery defiling the sacredness of the home, for both the black family and the white family. In the evidence available from female slaves themselves, in the form of escapees' testimony or post–Civil War remembrances, the specific injustices perpetrated on them as women are subsumed under the leading fact of slavery. The contrast between freedom and slavery was a more important one, to the black refugee women interviewed by Benjamin Drew in Canada in the 1850s, than any contrast between the condition of a male slave and a female slave. A document such as Linda Brent's autobiography, however—published seventeen years after her escape from slavery—focused on the sexual oppression of the female slave and the neglected bond of empathy that should have drawn the white

---

[11] Edmund Wilson, *Patriotic Gore* (New York: Oxford Press, 1966), p. 291; see also Taylor, *op. cit.*, pp. 147–148.

mistress to protect her. The escaped-slave narratives in this section, together with writings by the Grimké sisters and Mary Chesnut, give some suggestion of the tensions contained in the duplicitous sexual code of the antebellum South.

V. NINETEENTH-CENTURY ALTERNATIVES:
PIONEERS AND UTOPIANS

In the mid-nineteenth century, although the dominant image of woman's place was city-bred and city-propagated, the large majority of America's population lived on the land; most women worked out their life experience on farms and ranches, in small towns and rural communities. The movement of pioneer settlement westward meant that the experience of many women included a long overland journey and the frustrations of housekeeping without ready supplies. In frontier settlements, the stringencies of colonial settlement reappeared in some respects, with similar effect on women's circumstances: a skewed sex ratio put women very much in demand, and the difficulties of the wilderness environment superseded fine discrimination between male and female "legitimate spheres." There were great differences from colonial settlement, however, in that nineteenth-century pioneers were not separated by an ocean from their closest cultural and productive link, and their motivations were usually more worldly than religious. On the nineteenth-century frontier, the relative scarcity of women had a double potential—to generate a greater regard for women's self-determination, or to multiply the burdens to be borne as part of women's sphere. Pioneer communities did not escape the "sphere" of the cultural and social influence of the eastern United States.

One must assume, however, that the people who migrated westward had some dissatisfaction with the eastern United States, or a sense of better opportunities elsewhere. In this respect, the individual pioneer settlers of the West resemble the members of socialist and other "associative" communities that cropped up frequently in the mid-nineteenth century. The progressive settlement of the American continent can be regarded altogether, with more sense than whimsy, as a series of utopian endeavors. The founders of purposive socialist communities distinguished themselves from other nineteenth-century pioneers by their more scrupulous objections to the society they left, and their stricter formulations of how to create the ideal society. But in light of their similarities, and whatever divergence from eastern society the utopian and pioneer efforts share, some of their documents are grouped together in this section as "alternatives."

The question is: to what extent did such new communities offer real alternatives to women? Emigrants did not easily leave behind the "domestic mystique." In the westward migration of Harriet Noble's family to Michigan, or Elizabeth Smith Geer's to Oregon, as these women recount it, the rewards of pioneering were less apparent than the privations. Perhaps we should look instead at women participating in communities with avowedly perfectionist intentions. In the description given by a male communitarian, the "associative" scheme for emancipating women from domestic bondage was well designed to aid "the conciliation of the family interest, with all the other interests of society." Nevertheless the letter included here written by the women of Trumbull Phalanx, a Fourierist community, expresses empathy with the *suffering* of sisters around the world. As statements of "pioneering" or "utopian" alternatives for women, the efforts of Frances Wright or Victoria Woodhull—two "notorious women"—were more positive.

VI. SEXUALITY AND GYNECOLOGY:
THE NINETEENTH CENTURY

Biology *was* destiny for women to a much greater extent in past centuries than it need be today. A married woman in seventeenth-century New England, for example, might easily spend twenty-five years of her adult life always either pregnant or nursing. If pregnancies were complicated, or deliveries resulted in injury, married women saw this as their lot. Without sure and effective means of contraception, or good medical understanding of disturbances of the female reproductive organs, women's childbearing capacity was likely to demand considerable attention. Women did not, until the very late nineteenth century, have safe means to exert their will over their reproductive functions: they could be, in a very real sense, prisoners of their own bodies.

Women in the nineteenth century were limited first of all by their lack of medical knowledge. Well into the nineteenth century, medical science failed to go beyond using the catch-all "prolapsus uteri," or fallen womb, to denote most female problems after childbirth. Women, moreover, had almost no chance to participate in the advancement of gynecological knowledge. The professionalization of American medicine in the late eighteenth and early nineteenth centuries made medical degrees and doctor's licenses necessary to the practice of medicine—and women, excluded from medical schools, were prevented from acquiring either of these. Whereas women had traditionally been midwives and healers, by the mid-nineteenth century their competence in these areas was overwhelmed by the prestige of the medical profession. As medical practice became standardized and acquired institutional trappings, physicians displaced female midwives, in urban areas at least.[12]

Women's knowledge about their bodies was also a casualty of nineteenth-century sexual repressiveness. When the word "proper" led the designation of all aspects of women's behavior, frank discussion of female physiology, even between mother and daughter, foundered. Idealization of woman as unfailingly virtuous, pious, and genteel left no room for cognizance of either her sensual nature or her physical needs for good health. The rhetorical direction of the cult of true womanhood was to spiritualize the female until she was almost literally "disembodied." Totally defined by her sex (reproduction), still the true woman was sexless (devoid of sexual passion). The wishful distinction between man's frenetic aggressiveness in the marketplace and woman's static serenity in the home became a metaphor of the male's sexual role to seek, the female's merely to endure. Besides, the true woman's part as moral guardian of the home proscribed the "baser" passion of sex. The sexual content of marriage thus appeared a matter of tolerance, of necessary accommodation, to women who were affected by the cult of true womanhood.

Those women who were able to forge a positive view of their womanhood from the concept of woman's sphere—even the early feminists—persisted in repressing female sexuality in order to stress the Christian, moral content of women's strengths. Angelina Grimké, for example, admitted to her prospective husband Theodore Weld her conviction that "men in general, the vast majority, believe most seriously that women were made to gratify their animal appetites, *expressly* to minister to *their* pleasure—yea, Christian men too. My soul abhors such

---

[12] See Gerda Lerner, "The Lady and the Mill-girl," 7–9, on the professionalization of medicine.

a base letting down of the high dignity of my nature as a woman."[13] Because pleasure in and active seeking of sexual relations were supposed to be male prerogatives, woman's cooperation seemed a manifestation of her submissiveness or weakness. Women who rejected the idea of female weakness and submissiveness often had to reject any concept of a sexual role as well. In addition, feminist principles in the nineteenth century could logically mean denying one's sexual nature to avoid the immediate results of enjoying it: i.e., children, and possibly "female problems." (To continue with the example of Angelina Grimké: after her readings in human physiology reconciled her mind with the "compound relations" of marriage, she married Weld, and bore three children. Having purposely retired from her public-speaking career but not from her feminist principles, she found her health impaired, her activities restricted by a condition called "prolapsus uteri."[14])

Thus while nineteenth-century ideology portrayed woman's reproductive functions as her most important and most fulfilling ones, to individual women they could easily be the most hampering. The notion of woman's "delicacy" combined the ideal of female decorativeness and gentility with the fact that women's reproductive functions could cause them severe disabilities. No doubt the exaggerated stress on the female sphere as composed only of reproduction and domestic maintenance created nervous debility in many women. The "assumption that woman is a natural invalid," which Mary Livermore cites in subsequent pages, merely carried this view to its illogical conclusion.

The mass of contradictions contained in the Victorian approach to female sexuality emerges in documents such as the ones in this section. The intent to have women recognize their reproductive functions as their most glorious raison-d'etre often appears to clash with the demands of an exaggerated propriety. The office of acquainting women with "the laws of their being" was a powerful one, particularly in the hands of medical men. By the end of the nineteenth century, however, politically active feminists were aware of the manipulative possibilities of male monopoly of gynecological knowledge. Moreover, women had

[13] Angelina Grimké to Theodore Weld, March 4, 1838, in G. H. Barnes and D. L. Dumond (eds.), *Letters of Theodore Dwight Weld, Angelina Grimké Weld, and Sarah Grimké* (New York, 1934), Vol. II, p. 587.

[14] See Gerda Lerner, *The Grimké Sisters from South Carolina* (Boston: Houghton Mifflin Co., 1967), on Angelina Grimké's later life.

broken into the medical profession, and were providing women with a new perspective on their physical functioning.

VII. INDUSTRIALIZATION AND WOMEN'S WORK

As an influx of rural migrants and European immigrants swelled the urban population of America in the latter part of the nineteenth century, the proportion of women working for money wages rose. Women entered paid employment out of economic necessity. As daughters, wives, maiden aunts, and widows had always worked in the home or on the farm in families that could not afford leisure for any of their members, they now worked in the factory or shop. "Work" was always the content of most women's lives—except in the myth of true womanhood, which made the domestic role into part of woman's nature, her way of being, rather than something she *did*. Women's paid work outside the home, though it was undertaken to support their families, was a travesty of the domestic ideal of wife and mother. The social status of the employed woman remained low so long as the upper-class image of the woman at home, gracing her hearth, remained the object of aspiration.

Nevertheless the fact was that more women were seeking employment outside the home, at some time of their lives. Young unmarried women predominated among the female work force in the late nineteenth century, indicating that after marriage and motherhood most women reverted to the traditional role of economic dependence—unless their husbands were unable to earn a living wage. Widows and married women whose husbands were disabled or estranged constituted the second major grouping of working women. Only among blacks, and among immigrants whose children worked in industry with them, were there substantial numbers of mothers who held jobs when their husbands were also employed.[15]

All women who sought work outside the home, however—whether unmarried women supporting brothers and mothers, or young girls earning their keep, or widows or estranged wives trying to feed their children, or married women whose husbands' incomes were insufficient —all suffered repercussions from the idea that women's earning function was secondary, that women should and would be supported by some-

[15] Robert Smuts, *Women and Work in America* (New York: Schocken Paperbacks, 1971), chapter 2.

one, rather than support themselves. The result was that women were rarely paid at the same rate as men. In factories at the end of the century, women workers earned on the average only about half as much as men.[16] Need drove them to accept the low-paying, dead-end jobs that were available to them. From within and without the working class, women workers were accused, sporadically, of undercutting wages and unsettling the labor market. Young women living with their parents were assumed to be earning "pin money" and thus to be satisfied with less than a living wage. Women workers were treated as casual laborers, who had no prospect for advancement and no future in organization, because home and family comprised their natural interests.

In some aspects and for some individuals these accusations had truth, but they did not explain the disadvantages women worked under. In almost all industries and trades women were not hired into the same job classifications as men. Unskilled women were hired for the most monotonous, lowest-paid positions, in which they had no opportunities to advance their skills. In skilled trades, where men might receive apprenticeship training, women were assigned the least varied tasks. Even where men's and women's assignments were comparable, the "women's work," by being designated as such, brought lower compensation. Injustices provoked a few strong women organizers, but unions in the late nineteenth century bypassed most women. The focus of the American Federation of Labor on skilled workers left out most women in industry. Also, women's inferior employment position created false barriers between males and females who as workers had the same interests. Union men frequently called women unorganizable because their orientation toward marriage and economic support made them uncommitted as workers.

The woman employed outside the home was an anomaly by nineteenth-century standards of sex-stereotyped spheres of activity. This made working women subject to character aspersion for their entry into the unchaste, aggressive "male sphere" of gainful employment. The economic vulnerability that made women seek employment also made them vulnerable to sexual exploitation. As it appears in the 1884 study *The Working Girls of Boston*, excerpted in this section, positive effort had

[16] *Ibid.*, pp. 91–92.

to be made to combat the assumption that working girls were corrupted by their occupational surroundings, and were equivalent to prostitutes. On the other hand, the employment position of working women was not acknowledged as their essential work—by their employers, by union men, sometimes by themselves—although they endured its real hardships.

A frank statement of the ways in which women workers were regarded as different from laborers in general appeared in the United States Supreme Court decision in *Muller* v. *Oregon*,[17] which upheld the ten-hour workday for women employed in laundries. This decision came three years after the Court had struck down, as a violation of the employer's and employee's right to contract, a similar law limiting the working hours of male bakers.[18] In *Muller* v. *Oregon* the Court stated:

> The two sexes differ in structure of body, in the functions to be performed by each, in the amount of physical strength, in the capacity for long-continued labor, particularly when done standing, the influence of vigorous health upon the future well-being of the race, the self-reliance which enables one to assert full rights, and in the capacity to maintain the struggle for subsistence. This difference justifies a difference in legislation, and upholds that which is designed to compensate for some of the burdens which rest upon her. . . .[19]

Apart from the progress this decision allowed in limiting hours of work, the Court's reasoning is indicative of prevailing attitudes about women and their employment outside the home. Women were seen as different (by implication deficient) in "the self-reliance which enables one to assert full rights," and "the capacity to maintain the struggle for subsistence," because of their customary economic dependence on men, and the lack of acknowledgment of their productive capacity in the domestic role. The important productive capacity of women instead appeared in their reproductive capacity—"the well-being of the race." The Court also took cognizance of physical differences between men and women, linking these to differences in endurance. In practice, in industry, the argument of women's inferior strength tended to be used to shut women out of advancement opportunities, without relieving them of backbreaking menial toil.

[17] 208 U.S. 412 (1908).
[18] *Lochner* v. *N.Y.*, 198 U.S. 45 (1905).
[19] 208 U.S. 412, 422–23 (1908).

This section of documents deals with the content of women's work in an increasingly urban, industrial America, and with the new choices, if any, which industrial employments and advancing technology offered to women. Economic dependence on men was the premise underlying the formulation of women's domestic occupation—and domestic nature. As more women showed their competence to earn money wages in a variety of employments, the notion of all-consuming domesticity appeared more and more a mannerism.

VIII. LEGACY OF LEISURE: DISCONTENT

The last quarter of the nineteenth century proved the obsolescence of the literal if not the psychological limitation of woman's sphere to the home, as even economically secure women increasingly sought extra-domestic pursuits. It was not only that the Civil War had provoked a need for women's services, and women's wartime contributions became models of heroic action—although those years did set a powerful example. Urbanization, technological advance, and a declining birth rate brought a decrease in the amount of domestic work imposed on women. The more inclusive mass production and marketing of household necessities became, the more women's domestic role acquired the character of a consumer rather than a creator of commodities. As the birth rate declined (and it did throughout the nineteenth century, particularly in the upper economic brackets where women's leisure was doubly ensured by the presence of servants), childbearing was no longer a lifetime project, and child-rearing duties became less continuous.

The decades of pressure by women's rights advocates also had a number of effects by the later nineteenth century. Higher education was increasingly available to women, in both private and public institutions; and as always, broader education meant higher aspirations. Female suffrage, which in 1848 seemed too outlandish to be proposed by more than a bare majority of the first women's rights convention, was by the 1870s regularly discussed in society at large. There were visible examples of extraordinary women, such as Dr. Elizabeth Blackwell, who had braved their ways into all-male professions. Moreover the general contention presented by feminists, that women had the right to decide their own lives and priorities, was reflected among leisured women who had time to consider their purpose. With the increasing demand for women in the work force, the specter (and indeed the reality) of independent women appeared.

Such factors as these provoked restlessness among women who had economic support but no life work. Thorstein Veblen, whose rhetoric gave us the words still used to describe the position of upper-class women in industrial society, formulated his understanding of the phenomenon in *The Theory of the Leisure Class* (1898). He noted that the requirement for a woman to spend her time in vicarious leisure—that is, leisure that would reflect the status of her man—was greatly at variance with the impulse toward self-expression and workmanship. This explained why supposed advantages were really the cause of grievance:

> She is petted, and is permitted, or even required, to consume largely and conspicuously—vicariously for her husband or other natural guardian. She is exempted, or debarred, from useful employment—in order to perform leisure vicariously for the good repute of her natural (pecuniary) guardian. These offices are the conventional marks of the un-free, at the same time that they are incompatible with the human impulse to purposeful activity. But the woman is endowed with her share—which there is reason to believe is more than an even share—of the instinct of workmanship, to which futility of life or of expenditure is obnoxious. She must unfold her life activity in response to the direct, unmediated stimuli of the economic environment with which she is in contact.

Thus Veblen analyzed the discontent that fired the "New-Woman" movement. He also suggested its direction: "there is a demand, more or less serious, for emancipation from all relation of status, tutelage, or vicarious life . . . The demand comes from that portion of womankind which is excluded by the canons of good repute from all effective work, and which is closely reserved for a life of leisure and conspicuous consumption."[20]

Before Veblen wrote, perspicacious women recognized that their enforced leisure should and would drive them into activities outside their appointed domain. In 1873, Antoinette B. Blackwell, in the speech which appears in subsequent pages, called upon American women as the only "considerable American leisure class" to take up their social duty. Jane Addams' motives in the settlement house movement emerged from her revulsion against a pattern of life that dictated "uselessness" and a

[20] Thorstein Veblen, *The Theory of the Leisure Class* (New York: Mentor Paperback edition, 1953), pp. 231–232.

"feverish search after culture." The American tendency toward asso-
ciationism—noted among women as well as among men since the Jacksonian period—provided less ambitious channels for the expression of
women's energies. From the tradition of maternal associations and religious societies came women's clubs devoted to "self-culture," to civic
works, to social purposes. The gathering momentum of the women's
club movement was evidence not only that middle-class women had
time to spend outside the home, but also that they wanted to broaden
the range of their sights beyond the individual home. Through associations these women devoted themselves to self-improvement, but also to
the causes of philanthropy, public health, temperance, conservation,
education, and child and female labor regulation.[21] Suffragists comprised
only a minority, though of course a signal one, of the women who were
extending the spectrum of women's acknowledged capabilities.

The fact that many women's club activities and social reform endeavors grew out of, rather than in direct opposition to, the cult of
true womanhood, is testimony to the power of that ideology. Interest
in public health, social welfare work, employment conditions for females, and particularly, child labor, was consciously seen and justified
as an extension of woman's traditional role as moral and physical
nurturer. Since pure motives, self-sacrifice, and benevolent intentions
had been granted to the true woman to exercise inside the family circle,
these attributes framed the popular justification for the wider extension
of woman's influence. Many women involved in club or reform
activities were the first to say that their "outside" interests were really
undertaken in the service of the home, though on a larger scale—to
preserve the institution of family life and the continuation of a healthy
race.

The most sensitive participant-observers, however—such as Jane
Addams and Charlotte Perkins Gilman—recognized that there was a
fundamental opposition between the traditional upbringing of a female
for exclusive devotion within the family circle, and her desires to be a
contributing member of the complex urban society outside the home.
Addams noted how a girl's education for self-sacrifice at home, when
taken a logical step further and applied to the benefits of the larger
society, was stopped short by the "family claim." In Gilman's analysis
of the "sexuo-economic" factor in social evolution, the home revolving

---

[21] On the women's club movement, and social reform efforts of women between
the 1860s and 1920, see William O'Neill, *op. cit.*, pp. 33–70.

around the economically dependent woman was an anachronism, at odds with the direction of industrial society.

To what extent the proliferating activities of middle-class women implied a change in their consciousness and expectations is problematic. Certainly in many instances women's clubs or reform activities were only palliatives, occupying their energies, aiding their self-esteem in the short run, but suffering them to remain economically dependent, still in an ancillary relation and "sphere." Nevertheless, as the growing complexity and disorganization of a multi-ethnic, urban society demanded new social service positions, and women appeared to fill them, the range of "women's work" expanded. Dedicated women who achieved national prominence for their innovative work, such as Florence Kelley or Jane Addams, created models of female contributions. In thus breaking through the limitations imposed on women's personalities and on their physical and mental capacities, such activities helped to alter the general definition of women.

It still remained to integrate this newly expanded definition of woman's capabilities and interests with her roles as wife and mother. Most of the late nineteenth-century generation of women who initiated significant social-welfare work in cities did their work while unmarried or widowed. The first several classes of graduates from women's colleges (containing many of the women who became settlement house workers in the 1880s and 1890s) had a notably low rate of marriage and childbearing. The difficulties that the institution of "the home" and the nuclear family posed, for women's redefinition of their aims and capabilities, were recognized in effect by evasion. Only Charlotte Perkins Gilman, in her theoretical offensive against the home—in her separation of the institution of "the home" from "the family" and again from "marriage"—went beyond evasion to an attempt at resolution.

The documents collected here are organized into sections, which are partially chronological and partially thematic—not, however, with any presumption that the organizing themes are, or could be, all-inclusive. In introducing each selection I have purposely declined to prejudge its value and content by extracting a critical "point" for the headnote; on the contrary, the knowledge and inferences readers draw should be able to be various and extensive. To my mind the virtue of these sources is their refusal to lend themselves to one-sentence condensations. The contents of this volume, taken together, express a complex unity that is American women's condition from the beginning of Puritan settlement to the beginning of the twentieth century. In compiling and editing these documents I have been moved by the knowledge that women can learn much from other women, and by the hope that clearer understanding of our history will foster our new self-determination.

I
The Early Colonial Milieu:
Goodwives, Shrews, and Witches

The Trappan'd Maiden: Or, The Distressed Damsel*

Among the many English ballads printed in the seventeenth century that pertained to America, this one deals explicitly with the miseries of a female indentured servant.

THE TRAPPAN'D MAIDEN: OR, THE DISTRESSED DAMSEL

This Girl was cunningly Trappan'd, sent to Virginny from England,
Where she doth Hardship undergo, there is no Cure it must be so:
But if she lives to cross the Main, she vows she'll ne'r go there again.

TUNE OF *Virginny*, OR, *When that I was weary, weary, O.*

Give ear unto a Maid, that lately was betray'd,
    And sent into Virginny, O:
In brief I shall declare, what I have suffer'd there,
    When that I was weary, weary, weary, weary, O.

[Since] that first I came to this Land of Fame,
    Which is called Virginny, O,
The Axe and the Hoe have wrought my overthrow,
    When that I was weary, weary, weary, weary, O.

Five years served I, under Master Guy,
    In the land of Virginny, O,
Which made me for to know sorrow, grief and woe,
    When that I was weary, weary, weary, weary, O.

When my Dame says "Go" then I must do so,
    In the land of Virginny, O;
When she sits at Meat, then I have none to eat,
    When that I am weary, weary, weary, weary, O.

* From C. H. Firth (ed.), *An American Garland: being a Collection of Ballads relating to America, 1563-1759* (Oxford, 1915), pp. 251-253.

The Cloath[e]s that I brought in, they are worn very thin,
  In the land of Virginny, O,
Which makes me for to say, "Alas, and Well-a-day!"
  When that I am weary, weary, weary, weary, O.

Instead of Beds of Ease, to lye down when I please,
  In the Land of Virginny, O;
Upon a bed of straw, I lye down full of woe,
  When that I am weary, weary, weary, weary, O.

Then the Spider, she, daily waits on me,
  In the Land of Virginny, O;
Round about my bed, she spins her web [of thread],
  When that I am weary, weary, weary, weary, O.

So soon as it is day, to work I must away,
  In the Land of Virginny, O;
Then my Dame she knocks, with her tinder-box,
  When that I am weary, weary, weary, weary, O.

I have play'd my part both at Plow and Cart,
  In the Land of Virginny, O;
Billets from the Wood upon my back they load,
  When that I am weary, weary, weary, weary, O.

Instead of drinking Beer, I drink the water clear,
  In the Land of Virginny, O;
Which makes me pale and wan, do all that e'er I can,
  When that I am weary, weary, weary, weary, O.

If my Dame says "Go!" I dare not say no,
  In the Land of Virginny, O;
The Water from the Spring, upon my head I bring,
  When that I am weary, weary, weary, weary, O.

When the Mill doth stand, I'm ready at command,
  In the Land of Virginny, O;
The Morter for to make, which makes my heart to ake,
  When that I am weary, weary, weary, weary, O.

When the Child doth cry, I must sing "By-a-by!"
  In the Land of Virginny, O;

No rest that I can have, whilst I am here a Slave,
When that I am weary, weary, weary, weary, O.

A thousand woes beside, that I do here abide,
In the Land of Virginny, O;
In misery I spend my time that hath no end,
When that I am weary, weary, weary, weary, O.

Then let Maids beware, all by my ill-fare,
In the Land of Virginny, O;
Be sure to stay at home, for if you do here come,
You all will be weary, weary, weary, weary, O.

But if it be my chance, Homewards to advance,
From the Land of Virginny, O;
If that I, once more, land on English Shore,
I'll no more be weary, weary, weary, weary, O.

Examination of Mrs. Ann Hutchinson*

Ann Hutchinson's trial at the court at Newtown (Cambridge) was the focus of the "Antinomian crisis." Mrs. Hutchinson's exposition of John Cotton's doctrine at gatherings at her home had created a large following for her, which amounted in fact to a political split in the Massachusetts Bay colony, and a threat to the established leaders. John Winthrop, Governor, took the prosecutor's part in the examination of her before the colony's court.

NOVEMBER 1637

THE EXAMINATION OF MRS. ANN HUTCHINSON
AT THE COURT OF NEWTOWN

Mr. Winthrop, Governor: Mrs. Hutchinson, you are called here as one of those that have troubled the peace of the commonwealth and the churches here; you are known to be a woman that hath had a great share in the promoting and divulging of those opinions that are causes of this trouble, and to be nearly joined not only in affinity and affection with some of those the court had taken notice of and passed censure upon, but you have spoken divers things as we have been informed very prejudicial to the honour of the churches and ministers thereof, and you have maintained a meeting and an assembly in your house that hath been condemned by the general assembly as a thing not tolerable nor comely in the sight of God nor fitting for your sex, and notwithstanding that was cried down you have continued the same, therefore we have thought good to send for you to understand how things are, that if you be in an erroneous way we may reduce you that so you may become a profitable member here among us, otherwise if you be obstinate in your course that then the court may take such course that you may trouble

* Thomas Hutchinson, *The History of the Colony and Province of Massachusetts Bay*, edited from the author's own copies of Volumes I and II and his manuscript of Volume III, with a memoir and additional notes, by Lawrence Shaw Mayo (Cambridge: Harvard University Press, 1936), Volume II, Appendix II, pp. 366–391. Reprinted by permission of the President and Fellows of Harvard College. Copyright 1936 by the President and Fellows of Harvard College.

us no further, therefore I would intreat you to express whether you do not assent and hold in practice to those opinions and factions that have been handled in court already, that is to say, whether you do not justify Mr. Wheelwright's sermon and the petition.

Mrs. Hutchinson: I am called here to answer before you but I hear no things laid to my charge.

Gov.: I have told you some already and more I can tell you.

Mrs. H.: Name one Sir.

Gov.: Have I not named some already?

Mrs. H.: What have I said or done?

Gov.: Why for your doings, this you did harbour and countenance those that are parties in this faction that you have heard of.

Mrs. H.: That's matter of conscience, Sir.

Gov.: Your conscience you must keep or it must be kept for you.

Mrs. H.: Must not I then entertain the saints because I must keep my conscience.

Gov.: Say that one brother should commit felony or treason and come to his brother's house, if he knows him guilty and conceals him he is guilty of the same. It is his conscience to entertain him, but if his conscience comes into act in giving countenance and entertainment to him that hath broken the law he is guilty too. So if you do countenance those that are transgressors of the law you are in the same fact.

Mrs. H.: What law do they transgress?

Gov.: The law of God and of the state.

Mrs. H.: In what particular?

Gov.: Why in this among the rest, whereas the Lord doth say honour thy father and thy mother.

Mrs. H.: Ey Sir in the Lord.

Gov.: This honour you have broke in giving countenance to them.

Mrs. H.: In entertaining those did I entertain them against any act (for there is the thing) or what God hath appointed?

Gov.: You knew that Mr. Wheelwright did preach this sermon and those that countenance him in this do break a law.

Mrs. H.: What law have I broken?

Gov.: Why the fifth commandment.

Mrs. H.: I deny that for he saith in the Lord.

Gov.: You have joined with them in the faction.

Mrs. H.: In what faction have I joined with them?

Gov.: In presenting the petition.

Mrs. H.: Suppose I had set my hand to the petition what then?

Gov.: You saw that case tried before.

Mrs. H.: But I had not my hand to the petition.

Gov.: You have councelled them.

Mrs. H.: Wherein?

Gov.: Why in entertaining them.

Mrs. H.: What breach of law is that Sir?

Gov.: Why dishonouring of parents.

Mrs. H.: But put the case Sir that I do fear the Lord and my parents, may not I entertain them that fear the Lord because my parents will not give me leave?

Gov.: If they be the fathers of the commonwealth, and they of another religion, if you entertain them then you dishonour your parents and are justly punishable.

Mrs. H.: If I entertain them, as they have dishonoured their parents I do.

Gov.: No but you by countenancing them above others put honor upon them.

Mrs. H.: I may put honor upon them as the children of God and as they do honor the Lord.

Gov.: We do not mean to discourse with those of your sex but only this; you do adhere unto them and do endeavor to set forward this faction and so you do dishonour us.

Mrs. H.: I do acknowledge no such thing neither do I think that I ever put any dishonour upon you.

Gov.: Why do you keep such a meeting at your house as you do every week upon a set day?

Mrs. H.: It is lawful for me so to do, as it is all your practices and can you find a warrant for yourself and condemn me for the same thing? The ground of my taking it up was, when I first came to this land because I did not go to such meetings as those were, it was presently reported that I did not allow of such meetings but held them unlawful and therefore in that regard they said I was proud and did despise all ordinances, upon that a friend came unto me and told me of it and I to prevent such aspersions took it up, but it was in practice before I came therefore I was not the first.

Gov.: For this, that you appeal to our practice you need no confutation. If your meeting had answered to the former it had not been offensive, but I will say that there was no meeting of women alone, but your meeting is of another sort for there are sometimes men among you.

Mrs. H.: There was never any man with us.

Gov.: Well, admit there was no man at your meeting and that you was sorry for it, there is no warrant for your doings, and by what warrant do you continue such a course?

Mrs. H.: I conceive there lyes a clear rule in Titus, that the elder women should instruct the younger and then I must have a time wherein I must do it.

Gov.: All this I grant you, I grant you a time for it, but what is this to the purpose that you Mrs. Hutchinson must call a company together from their callings to come to be taught of you? . . .

Mrs. H.: . . . if you look upon the rule in Titus it is a rule to me. If you convince me that it is no rule I shall yield.

Gov.: You know that there is no rule that crosses another, but this rule crosses that in the Corinthians. But you must take it in this sense that elder women must instruct the younger about their business and to love their husbands and not to make them to clash.

Mrs. H.: I do not conceive but that it is meant for some publick times.

Gov.: Well, have you no more to say but this?

Mrs. H.: I have said sufficient for my practice.

Gov.: Your course is not to be suffered for, besides that we find such a course as this to be greatly prejudicial to the state, besides the occasion that it is to seduce many honest persons that are called to those meetings and your opinions being known to be different from the word of God may seduce many simple souls that resort unto you, besides that the occasion which hath come of late hath come from none but such as have frequented your meetings, so that now they are flown off from magistrates and ministers and this since they have come to you, and besides that it will not well stand with the commonwealth that families should be neglected for so many neighbours and dames and so much time spent, we see no rule of God for this, we see not that any should have authority to set up any other exercises besides what authority hath already set up and so what hurt comes of this you will be guilty of and we for suffering you.

Mrs. H.: Sir I do not believe that to be so.

Gov.: Well, we see how it is we must therefore put it away from you or restrain you from maintaining this course.

Mrs. H.: If you have a rule for it from God's word you may.

Gov.: We are your judges, and not you ours and we must compel you to it.

Mrs. H.: If it please you by authority to put it down I will freely let you for I am subject to your authority. . . .

Dep. Gov.: I would go a little higher with Mrs. Hutchinson. About three years ago we were all in peace. Mrs. Hutchinson from that time she came hath made a disturbance, and some that came over with her in the ship did inform me what she was as soon as she was landed. I being then in place dealt with the pastor and teacher of Boston and desired them to enquire of her, and then I was satisfied that she held nothing different from us, but within half a year after, she had vented divers of her strange opinions and had made parties in the country, and at length it comes that Mr. Cotton and Mr. Vane were of her judgment, but Mr. Cotton hath cleared himself that he was not of that mind, but now it appears by this woman's meeting that Mrs. Hutchinson hath so forestalled the minds of many by their resort to her meeting that now she hath a potent party in the country. Now if all these things have endangered us as from that foundation and if she in particular hath disparaged all our ministers in the land that they have preached a covenant of works, and only Mr. Cotton a covenant of grace, why this is not to be suffered, and therefore being driven to the foundation and it being found that Mrs. Hutchinson is she that hath depraved all the ministers and hath been the cause of what is fallen out, why we must take away the foundation and the building will fall.

Mrs. H.: I pray Sir prove it that I said they preached nothing but a covenant of works.

Dep. Gov.: Nothing but a covenant of works, why a Jesuit may preach truth sometimes.

Mrs. H.: Did I ever say they preached a covenant of works then?

Dep. Gov.: If they do not preach a covenant of grace clearly, then they preach a covenant of works.

Mrs. H.: No Sir, one may preach a covenant of grace more clearly than another, so I said.

Dep. Gov.: We are not upon that now but upon position.

Mrs. H.: Prove this then Sir that you say I said.

Dep. Gov.: When they do preach a covenant of works do they preach truth?

Mrs. H.: Yes Sir, but when they preach a covenant of works for salvation, that is not truth.

Dep. Gov.: I do but ask you this, when the ministers do preach a covenant of works do they preach a way of salvation?

Mrs. H.: I did not come hither to answer to questions of that sort.

Dep. Gov.: Because you will deny the thing.

Mrs. H.: Ey, but that is to be proved first.

Dep. Gov.: I will make it plain that you did say that the ministers did preach a covenant of works.

Mrs. H.: I deny that.

Dep. Gov.: And that you said they were not able ministers of the new testament, but Mr. Cotton only.

Mrs. H.: If ever I spake that I proved it by God's word.

Court: Very well, very well. . . .

Mr. Peters: We shall give you a fair account of what was said and desire that we may not be thought to come as informers against the gentlewoman, but as it may be serviceable for the country and our posterity to give you a brief account. This gentlewoman went under suspicion not only from her landing, that she was a woman not only difficult in her opinions, but also of an intemperate spirit. What was done at her landing I do not well remember, but as soon as Mr. Vane and ourselves came this controversy began yet it did reflect upon Mrs. Hutchinson and some of our brethren had dealt with her, and it so fell out that some of our ministry doth suffer as if it were not according to the gospel and as if we taught a covenant of works instead of a covenant of grace. Upon these and the like we did address ourselves to the teacher of that church, and the court then assembled being sensible of these things, and this gentlewoman being as we understood a chief agent, our desire to the teacher was to tell us wherein the difference lay between him and us, for the spring did then arise as we did conceive from this gentlewoman, and so we told him. He said that he thought it not according to God to commend this to the magistrates but to take some other course, and so going on in the discourse we thought it good to send for this gentlewoman, and she willingly came, and at the very first we gave her notice that such reports there were that she did conceive our ministry to be different from the ministry of the gospel, and that we taught a covenant of works, &c. and this was her table talk and therefore we desired her to clear herself and deal plainly. She was very tender at the first. Some of our brethren did desire to put this upon proof, and then her words upon that were. The fear of man is a snare why should I be afraid. These were her words. I did then take upon me to ask her this question. What difference do you conceive to be between your teacher and us? She did not request us that we should preserve her from danger or that we should be silent. Briefly, she told me there was a wide and a broad difference between our brother Mr. Cotton and our selves. I desired to know the difference. She answered that he preaches the covenant of grace and you the covenant of works and that you are not able ministers of the new testament and know no more than the apostles did before the resurrection of Christ. I did then put it to her, What do you conceive of such a brother? She answered he had not the seal of the spirit. And other things we asked her but generally the frame of her course was this, that she did conceive that we were not able ministers of the gospel. And that day being past our brother Cotton was sorry that she should lay us under a covenant of works, and could have wished she had not done so. The elders being there present we did charge them with her, and the teacher of the place said they would speak further with her, and after some time she answered that we were gone as far as the apostles were before Christ's ascension. And since that we have gone with tears some of us to her. . . .

[Six more ministers testify, agreeing with Peters.]

Gov.: Here are six undeniable ministers who say it is true and yet you deny that you did say that they did preach a covenant of works and that they were not able ministers of the gospel, and it appears plainly that you have spoken it, and whereas you say that is was drawn from you in a way of friendship, you did profess then that it was out of conscience that you spake and said The fear of man is a snare, wherefore shall I be afraid, I will speak plainly and freely.

Mrs. H.: That I absolutely deny, for the first question, was thus answered by me to them. They thought that I did conceive there was a difference between them and Mr. Cotton. At the first I was somewhat reserved, then said Mr. Peters I pray answer the question directly as fully and as plainly as you desire we should tell you our minds. Mrs. Hutchinson we come for plain dealing and telling you our hearts. Then I said I would deal as plainly as I could, and whereas they say I said they were under a covenant of works and in the state of the apostles why these two speeches cross one another. I might say they might preach a covenant of works as did the apostles, but to preach a covenant of works and to be under a covenant of works is another business.

Dep. Gov.: There have been six witnesses to prove this and yet you deny it.

Mrs. H.: I deny that these were the first words that were spoken.

Gov.: You make the case worse, for you clearly shew that the ground of your opening your mind was not to satisfy them but to satisfy your own conscience.

Mr. Peters: We do not desire to be so narrow to the court and the gentlewoman about times and seasons, whether first or after, but said it was. . . .

Gov.: Mrs. Hutchinson, the court you see hath laboured to bring you to acknowledge the error of your way that so you might be reduced, the time now grows late, we shall therefore give you a little more time to consider of it and therefore desire that you attend the court again in the morning.

THE NEXT MORNING

. . .

Mrs. H.: The ministers come in their own cause. Now the Lord hath said that an oath is the end of all controversy; though there be a sufficient number of witnesses yet they are not according to the word, therefore I desire they may speak upon oath.

Gov.: Well, it is in the liberty of the court whether they will have an oath or no and it is not in this case as in case of a jury. If they be satisfied they have sufficient matter to proceed. . . .

Gov.: For that which you alledge as an exception against the elders it is vain and untrue, for they are no prosecutors in this cause but are called to witness in the cause.

Mrs. H.: But they are witnesses of their own cause.

Gov.: It is not their cause but the cause of the whole country and they were unwilling that it should come forth, but that it was the glory and honour of God.

Mrs. H.: But it being the Lord's ordinance that an oath should be the end of all strife, therefore they are to deliver what they do upon oath.

Mr. Bradstreet: Mrs. Hutchinson, these are but circumstances and adjuncts to the cause, admit they should mistake you in your speeches you would make them to sin if you urge them to swear.

Mrs. H.: That is not the thing. If they accuse me I desire it may be upon oath.

Gov.: If the court be not satisfied they may have an oath.

[Debate follows about the ministers' speaking under oath, and about Mrs. Hutchinson bringing her own witnesses.]

Gov.: Mr. Cotton, the court desires that you declare what you do remember of the conference which was at that time and is now in question.

Mr. Cotton[1]: I did not think I should be called to bear witness in this cause and therefore did not labour to call to remembrance what was done; but the greatest passage that took impression upon me was to this purpose. The elders spake that they had heard that she had spoken some condemning words of their ministry, and among other things they did first pray her to answer wherein she thought their ministry did differ from mine, how the comparison sprang I am ignorant, but sorry I was that any comparison should be between me and my brethren and uncomfortable it was, she told them to this purpose that they did not hold forth a covenant of grace as I did, but wherein did we differ? why she said that they did not hold forth the seal of the spirit as he doth. Where is the difference there? say they, why saith she speaking to one or other of them, I know not to whom. You preach of the seal of the spirit upon a work and he upon free grace without a work or without respect to a work, he preaches the seal of the spirit upon free grace and you upon a work. I told her I was very sorry that she put comparisons between my ministry and their's, for she had said more than I could myself, and rather I had that she had put us in fellowship with them and not have made that discrepancy. She said, she found the difference. . . . And I must say that I did not find her saying they were under a covenant of works, nor that she said they did preach a covenant of works. . . .

Mr. Peters: I humbly desire to remember our reverend teacher. May it please you to remember how this came in. Whether do you not

1 Teacher of Boston church.

remember that she said we were not sealed with the spirit of grace, therefore could not preach a covenant of grace, and she said further you may do it in your judgment but not in experience, but she spake plump that we were not sealed.

Mr. Cotton: You do put me in remembrance that it was asked her why cannot we preach a covenant of grace? Why, saith she, because you can preach no more than you know, or to that purpose, she spake. Now that she said you could not preach a covenant of grace I do not remember such a thing. I remember well that she said you were not sealed with the seal of the spirit. . . .

Mrs. H.: If you please to give me leave I shall give you the ground of what I know to be true. Being much troubled to see the falseness of the constitution of the church of England, I had like to have turned separatist; whereupon I kept a day of solemn humiliation and pondering of the thing; this scripture was brought unto me—he that denies Jesus Christ to be come in the flesh is antichrist—This I considered of and in considering found that the papists did not deny him to be come in the flesh, nor we did not deny him—who then was antichrist? Was the Turk antichrist only? The Lord knows that I could not open scripture; he must by his prophetical office open it unto me. So after that being unsatisfied in the thing, the Lord was pleased to bring this scripture out of the Hebrews. He that denies the testament denies the testator, and in this did open unto me and give me to see that those which did not teach the new covenant had the spirit of antichrist, and upon this he did discover the ministry unto me and ever since, I bless the Lord, he hath let me see which was the clear ministry and which the wrong. Since that time I confess I have been more choice and he hath left me to distinguish between the voice of my beloved and the voice of Moses, the voice of John Baptist and the voice of antichrist, for all those voices are spoken of in scripture. Now if you do condemn me for speaking what in my conscience I know to be truth I must commit myself unto the Lord.

Mr. Nowel: How do you know that that was the spirit?

Mrs. H.: How did Abraham know that it was God that bid him offer his son, being a breach of the sixth commandment?

Dep. Gov.: By an immediate voice.

Mrs. H.: So to me by an immediate revelation.

Dep. Gov.: How! an immediate revelation.

Mrs. H.: By the voice of his own spirit to my soul. . . .

Gov.: Daniel was delivered by miracle do you think to be deliver'd so too?

Mrs. H.: I do here speak it before the court. I look that the Lord should deliver me by his providence. . . .

Mr. Bartholomew: I speak as a member of the court. I fear that her revelations will deceive.

Gov.: Have you heard of any of her revelations?

Mr. Barthol.: For my own part I am sorry to see her now here and I have nothing against her but what I said was to discover what manner of spirit Mrs. Hutchinson is of; only I remember as we were once going through Paul's church yard she then was very inquisitive after revelations and said that she had never had any great thing done about her but it was revealed to her beforehand.

Mrs. H.: I say the same thing again.

Mr. Barthol.: And also that she said that she was come to New-England but for Mr. Cotton's sake. As for Mr. Hooker (as I remember) she said she liked not his spirit, only she spake of a sermon of his in the Low Countries wherein he said thus—it was revealed to me yesterday that England should be destroyed. She took notice of that passage and it was very acceptable with her. . . .

Dep. Gov.: I desire Mr. Cotton to tell us whether you do approve of Mrs. Hutchinson's revelations as she hath laid them down.

Mr. Cotton: I know not whether I do understand her, but this I say, if she doth expect a deliverance in a way of providence—then I cannot deny it.

Dep. Gov.: No Sir we did not speak of that.

Mr. Cotton: If it be by way of miracle then I would suspect it.

Dep. Gov.: Do you believe that her revelations are true?

Mr. Cotton: That she may have some special providence of God to help her is a thing that I cannot bear witness against.

Dep. Gov.: Good Sir I do ask whether this revelation be of God or no?

Mr. Cotton: I should desire to know whether the sentence of the court will bring her to any calamity, and then I would know of her whether she expects to be delivered from that calamity by a miracle or a providence of God.

Mrs. H.: By a providence of God I say I expect to be delivered from some calamity that shall come to me.

Gov.: The case is altered and will not stand with us now, but I see a marvellous providence of God to bring things to this pass that they are. We have been hearkening about the trial of this thing and now the mercy of God by a providence hath answered our desires and made her to lay open her self and the ground of all these disturbances to be by revelations, . . . the ground work of her revelations is the immediate revelation of the spirit and not by the ministry of the word, and that is the means by which she hath very much abused the country that they shall look for revelations and are not bound to the ministry of the word, but God will teach them by immediate revelations and this hath been the ground of all these tumults and troubles, and I would that those were all cut off from us that trouble us, for this is the thing that hath been the root of all the mischief.

Court: We all consent with you. . . .

Gov.: Of all the revelations that ever I read of I never read the like ground laid as is for this. The Enthusiasts and Anabaptists had never the like.

Mr. Cotton: You know Sir, that their revelations broach new matters of faith and doctrine.

Gov.: So do these and what may they breed more if they be let alone. I do acknowledge that there are such revelations as do concur with the word but there hath not been any of this nature. . . .

Dep. Gov.: These disturbances that have come among the Germans have been all grounded upon revelations, and so they that have vented them have stirred up their hearers to take up arms against their prince and to cut the throats of one another, and these have been the fruits of them, and whether the devil may inspire the same into their hearts here I know not, for I am fully persuaded that Mrs. Hutchinson is deluded by the devil, because the spirit of God speaks truth in all his servants.

Gov.: I am persuaded that the revelation she brings forth is delusion.

All the court but some two or three ministers cry out we all believe it— we all believe it.

. . .

Gov.: The court hath already declared themselves satisfied concerning the things you hear, and concerning the troublesomeness of her spirit and the danger of her course amongst us, which is not to be suffered. Therefore if it be the mind of the court that Mrs. Hutchinson for these things that appear before us is unfit for our society, and if it be the mind of the court that she shall be banished out of our liberties and imprisoned till she be sent away, let them hold up their hands.

All but three.

Those that are contrary minded hold up yours,

Mr. Coddington and Mr. Colborn, only.

Mr. Jennison: I cannot hold up my hand one way or the other, and I shall give my reason if the court require it.

Gov.: Mrs. Hutchinson, the sentence of the court you hear is that you are banished from out of our jurisdiction as being a woman not fit for our society, and are to be imprisoned till the court shall send you away.

Mrs. H.: I desire to know wherefore I am banished?

Gov.: Say no more, the court knows wherefore and is satisfied.

Church Trial of Mistress Ann Hibbens*

The assembled First Church of Boston examined Mistress Ann Hibbens in September and December, 1640, for offense she had given to some of the brethren, stemming from her dispute with the town's joiners (carpenters). After a joiner had done some carpentry work in her house at her request, she had judged the work to be poorly done and the rate excessive, and went to other citizens and joiners (John Davis being one), asking their opinions of the work's value. Brother Davis brought the dispute before the church because of what he considered to be false accusations and contentious behavior on Mrs. Hibbens' part.

There appears to be no evidence of Mrs. Hibbens' reinstatement as a church member. In 1656, two years after the death of her husband, who was a well-respected member of the Boston community, Mrs. Hibbens was accused and convicted of witchcraft and executed.

This account of the trial comes from Robert Keayne's personal notebook, which was usually devoted to notes on John Cotton's sermons, but shows a record of some other church proceedings as well. Spelling and punctuation have been modernized, abbreviations spelled out, and a few words (in brackets) added for sense.

CHURCH TRIAL OF MISTRESS ANN HIBBENS

. . .

Pastor: All this that you now relate is only to excuse yourself and lessen your own fault and lay blame upon others; and therefore you have in an unsatisfied way sent from workman to workman, and from one to another, to view the work and to [ap]praise it; and when the elders and others that met at your own house about this did see reason that you should be satisfied, yet you have been so suspicious and used such speeches to accuse our Brother Davis and other workmen, when they would not speak as you do. Yet you have continued still to be so unsatisfied, that you have caused more expense of time than all your work is worth. And when our Teacher and the elders and myself, upon

* Reprinted from the manuscript of Robert Keayne's "Notes on John Cotton's Sermons," by permission of the Massachusetts Historical Society. "Hibbens Transcript," pp. 13–19, 23, 28–41, 43–47, 55–57, 61–64, used from typescript by permission of Anita Rutman, transcriber.

due search and examination of the matter, we did not find that there was any great wrong done to you—or if it were a wrong yet we thought you ought to have been satisfied and to stir no more in it—but such has been the unquiet frame of your spirit, that you would take no warning, nor hearken to our counsel and exhortation, but have still been stirring, to the offense of many of the congregation whose names and credits you have defamed, and we are unsatisfied also. Therefore consider what whether this has been according to the rule of Christian love; and therefore if you cannot give a better answer, you must expect the further proceedings of the church against you, as shall be most wholesome for your soul.

Elder Oliver: Sister, methinks [this]: the last meeting we had about this business when there was ten of us together, (five for you and five for our Brother Davis), and many witnesses examined, and the joiners professing as in the presence of God that they had rated it as low as ever as they could, and so low as we can get no other joiners in this town to do the like—and they brought it to ten pounds or thereabouts—and therefore methinks you should be satisfied and speak no more.

Mrs. Hibbens: There was a joiner from Salem and some others that saw it that did not reckon it above half the price of what he took for it.

Brother Penn: All that our Sister hath spoken tends not to any measure of repentance or sorrow for her sin, but to her further justification and excusing of herself, and casting blame upon others, which savors of great pride of spirit and a heart altogether untouched by any of those means that hath been used with her.

Sgt. Savage: I think if all other offenses were passed by, that hath been mentioned, yet she hath shed forth one sin in the face of the congregation worthy of reproof: and that is transgressing the rule of the apostle in usurping authority over him whom God hath made her head and husband, and in taking the power and authority which God hath given to him out of his hands; and when he was satisfied and sits down contented she is unsatisfied, and will not be content, but will stir in it, as if she were able to manage it better than her husband, which is a plain breach of the rule of Christ.

Pastor: That indeed is observed in her by diverse [people] as a great aggravation of her sin; in so much that some do think she doth but make a wisp of her husband. Yet this she alleged for herself: that her husband did give her leave to order and carry on this business to her own satisfaction.

Brother Corser: It is thought by many that it is an untruth which she speaks and yet it will be proved on oath that her husband would have had her contented and rest satisfied—and she would not.

Brother Hibbens: At the first I did give my wife leave to agree with the joiner, and to order the business with him as she thought good. Yet I must needs say in faithfulness to the church that when difference did arise about the work, my wife told me she had agreed with him to do it for forty s[hillings]—which I cannot affirm, having no witness but my wife's own affirmation, which he denied from the first. And therefore conceiving that the work was too much for the price, I told him [that] when it was done, what it came to more, I would give him, as two men should judge it worth. And I chose my Brother Davis, of whose faithfulness I am well satisfied, and was very willing to stand to that agreement he made, and did persuade my wife, and could have wished with all my heart she had been willing to have done the same. And I have had some exercise of spirit with her, that she hath not done so. . . .

Mrs. Hibbens: The Lord knoweth that in all this I have but only desired to find out the truth of a thing and to do them good with whom I had to deal. For there being a general complaint of oppression in work and workmen, and I finding this to exceed all reason—in so much as some cried out of the excess of it, and advised me to complain of it in the Court—and because the truth of it would hardly be found out by the joiners of this town, I was counseled to seek out to others in some other town, that would speak the truth, and when they had spoken it, would not be afraid to stand to it; which I did. And because I feared that some such things might be objected, that I did it for lucre of gain, while I might lawfully take that it is my own, yet to prevent that objection, though I found he had taken more by half than the work was worth yet I resolved not to purse one penny of it, but to dispose it to some other use.

Pastor: It is now late and we must draw to a conclusion. And therefore the church is to express themselves, whether we shall proceed to pass some censure upon her, as that of Admonition—for the further melting and humbling of her soul, if God so please; or if He leave her to obstinacy and impenitence, it may make way to the more speedy and finally cutting of her off by that great censure of Excommunication. . . .

[The church then proceeds to approve and deliver the censure of admonition against Mrs. Hibbens.]

Mrs. Hibbens, her next examination by the church, after her former Admonition: upon a second day of the week, appointed on purpose only for her business, to see how her formation Admonition had wrought upon her, and also to give account to Elders of other churches, or any strangers that should come, of the grounds of the church's former proceedings against her; because she conceived and had informed others as if the church had not dealt righteously with her. Therefore this meeting was not on the Lord's day, but appointed on purpose to be on a second day of the week, being the first day of the 12th month, 1640, that strangers might come. . . .

Pastor: Brother Davis, produce your witnesses, that our Sister Hibbens did accuse you and the joiners in the town of such a sinful confederacy before she dealt with you about it.

Brother Davis: She said we had committed such wickedness that the stones in the street and the beams in the house would cry for vengeance, and that the joiners had compacted together to deceive her. Our Brother Button, Mr. Oliver, and Mr. Leveret can witness. . . .

[Oliver, Leveret, and Button give witness.]

Brother Davis: If the pains and arbitrations of Brethren and godly men shall be censured, threatened, and called into question, when they have done to their best skill and judgment as in the sight of God, and have a reproach cast on their names, it will make all men unwilling to arbitrate anything. For I think she hath had at least twenty, or forty several meetings, and she rest in none of them except in one or two that speaks according to her mind, when we were not by. And so to be accused that we commit wickedness and did sin against our consciences, and that the wickedness was so great that the timbers of the house would cry to God for vengeance upon us for this unrighteous valuation of her work—

Brother Button: She expressed so much to me, and to our Brother Painter.

Mr. Cotton: Sister Hibbens, I pray speak to this point in the fear of God and presence of His church. For the thing you are accused of, and for which you are to give satisfaction first, is in this thing: whether you have so thought and spake against our Brethren, and yet did not deal with them in a church way; and whether you do allow yourself in any such thing or do judge yourself for it before the Lord.

Mrs. Hibbens: I, conceiving that I had great wrong, did take occasion to speak to our Pastor about it, unto whom it was the first that I let fall that word of my fear of an agreement among our joiners to keep out the prices of their work; and he bid me if I could prove any such thing, I should declare it to you, and you would take a course with them about it. I never spake of it to any but him only.

Pastor: It is true you did in private declare your grievance to me . . . and I thought you would be advised by me, but you were not, but in an unsatisfied way did go from one to another and inquire of this and that man. And though, as I hear, you have entertained deep prejudice against me, for revealing or speaking of what you imparted to me only in private, now, I did not open it to any—no, not to she that lies in my bosom, though she gave me occasion to reveal it—till I saw you remained still unsatisfied, and went from one to another . . .

Mr. Cotton: Then, Sister Hibbens, I pray, consider and express whether you do not see it in you as a breach of rule, that you should entertain such jealousies and speak so hardly of brethren . . . ?

Mrs. Hibbens: . . . my scruple is this, that they may be helped to see their evil, which I hope in time will come out; and therefore I thought it was my part to labor to search out and find the truth of it. I thought it was not ripe for church proceeding, but in that I did not show so much love to our Brother's soul as to use the right way of bringing him to a sight of his sin, but rather did speak of it to his disgrace, I confess to be my sin, and desire to judge my self and to be more sorry for it before the Lord.

Mr. Cotton: This you could not be brought to see when the church dealt with you, but you left them unsatisfied, which was one ground of your censure—but it is well that God hath helped you now to see it. Therefore, I pray, speak to another point which did aggravate your offense in the church: that though you owed subjection to your husband, and to take advice and counsel from him, but when he did advise you to be quiet and sit still and rest in their arbitration, as in the judgment of God by men, [still] you were unsatisfied, and did still stir up and down with an unquiet and restless spirit, as if you had more wit and care than your husband.

Mrs. Hibbens: My husband did give me leave for the satisfying of my spirit, to search farther into it, and to find out the truth.

Pastor: It was such a grant as Elisau granted to the young prophets when they desired to go seek the body of Eliah: he did refuse to let them go, and knew their journey would be unprofitable, yet when they were so earnest with him, and would take no denial, then he bid them go, but he knew it was in vain. And so it may be your husband yielded to you, but you should have been advised by your husband at first, though it was against your mind or will.

Capt. Gibbens: As this Sister hath made my heart sad, amongst diverse other Brethren, so I would be glad to hear some such expressions from her as may cause myself, with others, to rejoice. Therefore I desire she may not answer things in expressions and terms of will, but let her answer plainly, whether she did indeed accuse our Brethren that they did wickedly, and did sin against their conscience, or no.

Sister Hibbens: I do not remember that I did use any such words, but because two witnesses say so, I am willing to suspect my own self that I might do so.

Mr. Cotton: But if you did so, have you not cause, think you, to judge yourself for it as a Sin?

Mrs. Hibbens: I can say no more than what I have. I do not remember that I spake the words.

Teacher: But that is not the thing you are called to give answer to. Therefore speak plainly to the point. And to help you a little in it before, the thing is this: whether if these Brethren do testify as in the sight and presence of God, that they have done justly and according to a good conscience, then whether you are not bound to believe them, and to acknowledge that you were uncharitable in thinking and speaking so of your Brethren.

Mrs. Hibbens: Yes, I think I ought to believe them, and am to judge myself for it, and lay after such thoughts.

Sgt. Oliver: The answer she makes doth not reach the thing expected from her. Her answer expresseth no more than what any may say in the point of judgment; but that which now is expected from our Sister is penitency and brokenness of spirit for that wrong she hath done them, and those evil thoughts she hath taken up against them.

Pastor: Therefore speak punctually: are you indeed convinced in your conscience that you have wronged them, and do sit as God in the consciences of your Brethren to judge their conscience, which belongs only to God?

Mrs. Hibbens: I can say no more than what I have. I leave that to their own conscience to judge.

Elder Oliver: I desire to speak one word to our Sister, because she hath often affirmed that she doth not remember that she accused our Brethren of wicked and unconscionable dealing. Now I would ask you whether you do not remember such an expression as this, that if you should hold your tongue, the very beams of your house would cry to God for vengeance against them.

Mrs. Hibbens: Yes. I do remember I did so say, and I do think so still.

Elder Oliver: If you can remember those words, it doth plainly argue that you used the former then. So I marvel you should remember this and still justify it, and not the other.

Brother Penn: The answer of our Sister seems to be strange and intolerable . . .

Mr. Wells (probably from Roxbury): I do bless God with my heart and soul to see the patience and lenity of this church, and the wise dealing of the church in laboring to convince her and to bring so many witnesses to prove things. Therefore I do not marvel at the hardness of the heart of this Sister and her uncharitableness of these brethren [more] than I do at the lenity and wisdom and patience of the church in dealing with her. Neither did I come this day with any prejudice against the church in their proceedings with this Sister, so much as to see and hear what may be of use and profitable to ourselves and our church in any such proceedings. Only I think by what I have heard there is just cause in this church, or any other, to have proceeded to Admonition against any member for so many plain breaches of rule. Therefore I must needs justify and join with the church in what they have done, for I have observed all this day, that notwithstanding all the pains that hath been taken with her, yet her acknowledgments hath rather been forced, than voluntary; and that they have been very lean, and thin, and poor, and sparing, without any sign of sorrow and brokenness of spirit, for such great offenses laid to your charge . . .

Brother Penn: It seems to me our Sister hath an incorrigible spirit, for when she is called to acknowledgment for the sin and offense she hath given, she seeks to hide her sin by laying the cause of this carriage of hers [upon others] . . .

Mr. Winthrop: I perceive she hath carried on this business from the beginning with skill and patience, laboring to draw sometimes one and sometimes another to her own judgment, and making the things very heinous and great, setting it out with great aggravations and with a great lamentations of the sin of the parties that had to deal with her. And she cannot but remember that she used many hard expressions to me of their unconscionable dealing in the thing, and would never be satisfied till I had come and viewed her work, and to judge of it. And when I did undervalue it, upon my own want of experience in such work, yet when upon better grounds I altered my judgment, she would never be satisfied, and would know my reasons. And when I did give my reasons, yet she was still unsatisfied, and came again and again to know my reasons, till at last I was fain to turn my back upon her and to say no more. . . .

Brother Eliot: I think this should farther be pressed upon her spirit: her want of wifelike subjection to her husband, and in following his advice and not to do things contrary to it.

Mrs. Hibbens: You may remember, sir, that you have delivered it as an ordinance of God, that a man should hearken to the counsel of his wife—from that speech of God to Abraham, hearken to thy wife in all that she shall say to thee.

Mr. Cotton: Did you hear me say so, or deliver any such point?

Mrs. Hibbens: I was told you did deliver it before I came.

Mr. Cotton: If any told you so, they told you an untruth, for I dare confidently affirm that I never delivered any such thing.

Capt. Gibbens: I desire that our Sister would express who that was, which should tell her so; for myself sometimes dealing with her about her doing things contrary to the advice of her husband, she answered me thus: whether it is better to obey God or man, that judge you. By which she intimated to me that disobedience to the counsel of her godly husband was her obedience to God, and that God would have her to do what she did. So that it argues, she takes it for a principle that the husband must hearken to his wife in the counsel she shall give, and not the wife to the husband. And so she makes a cipher of her husband and his authority, which she should have in great respect.

Brother Fairbank: I conceive she is settled in that opinion, for myself having occasion to speak with her at our Pastor's house about the obedience of wives to husbands, she answered me from that speech of

God to Abraham—hearken to thy wife, in all that she shall say to thee.

Mr. Cotton: That is to be understood when a wife speaks as the oracles of God, according to the mind and will of God—as indeed then the speech of godly women were as oracles, and did declare the mind and counsel of God to their husbands, and then they were to hearken to them as to God. But that wives *now* should be always God's oracles to their husband, and that the husband should obey his wife, and not the wife the husband, that is a false principle. For God hath put another law upon women: wives, be subject to your husbands in all things. Except they should require something of you that is a plain sin, or a direct breach of rule, you ought to obey them and be subject to them in all things. Are you convinced therefore that you ought to hearken to the counsel of your husband, and that it is a sin in you at any time to transgress the will and appointment of your husband?

Mrs. Hibbens: Yes, sir, I do think that I am bound to obey my husband in all lawful things, and that it is a sin to do the contrary.

Pastor: And are you also convinced that it was a sin in you not to obey your husband in being satisfied with that appraisement of brethren, without further agitation?

Mrs. Hibbens: I have said that my husband gave me leave to wade farther, to find out the sin in this business.

Brother Fairbank: I desire it may be put to our Sister again, to declare who it was that told her that our Teacher did declare such a doctrine as she hath expressed.

Elder Oliver: I pray, Sister, satisfy the brethren in what they desire.

Mrs. Hibbens: It was my Sister Bellingham, that told me so, that you delivered such a thing at our Elder Leveret's daughter's marriage.

Mr. Bellingham: This I can testify, that it was neither the opinion nor practice of my wife—but if she had at any time given offense in any such way, she would speedily come in with submission and much melting of spirit.

Mr. Cotton: I know she was of another mind and therefore I doubt our Sister Hibbens did mistake our Sister Bellingham which is now dead. It was with some other expression that did alter that sense which you took it up in.

Pastor: I would have you, Sister, consider [what] the Lord [means], by all this accusation of the brethren, which makes them so jealous of the frame of your spirit and carriage toward your husband; and whether there is not much sin this way in your carriage to your husband, and therefore God leaves you in so great jealousy in the hearts of brethren in this thing, that though you may not be guilty at this time, yet in some such carriages formerly. . . .

[The final questioning of Mrs. Hibbens by Mr. Cotton then proceeds.]

Mr. Cotton: . . . [Now] for your uncharitable censurings, and judgings of your brethren: they have by oath cleared themselves of your prejudice; therefore you are bound to believe them. If you do not, you take upon you to judge their consciences, and so you thrust yourself into God's throne and seat, to know the hearts of men, which is God's peculiar prerogative which he will give to no other. Do you not think it is a sin for you to sit in God's throne? I pray speak.

Mrs. Hibbens: Yes, if I should do so, it were a great sin.

Mr. Cotton: Why, you do so, if after their clearing by oath you do not clear them in your conscience—if you do not believe them, but retain your uncharitable opinion of them still. Therefore, I pray, give God the glory. Do you believe now that they have spoken the truth, and that you have done them wrong, to entertain such thoughts of them as you have done?

Mrs. Hibbens: I dare not clear them, but I leave them on their consciences to God.

Mr. Cotton: I am sorry to hear you say so, and that your heart is so prejudiced against your brethren. The next, then, you are to consider of, is those lies and untruths that you are accused of in speaking about the work. I hope you will acknowledge that all lies or untruths are sins against God.

Mrs. Hibbens: I do not remember that I spake as they accuse me, or with that meaning as they gather, but if they say so, I must submit to it, because I cannot dispute them.

Mr. Cotton: Another offense you are to consider and to give satisfaction for, is your usurping authority over such a head and husband which God hath given to you, who is able to guide and direct you according to God. Now, do you think it is a breach of rule in a wife to transgress the will of her husband, when he requires that which is according to God?

Mrs. Hibbens: My husband did give me leave to search further into the foulness of this business. . . .

Pastor: We see the Lord hath not yet broken her spirit, nor there is nothing comes from her that tends to satisfactions. Therefore we must propound it to the church, what is farther to be done . . .

[Several men speak their approval of the censure of excommunication.]

Capt. Gibbens: This Sister of ours hath held forth many sins this day, in the face of the congregation, the least whereof deserves a sharp censure. She hath accused diverse of the brethren falsely, when no such things appear, and so hath borne false witness against the rule of the Word. She hath taken away their names and credits, what in her lies, which is as precious as life itself. She hath accused others to justify herself. She hath sat in the throne of God himself, as hath been shown her, in judging the consciences and hearts of her brethren. She hath usurped authority over her guide and head, whom she should have obeyed, and unto whom God hath put her in subjection, yet she hath exalted her own wit and will and way above his, to the great dishonor of God and of him. She hath committed one of those seven sins which Solomon saith God hates, that is to sow sedition and strife among brethren. And she has been eminent this way and not only amongst brethren, but she hath done her endeavor to sow discord between churches, and to set them at variance, and to hatch jealousies between them. And indeed I do not know what sin she is not guilty of. And all these are accompanied with impenitency and obstinacy, and therefore I think the church should be unfaithful to her soul if they should not proceed to a farther and sharper censure, and to cast her out from that society which she hath had so slight an esteem of . . .

Sgt. Oliver: For my own part, I look at the case of this Sister of ours to be somewhat like that of Miriam, which rose up against Moses and Aaron, whose leprosy appeared in the face of the Congregation—and there was a law for lepers, that the priest should search and view them, and if upon the search, they found leprosy appearing, the priest was to pronounce them leprous, and then they were to be thrust out for a time, till they were healed of that disease, from the congregation and the society of God's people. As this sister hath been diligently searched and viewed, and upon the search she is found leprous, and diverse spots are risen, and do manifestly appear to the congregation; therefore according to the law of God I think she ought to be pronounced unclean, and as a leprous person, to be put out from amongst us. And it appearing so plainly, I know not how with safety, or without danger of infecting others, we may keep her one week longer amongst us. It hath been too long forborne already, and there is danger that many hath been infected by the church's delay . . . Therefore I think the censure ought speedily to be applied and to cast her out of the church as leprous.

Mr. Hibbens: I humbly crave leave for a word or two of the congregation, in regard of that relation that is between us. I am sorry that I should have any occasion to speak, yet it is not to hinder the church in their proceedings. But what they shall conclude of, I shall sit down contented with. Only I would humbly propose one place, to your wise consideration, if it may be of any use to your direction; and to crave a little more patience and lenity that the Lord may sanctify that to my dear wife . . . If church would show their bowels of pity in sparing or respiting her censure for a time, the Lord may so bow the heart of my wife that she may give the church full satisfaction, which would be the rising of my soul. I shall wholly leave it with you.

[The church members then proceed to assent to the excommunication of Mrs. Hibbens. The Pastor delivers the sentence of excommunication.]

Ordinary Dealings at Suffolk County Court*

These entries from the records of the Suffolk County Court (Massachusetts), 1671–80, indicate some of the ways in which women came before the law.

ORDINARY DEALINGS AT SUFFOLK COUNTY COURT

Session of 28 January, 1672–73

Jasper Indian Sentanced

Jasper m^r Warren's Indian convict by his own confession in Court of committing Fornication. The Court Sentanceth him to bee whip't with fifteen Stripes or to pay Forty shillings in mony fine to the County & Fees of Court.

Joan Negro's Sentance

Joan m^r Warren's Negro convict by her own confession in Court of committing Fornication with Jasper Indian & that she had an illegitemate Childe. The Court Sentances her to bee whip't with fifteen Stripes or to pay Forty Shillings in Mony fine to the County & Fees of Court.

Mercy Veering's Sentance

Mercy Veering convict of uncivill carriage with Sammuell Smith, & bad language & carriages towards her husband John Veering. The Court Sentanceth her to bee whip't with twenty Stripes & to pay Fees of Court standing committed while the Sentance bee performed. Vpon her peticion the Court respites the Execucion of her Sentance till after her next delivery of Childe.

Samm: Smith's Sentance

Samuell Smith, convict of uncivill carriages to & too great familiarity with Mercy the wife of John Veering. The Court Sentanceth him to bee whip't with thirty Stripes. Vpon the humble peticion of the saide

* From *Records of Suffolk County Court: 1671–1680*, Publications of the Colonial Society of Massachusetts, Vol. XXIX (Boston, 1938), pp. 233, 302, 338, 436, 492, 558, 1063–1064.

Smith the Court reversed this judgment and Sentance him to pay ten pounds in mony fine to the County & Fees of Court & after his discharge to depart the Towne of Boston.

Session of 29 July, 1673

Scott's Sent[a]

Sarah Scott presented for Reviling & strikeing her Mother. Vpon due hearing of the case, The Court Sentances her to stand upon a Block or Stoole of two foote high in the Markett place in Boston upon a thursday immediately after lecture with an inscription upon her breast in a faire character For undutifull abusive & reviling speeches & carriages to her naturall mother & to give bond for her good behavio[r] till the next Court of this County 10[li] herselfe & 5[li] apeice two sureties & to pay Fees of Court.

Session of 28 October, 1673

Bedwell Fin[d] 40[s]

Mary Bedwell bound over to this Court to Answer for her railing & scurrilous Language & bad Speeches of which Shee was convict in Court. The Court Sentenc[d] her to bee whip't with fifteen Stripes or to pay Forty Shillings in mony as a Fine to the County & Fees of Court standing committed untill the Sentence bee performed.

Session of 28 April, 1674

Steward Admonish'[t]

Hanna Steward being committed to prison upon suspition of Stealing severall goods from her Master Jonathan Bridgham; which upon hearing could not bee fully proved ag[t] her The Court Admonished her & Order her to pay fees of Court & prison & soe dismissed her.

Stevens discharg[d]

Sarah Stevens committed to prizon upon her saying that she had Lyen with Christopher Lawson; which was fully evidenced against her; but shee denying in Court that shee had soe done The Court judging by her carriages & testimonies concerning her that shee was a distempered crazy woman discharged her.

Walsebee's discharge

The wife of David Walsebee of Brantery being presented for her Idleness & sottish carriage. upon hearing of the case The Court judge there is noe ground for the presentment & soe discharge her.

LICENSES

Anne Puglice upon certificate from the Selectmen of Boston had her Licence renewed to distill & retail strong waters by small quantities for ye yeare ensuing; provided shee did not sell to any of the inhabitants of the Town to drincke it in her house and George Puglice her husband as principall in ten pounds & Richard Collicot & William Bartholmew as Sureties in five pounds apeice acknowledged themselves respectiuely bound to the Treasuro^r of the County of Suffolke on condicion that Anne Puglice should observe all the Laws concerning distilling and retailing of strong waters & that shee should not sell any to the inhabitants of the Town to bee dranck in her house.

Session of 28 July, 1674

Order ab^t Hitt

Jn Answer to the request of Anne Hitt widdow & Administratrix to the Estate sometime Eliphalet Hitts of Boston deceased that Shee might haue Liberty to dispose of & put to Sale some part of that Estate for the paiment of debts & Legacies & maintenance of herselfe & Children: The Court Orders & Empowres the saide Anne Hitt (with the consent & advice) of those that are Sureties for her true Administracion upon the saide Estate) to dispose of & put to Sale the house & ground at Charlestown valued in the Jnventory at £:170. Shee rendring an Account of s^d Sale unto the Court of this County.

Session of 26 January, 1675

Hawkins Sentenced

Mary Hawkins convict in Court of bold whorish carriages & having a bastard Childe & impudent & pernicious Lying: The Court Sentenced her to bee whip't at a Carts tayle up from the dwelling house of John Hall in Boston formerly Ezekiel Foggs Lodgeing into the Town round about the Town house & soe to the prison with twenty five Stripes severely. & within one month following to bee whip't again severely with twenty Five stripes, paying Fees of Court & prison standing committed untill this Sentence bee performed.

[Mary Hawkins' petition

To yᵉ honʳᵈ Court of Assistants now siting at Boston
The humble petition of Mary Hawkins Humbly sheweth
That where as yoʳ pore petitioner hath through her very great sin & wickednes many ways agriuated, brought herselfe vnder the iust sentence of yᵉ Countie Court, one part of wᶜʰ hath bene already inflicted vpon me & though I can not but owne yᵗ I deserue not onely yᵉ other part to be inflicted, but by reason of my sin being so agreuated as It was, neuer to haue any countenans of fauour [showne] to me either from god or [man] yet considering gods wonderfull mercy to humble peniten [sinners] (though very hainous) calls vpon them to turne from the[re] wickednes & liue, & yᵗ yᵉ same spirit of Compashon he works in his people, imboldens me humbly to Supplicate yoʳ honʳˢ yᵗ you wil be pleased to remitt yᵗ other part of yᵉ punishment yᵗ is not yet inflicted, desireing yᵉ lord to worke still more & more in my soule a greater sence of my sin & giue me truly to repent & turne to him & to loath my selfe & sin wᶜʰ I hope in [some] weaker measure I doe, thus leaueing my condition in yᵉ lords & yoʳ hands praying for yoʳ honʳˢ I subscribe myselfe
yoʳ Honʳˢ pore afflicted prisoner
mary hokahans

In Ansʳ to this peticon this Court Judgeth it meet wᵗʰ the Consent of the [County] Court to Grant hir request & Remitts hir second punishment ordering the keep[ʳ] of the prison to Dissmiss hir from yᵉ prison & set hir at liberty]

Fogg Fined

Ezekiel Fogg convict in Court of wanton Lascivious & obscene carriages with Mary Hawkins, the saide Mary now having a bastard Childe; the saide Fogg since the discovery of her being with Childe having encouraged her escape & endeavoured to conveigh her from the hands of Justice: The Court Sentenced him to pay ten pounds in mony as a fine to the County & remit the Forfiture of his bond for non appearance to ten pounds in mony more & to pay Fees of Court standing committed untill the Sentence bee performed.

Session of 29 July, 1679

Phillips' Sent^a

Sarah Phillips Servant unto Wm Green of Boston convict^d in Court by her own confession of Stealing mony from her Ma^r rideing away in mans Apparrell and having a bastard Childe. She knoweth not (Shee Saith) by whome begotten, Sentenced to bee forthwith whip't with Fifteen Stripes and a Fortnight after to bee whip't again at Charlestown with Fifteen Stripes and to pay unto her ma^r Green 3^{ble} damages according to Law, hee defalkeing what hee hath already received, and to pay fees of Court and prison standing committ^d &c^a and order y^t in case her Ma^r do not discharge her of the prison upon her receiving her 2^d punishm^t the keeper is ordered to dispose of her for his Satisfaction and to pay the overplus to her Master.

Waters' Complaint

Upon complaint made to this Court by Elizabeth Waters that her Husband Wm Waters doth refuse to allow her victuals clothing or fireing necessary for her Support or liuelihood and hath acted many unkindnesses and cruelties towards her: The Court having sent for the s^d Wm Waters and heard both partys, do Order that the s^d Waters bee admonish't for his cruelty and unkindness to his wife, and that hee forthwith provide Suitable meate drinke and apparrell for his s^d wife for future at the Judgem^t of m^r Edward Rawson and m^r Richd Collacot or allow her five Shillings per weeke.

Smith Fin^d 10^s

John Smith and Mary his wife complained ag^t & convict^d by testimony of Suffering disorders in their house Sentenc^d to pay ten shillings mony fine to the County and fees of Court standing committ^d &c^a.

Salter Fine^d £.5.

Mary Salter Widdow convicted by testimony of retailing Rum without Licence Sentenc^d to pay Five pounds in money fine to the County according to Law and Fees of Court.

Burnell's complaint and Order

Upon complaint of Sarah Burnell Widdow of W[m] Burnell sometime of Boston dece[d] that her Son Samuel Burnell hath the Estate that was left by her s[d] Husband in his hands & refuseth to releive her or yeild her any Succor or maintenance therefrom: The Court Orders that the s[d] Widdow bee forthw[th] put into possession of the Chamber. Shee formerly had in her Son's house or other at the Judgem[t] of Cap[tn] John Richards and L[t] Daniel Turill and bee paid five Shillings in money per weeke by her Son untill the next Court of this County.

Mercy Short, Bewitched*

Cotton Mather described Mercy Short's possession by witchcraft in his 1692 essay "A Brand Pluck'd out of the Burning," after he had taken her into his home for observation. The following excerpt includes his record of her direct discourse when she was tormented by a "fit."

A BRAND PLUCK'D OUT OF THE BURNING

§ 1. Mercy Short had been taken Captive by our cruel and Bloody Indians in the East, who at the same time horribly Butchered her Father, her Mother, her Brother, her Sister, and others of her Kindred and then carried her, and three surviving Brothers with two Sisters, from Nieuchewannic unto Canada: after which our Fleet Returning from Quebeck to Boston, brought them with other prisoners that were then Redeemed. But altho she had then already Born the Yoke in her youth, Yett God Almighty saw it Good for her to Bear more of that Yoke, before seventeen years of her Life had Rolled away.

§ 2. It was in the Summer of the Year 1692, when sever[al] persons were committed unto the Gaol in Boston on suspicion of having an Hand in that most Horrid and Hellish Witchcraft, which had brought in the Divels upon several parts of the Country, at such a rate as is the just Astonishment of the world; Then it was that Mercy Short, being sent by her Mistress upon an Errand unto the prison, was asked by one of the Suspected Witches for a little Tobacco; and she affronted the Hag (t'was one Sarah Good, since executed at Salem) by throwing an Handful of Shavings at her and saying, That's Tobacco good enough for you. Whereupon that Wretched Woman bestowed some ill words upon her, and poor Mercy was taken with just such, or perhaps much worse, Fits as those which held the Bewitched people then Tormented by Invisible Furies in the County of Essex. A world of misery did shee endure, for diverse weeks together, and such as could not possibly bee

* From George Lincoln Burr (ed.), *Narratives of the Witchcraft Cases 1648–1706* (New York: Barnes & Noble Inc., 1946), pp. 259–260, 267–272. Reprinted by permission of Barnes & Noble Publishers. Copyright 1946 by Barnes & Noble Publishers.

inflicted upon her without the Immediate efficiency of some Agent, or Rational or Malicious; until God was pleased at length to hear the multiply'd prayers of His people for her Deliverance. There were many Remarkable Things in the molestations then given her; Whereof one was that they made her Fast for Twelve Days together. . . .

§ 13. Reader, If thou hadst a Desire to have seen a Picture of Hell, it was visible in the doleful Circumstances of Mercy Short! Here was one lying in Outer Darkness, haunted with the Divel and his Angels, deprived of all common Comforts, tortured with most cruciating Fires, Wounded with a thousand Pains all over, and cured immediately, that the Pains of those Wounds might bee repeated. . . .

§ 14. Her Discourses to *Them* were some of the most Surprising Things imaginable, and incredibly beyond what might have been expected, from one of her small Education or Experience. In the Times of her Tortures, Little came from her, besides direful Shrieks, which were indeed so frightful, as to make many people Quitt the Room. Only now and then any Expression of marvellous Constancy would bee heard from her; *e. g.* "Tho' you kill mee, I'l never do what you would have mee.—Do what you will, yett with the Help of Christ, I'l never touch your Book.—Do, Burn mee then, if you will; Better Burn here, then [than] Burn in Hell." But when her Torturer went off, Then t'was that her senses being still detained in a Captivity to Spectres, as the only object of them, Wee were Ear-witnesses to Disputacions that amazed us. Indeed Wee could not hear what They said unto her; nor could shee herself hear them ordinarily without causing them to say over again: But Wee could Hear Her Answers, and from her Answers Wee could usually gather the Tenour of Their Assaults. . . . But the cheef Argument held between Her and Them, was upon the Business of Signing the *Book*, by Them tendred unto Her.—In the Handling of this Argument, innumerable Things were uttered by her which would have been more Agreeable to One of a greater Elevation in Christianity; but omitting multitudes of such passages, I shall record a few, which were to This Purpose.

Oh You horrid Wretch! You make my very Heart cold within mee. It is an Hell to mee, to hear You speak so! What? Are You *God?* No, bee gone, You Divel! Don't pester mee any more with such horrid Blasphemies!

You! Do You say that You are *Christ!* No, You are a Divel, and I hope that Christ will shortly deliver mee from such a Divel.—The Christ of God came to seek and to save that which is Lost, such as I am; but as for You, You come to seek and confound all that you can light upon.

If You are *Christ,* Pray how came you by that Cloven Foot?—If You are a Christ I am sure you are a very odious One; You shall bee no Christ for mee.—Pray, go about Your Business; if You are Christ, yett I tell you plainly, You shall bee none of my Christ. I know of a Better Christ; and Him will I follow.—You, a Christ! No, You are a Beast. If You had not been a Beast, would You have asked of our Lord that Hee would give You leave to enter into an Herd of Swine!—I think truly, That Hogs are the fittest company for You!—Would You know my mind? Why then, I say this:—When You have become a Man, and have suffered a cruel Death on a Cross for me; and when you have Reconciled me to God, and been some Ages in Heaven powerfully Interceding for my Salvation from the Divel, —Then come to mee again, and I shall have something further to say to You.—In the meantime I say to You, In the Name of the Lord Jesus Christ, the Son of God, Beegone!

You pretend a precious deal of Love to mee indeed! If You Love mee so much, pray, why do you Starve mee? I am een famished; It is Nine Dayes now, that I have not eaten one bitt of Victuals.

Fine Promises! You'l bestow an Husband upon mee, if I'l bee your Servant. An Husband! What? A Divel! I shall then bee finely fitted with an Husband: No I hope the Blessed Lord Jesus Christ will marry my Soul to Himself yett before Hee has done with mee, as poor a Wretch as I am! —Fine Clothes! What? Such as Your Friend Sarah Good had, who hardly had Rags to cover her! Pray why did you not provide better for Her Then?—Never Dy! What? Is my Life in Your Hands? No, if it had, You had killed mee long before this Time!—Whats that?—So You can!—Do it then, if You can. Come, I dare You; here, I challenge You to do it. Kill mee if You can.—Poor Fool!—But hark Yee! If you can keep your Servants alive, the more false Wretch you, to lett the Halter choke the Witches that were hanged the t'other Day! tho' You promised them, that when the Halters were about their Necks, You would come and Rescue them!

You talk of carrying mee to Heaven! It makes mee think of Goody Carrier; pray whither did you carry her?—Heaven! What a foolish Question is that? Was I ever there? No, I never was there; but I hope I shall be there; and I believe what I have heard and read in the Word of God concerning it. I confess, You were once in Heaven; but God for Your Pride, hurled you thence; and You shall never come there again.—They that follow You, will mistake the Way to Heaven, I'l promise 'em. Hee that has the Divel for his Leader must bee content with Hell for his

Lodging.—Hell! Yee Lying Wretch, I have catch'd you in an hundred Lyes; Who would beleeve one Word You say? Yesterday or t'otherday, You told mee there was no Hell; and now You tell mee, that One may come out of Hell when they will. Pray then, Lett Sarah Good come; if I could see her, I am confident shee would tell mee that Hell is a terrible place; and I know there is no coming out.—But if all the Wood in this World were laid in One Fire, it would not bee so dreadful as Hell; that Hell, whither You carry all that follow You. They are out of there Wits that will serve such a Divel. . . .

Stay, One at once!—Well, And is that all that You have to say?—Pray then, Hear what I have to say.—I say this, That when You, yee filthy Witches, first gave yourselves to your Black Master there, it was the worst Dayes work that ever You did in Your Lives. And I seriously advise you all, to Repent of what You have done. I hope tis not altogether Too late, at least for some of you, to Repent.—Tho' you have done mee so much Wrong, yett I heartily wish you so much Good, as Repentance and Conversion.—O that you would fall down before the God against Whom you have sinned, and beg of Him, that for the sake of Jesus Christ, Hee would pardon your horrible sin.—If You won't take this Counsil, I think, twil bee no Hurt to wish that God would bring you out, and that you may Dy for what you have done and that the World may be no longer troubled with you.

Whats that? Must the Younger Women, do yee say, hearken to the Elder?—They must bee another Sort of Elder Women than You then! they must not bee Elder Witches, I am sure. Pray, do you for once Hearken to mee.—What a dreadful Sight are You! An Old Woman, an Old Servant of the Divel! You, that should instruct such poor, young Foolish Creatures as I am, to serve the Lord Jesus Christ, come and urge mee to serve the Divel! Tis an horrible Thing!—And pray, how durst You, after You had given yourself to the Divel, come to the Table of the Lord: I profess I wonder the Divel did not come and fetch you away alive!—But God is a long-suffering God!

Well; and what if I am Fatherless? How often have you told mee of That? No, I been't Fatherless. I have God for my Father and I don't Question but Hee'l provide well for me. Has not Hee upheld mee all the while? I had signed your Book before now, if God had not kept mee with His Grace. You had before now made an end of mee, if God had not stood by mee. And I beleeve that God will yett deliver mee out of your Cruel Hands.

You are Wicked Wretches. What do you show mee the Shape of that good Woman for? I know her. Shee's a good Woman. Shee never did mee any Hurt. Yett you would fain have mee cry out of her. But I will bee so far from crying out of Her that I will not cry out of You; I don't know what Tricks you have gott; but I hope God will keep mee from letting fall one word that may blast the Name of any Person in the World. I will never tell any body, who you are that have Tormented mee, only it may bee I may tell One Gentleman who will be as careful, that no Harm should come on't, as I can desire him.—How ever I hope God will find you out. . . .

Memorandum. T'was an ordinary thing for the Divel to persecute her with Stories of what this and that Body in the Town spoke against her. The Unjust and Absurd Reflections cast upon her by Rash People in the coffee-houses or elsewhere, Wee discerned that the Divel Reported such Passages unto her in her Fitts, to discourage her. But shee bore those Trials as well as the rest.

§ 15. But when shee had so much Release from the captivating Impressions of the Wretches that haunted her, as to bee able to see and hear the Good People about her in the Room, Shee underwent another sort of plague, which I don't Remember that ever I observed in more than One or Two Bewitched person[s] besides her. Her Tortures were turned into Frolicks; and Shee became as extravagant as a Wild-cat. Shee now had her Imaginacion so strangely disordered, that shee must not Acknowledge any of her Friends; but tho' shee Retained a Secret Notion, Who wee were, yett shee might by no means confess it. Shee would sometimes have diverse of these Fitts in a Day, and shee was always excessively Witty in them; never downright Profane, but yett sufficiently Insolent and Abusive to such as were about her. And in these Fitts also shee took an extraordinary Liberty (which I have likewise noted in some other possessed Persons) to animadvert upon all People, that had any thing in their Apparrel that savoured of Curiosity or Ornament. Her Apprehension, Understanding, and Memory, were now Riper than ever in her Life; and yett, when shee was herself, Shee could Remember the other Accidents of her Afflictions but Forgot almost everything that passed in these Ludicrous Intervals. . . .

Susanna Martin, on Trial for Witchcraft*

In his vindication of the Salem witchcraft trials, *The Wonders of the Invisible World* (1693), Cotton Mather included this account of the trial of Susanna Martin, in which typical evidences of her practice of witchcraft were brought forward. She had long been accused, and, after this trial, was executed on July 19, 1692.

THE TRYAL OF SUSANNA MARTIN, AT THE COURT OF OYER AND TERMINER, HELD BY ADJOURNMENT AT SALEM, JUNE 29, 1692

I. Susanna Martin, pleading Not Guilty to the Indictment of Witchcraft brought in against her, there were produced the evidences of many persons very sensibly and grievously Bewitched; who all complaned of the prisoner at the Bar, as the person whom they Believed the cause of their Miseries. And now, as well as in the other Trials, there was an extraordinary endeavour by Witchcrafts, with Cruel and Frequent Fits, to hinder the poor sufferers from giving in their complaints; which the Court was forced with much patience to obtain, by much waiting and watching for it. . . .

IV. John Atkinson Testify'd, That he Exchanged a Cow with a Son of Susanna Martins, whereat she muttered, and was unwilling he should have it. Going to Receive this Cow, tho' he Hamstring'd her, and Halter'd her, she of a Tame Creature grew so mad, that they could scarce get her along. She broke all the Ropes that were fastned unto her, and though she were Ty'd fast unto a Tree, yet she made her Escape, and gave them such further Trouble, as they could ascribe to no cause but Witchcraft.

V. Bernard Peache testify'd, That being in Bed on a Lords-day Night, he heard a scrabbling at the Window, whereat he then saw Susanna

* George Lincoln Burr (ed.), *Narratives of the Witchcraft Cases 1648–1706* (New York: Barnes & Noble Inc., 1946), pp. 229, 231–232, 234–236. Reprinted by permission of Barnes & Noble Publishers. Copyright 1946 by Barnes & Noble Publishers.

Martin come in, and jump down upon the Floor. She took hold of this Deponents Feet, and drawing his Body up into an Heap, she lay upon him near Two Hours; in all which time he could neither speak nor stirr. At length, when he could begin to move, he laid hold on her Hand, and pulling it up to his mouth, he bit three of her Fingers, as he judged, unto the Bone. Whereupon she went from the Chamber, down the Stairs, out at the Door. This Deponent thereupon called unto the people of the House, to advise them of what passed; and he himself did follow her. The people saw her not; but there being a Bucket at the Left-hand of the Door, there was a drop of Blood found on it; and several more drops of Blood upon the Snow newly fallen abroad. There was likewise the print of her two Feet just without the Threshold; but no more sign of any Footing further off: . . .

VI. Robert Downer testifyed, That this Prisoner being some years ago prosecuted at Court for a Witch, he then said unto her, He believed she was a Witch. Whereat she being dissatisfied, said, That some Shee-Devil would Shortly fetch him away! Which words were heard by others, as well as himself. The Night following, as he lay in his Bed, there came in at the Window the likeness of a Cat, which Flew upon him, took fast hold of his Throat, lay on him a considerable while, and almost killed him. At length he remembred what Susanna Martin had threatned the Day before; and with much striving he cryed out, "Avoid, thou Shee-Devil! In the Name of God the Father, the Son, and the Holy Ghost, Avoid!" Whereupon it left him, leap'd on the Floor, and Flew out at the Window.

And there also came in several Testimonies, that before ever Downer spoke a word of this Accident, Susanna Martin and her Family had related, How this Downer had been Handled! . . .

VIII. William Brown testify'd, that Heaven having blessed him with a most Pious and prudent wife, this wife of his one day mett with Susanna Martin; but when she approch'd just unto her, Martin vanished out of sight, and left her extremely affrighted. After which time, the said Martin often appear'd unto her, giving her no little trouble; and when she did come, she was visited with Birds that sorely peck't and Prick'd her; and sometimes a Bunch, like a pullets egg, would Rise in her throat, ready to Choak her, till she cry'd out, "Witch, you shan't choak me!" While this good Woman was in this Extremity, the Church appointed a Day of Prayer, on her behalf; whereupon her Trouble ceas'd; she saw not Martin as formerly; and the Church, instead of their Fast, gave Thanks for her Deliverance. But a considerable while after, she being Summoned to give in some Evidence at the Court, against this Martin, quickly thereupon this Martin came behind her, while she was milking her Cow, and said unto her, "For thy defaming me at Court, I'l make thee the miserablest Creature in the World." Soon after which, she fell into a strange kind of Distemper, and became horribly Frantick, and uncapable of any Reasonable Action; the Physicians declaring, that her Distemper was preternatural, and that some Devil had certainly Bewitched her; and in that Condition she now remained.

IX. Sarah Atkinson testify'd, That Susanna Martin came from Amesbury to their House at Newbury, in an extraordinary Season, when it was not fit for any one to Travel. She came (as she said unto Atkinson) all that long way on Foot. She brag'd and show'd how dry she was; nor could it be perceived that so much as the Soles of her Shoes were wet. Atkinson was amazed at it; and professed, that she should her self have been wet up to the knees, if she had then came so far; but Martin reply'd, She scorn'd to be Drabbled! It was noted, that this Testimony upon her Trial cast her in a very singular Confusion.

X. . . . It was further testify'd by [John Pressy], That after he had given in some Evidence against Susanna Martin, many years ago, she gave him foul words about it; and said, He should never prosper more; particularly, That he should never have more than two Cows; that tho' he were never so likely to have more, yet he should never have them. And that from that very Day to this, namely for Twenty Years together, he could never exceed that Number; but some strange thing or other still prevented his having of any more.

XI. Jervis Ring testifyed, that about seven years ago, he was oftentimes and grievously Oppressed in the Night, but saw not who Troubled him, until at last he, Lying perfectly Awake, plainly saw Susanna Martin approach him. She came to him, and forceably Bit him by the Finger; so that the Print of the Bite is now so long after to be seen upon him.

XII. But besides all of these Evidences, there was a most wonderful Account of one Joseph Ring, produced on this Occasion.

This man has been strangely carried about by Dæmons, from one Witch-Meeting to another, for near two years together; and for one Quarter of this Time, they have made him and kept him Dumb, tho' he is now again able to speak. There was one T. H. who having, as tis judged, a Design of engaging this Joseph Ring in a Snare of Devillism, contrived a wile, to bring this Ring two Shillings in Debt unto him.

Afterwards, this poor man would be visited with unknown shapes, and this T. H. sometimes among them; which would force him away with them, unto unknown Places, where he saw meetings, Feastings, Dancings; and after his Return, wherein they hurried him along thro' the Air, he gave Demonstrations to the Neighbours, that he had indeed been so transported. When he was brought unto these Hellish meetings, one of the First things they still did unto him, was to give him a knock on the Back, whereupon he was ever as if Bound with Chains, uncapable of Stirring out of the place, till they should Release him. He related, that there often came to him a man, who presented him a Book, whereto he would have him set his Hand; promising to him, that he should then have even what he would; and presenting him with all the Delectable Things, persons, and places, that he could imagine. But he refusing to subscribe, the business would end with dreadful Shapes, Noises, and Screeches, which almost scared him out of his witts. Once with the Book, there was a Pen offered him, and an Inkhorn with Liquor in it, that seemed like Blood: but he never toucht it.

This man did now affirm, that he saw the Prisoner at several of those Hellish Randezvouzes.

Note, This Woman was one of the most Impudent, Scurrilous, wicked creatures in the world; and she did now throughout her whole Trial discover herself to be such an one. Yet when she was asked, what she had to say for her self? her Cheef Plea was, That she had Led a most virtuous and Holy Life!

II

An Achieving Society: The Eighteenth Century

The Lady's New Year's Gift, or, *Advice to a Daughter* by George Savile, Marquis of Halifax*

This "pocket" book was first published in London in 1688, and ran through fifteen editions between 1688 and 1765. Frequently advertised in colonial newspapers and recommended for ladies' libraries, particularly in the South, it provided a model of decorum for eighteenth-century colonial ladies to emulate.

ADVICE TO A DAUGHTER

That which challengeth the next place in your Thoughts, is, How to live with a *Husband:* And though that is so large a Word, that few *Rules* can be fix'd to it which are unchangeable, the *Methods* being as various as the *Tempers* of *Men* to which they must be suited; yet I cannot omit some *General Observations*, which, with the help of your own, may the better direct you in the part of your Life upon which your *Happiness* most dependeth.

It is one of the Disadvantages belonging to your Sex, that young Women are seldom permitted to make their own *Choice;* their Friends Care and Experience are thought safer Guides to them, than their own *Fancies;* and their *Modesty* often forbiddeth them to refuse when their Parents recommend, though their *inward Consent* may not entirely go along with it: In this case there remaineth nothing for them to do, but to endeavour to make that easie which falleth to their *Lot,* and by a wise use of every thing they may dislike in a *Husband,* turn that by degrees to be very supportable, which, if neglected, might in time beget an *Aversion.*

You must first lay it down for a Foundation in general, That there is *Inequality* in *Sexes,* and that for the better Oeconomy of the World; the *Men,* who were to be the Law-givers, had the larger share of *Reason* bestow'd upon them; by which means your Sex is the better prepar'd

---

* Advice to a Daughter (London, 1688), pp. 24–42, 44–45, 57–61. Reprinted by permission of Harvard College Library.

for the *Compliance* that is necessary for the performance of those *Duties* which seem'd to be most properly assign'd to it. This looks a little uncouthly at the first appearance; but upon examination it will be found, that *Nature* is so far from being unjust to you, that she is partial on your side: She hath made you such large *Amends* by other Advantages, for the seeming *Injustice* of the first Distribution, that the Right of Complaining is come over to our Sex; you have it in your power not only to free your selves, but to subdue your Masters; and without violence throw both their *Natural* and *Regal Authority* at your Feet. We are made of differing *Tempers*, that our *Defects* might be mutually supplied: Your *Sex* wanteth our *Reason* for your *Conduct*, and our *Strength* for your *Protection: Ours* wanteth your *Gentleness* to soften, and to entertain us. The first part of our Life is a good deal of it subjected to you in the *Nursery*, where you Reign without Competition, and by that means have the advantage of giving the first *Impressions;* after you have stronger Influences, which well manag'd, have more force in your behalf, than all our *Privileges* and *Jurisdictions* can pretend to have against you. You have more strength in your *Looks*, than we have in our *Laws;* and more power by your *Tears*, than we have by our *Arguments*.

It is true, that the *Laws* of *Marriage* run in a harsher stile towards your *Sex*. *Obey* is an ungentle word, and less easie to be digested, by making such an unkind distinction in the Terms of Contract, and so very unsuitable to the excess of *Good Manners*, that generally goes before it; besides, the *universality* of the Rule seemeth to be a *Grievance*, and it appeareth reasonable, that there might be an *Exemption* for extraordinary Women, for ordinary Rules, to take away the just Exception that lieth against the false measure of *general Equality:* it may be alledged by the *Council* retained by your Sex, as there is in all other Laws an Appeal from the *Letter* to *Equity* in Cases that require it; It is reasonable, that some *Court* of a larger *Jurisdiction* might be erected, where some Wives might resort and plead, *especially*, and in such Instances, where Nature is so kind as to raise them above the *level* of their own Sex, that they might have *Relief*, and obtain a *Mitigation* in their own particular, of a Sentence which was given generally against *Womankind*.

The causes of *Separation* are now so very course, that few are *confident* enough to buy their *Liberty* at the price of having Modesty so exposed, and for *disparity of Minds*, which above all other things re-

quireth a *Remedy*, the *Laws* have made no *provision;* so little refin'd
are numbers of Men, by whom they are compil'd. This, and a great deal
more might be said to give a colour to this Complaint; but the Answer
is, in short, That the *Institution* of *Marriage* is too sacred to admit of a
Liberty of *Objection* to it: that the Supposition of your being the
weaker Sex, having without all doubt a good Foundation, maketh it
reasonable to subject it to the *Masculine Dominion;* that no *Rule* can be
so *perfect,* as not to admit some *Exceptions;* but the Law presumeth
there would be so few found in this Case, who would have a sufficient
Right to such a Privilege, that it is safer some *Injustice* should be
conniv'd at in a very few Instances, than to break into an Establishment
upon which the Order of Humane Society doth so much depend. You
are therefore to make the best of what is *setled* by Law, and not vainly
imagine, that it will be *changed* for your sake. But that you may not be
discouraged, as if you lay under the weight of an *incurable Grievance,*
you are to know, that by a *wise* and *dexterous* Conduct, it will be in
your power to *retrieve* your self from any thing that looketh like a
disadvantage in it. For your better direction, I will give a hint of the
most *ordinary Causes* of *Dissatisfaction* between Man and Wife, that
you may be able by such a *Warning* to live so upon your *Guard,* that
when you shall be married, you may know how to *cure* your Husband's
Mistakes, and to *prevent* your own.

First then, you are to consider, you live in a time which hath rendred
some kind of Frailties so habitual, that they lay claim to large *Grains* of
Allowance. The World in this is somewhat unequal, and our Sex
seemeth to play the *Tyrant,* in distinguishing *partially* for our selves, by
making that in the utmost degree *Criminal* in the *Woman,* which in a
Man passeth under a much *gentler Censure.* The Root and Excuse of
this Injustice is the *Preservation* of Families from any Mixture that may
bring a Blemish to them: And whilst the *Point* of *Honour* continues to
be so plac'd, it seems unavoidable to give your *Sex* the greater share of
the Penalty. But if in this it lieth under any *Disadvantage,* you are more
than recompens'd; by having the *Honour* of *Families* in your keeping.
The Consideration so great a Trust must give you, maketh full amends;
and this Power the World hath lodg'd in you can hardly fail to restrain
the Severity of an *ill* Husband, and to improve the Kindness and
Esteem of a *good* one. This being so, remember, That next to the
danger of *committing* the Fault your self, the greatest is that of *seeing*
it in your *Husband.* Do not seem to look or hear that way: If he is a

Man of Sence, he will reclaim himself; the Folly of it, is of it self sufficient to cure him: If he is not so, he will be provok'd, but not reform'd. To expostulate in these looketh like declaring War, and Preparing for Reprisals; which to a *thinking Husband* would be a dangerous Reflexion. Besides, it is so course a Reason which will be assign'd for a lady's too great Warmth upon such an occasion, that Modesty no less than Prudence ought to restrain her; since such an undecent Complaint makes a *Wife* much more Ridiculous, than the Injury that provoketh her to it. But it is yet worse, and more unskilful, to *blaze* it in the World, expecting it should rise up in Arms to take her part: Whereas she will find, it can have no other Effect, than that she will be served up in all Companies, as the *reigning Jest* at that time; and will continue to be the common Entertainment, till she is rescu'd by some *newer Folly* that cometh upon the Stage, and driveth her away from it. The Impertinence of such Methods is so plain, that it doth not deserve the Pains of being laid open. Be assur'd, that in these Cases your *Discretion* and *Silence* will be the most *prevailing Reproof;* and an *affected Ignorance,* which is seldom a *Vertue,* is a great one here: And when your *Husband* seeth how unwilling you are to be uneasie, there is no stronger Argument to persuade him not to be unjust to you. Besides, it will naturally make him more *yielding* in other things: And whether it be to *cover* or *redeem* his *Offence,* you may have the good Effect of it whilst it lasteth, and all that while have the most reasonable Ground that can be, of presuming, such a Behaviour at last will intirely convert him. There is nothing so glorious to a *Wife,* as a Victory so gain'd: A Man so reclaim'd, is for ever after subjected to her *Vertue;* and her *bearing* for a time, is more than rewarded by a Triumph that will continue as long as her Life.

The next thing I will suppose, is, That your *Husband* may love *Wine* more than is convenient. It will be granted, That though there are Vices of a deeper dye, there are none that have greater *Deformities* than this, when it is not restrain'd: But with all this, the same Custom which is the more to be lamented for its being so general, should make it less uneasie to every one in particular who is to suffer by the Effects of it: So that in the first place, it will be no new thing if you have a *Drunkard* for your *Husband;* and there is by too frequent Examples evidence enough, that such a thing may happen, and yet a *Wife* may live too without being miserable. . . .

I am tempted to say (if the Irregularity of the Expression could in strictness be justified) That a *Wife* is to thank God her *Husband* hath *Faults*. Mark the seeming Paradox, my Dear, for your own Instruction, it being intended no further. A *Husband* without *Faults* is a dangerous Observer; he hath an Eye so piercing, and seeth every thing so plain, that it is expos'd to his Censure; and though I will not doubt but that your *Vertue* will disappoint the sharpest Enquiries, yet few Women can bear the having all they say or do *represented* in the clear Glass of an Understanding without *Faults*. Nothing sofneth the *Arrogance* of our *Nature*, like a Mixture of some *Frailties* . . . The *Faults* and *Passions* of *Husbands* bring them down to you, and make them content to live upon less unequal Terms, than Faultless Men would be willing to stoop to. . . .

Consider, that where the Man will give such frequent Intermissions of the use of his *Reason*, the *Wife* insensibly getteth a Right of *Governing* in the Vacancy, and that raiseth her *Character* and *Credit* in the Family, to a higher pitch than perhaps could be done under a *sober Husband*, who never putteth himself into an Incapacity of holding therein. If these are not Intire *Consolations*, at least they are *Remedies* to some Degree: . . .

The last supposition I will make is, That your *Husband* should be *weak* and *incompetent* to make use of the Privileges that belong to him; it will be yielded, that such a one leaveth room for a great many Objections; but God Almighty seldom sendeth a *Grievance* without a *Remedy*, or at least such a Mitigation as taketh away a great part of the sting, and the smart of it. To make such a *Misfortune* less heavy, you are to cling to your Observations. That a *Wife* very often maketh the better Figure, for her *Husbands* making no great one; . . . If you will be more ashamed in some Cases, of such a *Husband*, you will be less afraid than you would perhaps be of a wise one; his *Unseasonable Weakness*, may no doubt sometimes grieve you, but then set against this, that it giveth you the *Dominion*, if you will make the right use of it; it is next to his being dead, in which case the Wife hath right to Administer; therefore be sure, if you have such an Ideot, that none, except your self, may have the benefit of the forfeiture: Such a Fool is a dangerous Beast, if others have the keeping of him; and you must be very dextrous, if when your *Husband* shall resolve to be an *Ass*, you do not take care he may be *your Ass;* but you must go skillfully about it, and above all things, take heed of distinguishing in publick what kind of *Husband* he is; your inward thoughts must not hinder the outward payment of the consideration that is due to him; your *slighting* him in *Company*, besides, that it would, to a discerning By-stander, give too great encouragement for the making nearer application to you, is in it self such an indecent way of assuming, that it may provoke the same Creature to break loose, and to shew his *Dominion* for his Credit, which he was content to forget for his Ease: In short, the surest and the most approved method will be to do like a wise *Minister* to an easy *Prince*; first give him the Orders you afterwards receive from him; with all this, that which you are to pray for, is a *Wise Husband*, one that by knowing how to *Master*, for the very reason will not let you feel the weight of it; one whose Authority is so soften'd by his Kindness, that it giveth you ease without abridging your *Liberty*; one that will return so much freedom for your *Just Esteem* of him, that you will never want *power*, though you will seldom care to use it; such a *Husband* is as much above all the other Kindnesses of them, as a *rational subjection* to a Prince, great in himself, is to be preferr'd before the disquiet and uneasiness of *Unlimited Liberty*.

Sarah Osborn's Religious Conversion*

Sarah Osborn, noted for her piety during her long life in Newport, Rhode Island, was born in London in 1714. Her family emigrated to the Colonies in 1722 and settled in Newport in 1729. The following part of her memoirs, which includes her experience during the "Great Awakening" in New England, was completed in 1743. She lived until 1796, acting as religious mentor to younger people, giving religious instruction in her home, and teaching school to support herself.

SARAH OSBORN'S RELIGIOUS CONVERSION

. . . I thought I trusted in God; and used frequently, in times of trial, to go and pour out my complaints to him, thinking he was my only support. But I dare not now be positive, or really conclude, that I know what it was to put my trust in God; for my conduct after this seems so inconsistent with grace, that I dare not say I had one spark of it then; but rather think I was only under a common work of the Spirit: Though some times I think I had true grace, though very weak. . . . After this (O that with deep humility of soul, with sorrow and shame, I could speak of it) I relapsed again, and was full of vanity. I kept company with a young man, something against my parents' will. But that was owing to false reports raised of him; for at first they liked him. I made resolutions, that, after I was married, I would lead a new life, flattering myself that then I should not have the hinderances which I now had. I used bitterly to reflect upon myself, when I had given myself liberty to be merry; for though I appeared outwardly so, I had no real pleasure: But still put off repentance, or an entire breaking off from vanity, till a more convenient season; and so resisted the Spirit of God. . . . In process of time, I was married to Mr. Samuel Wheaten, being in my eighteenth year, October 21, 1731, and went with my husband, then next winter, to see his friends in the country; where I stayed almost five months; and was almost all the time under strong convic-

* Samuel Hopkins (ed.), *Memoirs of the Life of Mrs. Sarah Osborn* (Worcester, Mass.: Leonard Worcester, 1799), pp. 15–21, 39, 42–43, 45–46, 49–55.

tions. Oh, how I did sweat and tremble for fear my convictions should wear off again, and plead with God to set home strong convictions, and never, never suffer them to cease, till they ended in a sound and saving conversion. . . .

. . . From this time I had a hope again, at times, that Christ was mine. But it was some years after before it pleased God to answer it fully, by giving me an assurance of it. . . .

After I came home, I met with much affliction in many respects. It seemed to me that the whole world were in arms against me. I thought I was the most despised creature living upon earth. I used to pray to God in secret to relieve me; but did not, as I ought, see his hand in permitting it so to be, as a just punishment for my vile sins: And therefore was not humbled under it as I ought; but let nature rise, and acted very imprudently, in many respects. I was then with child, and often lamented that I was to bring a child into such a world of sorrow: But some times found a disposition to dedicate my babe to God, while in the womb; and did so, at all seasons of secret prayer. And after it was born, my husband being at sea, I could not rest till I had solemnly given it up to God in baptism. And I thought that I did indeed give up both myself and it to God.

I met with many trials in my lying in, it being an extreme cold season. My child was born on Oct. 27, 1732. The next spring, my husband returned home; but went to sea again, and died abroad in November, 1733. I was then in my twentieth year. The news of my husband's death came to me on the first of the next April. . . . But God appeared wonderfully for my support. I saw his hand, and was enabled to submit with patience to his will. I daily looked round me, to see how much heavier the hand of God was laid on some others, than it was on me, where they were left with a large number of children, and much involved in debt. And I had but one to maintain; and, though poor, yet not involved. Others, I saw, as well as myself, had their friends snatched from them by sudden accidents. The consideration of these things, together with the thoughts of what I deserved, stilled me so, that though the loss of my companion, whom I dearly loved, was great; yet the veins of mercy, which I saw running through all my afflictions, were so great likewise, that, with Job, I could say, "The Lord gave, and the Lord hath taken away, and blessed be the name of the Lord."

. . . As before this affliction every one seemed to be enemies to me, so from that time, all became friends. My parents treated me very tenderly; and God inclined every one who saw me to be kind to me. My brother was come into New-England: And being a single man, we went to housekeeping together. But in three months after he married, and I soon found it would not do to live as before; and began to be thoughtful how I should do. I could see no way in which I could get a living. All doors seemed to be shut. But I verily believed that God would point out a way for me. And accordingly, the very day I came to a resolution to move as soon as I could, a stranger to my case, who kept a school a little way off, came to me, and told me that she only waited for a fair wind to go to Carolina; and, if it would suit me, I should have her chamber and schollars; which I joyfully accepted. Thus the widow's God remarkably provided for me. This was on Nov. 19, 1734. I was then placed in a family, who discovered a great deal of affection for me; and in all respects used me as tenderly as if I had been a near relation.

. . . The instances of the remarkable hand of God in his providence, in ordering my temporal affairs, are innumerable. But, oh vile wretch! after all this I grew slack again, and got into a cold, lifeless frame. As I grew better in bodily health, my soul grew sick. I daily laid up a stock for repentance. But, through rich grace, I was again convinced of my stupidity, and began to be more diligent in attending on the means of grace. But I found I could not profit by the word preached: Nothing reached my heart; all seemed but skin deep: And the more I went to meeting, the more I found it so. Then I began to think I must take some other course. . . .

. . . [And] O, when I had finished writing my covenant, which was on the 26th of March, 1737, and came to spread it before God, and with prayers and tears to deliver it to him as my own act and deed, it verily seemed to me that all the heavens rang with acclamations of joy, that such a prodigal as I was returned to my God and Father. . . .

These were happy days—But now how shall I speak! Oh, that I may do it with a heart truly broken for my sins! After all this, I began to grow more conformed to the world. Things which, when I was thus lively, appeared insipid, and indeed odious to me, began to grow more tolerable, and by degrees in a measure pleasant. And depraved nature and Satan together pleaded for them thus, "That there was a time for all things; and singing and dancing now and then, with a particular friend, was an innocent diversion. Who did I see, besides myself, so precise and strict? Other christians allowed themselves in such things, who, I had reason to think, were far superior to me in grace; especially one with whom I was very intimate. Sure, if it was sin, she would not allow herself in it. It was for extraordinary christians, such as ministers, and others who were eminent for piety, to avoid the practice of such things, and not for *me*. Who did I think I was, that I should pretend to outdo other christians? They could talk of worldly things. What ailed me?" Thus the devil and carnal reasoning argued me out of a great part of my resolutions for strict godliness; and, in short, made me, in a sort, believe that it was only pride and hypocrisy, and to be seen of men, that had ever made me pretend to it.

Thus I sunk by degrees lower and lower, till I had at last almost lost all sense of my former experiences. I had only the bare remembrance of them, and they seemed like dreams or delusion; at some times. At others again, I had some revivals. . . . But I knew I was a dreadful backslider, and had dealt treacherously with God . . .

In Sept. 1740, God in mercy sent his dear servant Whitefield[1] here, which in some measure stirred me up. But when Mr. Tennent[2] came soon after, it pleased God to bless his preaching so to me, that it roused me. But I was all the winter after exercised with dreadful doubts and fears about my state. I questioned the truth of all I had experienced, and feared I had never yet passed through the pangs of the new birth, or ever had one spark of grace.

. . . I continued thus till March, 1741. And then it pleased God to return Mr. Tennent to us again, and he preached twenty one sermons here. But while he was here, I was more than ever distressed. I had lost the sensible manifestations of Christ's love. . . . And [Mr. Tennent] struck directly at those things, for which I had so foolishly and wickedly pleaded christian example, such as singing songs, dancing and foolish jesting, which is not convenient. He said, he would not say there was no such thing as a dancing christian, but he had a very mean opinion of such as could bear to spend their time so, when it is so short, and the work for eternity so great. Then, and not till then, was I fully con-

---

[1] George Whitefield, English evangelical preacher who undertook a speaking tour in the American Colonies in 1739–41. He kindled the "great and general revival of religion" in the 1740s. —Ed.

[2] Gilbert Tennent, a "New Light" Presbyterian minister from New Jersey who benefited in prestige and following from his association with Whitefield during the latter's visits to America. —Ed.

vinced what prodigal wasters of precious time such things were. And, through grace, I have abhorred them all ever since.

. . . After I was thus revived, my longings to be made useful in the world returned, and I earnestly pleaded with God that he would not suffer me to live any longer an unprofitable servant; but would point out some way, in which I might be useful: And that I might now be as exemplary for piety, as I had been for folly. And it pleased God so to order it, that I had room to hope my petitions were both heard, and in a measure answered. For soon after this a number of young women, who were awakened to a concern for their souls, came to me, and desired my advice and assistance, and proposed to join in a society, provided I would take the care of them. To which, I trust with a sense of my own unworthiness, I joyfully consented. And much sweetness we enjoyed in these meetings. . . .

About this time I had the offer of a second marriage, with one who appeared to be a real christian (and I could not think of being unequally yoked with one who was not such). I took the matter into serious consideration. I foresaw there were difficulties which I must unavoidably encounter; and many duties would be incumbent on me, to which I had been a stranger: Particularly, in my being a mother in law to three sons, which my proposed husband had by a first wife. But after weighing all circumstances, as well as I could, in my mind, and earnest prayer, which God enabled me to continue in for some time, I concluded it was the will of God, that I should accept of the offer, and accordingly was married to Mr. Henry Osborn, on the fifth day of May, 1742. . . .

Soon after this, we fell into disagreeable and difficult worldly circumstances, with respect to living and paying the debts we owed. My greatest concern was with respect to the latter, lest we should not be able to do justice, and so wrong our creditors, and bring dishonor on God, and our profession. Under this pressure and distress, I was relieved and supported by the following words of Scripture, "Let your conversation be without covetousness, and be content with such things as ye have; for he hath said, I will never leave thee, nor forsake thee." I lived cheerfully, upon this promise, for a considerable time. And God ordered things so that our creditors were paid to their satisfaction.

I have often thought God has so ordered it throughout my days hitherto, that I should be in an afflicted, low condition, as to worldly circumstances, and inclined the hearts of others to relieve me in all my distresses, on purpose to suppress that pride of my nature, which doubtless would have been acted out greatly to his dishonor, had I enjoyed health, and had prosperity, so as to live independent of others. I will therefore think it best for me; . . . [and], on account of my poverty, I never was despised.

Letter from an Indentured Servant*

This is one of the few available firsthand accounts of the condition of a female servant in the southern Colonies in the eighteenth century.

ELIZABETH SPRIGS TO JOHN SPRIGS

TO MR. JOHN SPRIGS WHITE SMITH IN WHITE CROSS STREET
NEAR CRIPPLE GATE LONDON

Honred Father   Maryland Sept'r 22'd 1756.

My being for ever banished from your sight, will I hope pardon the Boldness I now take of troubling you with these, my long silence has been purely owing to my undutifullness to you, and well knowing I had offended in the highest Degree, put a tie to my tongue and pen, for fear I should be extinct from your good Graces and add a further Trouble to you, but too well knowing your care and tenderness for me so long as I retain my Duty to you, induced me once again to endeavour if possible, to kindle up that flame again. O Dear Father, belive what I am going to relate the words of truth and sincerity, and Ballance my former bad Conduct [to] my sufferings here, and then I am sure you'll pitty your Destress[ed] Daughter, What we unfortunat English People suffer here is beyond the probability of you in England to Conceive, let it suffice that I one of the unhappy Number, am toiling almost Day and Night, and very often in the Horses druggery, with only this comfort that you Bitch you do not halfe enough, and then tied up and whipp'd to that Degree that you'd not serve an Annimal, scarce any thing but Indian Corn and Salt to eat and that even begrudged nay many Negroes are better used, almost naked no shoes nor stockings to wear, and the comfort after slaving dureing Masters pleasure, what rest we can get is to rap ourselves up in a Blanket and ly upon the Ground, this is the deplorable Condition your poor Betty endures, and now I

* Isabel Calder (ed.), *Colonial Captivities, Marches, and Journeys* (New York: The Macmillan Company, 1935), pp. 151-152. Reprinted by permission of Mrs. Alfred Howe Terry for the National Society of Colonial Dames of America in the State of Connecticut. Copyright 1935 by The Macmillan Co.

beg if you have any Bowels of Compassion left show it by sending me some Relief, C[l]othing is the principal thing wanting, which if you should condiscend to, may easely send them to me by any of the ships bound to Baltimore Town Patapsco River Maryland, and give me leave to conclude in Duty to you and Uncles and Aunts, and Respect to all Friends

Honred Father
Your undutifull and Disobedient Child
Elizabeth Sprigs

Please to direct for me
at Mr. Rich'd Crosses to
be left at Mr. Luxes Merc't
in Baltimore Town Patapsco River
Maryland

Sally Wister's Revolutionary War-Time Diary*

The following journal was kept by fifteen-year-old Sally Wister, as if addressed to her friend Deborah Norris in Philadelphia. The Wister family were Philadelphians but had removed to a relative's country house when it became evident (shortly after the battle of Brandywine) that the British would occupy the city.

SALLY WISTER'S REVOLUTIONARY WAR-TIME DIARY

September, 1777

Yesterday, which was the 24th of September, two Virginia officers called at our house, and informed us that the British army had crossed the Schuylkill. Presently after, another person stopped, and confirmed what they had said, and that General Washington and army were near Pottsgrove. Well, thee may be sure we were sufficiently scared; however, the road was very still till evening. About seven o'clock we heard a great noise. To the door we all went. A large number of waggons, with about three hundred of the Philadelphia militia. They begged for drink, and several pushed into the house. One of those that entered was a little tipsy, and had a mind to be saucy. I then thought it time for me to retreat; so figure me (mightily scared, as not having presence of mind enough to face so many of the military) running in at one door, and out at another, all in a shake with fear; but after a little, seeing the officers appear gentlemanly and the soldiers civil, I called reason to my aid. My fears were in some measure dispelled, tho' my teeth rattled, and my hand shook like an aspen leaf. They did not offer to take their quarters with us; so, with many blessings, and as many adieus, they marched off. . . .

Fifth Day, September 26th.

We were unusually silent all the morning; no passengers came by the house, except to the mill, and we don't place much dependence on mill news. About 12 o'clock, cousin Jesse heard that General Howe's army

* Reprinted from *Pennsylvania Magazine of History and Biography*, IX: 319–324, 326–327, 332–333; X: 51–52, 55–57.

had moved down towards Philadelphia. Then, my dear, our hopes and fears were engaged for you. However, my advice is, summon up all your resolution, call Fortitude to your aid, don't suffer your spirits to sink, my dear; there's nothing like courage; 'tis what I stand in need of myself, but unfortunately have but little of it in my composition. I was standing in the kitchen about 12, when somebody came to me in a hurry, screaming, "Sally, Sally, here are the light horse!" This was by far the greatest fright I had endured; fear tack'd wings to my feet; I was at the house in a moment; at the porch I stopt, and it really was the light horse. I ran immediately to the western door, where the family were assembled, anxiously waiting for the event. They rode up to the door and halted, and enquired if we had horses to sell; he answered negatively. "Have not you, sir," to my father, "two black horses?"— "Yes, but have no mind to dispose of them." My terror had by this time nearly subsided. The officer and men behaved perfectly civil; the first drank two glasses of wine, rode away, bidding his men to follow, which, after adieus in number, they did. The officer was Lieutenant Lindsay, of Bland's regiment, Lee's troop. The men, to our great joy, were Americans, and but 4 in all. What made us imagine them British, they wore blue and red, which with us is not common. It has rained all this afternoon, and, to present appearances, will all night. In all probability the English will take possession of the city to-morrow or next day. What a change it will be! . . .

Nothing worth relating has occurred this afternoon. Now for trifles. I have set a stocking on the needles, and intend to be mighty industrious. This evening our folks heard a very heavy cannon. We suppose it to be fired by the English. The report seem'd to come from Philadelphia. We hear the American army will be within five miles of us tonight. The uncertainty of our position engrosses me quite. Perhaps to be in the midst of war, and ruin, and the clang of arms. But we must hope the best. . . .

Second Day, October 19th.

Now for new and uncommon scenes. As I was lying in bed, and ruminating on past and present events, and thinking how happy I should be if I could see you, Liddy came running into the room, and said there was the greatest drumming, fifing, and rattling of waggons that ever she had heard. What to make of this we were at a loss. We dress'd and down stairs in a hurry. Our wonder ceased. The British had left Germantown, and our army were marching to take possession. It was the general opinion they would evacuate the capital. Sister B. and myself, and G. E. went about half a mile from home, where we cou'd see the army pass. Thee will stare at my going, but no impropriety, in my opine, or I should not have gone. We made no great stay, but return'd with excellent appetites for our breakfast. Several officers call'd to get some refreshments, but none of consequence till the afternoon. Cousin P. and myself were sitting at the door; I in a green skirt, dark short gown, etc. Two genteel men of the military order rode up to the door: "Your servant, ladies," etc.; ask'd if they could have quarters for General Smallwood. Aunt F. thought she could accommodate them as well as most of her neighbors,—said they could. One of the officers dismounted, and wrote "Smallwood's Quarters" over the door, which secured us from straggling soldiers. After this he mounted his steed and rode away. When we were alone, our dress and lips were put in order for conquest, and the hopes of adventures gave brightness to each before passive countenance. . . . Dr. Gould usher'd the gentlemen into our parlour, and introduc'd them,—"General Smallwood, Captain Furnival, Major Stodard, Mr. Prig, Captain Finley, and Mr. Clagan, Colonel Wood, and Colonel Line." These last two did not come with the General. They are Virginians, and both indispos'd. The General and suite, are Marylanders. Be assur'd, I did not stay long with so many men, but secur'd a good retreat, heart-safe, so far. Some sup'd with us, others at Jesse's. They retir'd about ten, in good order. How new is our situation! I feel in good spirits, though surrounded by an army, the house full of officers, the yard alive with soldiers,—very peaceable sort of people, tho'. They eat like other folks, talk like them, and behave themselves with elegance; so I will not be afraid of them, that I won't. Adieu. I am going to my chamber to dream, I suppose, of bayonets and swords, sashes, guns, and epaulets. . . .

Second Day, 26th October.

The General and officers drank tea with us, and stay'd part of the evening. After supper I went with aunt, where sat the General, Colonel Line, and Major Stodard. So Liddy and I seated ourselves at the table in order to read a verse-book. The Major was holding a candle for the General, who was reading a newspaper. He look'd at us, turn'd away his eyes, look'd again, put the candlestick down, up he jumps, out of the door he went. "Well," said I to Liddy, "he will join us when he comes in." Presently he return'd, and seated himself on the table. "Pray, ladies, is there any songs in that book?" "Yes, many." "Can't you favor me with a sight of it?" "No, Major; 'tis a borrow'd book." "Miss Sally, can't you sing?" "No." Thee may be sure I told the truth there. Liddy, saucy girl, told him I could. He beg'd, and I deny'd; for my voice is not much better than the voice of a raven. We talk'd and laugh'd for an hour. He is clever, amiable, and polite. He has the softest voice, never pronounces the *r* at all.

I must tell thee, to-day arriv'd Colonel Guest and Major Leatherberry; the former a smart widower, the latter a lawyer, a sensible young fellow, and will never swing for want of tongue. Dr. Diggs came Second day; a mighty disagreeable man. We were oblig'd to ask him to tea. He must needs pop himself between the Major and me, for which I did not thank him. After I had drank tea, I jump'd from the table, and seated myself at the fire. The Major follow'd my example, drew his chair close to mine, and entertain'd me very agreeably. Oh, Debby; I have a thousand things to tell thee. I shall give thee so droll an account of my adventures that thee will smile. "No occasion of that, Sally," methinks I hear thee say, "for thee tells me every trifle." But, child, thee is mistaken, for I have not told thee half the civil things that are said of us *sweet* creatures at "General Smallwood's Quarters.". . .

December 5th, Sixth Day.

Oh, gracious Debby, I am all alive with fear. The English have come out to attack (as we imagine) our army, three miles this side. What will become of us, only six miles distant? We are in hourly expectation of an engagement. I fear we shall be in the midst of it. Heaven defend us from so dreadful a sight. The battle of Germantown, and the horrors of that day, are recent in my mind. It will be sufficiently dreadful, if we are only in hearing of the firing, to think how many of our fellow creatures are plung'd into the boundless ocean of eternity, few of them prepar'd to meet their fate. But they are summon'd before an all-merciful judge, from whom they have a great deal to hope.

Seventh Day, December 6th.

No firing this morn. I hope for one more quiet day.

Seventh Day, Noon, 4 o'clock.

I was much alarm'd just now, sitting in the parlour, indulging melancholy reflections, when somebody burst open the door. "Sally, here's Major Stodard." I jumped. Our conjectures were various concerning his coming. The poor fellow, from great fatigue and want of rest, together with being expos'd to the night air, had caught cold, which brought on a fever. He cou'd scarcely walk, and I went into aunt's to see him. I was surpris'd. Instead of the lively, alert, blooming Stodard, who was on his feet the instant we enter'd, he look'd pale, thin, and dejected, too weak to rise, and "How are you, Miss Sally?" "How does thee do, Major?" I seated myself near him, inquir'd the cause of his indisposition, ask'd for the General, receiv'd his compliments. Not willing to fatigue him with too much chat, I bid him adieu. . . .

First Day, Morn, December 7th.
I trip'd into aunt's. There sat the Major, rather more like himself. How natural it was to see him. "Good morning, Miss Sally." "Good morrow, Major, how does thee do to-day?" "I feel quite recover'd, Sally." "Well, I fancy this indisposition has sav'd thy head this time." Major: "No ma'am; for if I hear a firing, I shall soon be with them." That was heroic. About eleven I dress'd myself, silk and cotton gown. It is made without an apron. I feel quite awkwardish, and prefer the girlish dress. . . .

Fourth Day, June 3, 1778
. . . About nine I took my work and seated myself in the parlour. Not long had I sat, when in came Dandridge,—the handsomest man in existence, at least that I had ever seen. But stop here, while I just say, the night before, chatting upon dress, he said he had no patience with those officers who, every morn, before they went on detachments, would wait to be dress'd and powder'd. "I am," said I, "excessively fond of powder, and think it very becoming." "Are you?" he reply'd. "I am very careless, as often wearing my cap thus" (turning the back part before) "as any way." I left off where he came in. He was powder'd very white, a (pretty colored) brown coat, lapell'd with green, and white waistcoat, etc. . . . He made a truly elegant figure. "Good morning, Miss Sally. You are very well, I hope." "Very well. Pray sit down," which he did, close by me. "Oh, dear," said I, "I see thee is powder'd." "Yes, ma'am. I have dress'd myself off for you." Will I be excused, Debby, if I look upon his being powder'd in the light of a compliment to me? . . .

'Tis impossible to write a regular account of our conversation. Be it sufficient to say that we had a multiplicity of chat.

About an hour since, sister II. came to me and said Captain Dandridge was in the parlour, and had ask'd for me. I went in. He met me, caught my hands. "Oh, Miss Sally, I have a beautiful sweetheart for you." "Poh! ridiculous! Loose my hands." "Well, but don't be so cross." "Who is he?" "Major Clough. I have seen him. Ain't he pretty, to be sure? I am going to headquarters. Have you any commands there?" "None at all; but" (recollecting), "yes, I have. Pray, who is your commanding officer?" "Colonel Bland, ma'am." "Please give my compliments to him, and I shou'd be glad if he would send thee back with a little more manners." He reply'd wickedly, and told me I had a little spiteful heart. But he was intolerably saucy; said he never met with such ladies. "You're very ill-natur'd, Sally." And, putting on the sauciest face, "Sally, if Tacy V*nd*r*n won't have me, will you?" "No, really; none of her discarded lovers." "But, provided I prefer you to her, will you consent?" "No, I won't." "Very well, madam." And after saying he would return to-morrow, among a hundred other things, he elegantly walk'd out of the room. . . .

Sixth Day, June 5th, Morn, 11 o'clock.

Last night we were a little alarm'd. I was awaken'd about 12, with somebody's opening the chamber door. I observ'd cousin Prissa talking to mamma. I asked what was the matter. "Only a party of light horse." "Are they Americans?" I quickly said. She answer'd in the affirmative, (which dispell'd my fears), and told me Major Jameson commanded, and that Captains Call and Nixon were with him. With that intelligence she left us. I revolved in my mind whether or not Jameson would renew his acquaintance; but Morpheus buried all my ideas, and this morning I rose by, or near seven, dress'd in my light chintz, which is made gown-fashion, kenton handkerchief, and linen apron. . . .

Dress'd as above, down I came, and went down to our kitchen, which is a small distance from the house. As I came back, I saw Jameson at the window. He met me in the entry, bow'd:—"How do you do, Miss Sally?" After the compliments usual on such occasions had pass'd, I invited him into our parlour. He followed me in. We chatted very sociably. . . .

I ask'd him whether Dandridge was on this side the Delaware. He said, "Yes." I wanted sadly to hear his opinion, but he said not a word.

The conversation turn'd upon the British leaving Philadelphia. He firmly believ'd they were going. I sincerely wish'd it might be true, but was afraid to flatter myself. I had heard it so often that I was quite faithless, and express'd my approbation of Pope's 12th beatitude, "Blessed are they that expect nothing, for they shall not be disappointed." He smil'd, and assur'd me they *were* going away.

He was summon'd to breakfast. I ask'd him to stay with us. He declin'd the invitation with politeness, adding that he was in a hurry,— oblig'd to go to camp as soon as he could. He bow'd, "Your servant, ladies," and withdrew immediately. After breakfast they set off for Valley Forge, where Gen'l Washington's army still are.

A Friend's Journal in Philadelphia by Ann Head Warder*

Ann Head, an English Quaker, married a Philadelphia Quaker shipping merchant, John Warder, after he took up residence in London in 1776. In 1786, business called him back to Philadelphia, where the couple stayed in his mother's house, thus being placed in the midst of Philadelphia Friends' social life. The extracts from Ann Head Warder's diary here begin during their Philadelphia stay in 1786, when she was twenty-eight.

A PHILADELPHIA FRIEND'S JOURNAL

6 mo. 11th.—In the forenoon went to Market Street Meeting which I think is full double the size of Gracechurch street. It has five doors, one each side the minister's gallery, near which I sit though much courted by beckoners to come under it, which I refused, though not without feeling some pleasure, as sister Hannah had given me a very different account of their Friends. We dined at dear uncle John Head's, for whom my heart is always filled with pleasure at seeing which happens pretty frequent, as the greatest sociability subsist in this place. He has by his first wife a daughter married, with a large family. His second wife left him with three children. Uncle has not so much vivacity as our beloved parent in full health used to possess, and is now sixty two. At six went again to meeting, the day being so warm it was omitted in the afternoon. Returned home to supper when we met Brother and Sister Vaux with their only two children. The mode of dressing children here is not so becoming as with us, and I have scarcely seen a white frock since my arrival; their colored ones are very inferior to what we use, which with blue and yellow skirts and their necks entirely covered to preserve them, complete a dress very inconsistent with the mothers' appearance when from home, for not a woman has visited me but what was elegant enough for any bride. Indeed we could almost persuade ourselves that was the case from so much

* Reprinted from *Philadelphia Magazine of History and Biography*, XVII: 446–449, 451–453; XVIII: 51–52, 60.

saluting—which is a practice here considerably out of use. A young girl esteems it an insult for a man to offer any such thing—the strictest delicacy subsists, beyond what I ever expected to find, particularly as they are more and much earlier exposed to men's company. . . .

6 mo. 13th.—The forenoon as usual engaged with company. The family dined at Billy Morris's. We had a very genteel dinner, indeed I think from my present observation that people here are more superb in their entertainments than with us. Provisions of every kind are cheaper, but the greatest luxury is the abundance of fruit. We have pineapples, strawberries, cherries, peas. We remained the evening 'till twelve o'clock, which doings we have been guilty of every night— supping late and chatting after; sometimes a walk after dark, which is much the practice here owing to the extreme heat of the day. I dread the increase about two months hence.

6 mo. 14th.—In the afternoon, the weather being cool, Johnny, sister Vaux and myself in a phaeton, and Billy Prichard and Sally Parker in a chair, took a ride of ten miles along the banks of the Schuylkill, with which I was much pleased. Several friends called in during the evening, which I find is occasioned by the intense heat of the Summer—they walk most after dark and sit much on their porches, which as a *mother* I think expose girls too early to the acquaintance of men.

6 mo. 16th.—Drank tea at Uncle Roberts, brother Jerry's first wife was his daughter; Richard Vaux also married another; she is destitute of beauty but an agreeable woman.

6 mo. 18th.—Being engaged to dine at Thomas Eddy's was induced to attend the meeting nearest their house, which being esteemed a cool one proved a double inducement. I dread the heat most where a number of people are gathered together. It was a pretty house called the Hill or Pine Street Meeting, not near so large as Market Street Meeting, but many friends were there who I knew from their attention in calling upon me. After tea returned home where we found Billy Parker and Harry Capper sitting at the door. At supper Dr. Foulke and Jacky Fry joined us. People talk about Sally Parker and him. Girls run so thick and lads so thin that if two are seen together several times people will talk. We can't find any body in particular to joke Jerry and Dick about, they are attentive to all when thrown in their way, but engaged to none. Jerry says that in Winter the girls look so blooming by a good fire that he is induced to think about matrimony, and almost determined if they can stand the next Summer. Then the sultry heat discovers such

poor relaxed, unhealthy constitutions that his resolutions vanish—they both talk of English wives in which more health, spirits, and beauty are to be found than here. I told him our husbands are obliged to exceed theirs in obedience. He says that a good curtain lecture sometimes from a wife who would render herself at others lively and agreeable to him and his friends would be more bearable than lumps of dead or inanimate flesh. I have threatened the destruction of their pig tails before I will consent to introduce them as my nephews in our country, which they both acknowledge will be cheerfully resigned. . . .

6 mo. 25th.—Went to Market street meeting morning and evening, the violent heat preventing my expecting to profit in the least by going in the afternoon; indeed without the frequent use of fans we must be melted down. Our meetings were large, particularly in the evening, when Thomas Colley and many other public Friends were present. One woman Friend appeared in supplication and whilst she was speaking Betsy Roberts (Nancy Vaux's sister) walked into the gallery and knelt down, and as soon as the first had finished, began very loud. Last first day evening there were three followed each other in that manner, and I could not help being struck with their appearance both having drab silk gowns and black pasteboard bonnets on; brown is thought gayer, so much for custom. To see an old man stand up with a mulberry coat, nankeen waistcoat and breeches with white stockings, would look singular in England. My cap is the admiration of plain and gay, and had I that which I wore some years ago many would have asked for the pattern. They all wear a round one the border drawn close to the face without a pleat piece, some plain others quilled with narrow ribbon puffed—a consistency is wanted, their bonnets are more Friendly and gowns less so. . . .

7th mo. 3d.—This day I accomplished more needlework than almost altogether since my arrival, for with one engagement or another I could scarce get more done than making caps and mending stockings, and that with some difficulty. My husband had a mind for a thin napping gown for coolness, so after dinner I began one and with a little help finished by evening. For my own part I have made no alteration in my dress on account of the weather, though sometimes I have felt a good deal oppressed, yet resolution would not let me wear short gowns, which are common here. . . .

7 mo. 16th.—My spirits somewhat depressed this forenoon, which were rather increased by mother telling me that Sister Morris and Emlen thought I rather slighted them by my few visits, and conscious that every moment of my time seemed too much engaged with such trifles, I could not help weeping which did me good. We went to Bank Meeting, which was a favored one, where William Savery long addressed us in such a lively manner I scarce ever heard; indeed he is a wonderful man and though wrong to follow preachers I would like to more frequently attend his meetings. . . .

9th mo. 22d.—After dinner prepared for a general ramble among my friends. First called on Hessy Fisher, who was rather unwell; then to Abijah Dawes, where I saw Sally; then to my much valued friend Sally Waln who was sitting very comfortably with Nicholas, who has not long returned from New England. After calling on Tommy Fisher went to James Pemberton's, whose wife has lately met with so severe loss in the death of Robert Morton. On the way home stopped at Uncle Head's, where was much company, and was given four bunches of grapes, with some of his best plums and peaches. I darned a place in my light calico gown torn some weeks ago, have had no time before to darn it, in which situation I have now a great heap of work that decreases very slowly through gossiping about, which is unavoidable without giving my kind friends offense, for the great number before I have got once around renders it necessary to begin again. It is a life I would not continue on any account, though here rather desirable, the time, which without variety must appear much longer. It is a custom to visit here more than with us, and they destroy the social freedom of it by too much dressing. . . .

1 mo. 13th.—Before dinner I went to my husband's room and found him preparing to accompany his brother Jerry to his country place about fourteen miles from here, which distressed me not a little. Nothing that I could say would prevail, he was determined and resolute, for with such a cold and exposing himself to the cutting cold wind, besides going into a damp house and bed, caused fear which I cannot express. After dinner visited friend Armat, who is rather an ancient widow, where I met Benedict Dorsey's wife, who related to me what Friends' situation was in the first settlement of this country; when the men and women toiled together to clear the land, without being able to procure

what we esteem the common necessaries of life. One day a worthy woman returning from her labor to provide something for her own and companions' dinner, and remembering that she had not nor could obtain nothing but very ordinary bread sat down and wept. A favorite cat came to her repeatedly which induced her to follow her into the woods, where she found that the animal had killed a fine fat rabbit, on which all dined.

Letters from Eliza Southgate
to Her Cousin Moses Porter*

Eliza Southgate, born in 1783 in Maine, had the advantages of wealth, family, and education. The following letters were written when she was seventeen to eighteen years old and had been to school in Boston and Medford.

LETTERS FROM ELIZA SOUTHGATE TO HER COUSIN MOSES PORTER

September, 1800

. . . As I look around me I am surprised at the happiness which is so generally enjoyed in families, and that marriages which have not love for a foundation on more than one side at most, should produce so much apparent harmony. I may be censured for declaring it as my opinion that not one woman in a hundred marries for love. A woman of taste and sentiment will surely see but a very few whom she could love, and it is altogether uncertain whether either of them will particularly distinguish her. If they should, surely she is very fortunate, but it would be one of fortune's random favors and such as we have no right to expect. The female mind I believe is of a very pliable texture; if it were not we should be wretched indeed. Admitting as a known truth that few women marry those whom they would prefer to all the world if they could be viewed by them with equal affection, or rather that there are often others whom they could have preferred if they had felt that affection for them which would have induced them to offer themselves, —admitting this as a truth not to be disputed,—is it not a subject of astonishment that happiness is not almost banished from this connexion? Gratitude is undoubtedly the foundation of the esteem we commonly feel for a husband. One that has preferred us to all the world, one that has thought us possessed of every quality to render him happy, surely merits our gratitude. If his character is good—if he is not displeasing in his person or manners—what objection can we make that will not be

* From Clarence Cook (ed.), *A Girl's Life Eighty Years Ago: Letters of Eliza Southgate Bowne* (New York, 1887), pp. 37-41, 55-57, 58-62, 101-102, 104-105.

thought frivolous by the greater part of the world?—yet I think there are many other things necessary for happiness, and the world should never compel me to marry a man because I could not give satisfactory reasons for not liking him. I do not esteem marriage absolutely essential to happiness, and that it does not always bring happiness we must every day witness in our acquaintance. A single life is considered too generally as a reproach; but let me ask you, which is the most despicable—she who marries a man she scarcely thinks *well* of—to avoid the reputation of an old maid—or she, who with more delicacy, than marry one she could not highly esteem, preferred to live single all her life, and had wisdom enough to despise so mean a sacrifice, to the opinion of the rabble, as the woman who marries a man she has not much love for—must make. I wish not to alter the laws of nature—neither will I quarrel with the rules which custom has established and rendered indispensably necessary to the harmony of society. But every being who has contemplated human nature on a large scale will certainly justify me when I declare that the inequality of privilege between the sexes is very sensibly felt by us females, and in no instance is it greater than in the liberty of choosing a partner in marriage; true, we have the liberty of refusing those we don't like, but not of selecting those we do. This is undoubtedly as it should be. But let me ask you, what must be that love which is altogether voluntary, which we can withhold or give, which sleeps in dullness and apathy till it is requested to brighten into life? Is it not a cold, lifeless dictate of the head,—do we not weigh all the conveniences and inconveniences which will attend it? And after a long calculation, in which the heart never was consulted, we determine whether it is most prudent to love or not.

How I should despise a soul so sordid, so mean! How I abhor the heart which is regulated by mechanical rules, which can say "thus far will I go and no farther," whose feelings can keep pace with their convenience, and be awakened at stated periods,—a mere piece of clockwork which always moves right! How far less valuable than that being who has a soul to govern her actions, and though she may not always be coldly prudent, yet she will sometimes be generous and noble, and that the other never can be. After all, I must own that a woman of delicacy never will suffer her esteem to ripen into love unless she is convinced of a return. Though our first approaches to love may be involuntary, yet I should be sorry if we had no power of controlling them if occasion required. There is a happy conformity or pliability in the female mind which seems to have been a gift of nature to enable them to be happy with so few privileges,—and another thing, they have more gratitude in their dispositions than men, and there is a something particularly gratifying to the heart in being beloved, if the object is worthy. . . . Indeed, I believe no woman of delicacy suffers herself to think she could love any one before she had discovered an affection for her. For my part I should never ask the question of myself—do I love such a one, if I had reason to think he loved me—and I believe there are many who love that never confessed it to themselves. My Pride, my delicacy, would all be hurt if I discovered such *unasked* for love, even in my own bosom. I would strain every nerve and rouse every faculty to quell the first appearance of it. There is no danger, however. I could never love without being beloved, and I am confident in my own mind that no person whom I could love would ever think me sufficiently worthy to love me. But I congratulate myself that I am at liberty to refuse those I don't like, and that I have firmness enough to brave the sneers of the world and live an old maid, if I never find one I can love. . . .

May, 1801

. . . I believe I possess decent talents and should have been quite another being had they been properly cultivated. But as it is, I can never get over some little prejudices which I have imbibed long since, and which warp all the faculties of my mind. I was pushed on to the stage of action without one principle to guide my actions,—the impulse of the moment was the only incitement. I have never committed any grossly imprudent action, yet I have been folly's darling child. I trust they were rather errors of the head than the heart, for we have all a kind of inherent power to distinguish between right and wrong, and if before the heart becomes contaminated by the maxims of society it is left to act from impulse though it have no fixt principle, yet it will not materially err. Possessing a gay lively disposition, I pursued pleasure with ardor. I wished for admiration, and took the means which would be most likely to obtain it. I found the mind of a female, if such a thing existed, was thought not worth cultivating. I disliked the trouble of thinking for myself and therefore adopted the sentiments of others—fully convinced to adorn my person and acquire a few little accomplishments was sufficient to secure me the admiration of the society I frequented. I cared but little about the mind. I learned to flutter about with a thoughtless gaiety—a mere feather which every breath had power to move. I left school with a head full of something, tumbled in without order or connection. I returned home with a determination to put it in more order; I set about the great work of culling the best part to make a few sentiments out of—to serve as a little ready change in my commerce with the world. But I soon lost all patience (a virtue I do not possess in an eminent degree), for the greater part of my ideas I was obliged to throw away without knowing where I got them or what I should do with them; what remained I pieced as ingeniously as I could into a few patch-work opinions,—they are now almost worn threadbare, and as I am about quilting a few more, I beg you will send me any spare ideas you may chance to have that will answer my turn. . . .

June, 1801

As to the qualities of mind peculiar to each sex, I agree with you that sprightliness is in favor of females and profundity of males. Their education, their pursuits would create such a quality even tho' nature had not implanted it. The business and pursuits of men require deep thinking, judgment, and moderation, while, on the other hand, females are under no necessity of dipping deep, but merely "skim the surface," and we too commonly spare ourselves the exertion which deep researches require, unless they are absolutely necessary to our pursuits in life. We rarely find one giving themselves up to profound investigation for amusement merely. Necessity is the nurse of all the great qualities of the mind; it explores all the hidden treasures and by its stimulating power they are "polished into brightness." Women who have no such incentives to action suffer all the strong energetic qualities of the mind to sleep in obscurity; sometimes a ray of genius gleams through the thick clouds with which it is enveloped, and irradiates for a moment the darkness of mental night; yet, like a comet that shoots wildly from its sphere, it excites our wonder, and we place it among the phenomenons of nature, without searching for a natural cause. Thus it is the qualities with which nature has endowed us, as a support amid the misfortunes of life and a shield from the allurements of vice, are left to moulder in ruin. In this dormant state they become enervated and impaired, and at last die for *want of exercise*. The little airy qualities which produce sprightliness are left to flutter about like feathers in the wind, the sport of every breeze.

Women have more fancy, more lively imaginations than men. That is easily accounted for: a person of correct judgment and accurate discernment will never have that flow of ideas which one of a different character might,—every object has not the power to introduce into his mind such a variety of ideas, he rejects all but those closely connected with it. On the other hand, a person of small discernment will receive every idea that arises in the mind, making no distinction between those nearly related and those more distant, they are all equally welcome, and consequently such a mind abounds with fanciful, out-of-the-way ideas. Women have more imagination, more sprightliness, because they have less discernment. I never was of opinion that the pursuits of the sexes ought to be the same; on the contrary, I believe it would be destructive to happiness, there would a degree of rivalry exist, incompatible with the harmony we wish to establish. I have ever thought it necessary that each should have a separate sphere of action,—in such a case there could be no clashing unless one or the other should leap their respective bounds. Yet to cultivate the qualities with which we are endowed can never be called infringing the prerogatives of man. Why, my dear Cousin, were we furnished with such powers, unless the improvement of them would conduce to the happiness of society? Do you suppose the mind of woman the only work of God that was "made in vain." The cultivation of the powers we possess, I have ever thought a privilege (or I may say duty) that belonged to the human species, and not man's exclusive prerogative. Far from destroying the harmony that ought to subsist, it would fix it on a foundation that would not totter at every jar. Women would be under the same degree of subordination that they now are; enlighten and expand their minds, and they would perceive the necessity of such a regulation to preserve the order and happiness of society. Yet you require that their conduct should be always guided by that reason which you refuse them the power of exercising. I know it is generally thought that in such a case women would assume the right of commanding. But I see no foundation for such a supposition,—not a blind submission to the will of another which neither honor nor reason dictates. It would be criminal in such a case to submit, for we are under a prior engagement to conduct in all things according to the dictates of reason. I had rather be the meanest reptile that creeps the earth, or cast upon the wide world to suffer all the ills "that flesh is heir to," than live a slave to the despotic will of another.

I am aware of the censure that will ever await the female that attempts the vindication of her sex, yet I dare to brave that censure that I know to be undeserved. It does not follow (O what a pen!) that every female who vindicates the capacity of the sex is a disciple of Mary Wolstoncraft. Though I allow her to have said many things which I cannot but approve, yet the very foundation on which she builds her work will be apt to prejudice us so against her that we will not allow her the merit she really deserves,—yet, prejudice set aside, I confess I admire many of her sentiments, notwithstanding I believe should any one adopt her principles, they would conduct in the same manner, and upon the whole her life is the best comment on her writings. Her style is nervous and commanding, her sentiments appear to carry conviction along with them, but they will not bear analyzing. I wish to say something on your *natural refinement*, but I shall only have room to touch upon it if I begin, "therefore I'll leave it till another time."

May, 1802

. . . Solitary happiness I have no idea of, 'tis only in the delightful sympathies of friendship, similarity of sentiments, that genuine happiness can be enjoyed. Your mind is cultivated and enlarged, your sentiments delicate and refined, you could not expect to find many with whom you could converse on a perfect equality,—or rather many whose sentiments could assimilate with yours. Were I a man, I should think it cowardly to bury myself in solitude,—nay, I should be unwilling to confess I felt myself unable to preserve my virtue where there were temptations to destroy it, there is no merit in being virtuous when there is no struggle to preserve that virtue. 'Tis in the midst of temptations and allurements that the active and generous virtues must be exerted in their full force. One virtuous action where there were temptations and delusions to surmount would give more delight to my own heart, more real satisfaction than a whole life spent in more negative goodness, he must be base indeed who can voluntarily act wrong when no allurement draws him from the path of virtue. You say you never dip't much into the pleasures of *high life* and therefore should have but little to regret on that score. In the choice of life one ought to consult their own dispositions and inclinations, their own powers and talents. We all have a preference to some particular mode of life, and we surely ought to endeavor to arrive at that which will more probably ensure us most happiness. I have often thought what profession I should choose were I a man. I might then think very differently from what I do now, yet I have always thought if I felt conscious of possessing brilliant talents, the *law* would be my choice. Then I might hope to arrive at an eminence which would be gratifying to my feelings. I should then hope to be a public character, respected and admired,—but unless I was convinced I possessed the talents which would distinguish me as a speaker I would be anything rather than a lawyer;—from the dry sameness of such employments as the business of an office all my feelings would revolt, but to be an eloquent speaker would be the delight of my heart. I thank Heaven I was *born* a women. I have now only patiently to wait till some clever fellow shall take a fancy to me and place me in a situation, I am determined to make the best of it, let it be what it will. We ladies, you know, possess that "sweet pliability of temper" that disposes us to enjoy any situation, and we must have no choice in these things till we find what is to be our destiny, then we must consider it the best in the world. But remember, I desire to be thankful I am not a man. I should not be content with moderate abilities—nay, I should not be content with mediocrity in any thing, but as a woman I am equal to the generality of my sex, and I do not feel that great desire of fame I think I should if I was a man. . . .

1802

I hardly know what to say to you, Cousin, you have attacked my system with a kind of fury that has entirely obscured your judgment, and instead of being convinced of its impracticability, you appear to fear its justness. You tell me of some excellent effects of my system, but pardon me for thinking they are dictated by prejudice rather than reason. I feel fully convinced in my own mind that no such effects could be produced. You ask if this plan of education will render one a more dutiful child, a more affectionate wife, &c, &c., surely it will,—those virtues which now are merely practised from the momentary impulse of the heart, will then be adhered to from principle, a sense of duty, and a mind sufficiently strengthened not to yield implicitly to every impulse, will give a degree of uniformity, of stability to the female character, which it evidently at present does not possess. From having no fixed guide for our conduct we have acquired a reputation for caprice, which we justly deserve. I can hardly believe you serious when you say that "the enlargement of the mind will inevitably produce superciliousness and a desire of ascendancy,"—I should much sooner expect it from an ignorant, uncultivated mind. We cannot enlarge and improve our minds without perceiving our weakness, and wisdom is always modest and unassuming,—on the contrary a mind that has never been exerted knows not its deficiencies and presumes much more on its powers than it otherwise would. . . .

You undoubtedly think I am acting out of my sphere in attempting to discuss this subject, and my presumption probably gave rise to that idea, which you expressed in your last, that however unqualified a woman might be she was always equipt for the discussion of any subject and overwhelmed her hearers with her "clack." On what subjects shall I write you? I shall either fatigue and disgust you with female trifles, or shock you by stepping beyond the limits you have prescribed.

III
The Cult of Domesticity Versus Social Change

ON "Proper Conduct of the Wife Towards Her Husband" by Samuel Jennings*

Jennings' book, *The Married Lady's Companion, or Poor Man's Friend*, is an early example of a nineteenth-century guide to morals and manners, combining sermonizing with advice on health and hygiene.

PROPER CONDUCT OF THE WIFE TOWARDS HER HUSBAND

1. As it is your great wish and interest, to enjoy much of your husband's company and conversation, it will be important to acquaint yourself with his temper, his inclination, and his manner, that you may render your house, your person, and your disposition quite agreeable to him. By observing with accuracy, and guarding your words and actions with prudence, you may quickly succeed according to your wishes.

2. Here perhaps you ask, why so much pains necessary on my part? I will answer your question candidly. Your choice in forming the connexion, was at best a passive one. Could you have acted the part of a courtier and made choice of a man whose disposition might have corresponded precisely with yours, there would have been less to do afterwards. But under present circumstances, it is your interest to adapt yourself to your husband, whatever may be his peculiarities. Again, nature has made man the stronger, the consent of mankind has given him superiority over his wife, his inclination is, to claim his natural and acquired rights. He of course expects from you a degree of condescension, and he feels himself the more confident of the propriety of his claim, when he is informed, that St. Paul adds his authority to its support. "Wives submit yourselves unto your own husbands, as unto the Lord, for the husband is the head of his wife."

3. In obedience then to this precept of the gospel, to the laws of custom and of nature, you ought to cultivate a cheerful and happy submission. "The way of virtue is the way of happiness." The truth of

* From Samuel K. Jennings, *The Married Lady's Companion, or Poor Man's Friend* (rev. 2d. ed.; New York: Lorenzo Dow, 1808), pp. 61–68.

this maxim will be verified to you in your conformity to this duty. By such submission, you will secure to yourself the advantages of a willing obedience on the part of your husband to the counter part of Paul's command, "Husbands love your wives as your own flesh," &c.

4. The great attention and submission practised by most men in time of courtship are well calculated to raise in the female mind, false expectation of an uniform continuance of the same officiousness after marriage. For the honey moon you may not be disappointed. But the charge of a family will soon teach any man, that he has something more to do than live a life of courtship. The discharge of his duty as a father, a friend, and a citizen, will gradually divert him in some degree from that punctilious attention to your person, with which you are so highly pleased.

5. Should you begin to discover this change, be careful to conduct yourself with discretion. By no means upbraid him, nor suffer jealousy to take possession of your breast. If you once admit this passion, it may terminate in your ruin. It will lead you to consider every seeming inattention, as a proof of his want of affection. You will conclude, *he is tired of his toy and is looking out for another.* This thought, once admitted, will have an infatuating influence over your mind. Not only your actions will express your suspicion, but you will unguardedly speak it out, perhaps in terms of reproach.—Your good husband, stabbed to the very heart, may possibly with eyes full of tears clasp you in his arms and assure you of his love. But all will be vain, jealousy once admitted contaminates the soul. He will scarcely turn his back, before the old impression will revive.

His tears and entreaties will be considered as evidence of his guilt, and you will wretchedly settle upon this conclusion. *"I am disagreeable, he is gone to caress the happy fair one whose company is preferred."*

6. As you regard your own bliss, speedily check all thoughts of this kind, as soon as they arise in your mind. If indulged, they will have a baneful effect upon your temper, and spread a gloom over your countenance, so as to strip you of every charm. Your husband, repelled from time to time, will at length become indifferent, and leaving you to languish in your distress, he will seek for amusement where it may be found. And thus you will bring upon yourself the very evil, against which you would make your mistaken defence.

7. If you have already proved the truth of these reflections by sad experience, I know you are ready to excuse yourself, because the whole

proceeded from the most sincere affection. But you should consider that the anxiety and distress which are so often depicted in your countenance, might, with equal propriety, lead your companion to doubt the sincerity of your love. And for any thing you know to the contrary, a suspicion of this kind is at the bottom of the whole mischief. Do not act like stubborn children, rejecting that happiness which is entirely in your own power.

8. If he do not come in, the very hour or day that you expect him, instead of accusing him with neglect, be the considerate woman, and take into view the various and unavoidable delays with which he must meet in transacting his business. And be assured, for I speak from experience, that in many instances he sacrifices his most sincere wishes to be with you, for what he considers necessary for the present. He is bound to provide for you and your children. In easy circumstances there is most satisfaction, and he feels a strong desire to secure this foundation for your future happiness. Receive him then with gladness as often as he comes in, shew him that you are happy in his company, and let the preparations made for his reception prove to him that he holds a considerable share in your thoughts and affections when he is absent. Such conduct will endear you to his heart, and secure to you all the attention and regard you so ardently desire.

9. Do not suppose, that my plan implies that the husband has nothing to do. So far from this he is bound "To love and cherish his wife, as his own flesh." But I repeat it, this obligation seems, in a great degree, to rest on the condition of a loving and cheerful submission on the part of the wife. Here again perhaps you object and say, "Why not the husband, first shew a little condescension as well as the wife?" I answer for these plain reasons. It is not his disposition; it is not the custom but with the henpecked; it is not his duty; it is not implied in the marriage contract; it is not required by law or gospel.

10. I presume you are not one of those ladies who indulge a mean opinion of their companions, and are indeed ashamed of them. This can happen in no case where there is not a want of information and judgment. If you stooped in marrying him, do not indulge the thought, that you added to his respectability. Never tell him "you lifted him out of the ashes." For it will be hard for you to extricate yourself from this difficulty. "If you stooped of necessity, because you could get no one else, the obligation is on your own side. If you stooped of choice, who ought to be blamed but yourself? Besides it will be well to remember

that when you became his wife, he became your head, and your supposed superiority was buried in that voluntary act.

There are women in the world, who arrogate to themselves superior skill in the management of an estate, suppose they have great judgment in the value of property, and therefore wrest every thing out of the hands of their husbands, and convert the poor men into perfect cyphers. I hold the disposition and conduct of such women in great contempt, and I pity the *poor inoffensive creature of a man*, who can submit to be so degraded. *Yet it must be acknowledged, that where the man falls into the hands of a termagant*, he may find it *necessary to purchase peace on any terms.*

Men and women appear to best advantage each in their own proper station. Had it been my lot, to have taken one of those *manlike ladies*, whenever there happened to be company at my house, I should have made it my business, to brush the floor, rub the furniture, wash the tea equipage, scold the maids, talk about the kitchen and dairy, &c. and apologize as I proceeded, by giving intimation, that I had made an exchange of provinces with my good wife, by way of mutual accommodation.

Such conduct would at least shew, how awkwardly a man appears in acting the part of a woman, and of course would lead a woman of common sense to conclude, that she could not appear to much better advantage, when engaged in the capacity of a man.

If it were to save appearances only, the husband ought at least to *seem* to be the head. And therefore if you are determined to rule him, adopt the following plan. "When any article of property is to be bought or sold, take him aside, teach him the price to be given or received, point out the kind of payment, the time when to be paid, &c. &c. let the whole business be properly adjusted, and then let the poor fellow go forward and seem to act like a man." It is shocking to every man of sense, to see a woman interfere publicly, fly into a passion, and declare *point blank* the thing shall not be. Indeed if she had the true spirit of a woman, she would blush to acknowledge herself the wife of such a dastardly man as would submit to such treatment.

ON American Women and American Wives
by Alexis de Tocqueville*

The young French nobleman Tocqueville, visiting America in 1830–31, applied the same perspicacity and European perspective to his observation of American women as to his assessment of the general American character.

On AMERICAN WOMEN AND AMERICAN WIVES

EDUCATION OF YOUNG WOMEN IN THE UNITED STATES

No free communities ever existed without morals; and, as I observed in the former part of this work, morals are the work of woman. Consequently, whatever affects the condition of women, their habits and their opinions, has great political importance in my eyes. Amongst almost all Protestant nations young women are far more the mistresses of their own actions than they are in Catholic countries. This independence is still greater in Protestant countries, like England, which have retained or acquired the right of self-government; the spirit of freedom is then infused into the domestic circle by political habits and by religious opinions. In the United States the doctrines of Protestantism are combined with great political freedom and a most democratic state of society; and nowhere are young women surrendered so early or so completely to their own guidance. Long before an American girl arrives at the age of marriage, her emancipation from maternal control begins; she has scarcely ceased to be a child when she already thinks for herself, speaks with freedom, and acts on her own impulse. The great scene of the world is constantly open to her view; far from seeking concealment, it is every day disclosed to her more completely, and she is taught to survey it with a firm and calm gaze. Thus the vices and dangers of society are early revealed to her; as she sees them clearly, she views them without illusions, and braves them without fear; for she is full of reliance on her own strength, and her reliance seems to be shared by all who are about her. An American girl scarcely ever displays that

* From Alexis de Tocqueville, *Democracy in America*, trans. Henry Reeve (rev. ed.; New York: Colonial Press, 1889), Vol. II, pp. 208–213, 221–224.

virginal bloom in the midst of young desires, or that innocent and in-
genuous grace which usually attends the European woman in the transition from girlhood to youth. It is rarely that an American woman at
any age displays childish timidity or ignorance. Like the young women
of Europe, she seeks to please, but she knows precisely the cost of
pleasing. If she does not abandon herself to evil, at least she knows that
it exists; and she is remarkable rather for purity of manners than for
chastity of mind. I have been frequently surprised, and almost frightened, at the singular address and happy boldness with which young
women in America contrive to manage their thoughts and their language amidst all the difficulties of stimulating conversation; a philosopher would have stumbled at every step along the narrow path which
they trod without accidents and without effort. It is easy indeed to
perceive that, even amidst the independence of early youth, an American woman is always mistress of herself; she indulges in all permitted
pleasures, without yielding herself up to any of them; and her reason
never allows the reins of self-guidance to drop, though it often seems
to hold them loosely.

In France, where remnants of every age are still so strangely mingled
in the opinions and tastes of the people, women commonly receive a
reserved, retired, and almost cloistral education, as they did in aristocratic times; and then they are suddenly abandoned, without a guide
and without assistance, in the midst of all the irregularities inseparable
from democratic society. The Americans are more consistent. They
have found out that in a democracy the independence of individuals
cannot fail to be very great, youth premature, tastes ill-restrained,
customs fleeting, public opinion often unsettled and powerless, paternal
authority weak, and marital authority contested. Under these circumstances, believing that they had little chance of repressing in woman the
most vehement passions of the human heart, they held that the surer
way was to teach her the art of combating those passions for herself.
As they could not prevent her virtue from being exposed to frequent
danger, they determined that she should know how best to defend it;
and more reliance was placed on the free vigor of her will than on safeguards which have been shaken or overthrown. Instead, then, of incul-
cating mistrust of herself, they constantly seek to enhance their confidence in her own strength of character. As it is neither possible nor
desirable to keep a young woman in perpetual or complete ignorance,
they hasten to give her a precocious knowledge on all subjects. Far

from hiding the corruptions of the world from her, they prefer that she should see them at once and train herself to shun them; and they hold it of more importance to protect her conduct than to be over-scrupulous of her innocence.

Although the Americans are a very religious people, they do not rely on religion alone to defend the virtue of woman; they seek to arm her reason also. In this they have followed the same method as in several other respects; they first make the most vigorous efforts to bring individual independence to exercise a proper control over itself, and they do not call in the aid of religion until they have reached the utmost limits of human strength. I am aware that an education of this kind is not without danger; I am sensible that it tends to invigorate the judgment at the expense of the imagination, and to make cold and virtuous women instead of affectionate wives and agreeable companions to man. Society may be more tranquil and better regulated, but domestic life has often fewer charms. These, however, are secondary evils, which may be braved for the sake of higher interests. At the stage at which we are now arrived the time for choosing is no longer within our control; a democratic education is indispensable to protect women from the dangers with which democratic institutions and manners surround them.

THE YOUNG WOMAN IN THE CHARACTER OF A WIFE

In America the independence of woman is irrecoverably lost in the bonds of matrimony: if an unmarried woman is less constrained there than elsewhere, a wife is subjected to stricter obligations. The former makes her father's house an abode of freedom and of pleasure; the latter lives in the home of her husband as if it were a cloister. Yet these two different conditions of life are perhaps not so contrary as may be supposed, and it is natural that the American women should pass through the one to arrive at the other.

Religious peoples and trading nations entertain peculiarly serious notions of marriage: the former consider the regularity of woman's life as the best pledge and most certain sign of the purity of her morals; the latter regard it as the highest security for the order and prosperity of the household. The Americans are at the same time a puritanical people and a commercial nation: their religious opinions, as well as their trading habits, consequently lead them to require much abnegation on the part of woman, and a constant sacrifice of her pleasures to her duties which is seldom demanded of her in Europe. Thus in the United States the inexorable opinion of the public carefully circumscribes woman within the narrow circle of domestic interests and duties, and forbids her to step beyond it.

Upon her entrance into the world a young American woman finds these notions firmly established; she sees the rules which are derived from them; she is not slow to perceive that she cannot depart for an instant from the established usages of her contemporaries, without putting in jeopardy her peace of mind, her honor, nay even her social existence; and she finds the energy required for such an act of submission in the firmness of her understanding and in the virile habits which her education has given her. It may be said that she has learned by the use of her independence to surrender it without a struggle and without a murmur when the time comes for making the sacrifice. But no American woman falls into the toils of matrimony as into a snare held out to her simplicity and ignorance. She has been taught beforehand what is expected of her, and voluntarily and freely does she enter upon this engagement. She supports her new condition with courage, because she chose it. As in America paternal discipline is very relaxed and the conjugal tie very strict, a young woman does not contract the latter without considerable circumspection and apprehension. Precocious marriages are rare. Thus American women do not marry until their understandings are exercised and ripened; whereas in other countries most women generally only begin to exercise and to ripen their understandings after marriage.

I by no means suppose, however, that the great change which takes place in all the habits of women in the United States, as soon as they are married, ought solely to be attributed to the constraint of public opinion: it is frequently imposed upon themselves by the sole effort of their own will. When the time for choosing a husband is arrived, that cold and stern reasoning power which has been educated and invigorated by the free observation of the world, teaches an American woman that a spirit of levity and independence in the bonds of marriage is a constant subject of annoyance, not of pleasure; it tells her that the amusements of the girl cannot become the recreations of the wife, and that the sources of a married woman's happiness are in the home of her husband. As she clearly discerns beforehand the only road which can lead to domestic happiness, she enters upon it at once, and follows it to the end without seeking to turn back.

The same strength of purpose which the young wives of America display, in bending themselves at once and without repining to the austere duties of their new condition, is no less manifest in all the great trials of their lives. In no country in the world are private fortunes more precarious than in the United States. It is not uncommon for the same man, in the course of his life, to rise and sink again through all the grades which lead from opulence to poverty. American women support these vicissitudes with calm and unquenchable energy: it would seem that their desires contract, as easily as they expand, with their fortunes.

The greater part of the adventurers who migrate every year to people the western wilds, belong, as I observed in the former part of this work, to the old Anglo-American race of the Northern States. Many of these men, who rush so boldly onwards in pursuit of wealth, were already in the enjoyment of a competency in their own part of the country. They take their wives along with them, and make them share the countless perils and privations which always attend the commencement of these expeditions. I have often met, even on the verge of the wilderness, with young women, who after having been brought up amidst all the comforts of the large towns of New England, had passed, almost without any intermediate stage, from the wealthy abode of their parents to a comfortless hovel in a forest. Fever, solitude, and a tedious life had not broken the springs of their courage. Their features were impaired and faded, but their looks were firm: they appeared to be at once sad and resolute. I do not doubt that these young American women had amassed, in the education of their early years, that inward strength which they displayed under these circumstances. The early culture of the girl may still therefore be traced, in the United States, under the aspect of marriage: her part is changed, her habits are different, but her character is the same.

HOW THE AMERICANS UNDERSTAND THE EQUALITY OF THE SEXES

I have shown how democracy destroys or modifies the different inequalities which originate in society; but is this all? or does it not ultimately affect that great inequality of man and woman which has seemed, up to the present day, to be eternally based in human nature? I believe that the social changes which bring nearer to the same level the father and son, the master and servant, and superiors and inferiors generally speaking, will raise woman and make her more and more the equal of man. But here, more than ever, I feel the necessity of making myself clearly understood; for there is no subject on which the coarse and lawless fancies of our age have taken a freer range.

There are people in Europe who, confounding together the different characteristics of the sexes, would make of man and woman beings not only equal but alike. They would give to both the same functions, impose on both the same duties, and grant to both the same rights; they would mix them in all things—their occupations, their pleasures, their business. It may readily be conceived, that by thus attempting to make one sex equal to the other, both are degraded; and from so preposterous a medley of the works of nature nothing could ever result but weak men and disorderly women.

It is not thus that the Americans understand that species of democratic equality which may be established between the sexes. They admit, that as nature has appointed such wide differences between the physical and moral constitution of man and woman, her manifest design was to give a distinct employment to their various faculties; and they hold that improvement does not consist in making beings so dissimilar do pretty nearly the same things, but in getting each of them to fulfil their respective tasks in the best possible manner. The Americans have applied to the sexes the great principle of political economy which governs the manufactures of our age, by carefully dividing the duties of man from those of woman, in order that the great work of society may be the better carried on.

In no country has such constant care been taken as in America to trace two clearly distinct lines of action for the two sexes, and to make them keep pace one with the other, but in two pathways which are always different. American women never manage the outward concerns of the family, or conduct a business, or take a part in political life; nor are they, on the other hand, ever compelled to perform the rough labor of the fields, or to make any of those laborious exertions which demand the exertion of physical strength. No families are so poor as to form an exception to this rule. If on the one hand an American woman cannot escape from the quiet circle of domestic employments, on the other hand she is never forced to go beyond it. Hence it is that the women of America, who often exhibit a masculine strength of understanding and a manly energy, generally preserve great delicacy of personal appearance and always retain the manners of women, although they sometimes show that they have the hearts and minds of men.

Nor have the Americans ever supposed that one consequence of democratic principles is the subversion of marital power, of the confusion of the natural authorities in families. They hold that every association must have a head in order to accomplish its object, and that the natural head of the conjugal association is man. They do not therefore deny him the right of directing his partner; and they maintain, that in the smaller association of husband and wife, as well as in the great social community, the object of democracy is to regulate and legalize the powers which are necessary, not to subvert all power. This opinion is not peculiar to one sex, and contested by the other: I never observed that the women of America consider conjugal authority as a fortunate usurpation of their rights, nor that they thought themselves degraded by submitting to it. It appeared to me, on the contrary, that they attach a sort of pride to the voluntary surrender of their own will, and make it their boast to bend themselves to the yoke, not to shake it off. Such at least is the feeling expressed by the most virtuous of their sex; the others are silent; and in the United States it is not the practice for a guilty wife to clamor for the rights of women, whilst she is trampling on her holiest duties.

It has often been remarked that in Europe a certain degree of contempt lurks even in the flattery which men lavish upon women: although a European frequently affects to be the slave of woman, it may be seen that he never sincerely thinks her his equal. In the United States men seldom compliment women, but they daily show how much they esteem them. They constantly display an entire confidence in the understanding of a wife, and a profound respect for her freedom; they have decided that her mind is just as fitted as that of a man to discover the plain truth, and her heart as firm to embrace it; and they have never sought to place her virtue, any more than his, under the shelter of prejudice, ignorance, and fear. It would seem that in Europe, where man so easily submits to the despotic sway of women, they are nevertheless curtailed of some of the greatest qualities of the human species, and considered as seductive but imperfect beings; and (what may well provoke astonishment) women ultimately look upon themselves in the same light, and almost consider it as a privilege that they are entitled to show themselves futile, feeble, and timid. The women of America claim no such privileges.

Again, it may be said that in our morals we have reserved strange immunities to man; so that there is, as it were, one virtue for his use, and another for the guidance of his partner; and that, according to the opinion of the public, the very same act may be punished alternately as a crime or only as a fault. The Americans know not this iniquitous division of duties and rights; amongst them the seducer is as much dishonored as his victim. It is true that the Americans rarely lavish upon women those eager attentions which are commonly paid them in Europe; but their conduct to women always implies that they suppose them to be virtuous and refined; and such is the respect entertained for the moral freedom of the sex, that in the presence of a woman the most guarded language is used, lest her ear should be offended by an expression. In America a young unmarried woman may, alone and without fear, undertake a long journey.

The legislators of the United States, who have mitigated almost all the penalties of criminal law, still make rape a capital offence, and no crime is visited with more inexorable severity by public opinion. This may be accounted for; as the Americans can conceive nothing more precious than a woman's honor, and nothing which ought so much to be respected as her independence, they hold that no punishment is too severe for the man who deprives her of them against her will. In France, where the same offence is visited with far milder penalties, it is frequently difficult to get a verdict from a jury against the prisoner. Is this a consequence of contempt of decency or contempt of women? I cannot but believe that it is a contempt of one and of the other.

Thus the Americans do not think that man and woman have either the duty or the right to perform the same offices, but they show an equal regard for both their respective parts; and though their lot is different, they consider both of them as beings of equal value. They do not give to the courage of woman the same form or the same direction as to that of man; but they never doubt her courage: and if they hold that man and his partner ought not always to exercise their intellect and understanding in the same manner, they at least believe the understanding of the one to be as sound as that of the other, and her intellect to be as clear. Thus, then, whilst they have allowed the social inferiority of woman to subsist, they have done all they could to raise her morally and intellectually to the level of man; and in this respect they appear to me to have excellently understood the true principle of democratic improvement. As for myself, I do not hesitate to avow that, although the women of the United States are confined within the narrow circle of domestic life, and their situation is in some respects one of extreme dependence, I have nowhere seen woman occupying a loftier position; and if I were asked, now that I am drawing to the close of this work, in which I have spoken of so many important things done by the Americans, to what the singular prosperity and growing strength of that people ought mainly to be attributed, I should reply—to the superiority of their women.

Lucy Larcom's Factory Experience*

Lucy Larcom went to work in the Lowell mills in 1835, at the age of eleven, after her father's death signaled the end of her idyllic rural childhood in Beverly, Massachusetts, and compelled the bereaved widow and children to support themselves. Larcom alternated work at the mills with her own education for several years, until she took a position teaching school in the Midwest. Her contributions to the Lowell operatives' magazines initiated her career as a poet and educator of girls. The following memoir of her early experience was published when she was sixty-five, four years before her death.

LUCY LARCOM'S FACTORY EXPERIENCE

I went to my first day's work in the mill with a light heart. The novelty of it made it seem easy, and it really was not hard, just to change the bobbins on the spinning-frames every three quarters of an hour or so, with half a dozen other little girls who were doing the same thing. When I came back at night, the family began to pity me for my long, tiresome day's work, but I laughed and said,—

"Why, it is nothing but fun. It is just like play."

And for a little while it was only a new amusement; I liked it better than going to school and "making believe" I was learning when I was not. . . .

There were compensations for being shut in to daily toil so early. The mill itself had its lessons for us. But it was not, and could not be, the right sort of life for a child, and we were happy in the knowledge that, at the longest, our employment was only to be temporary.

When I took my next three months at the grammar school, everything there was changed, and I too was changed. The teachers were kind, and thorough in their instruction; and my mind seemed to have been ploughed up during that year of work, so that knowledge took root in it easily. It was a great delight to me to study, and at the end of

* From Lucy Larcom, *A New England Girlhood* (Boston: Houghton Mifflin, 1889), pp. 153–157, 160, 166, 178–179, 188–193.

the three months the master told me that I was prepared for the high school.

But alas! I could not go. The little money I could earn—one dollar a week, besides the price of my board—was needed in the family, and I must return to the mill. It was a severe disappointment to me, though I did not say so at home. . . .

I began to reflect upon life rather seriously for a girl of twelve or thirteen. What was I here for? What could I make of myself? Must I submit to be carried along with the current, and do just what everybody else did? No: I knew I should not do that, for there was a certain Myself who was always starting up with her own original plan or aspiration before me, and who was quite indifferent as to what people generally thought. . . .

When I thought what I should best like to do, my first dream— almost a baby's dream—about it was that it would be a fine thing to be a school-teacher, like Aunt Hannah. . . .

All my thoughts about my future sent me back to Aunt Hannah and my first infantile idea of being a teacher. I foresaw that I should be that before I could be or do anything else. It had been impressed upon me that I must make myself useful in the world, and certainly one could be useful who could "keep school" as Aunt Hannah did. I did not see anything else for a girl to do who wanted to use her brains as well as her hands. So the plan of preparing myself to be a teacher gradually and almost unconsciously shaped itself in my mind as the only practicable one. I could earn my living in that way,—an all-important considera- tion. . . .

The transition from childhood to girlhood, when a little girl has had an almost unlimited freedom of out-of-door life, is practically the toning down of a mild sort of barbarianism, and is often attended by a pain- fully awkward self-consciousness. I had an innate dislike of conven- tionalities. I clung to the child's inalienable privilege of running half wild; and when I found that I really was growing up, I felt quite re- bellious.

I was as tall as a woman at thirteen, and my older sisters insisted upon lengthening my dresses, and putting up my mop of hair with a comb. I felt injured and almost outraged because my protestations against this treatment were unheeded; and when the transformation in my visible appearance was effected, I went away by myself and had a good cry, which I would not for the world have had them know about, as that would have added humiliation to my distress. And the greatest pity about it was that I too soon became accustomed to the situation. I felt like a child, but considered it my duty to think and behave like a woman. I began to look upon it as a very serious thing to live. The untried burden seemed already to have touched my shoulders. For a time I was morbidly self-critical, and at the same time extremely reserved. The associates I chose were usually grave young women, ten or fifteen years older than myself; but I think I felt older and appeared older than they did. . . .

One great advantage which came to these many stranger girls through being brought together [at Lowell], away from their own homes, was that it taught them to go out of themselves, and enter into the lives of others. Home-life, when one always stays at home, is necessarily narrowing. That is one reason why so many women are petty and unthoughtful of any except their own family's interests. We have hardly begun to live until we can take in the idea of the whole human family as the one to which we truly belong. To me, it was an incalculable help to find myself among so many working-girls, all of us thrown upon our own resources, but thrown much more upon each others' sympathies. . . .

My married sisters had families growing up about them, and they liked to have us younger ones come and help take care of their babies. One of them sent for me just when the close air and long days' work were beginning to tell upon my health, and it was decided that I had better go. The salt wind soon restored my strength, and those months of quiet family life were very good for me.

Like most young girls, I had a motherly fondness for little children, and my two baby-nephews were my pride and delight. . . . My sister had no domestic help besides mine, so I learned a good deal about general housework. A girl's preparation for life was, in those days, considered quite imperfect, who had no practical knowledge of that kind. We were taught, indeed, how to do everything that a woman might be called upon to do under any circumstances, for herself or for the household she lived in. It was one of the advantages of the old simple way of living, that the young daughters of the house were, as a matter of course, instructed in all these things. They acquired the habit of being ready for emergencies, and the family that required no outside assistance was delightfully independent.

A young woman would have been considered a very inefficient being who could not make and mend and wash and iron her own clothing, and get three regular meals and clear them away every day, besides keeping the house tidy, and doing any other neighborly service, such as sitting all night by a sick-bed. To be "a good watcher" was considered one of the most important of womanly attainments. People who lived side by side exchanged such services without waiting to be asked, and they seemed to be happiest of whom such kindnesses were most expected. . . .

I found my practical experience of housekeeping and baby-tending very useful to me afterwards at the West, in my sister Emilie's family, when she was disabled by illness. I think, indeed, that every item of real knowledge I ever acquired has come into use somewhere or somehow in the course of the years. But these were not the things I had most wished to do. The whole world of thought lay unexplored before me,—a world of which I had already caught large and tempting glimpses, and I did not like to feel the horizon shutting me in, even to so pleasant a corner as this. And the worst of it was that I was getting too easy and contented, too indifferent to the higher realities which my work and my thoughtful companions had kept keenly clear before me. I felt myself slipping into an inward apathy from which it was hard to rouse myself. I could not let it go on so. I must be where my life could expand.

It was hard to leave the dear little fellow I had taught to walk and to talk, but I knew he would not be inconsolable. So I only said "I must go,"—and turned my back upon the sea, and my face to the banks of the Merrimack.

When I returned I found that I enjoyed even the familiar, unremitting clatter of the mill, because it indicated that something was going on. I liked to feel the people around me, even those whom I did not know, as a wave may like to feel the surrounding waves urging it forward, with or against its own will. I felt that I belonged to the world, that there was something for me to do in it, though I had not yet found out what. Something to do; it might be very little, but still it would be my own work.

"Susan Miller," a Story by F. G. A.,
a Lowell Operative*

This story originally appeared in *The Lowell Offering,* a magazine that published mill girls' writing.

SUSAN MILLER

CHAPTER I

"Mother, it is all over now," said Susan Miller, as she descended from the chamber where her father had just died of *delirium tremens.*

Mrs. Miller had for several hours walked the house, with that ceaseless step which tells of fearful mental agony: and when she had heard from her husband's room some louder shriek or groan, she had knelt by the chair or bed which was nearest, and prayed that the troubled spirit might pass away. But a faintness came over her, when a long interval of stillness told that her prayer was answered; and she leaned upon the railing of the stairway for support, as she looked up to see the first one who should come to her from the bed of death.

Susan was the first to think of her mother: and when she saw her sink, pale, breathless, and stupified upon a stair, she sat down in silence, and supported her head upon her own bosom. Then for the first time was she aroused to the consciousness that she was to be looked upon as a stay and support; and she resolved to bring from the hidden recesses of her heart, a strength, courage, and firmness, which should make her to her heart-broken mother, and younger brothers and sisters, what *he* had not been for many years, who was now a stiffening corpse.

At length she ventured to whisper words of solace and sympathy, and succeeded in infusing into her mother's mind a feeling of resignation to the stroke they had received.—She persuaded her to retire to her bed, and seek the slumber which had been for several days denied them; and then she endeavored to calm the terror-stricken little ones, who were

* From *Mind amongst the Spindles;* a Miscellany wholly composed by the factory girls, selected from *The Lowell Offering;* with an Introduction by the English editor, and a Letter from Harriet Martineau (Boston: Jordan, Swift and Wiley, 1845), pp. 81–92.

THE CULT OF DOMESTICITY VERSUS SOCIAL CHANGE

screaming because their father was no more. The neighbors came in and proffered every assistance; but when Susan retired that night to her own chamber, she felt that she must look to HIM for aid, who alone could sustain through the tasks that awaited her.

Preparations were made for the funeral; and though every one knew that Mr. Miller had left his farm deeply mortgaged, yet the store-keeper cheerfully trusted them for articles of mourning, and the dress-maker worked day and night, while she expected never to receive a remuneration. The minister came to comfort the widow and her children. He spoke of the former virtues of him who had been wont to seek the house of God on each returning Sabbath, and who had brought his eldest children to the font of baptism, and been then regarded as an example of honesty and sterling worth; and when he adverted to the one failing which had brought him to his grave in the very prime of manhood, he also remarked, that he was now in the hands of a merciful God.

The remains of the husband and father were at length removed from the home which he had once rendered happy, but upon which he had afterwards brought poverty and distress, and laid in that narrow house which he never more might leave, till the last trumpet should call him forth; and when the family were left to that deep silence and gloom which always succeed a death and burial, they began to think of the trials which were yet to come.

Mrs. Miller had been for several years aware that ruin was coming upon them. She had at first warned, reasoned, and expostulated; but she was naturally of a gentle and almost timid disposition; and when she found that she awakened passions which were daily growing more violent and ungovernable, she resolved to await in silence a crisis which sooner or later would change their destiny. Whether she was to follow her degenerate husband to his grave, or accompany him to some low hovel, she knew not; she shrunk from the future, but faithfully discharged all present duties, and endeavored, by a strict economy, to retain at least an appearance of comfort in her household.

To Susan, her eldest child, she had confided all her fears and sorrows; and they had watched, toiled, and sympathized together. But when the blow came at last, when he who had caused all their sorrow and anxiety was taken away by a dreadful and disgraceful death, the long-enduring wife and mother was almost paralyzed by the shock.

But Susan was young; she had health, strength, and spirits to bear her up, and upon her devolved the care of the family, and the plan for its future support. Her resolution was soon formed; and without saying a word to any individual, she went to Deacon Rand, who was her father's principal creditor.

It was a beautiful afternoon in the month of May, when Susan left the house in which her life had hitherto been spent, determined to know, before she returned to it, whether she might ever again look upon it as her home. It was nearly a mile to the deacon's house, and not a single house upon the way. The two lines of turf in the road, upon which the bright green grass was springing, showed that it was but seldom travelled; and the birds warbled in the trees, as though they feared no disturbance. The fragrance of the lowly flowers, the budding shrubs, and the blooming fruit-trees, filled the air; and she stood for a moment to listen to the streamlet which she crossed upon a rude bridge of stones. She remembered how she had loved to look at it in summer, as it murmured along among the low willows and alder bushes; and how she had watched it in the early spring, when its swollen waters forced their way through the drifts of snow which had frozen over it, and wrought for itself an arched roof, from which the little icicles depended in diamond points and rows of beaded pearls. She looked also at the meadow, where the grass was already so long and green; and she sighed to think that she must leave all that was so dear to her, and go where a ramble among fields, meadows, and orchards, would be henceforth a pleasure denied to her.

CHAPTER II

When she arrived at the spacious farm-house, which was the residence of the deacon, she was rejoiced to find him at home and alone. He laid aside his newspaper as she entered, and, kindly taking her hand, inquired after her own health and that of her friends. "And now, deacon," said she, when she had answered all his questions, "I wish to know whether you intend to turn us all out of doors, as you have a perfect right to do— or suffer us still to remain, with a slight hope that we may sometime pay you the debt for which our farm is mortgaged."

"You have asked me a very plain question," was the deacon's reply, "and one which I can easily answer. You see that I have here a house, large enough and good enough for the president himself, and plenty of every thing in it and around it; and how in the name of common sense and charity, and religion, could I turn a widow and fatherless children out of their house and home! Folks have called me mean, and stingy, and close-fisted; and though in my dealings with a rich man I take good care that he shall not overreach me, yet I never stood for a cent with a poor man in my life. But you spake about some time paying me; pray, how do you hope to do it?"

"I am going to Lowell," said Susan quietly, "to work in the factory, the girls have high wages there now, and in a year or two Lydia and Eliza can come too; and if we all have our health, and mother and James get along well with the farm and the little ones, I hope, I do think, that we can pay it all up in the course of seven or eight years."

"That is a long time for you to go and work so hard, and shut yourself up so close at your time of life," said the deacon, "and on many other accounts I do not approve of it."

"I know how prejudiced the people here are against factory girls," said Susan, "but I should like to know what real good *reason* you have for disapproving of my resolution. You cannot think there is anything really wrong in my determination to labor, as steadily and as profitably as I can, for myself and the family."

"Why, the way that I look at things is this," replied the deacon: "whatever is not right, is certainly wrong; and I do not think it right for a young girl like you, to put herself in the way of all sorts of temptation. You have no idea of the wickedness and corruption which exist in that town of Lowell. Why, they say that more than half of the girls have been in the house of correction, or the county gaol, or some other vile place; and that the other half are not much better; and I should not think you would wish to go and work, and eat, and sleep, with such a low, mean, ignorant, wicked set of creatures."

"I know such things are said of them, deacon, but I do not think they are true. I have never seen but one factory girl, and that was my cousin Esther, who visited us last summer. I do not believe there is a better girl in the world than she is; and I cannot think she would be so contented and cheerful among such a set of wretches as some folks think factory girls must be. There may be wicked girls there; but among so many, there must be some who are good; and when I go there, I shall try to keep out of the way of bad company, and I do not doubt that cousin Esther can introduce me to girls who are as good as any with whom I have associated. If she cannot I will have no companion but her, and spend the little leisure I shall have in solitude, for I am determined to go."

"But supposing, Susan, that all the girls there were as good, and sensible, and pleasant as yourself—yet there are many other things to be considered. You have not thought how hard it will seem to be boxed up fourteen hours in a day, among a parcel of clattering looms, or whirling spindles, whose constant din is of itself enough to drive a girl out of her wits; and then you will have no fresh air to breathe, and as likely as not come home in a year or two with a consumption, and wishing you had staid where you would have had less money and better health. I have also heard that the boarding women do not give the girls food which is fit to eat, nor half enough of the mean stuff they do allow them, and it is contrary to all reason to suppose that folks can work, and have their health, without victuals to eat."

"I have thought of all these things, deacon, but they do not move me. I know the noise of the mills must be unpleasant at first, but I shall get used to that; and as to my health, I know that I have as good a constitution to begin with as any girl could wish, and no predisposition to consumption, nor any of those diseases which a factory life might otherwise bring upon me. I do not expect all the comforts which are common to country farmers; but I am not afraid of starving, for cousin Esther said, that she had an excellent boarding place, and plenty to eat, and drink, and that which was good enough for anybody. But if they do not give us good meat, I will eat vegetables alone, and when we have bad butter, I will eat my bread without it."

"Well," said the deacon, "if your health is preserved, you may lose some of your limbs. I have heard a great many stories about girls who had their hands torn off by the machinery, or mangled so that they could never use them again; and a hand is not a thing to be despised, nor easily dispensed with. And then, how should you like to be ordered about, and scolded at, by a cross overseer?"

"I know there is danger," replied Susan, "among so much machinery, but those who meet with accidents are but a small number, in proportion to the whole, and if I am careful I need not fear any injury. I do not believe the stories we hear about bad overseers, for such men would not be placed over so many girls; and if I have a cross one, I will give no reason to find fault; and if he finds fault without reason, I will leave him, and work for some one else.—You know that I must do something, and I have made up my mind what it shall be."

"You are a good child, Susan," and the deacon looked very kind when he told her so, "and you are a courageous, noble-minded girl. I am not afraid that *you* will learn to steal, and lie, and swear, and neglect your Bible and the meeting-house; but lest anything unpleasant should happen, I will make you this offer: I will let your mother live upon the farm, and pay me what little she can, till your brother James is old enough to take it at the halves; and if you will come here, and help my wife about the house and dairy, I will give you 4s. 6d. a-week, and you shall be treated as a daughter—perhaps you may one day be one."

The deacon looked rather sly at her, and Susan blushed; for Henry Rand, the deacon's youngest son, had been her playmate in childhood, her friend at school, and her constant attendant at all the parties and evening meetings. Her young friends all spoke of him as her lover, and even the old people had talked of it as a very fitting match, as Susan, besides good sense, good humor, and some beauty, had the health, strength and activity which are always reckoned among the qualifications for a farmer's wife.

Susan knew of this; but of late, domestic trouble had kept her at home, and she knew not what his present feelings were. Still she felt that they must not influence her plans and resolutions. Delicacy forbade that she should come and be an inmate of his father's house, and her very affection for him had prompted the desire that she should be as independent as possible of all favors from him, or his father; and also the earnest desire that they might one day clear themselves of debt. So she thanked the deacon for his offer, but declined accepting it, and arose to take leave.

"I shall think a great deal about you, when you are gone," said the deacon, "and will pray for you, too. I never used to think about the sailors, till my wife's brother visited us, who had led for many years a sea-faring life; and now I always pray for those who are exposed to the dangers of the great deep. And I will also pray for the poor factory girls who work so hard and suffer so much."

"Pray for me, deacon," replied Susan in a faltering voice, "that I may have strength to keep a good resolution."

She left the house with a sad heart; for the very success of her hopes and wishes had brought more vividly to mind the feeling that she was really to go and leave for many years her friends and home.

She was almost glad that she had not seen Henry; and while she was wondering what he would say and think, when told that she was going to Lowell, she heard approaching footsteps, and looking up, saw him coming towards her. The thought—no, the idea, for it had not time to form into a definite thought—flashed across her mind, that she must now arouse all her firmness, and not let Henry's persuasion shake her resolution to leave them all, and go to the factory.

But the very indifference with which he heard of her intention was of itself sufficient to arouse her energy. He appeared surprised, but otherwise wholly unconcerned, though he expressed a hope that she would be happy and prosperous, and that her health would not suffer from the change of occupation.

If he had told her that he loved her—if he had entreated her not to leave them, or to go with the promise of returning to be her future companion through life—she could have resisted it; for this she had resolved to do; and the happiness attending an act of self-sacrifice would have been her reward.

She had before known sorrow, and she had borne it patiently and cheerfully; and she knew that the life which was before her would have been rendered happier by the thought, that there was one who was deeply interested for her happiness, and who sympathized in all her trials.

When she parted from Henry it was with a sense of loneliness, of utter desolation, such as she had never before experienced. She had never before thought that he was dear to her, and that she had wished to carry in her far-off place of abode the reflection that she was dear to him. She felt disappointed and mortified, but she blamed not him, neither did she blame herself; she did not know that any one had been to blame. Her young affections had gone forth as naturally and as involuntarily as the vapors rise to meet the sun. But the sun which had called them forth had now gone down, and they were returning in cold drops to the heart-springs from which they had arisen; and Susan resolved that they should henceforth form a secret fount, whence every other feeling should derive new strength and vigor. She was now more firmly resolved that her future life should be wholly devoted to her kindred, and thought not of herself but as connected with them.

CHAPTER III

It was with pain that Mrs. Miller heard of Susan's plan; but she did not oppose her. She felt that it must be so, that she must part with her for her own good and the benefit of the family; and Susan hastily made preparations for her departure.

She arranged everything in and about the house for her mother's convenience; and the evening before she left she spent in instructing Lydia how to take her place, as far as possible, and told her to be always cheerful with mother, and patient with the younger ones, and to write a long letter every two months (for she could not afford to hear oftener), and to be sure and not forget her for a single day.

Then she went to her own room; and when she had reexamined her trunk, bandbox, and basket, to see that all was right, and laid her riding-dress over the great armchair, she sat down by the window to meditate upon her change of life.

She thought, as she looked upon the spacious, convenient chamber in which she was sitting, how hard it would be to have no place to which she could retire and be alone, and how difficult it would be to keep her things in order in the fourth part of a small apartment, and how possible it was that she might have unpleasant room-mates, and how probable that every day would call into exercise all her kindness and forbearance. And then she wondered if it would be possible for her to work so long, and save so much, as to render it possible that she might one day return to that chamber and call it her own. Sometimes she wished she had not undertaken it, that she had not let the deacon know that she hoped to be able to pay him; she feared that she had taken a burden upon herself which she could not bear, and sighed to think that her lot should be so different from that of most young girls.

She thought of the days when she was a little child; when she played with Henry at the brook, or picked berries with him on the hill; when her mother was always happy, and her father always kind; and she wished that the time could roll back, and she could again be a careless little girl.

She felt, as we sometimes do, when we shut our eyes and try to sleep, and get back into some pleasant dream, from which we have been too suddenly awakened. But the dream of youth was over, and before her was the sad waking reality of a life of toil, separation, and sorrow.

When she left home the next morning, it was the first time she had ever parted from her friends. The day was delightful, and the scenery beautiful; a stage-ride was of itself a novelty to her, and her companions pleasant and sociable; but she felt very sad, and when she retired at night to sleep in a hotel, she burst into tears.

Those who see the factory girls in Lowell, little think of the sighs and heart-aches which must attend a young girl's entrance upon a life of toil and privation, among strangers.

To Susan, the first entrance into a factory boarding-house seemed something dreadful. The rooms looked strange and comfortless, and the women cold and heartless; and when she sat down to the supper-table, where, among more than twenty girls, all but one were strangers, she could not eat a mouthful. She went with Esther to their sleeping apartment, and, after arranging her clothes and baggage, she went to bed, but not to sleep.

The next morning she went into the mill; and at first the sight of so many bands, and wheels, and springs, in constant motion was very frightful. She felt afraid to touch the loom, and she was almost sure that she could never learn to weave; the harness puzzled and the reed perplexed her; the shuttle flew out, and made a new bump upon her head; and the first time she tried to spring the lathe, she broke out a quarter of the treads. It seemed as if the girls all stared at her, and the overseers watched every motion, and the day appeared as long as a month had been at home. But at last it was night; and O, how glad was Susan to be released! She felt weary and wretched, and retired to rest without taking a mouthful of refreshment. There was a dull pain in her head, and a sharp pain in her ankles; every bone was aching, and there was in her ears a strange noise, as of crickets, frogs, and jews-harps, all mingling together, and she felt gloomy and sick at heart. "But it won't seem so always," said she to herself; and with this truly philosophical reflection, she turned her head upon a hard pillow, and went to sleep.

Susan was right, it did not seem so always. Every succeeding day seemed shorter and pleasanter than the last; and when she was accustomed to the work, and had become interested in it, the hours seemed shorter, and the days, weeks, and months flew more swiftly by than they had ever done before. She was healthy, active, and ambitious, and was soon able to earn as much as her cousin, who had been a weaver several years.

Wages were then much higher than they are now; and Susan had the pleasure of devoting the avails of her labor to a noble and cherished purpose. There was a definite aim before her, and she never lost sight of the object for which she left her home, and was happy in the prospect of fulfilling that design. And it needed all this hope of success, and all her strength of resolution, to enable her to bear up against the wearing influences of a life of unvarying toil. Though the days seemed shorter than at first, yet there was a tiresome monotony about them. Every morning the bells pealed forth the same clangor, and every night brought the same feeling of fatigue. But Susan felt, as all factory girls feel, that she could bear it for a while. There are few who look upon factory labor as a pursuit for life. It is but a temporary vocation; and most of the girls resolve to quit the mill when some favorite design is accomplished. Money is their object—not for itself, but for what it can perform; and pay-days are the landmarks which cheer all hearts, by assuring them of their progress to the wished-for goal.

Susan was always very happy when she enclosed the quarterly sum to Deacon Rand, although it was hardly won, and earned by the deprivation of many little comforts, and pretty articles of dress, which her companions could procure. But the thought of home, and the future happy days which she might enjoy in it, was the talisman which ever cheered and strengthened her.

She also formed strong friendships among her factory companions, and became attached to her pastor, and their place of worship. After the first two years she had also the pleasure of her sister's society, and in a year or two more, another came. She did not wish them to come while very young. She thought it better that their bodies should be strengthened, and their minds educated in their country home; and she also wished, that in their early girlhood they should enjoy the same pleasures which had once made her own life a very happy one.

And she was happy now; happy in the success of her noble exertions, the affection and gratitude of her relatives, the esteem of her acquaintances, and the approbation of conscience. Only once was she really disquieted. It was when her sister wrote that Henry Rand was married to one of their old school-mates. For a moment the color fled from her cheek, and a quick pang went through her heart. It was but for a moment; and then she sat down and wrote to the newly-married couple a letter, which touched their hearts by its simple fervent wishes for their happiness, and assurances of sincere friendship.

Susan had occasionally visited home, and she longed to go, never to leave it; but she conquered the desire, and remained in Lowell more than a year after the last dollar had been forwarded to Deacon Rand. And then, O, how happy was she when she entered her chamber the first evening after her arrival, and viewed its newly-painted wainscoting, and brightly-colored paper-hangings, and the new furniture with which she had decorated it; and she smiled as she thought of the sadness which had filled her heart the evening before she first went to Lowell.

She now always thinks of Lowell with pleasure, for Lydia is married here, and she intends to visit her occasionally, and even sometimes thinks of returning for a little while to the mills. Her brother James has married, and resides in one half of the house, which he has recently repaired; and Eliza, though still in the factory, is engaged to a wealthy young farmer.

Susan is with her mother and younger brothers and and sisters. People begin to think she will be an old maid, and she thinks herself that it will be so. The old deacon still calls her a good child, and prays every night and morning for the factory girls.

FROM *Woman in America*
by Mrs. A. J. Graves*

Graves intended this book as her contribution to the elucidation of "woman's sphere."

From WOMAN IN AMERICA

Next to the obligations which woman owes directly to her God, are those arising from her relation to the family institution. That *home* is her appropriate and appointed sphere of action there cannot be a shadow of doubt; for the dictates of nature are plain and imperative on this subject, and the injunctions given in Scripture no less explicit. Upon this point there is nothing equivocal or doubtful; no passage admitting of an interpretation varying with the judgments or inclinations of those who read. . . . "Let your women keep silence in the churches"—be "keepers at home"—taught "to guide the house." . . . And as no female of the present day can be so presumptuous as to suppose herself included in the miraculous *exceptions* mentioned in Scripture, these apostolic injunctions are doubtless to be considered as binding upon all: and if different views have been advocated, and a different practice has in many instances prevailed, the writer of these pages cannot but look upon such views and such practices as in direct violation of the apostle's commands, and as insidiously sapping the very foundations of the family institution.

The family institution is of God's own appointment, and He has ordered it for the best and wisest purposes. In His own Word we find that the spiritual welfare of the family is a paramount object in establishing the marriage relation. It was not for man's benefit alone that a helpmate was given him, and that he was to be the husband of one wife; for the holy prophet declares the revealed will of God when he says, "And did He not make *one?* yet had He the residue of the Spirit. And wherefore *one? That He might seek a godly seed.*" The Scriptures are full of

* Mrs. A. J. Graves, *Woman in America: Being an Examination into the Moral and Intellectual Condition of American Female Society* (New York: Harper and Bros., 1841), pp. 143–149, 152–164.

express as well as incidental instruction on this point. We read there that the spiritual interests of children are specially committed to the care of parents, and that there is a blessing promised, or a curse denounced, according to their faithfulness or unfaithfulness in this charge. . . . It is not in our power, we know, to give new hearts to our children; yet towards the attainment of this blessing God has assigned us a work to perform, which He has graciously promised to perfect for us. As reasonably might we expect a harvest from the field we have left untilled and unsown, as to look for the fruits of righteousness in our sons and daughters, if we leave them to grow up from youth to maturity without religious instruction. Some pious parents rely upon their prayers for the conversion of their children; but in this we are called upon to labour as well as to pray. Fervent prayer, we may hope, will be answered with a blessing; but, though it is declared that it availeth *much*, it is nowhere said that it availeth *everything*. . . .

Seeing, then, that the family institution is of Divine appointment, and the Holy Scriptures enjoin upon fathers to be faithful as teachers and rulers in causing their households to "keep the way of the Lord"; at the same time requiring of mothers that they be "keepers at home," that by the influence of their presence, example and instruction they may most effectually promote the welfare of their families, should not all Christian parents honour and cherish this institution far above whatever man has sought out or devised? And they should maintain a jealous watchfulness over the religious movements of the times, lest they be carried away by the spirit of the age contrary to the spirit of the Gospel. The present state of the world, with its stirring appeals, its strong excitements, its public teachings of every kind, and its public occupations and diversions, powerfully tends to depreciate and weaken individual mind and character, and the sacred bonds and responsibilities connected with the domestic relations. By taking a brief survey, therefore, of the state of society, in some of its most prominent characteristics, as it now exists, we shall be the better enabled to judge how far, in following its spirit, even Christian women have deviated from the strict line of duty in regard to their domestic responsibilities.

One of the most striking characteristics of the times is the universality of organized associations, and the high-wrought excitement so frequently produced by them. In these associations, where great numbers assemble together, whatever may be the object intended to be effected, there is a predominating influence which rules all minds, and communicates, as if by contagion, from one to another. When thus uniting in masses, men unconsciously give up their individual opinions, feelings, and judgments, and yield to the voice and the will of those around them. The power of sympathy, so potent in the human breast, makes the nerves of all thrill in unison, every heart throb with the same emotions, and every understanding submit to the same convictions, whether of truth or error, as though one spirit, and heart, and mind animated the whole. . . .

In such union there is a might which has accomplished widespread desolation and ruin, and glorious achievements too, so strikingly manifesting the power of man that he has been ready to deem himself as God in wisdom and greatness. When man is alone, he can form a just estimate of his strength and his weakness; of what God has enabled him to do, and what is denied to human agency. But when he combines his strength with that of others, and sees mighty results, he is tempted to think himself omnipotent. . . .

As a necessary consequence of this all-pervading spirit of association, there is at the present day a striking deficiency of individual and of private action. Our present schemes for human improvement are of a nature to weaken personal effort, to draw mankind from their homes, and to repress the high and holy influences flowing from our social instincts. The education of our youth must be carried on in *masses*, and hence the crowded schoolroom is deemed the most fitting place for the acquisition of knowledge, and the excitement of competition more favourable to its attainment than the love of it for its own sake, based on the instinctive *desire to know*, so early and so powerfully exhibited in childhood.

. . . The duty of charity is performed by societies instead of individuals, and thus it fails of its most beneficent effect, both as it regards the giver and the receiver. Neither men nor women think, feel, or act for themselves, and from this it is that we see so few instances of individual greatness, either moral or intellectual. . . .

Men may be personally more free, but their minds they have surrendered to be controlled by others, by the mass, by the omnipotence of public opinion. "Patient thought," which alone made a Newton, is given up for the ephemeral instruction of the public lecturer; and knowledge must be gained with steam-power rapidity, for we cannot wait the slow results of self-education. Hence the superficial character of our current literature: reviews, magazines, and fictitious narratives;

picture-books of all kinds, and scenic illustrations for all ages; but how few works of real enduring worth, leading men to think deeply, and think for themselves. We seek to be released as much as possible from the labour of thought, and require our authors to illustrate and explain the truths they would teach as though they were writing for children.

Another distinctive feature of the age, in all its great movements, whether political or moral, is an impatience for quick returns to our labours, and a constant studying to enlist the passions of the masses, to hurry onward whatever is undertaken. Instead of addressing the reason, and endeavouring to enlighten the judgment by a sober exhibition of truth, some point is seized upon which will best arouse the feelings. . . . Too impatient to wait for the gradual but enduring growth of principle, we call to our aid the more active and impetuous elements of man's nature, that we may realize more sudden and visible results, though these results may be but of momentary duration, quickly forced into maturity, and as rapidly declining into decay. It is not in the pursuit of riches only that men are making so much haste; but the same bustling, hurrying spirit has entered into undertakings whose high ends can only be attained by those who move calmly and steadily forward—their souls filled with a love for all that is great and good, too deep for noisy utterance, and their spirits nerved for every difficulty by the strength of well-considered and abiding principles. . . .

We would not undervalue the good, nor should we overlook the evils either necessarily or incidentally connected with this spirit of association; and we allude to it only for the purpose of showing its effects upon the character and usefulness of woman. Our chief aim throughout these pages is to prove that her domestic duties have a paramount claim over everything else upon her attention—that *home* is her appropriate sphere of action; and that whenever she neglects these duties, or goes out of this sphere of action to mingle in any of the great public movements of the day, she is deserting the station which God and nature have assigned to her. She can operate far more efficiently in promoting the great interests of humanity by supervising her own household than in any other way. Home, if we may so speak, is the cradle of the human race; and it is here the human character is fashioned either for good or for evil. It is the "nursery of the future man and of the undying spirit"; and woman is the nurse and the educator. Over infancy she has almost unlimited sway; and in maturer years she may powerfully counteract the evil influences of the world by the talisman of her strong, enduring love, by her devotedness to those intrusted to her charge, and by those lessons of virtue and of wisdom which are not of the world.

And is not this a sphere wide enough and exalted enough to satisfy her every wish? Whatever may be her gifts or acquirements, here is ample scope for their highest and noblest exercise. If her bosom burns with ardent piety, here she will find hearts to be kindled into devotion, and souls to be saved. Is she a patriot? It is here she can best serve her country, by training up good citizens, just, humane, and enlightened legislators. Has she a highly-cultivated intellect? Let her employ it, then, in leading those young, inquiring minds, which look up to her for guidance, along the pleasant paths of knowledge. Does her spirit burn within her to promote the prosperity of Zion? From this sacred retreat she may send forth a messenger of salvation to preach repentance to a fallen world; a Brainard or a Martyn, to bear the glad tidings of the Gospel to the untutored savage, or to the benighted heathen of other climes. Oh! that the mind of woman were enlightened fully to discern the extent and the importance of her domestic duties—to appreciate her true position in society; for then she would be in no danger of wandering from her proper sphere, or of mistaking the design of her being.

That woman should regard home as her appropriate domain is not only the dictate of religion, but of enlightened human reason. Well-ordered families are the chief security for the permanent peace and prosperity of the state, and such families must be trained up by enlightened female influence acting within its legitimate sphere. Again, there is a tendency in human nature to extremes, in all the changes through which society is passing, from one age to another; and the wisdom of God has devised certain influences to counteract these excesses. The domestic institution, which may be rendered so potential through the properly-directed influence of woman, contains within it a counterbalancing power to regulate and control the passions which give too great an impetus to the social machine. If man's duties lie abroad, woman's duties are within the quiet seclusion of home. If his greatness and power are most strikingly exhibited in associated action upon associated masses, her true greatness and her highest efficiency consist in individual efforts upon individual beings. The religion and the politics of man have their widest sphere in the world without; but the religious zeal and the patriotism of woman are most beneficially and powerfully exerted upon the members of her household. It is in her home that her strength lies; it is here that the gentle influence, which is the secret of her might, is most successfully employed; and this she loses as soon as she descends from her calm height into the world's arena. . . .

In this age of excitement, it is specially incumbent upon woman to exert her utmost influence, to maintain unimpaired the sacredness and the power of the family institution. "The causes of external excitement," says a late writer, "are increasing, and along with them the current seems to set from, rather than to, the domestic circle; and parental influences are in danger of being overwhelmed. There are more things out of doors, and fewer things within doors. The right of father, and mother, and home is in danger of becoming obsolete amid the thousand things that are crowding on the minds, and awakening the wonder, and the enterprise and ambition of the vigorous and the young. It cannot justly excite our astonishment, then, to find the value of home depreciated, its influences weakened, and its restraints less regarded. Sons often seem to look upon the parental abode as the place of mere boarding and lodging; and the opportunities for parental inspection, and the culture of the social feelings which chasten and sweeten life, become circumscribed to the few fleeting moments of a hurried repast. And thus becomes formed a taste for everything abroad and for but little at home. . . .

"Do we behold the family establishment in danger of waning before the excitements of the age? its restraints in danger of being diminished? its hallowed institutions in danger of being overwhelmed? Then there is the louder call upon the fidelity of all who can exert the smallest counteracting influence?"

Such is the language of this writer, and such his appeal to those who stand upon the watchtowers of Zion, to give timely notice of the approach of every danger. But may not the same appeal be made with equal force to the religious women of our country? for it is to them chiefly that we must look for aid in elevating the family institution to that high and commanding position in society which will cause it to be honoured and valued as God designed it should be. . . . In this Eden woman has been placed as a help meet for man; and a work has been given her to do, and pleasures have been given her to be enjoyed, sufficient to retain her a willing resident within its bounds.

Amid the prevailing neglect of household duty, there are, we rejoice to see, some indications of the approach of a brighter day. The awakened interest on the subject of maternal responsibility, which has given rise to our numerous Maternal Associations, will, we trust, be speedily followed by the best and happiest results. And if it has been deemed necessary so far to follow the tendencies of the age as to bring in the spirit of association and of combined action, we still fervently hope that mothers will remember that, though associations may accomplish great things, yet it is only by the individual influence of each one upon her own household that the great end of these associations can be accomplished. The very existence of such associations is, perhaps, the strongest evidence we could have of the lamentable neglect that has prevailed in relation to this matter; for if mothers had studied their Bibles aright, and duly reflected on its directions, they would have needed no farther counsel to instruct them in the duties they owe to their offspring. We would fain hope that these associations are the harbingers of better things to come; that the time is not distant when every American mother shall duly appreciate her domestic responsibilities; and when our homes shall be made attractive by the pure and satisfying enjoyments which religion, intellect, and the social affections have gathered around them. Then, when our husbands and our sons go forth into the busy and turbulent world, we may feel secure that they will walk unhurt amid its snares and temptations. Their hearts will be at home, where their treasure is; and they will rejoice to return to its sanctuary of rest, there to refresh their wearied spirits, and renew their strength for the toils and conflicts of life.

Petition for a Ten-Hour Workday*

The organization of Female Labor Reform Associations in Lowell and other mill towns during the 1840s gave evidence that conditions for workers in the New England textile industry were not so idyllic as factory owners would boast. The operatives who edited *The Factory Girl* (New Market, N.H.), *Factory Girl's Garland* (Exeter, N.H.), and *The Voice of Industry* (Lowell, Mass.) refused to accept the *Lowell Offering's* serene picture of factory life as anything but factory agents' public relations work. A part-editor of *The Voice of Industry*, Sarah Bagley was also a leader in mill-girls' organization to prevent their exploitation. She helped to organize the 1845 campaign to petition the Massachusetts Legislature for a restriction of the workday to ten hours. The following is the report of the House Committee that received the petitions and heard petitioners' testimony—but preferred to believe the mill owners' portrayal of the conditions of factory life and work.

PETITION FOR A TEN-HOUR WORKDAY

COMMONWEALTH OF MASSACHUSETTS

House of Representatives, March 12, 1845

The Special Committee to which was referred sundry petitions relating to the hours of labor, have considered the same and submit the following

REPORT:

The first petition which was referred to your committee, came from the city of Lowell, and was signed by Mr. John Quincy Adams Thayer, and eight hundred and fifty others, "peaceable, industrious, hard working men and women of Lowell." The petitioners declare that they are confined "from thirteen to fourteen hours per day in unhealthy apartments," and are thereby "hastening through pain, disease and privation, down to a premature grave." They therefore ask the Legislature "to

* *Documents Printed by Order of the House of Representatives of the Commonwealth of Massachusetts during the Session of the General Court* A.D. *1845*, Number 50 (Boston: Dutton and Wentworth, State Printers, 1845).

pass a law providing that ten hours shall constitute a day's work," and that no corporation or private citizen "shall be allowed, except in cases of emergency, to employ one set of hands more than ten hours per day."

The second petition came from the town of Fall River, and is signed by John Gregory and four hundred and eighty-eight others. These petitions ask for the passage of a law to constitute "ten hours a day's work in *all corporations* created by the Legislature."

The third petition signed by Samuel W. Clark and five hundred others, citizens of Andover, is in precisely the same words as the one from Fall River.

The fourth petition is from Lowell, and is signed by James Carle and three hundred others. The petitioners ask for the enactment of a law making "ten hours a day's work, where no specific agreement is entered into between the parties."

The whole number of names on the several petitions is 2,139, of which 1,151 are from Lowell. A very large proportion of the Lowell petitioners are females. Nearly one half of the Andover petitioners are females. The petition from Fall River is signed exclusively by males.

In view of the number and respectability of the petitioners who had brought their grievances before the Legislature, the Committee asked for and obtained leave of the House to send for "persons and papers," in order that they might enter into an examination of the matter, and report the result of their examination to the Legislature as a basis for legislative action, should any be deemed necessary.

On the 13th of February, the Committee held a session to hear the petitioners from the city of Lowell. Six of the female and three of the male petitioners were present, and gave in their testimony.

The first petitioner who testified was Eliza R. Hemmingway. She had worked 2 years and 9 months in the Lowell Factories; 2 years in the Middlesex, and 9 months in the Hamilton Corporations. Her employment is weaving,—works by the piece. The Hamilton Mill manufactures cotton fabrics. The Middlesex, woollen fabrics. She is now at work in the Middlesex Mills, and attends one loom. Her wages average from $16 to $23 a month exclusive of board. She complained of the hours for labor being too many, and the time for meals too limited. In the summer season, the work is commenced at 5 o'clock, A.M., and continued till 7 o'clock, P.M., with half an hour for breakfast and three quarters of an hour for dinner. During eight months of the year, but half an hour is

allowed for dinner. The air in the room she considered not to be wholesome. There were 293 small lamps and 61 large lamps lighted in the
room in which she worked, when evening work is required. These
lamps are also lighted sometimes in the morning.—About 130 females,
11 men, and 12 children (between the ages of 11 and 14,) work in the
room with her. She thought the children enjoyed about as good health
as children generally do. The children work but 9 months out of 12.
The other 3 months they must attend school. Thinks that there is no
day when there are less than six of the females out of the mill from
sickness. Has known as many as thirty. She, herself, is out quite often,
on account of sickness. There was more sickness in the Summer than in
Winter months; though in the Summer, lamps are not lighted. She
thought there was a general desire among the females to work but ten
hours, regardless of pay. Most of the girls are from the country, who
work in the Lowell Mills. The average time which they remain there is
about three years. She knew one girl who had worked there 14 years.
Her health was poor when she left. Miss Hemmingway said her health
was better where she now worked, than it was when she worked on the
Hamilton Corporation.

She knew of one girl who last winter went into the mill at half past
4 o'clock, A.M. and worked till half past 7 o'clock P.M. She did so to
make more money. She earned from $25 to $30 per month. There is
always a large number of girls at the gate wishing to get in before the
bell rings. On the Middlesex Corporation one fourth part of the females
go into the mill before they are obliged to. They do this to make more
wages. A large number come to Lowell to make money to aid their
parents who are poor. She knew of many cases where married women
came to Lowell and worked in the mills to assist their husbands to pay
for their farms. The moral character of the operatives is good. There
was only one American female in the room with her who could not
write her name.

Miss Sarah G. Bagley said she had worked in the Lowell Mills eight
years and a half,—six years and a half on the Hamilton Corporation, and
two years on the Middlesex. She is a weaver, and works by the piece.
She worked in the mills three years before her health began to fail. She
is a native of New Hampshire, and went home six weeks during the
summer. Last year she was out of the mill a third of the time. She thinks
the health of the operatives is not so good as the health of females who

do house-work or millinery business. The chief evil, so far as health is concerned, is the shortness of time allowed for meals. The next evil is the length of time employed—not giving them time to cultivate their minds. She spoke of the high moral and intellectual character of the girls. That many were engaged as teachers in the Sunday schools. That many attended the lectures of the Lowell Institute; and she thought, if more time was allowed, that more lectures would be given and more girls attend. She thought that the girls generally were favorable to the ten hour system. She had presented a petition, same as the one before the Committee, to 132 girls, most of whom said that they would prefer to work but ten hours. In a pecuniary point of view, it would be better, as their health would be improved. They would have more time for sewing. Their intellectual, moral, and religious habits would also be benefited by the change.

Miss Bagley said, in addition to her labor in the mills, she had kept evening school during the winter months, for four years, and thought that this extra labor must have injured her health.

Miss Judith Payne testified that she came to Lowell 16 years ago, and worked a year and a half in the Merrimack Cotton Mills, left there on account of ill health, and remained out over seven years. She was sick most of the time she was out. Seven years ago she went to work in the Boott Mills, and has remained there ever since; works by the piece. She has lost, during the last seven years, about one year from ill health. She is a weaver, and attends three looms. Last pay-day she drew $14.66 for five weeks work; this was exclusive of board. She was absent during the five weeks but half a day. She says there is a very general feeling in favor of the ten hour system among the operatives. She attributes her ill health to the long hours of labor, the shortness of time for meals, and the bad air of the mills. She had never spoken to Mr. French, the agent, or to the overseer of her room, in relation to these matters. She could not say that more operatives died in Lowell than other people.

Miss Olive J. Clark.—She is employed on the Lawrence Corporation; has been there five years; makes about $1.62½ per week, exclusive of board. She has been home to New Hampshire to school. Her health never was good. The work is not laborious; can sit down about a quarter of the time. About fifty girls work in the spinning-room with her, three of whom signed the petition. She is in favor of the ten hour system, and thinks that the long hours had an effect upon her health. She is kindly treated by her employers. There is hardly a week in which there is not some one out on account of sickness. Thinks the air is bad, on account of the small particles of cotton which fly about. She has never spoken with the agent or overseer about working only ten hours.

Miss Celicia Phillips has worked four years in Lowell. Her testimony was similar to that given by Miss Clark.

Miss Elizabeth Rowe has worked in Lowell 16 months, all the time on the Lawrence Corporation, came from Maine, she is a weaver, works by the piece, runs four looms. "My health," she says, "has been very good indeed since I worked there, averaged three dollars a week since I have been there besides my board; have heard very little about the hours of labor being too long." She consented to have her name put on the petition because Miss Phillips asked her to. She would prefer to work only ten hours. Between 50 and 60 work in the room with her. Her room is better ventilated and more healthy than most others. Girls who wish to attend lectures can go out before the bell rings; my overseer lets them go, also Saturdays they go out before the bell rings. It was her wish to attend 4 looms. She has a sister who has worked in the mill 7 years. Her health is very good. Don't know that she has ever been out on account of sickness. The general health of the operatives is good. Have never spoken to my employers about the work being too hard, or the hours too long. Don't know any one who has been hastened to a premature grave by factory labor. I never attended any of the lectures in Lowell on the ten hour system. Nearly all the female operatives in Lowell work by the piece; and of the petitioners who appeared before the Committee, Miss Hemingway, Miss Bagby, Miss Payne, and Miss Rowe work by the piece, and Miss Clark and Miss Phillips by the week.

Mr. Gilman Gale, a member of the city council, and who keeps a provision store, testified that the short time allowed for meals he thought the greatest evil. He spoke highly of the character of the operatives and of the agents; also of the boarding houses and the public schools. He had two children in the mills who enjoyed good health. The mills are kept as clean and as well ventilated as it is possible for them to be.

Mr. Herman Abbott had worked in the Lawrence Corporation 13 years. Never heard much complaint among the girls about the long hours, never heard the subject spoken of in the mills. Does not think it would be satisfactory to the girls to work only ten hours, if their wages were to be reduced in proportion. Forty-two girls work in the room with him. The girls often get back to the gate before the bell rings.

Mr. John Quincy Adams Thayer has lived in Lowell 4 years, "works at physical labor in the summer season, and mental labor in the winter." Has worked in the big machine shop 24 months, off and on; never worked in a cotton or woollen mill. Thinks that the mechanics in the machine shop are not so healthy as in other shops; nor so intelligent as the other classes in Lowell. He drafted the petition. Has heard many complain of the long hours.

Mr. S. P. Adams, a member of the House from Lowell, said he worked in the machine shop, and the men were as intelligent as any other class, and enjoyed as good health as any persons who work in-doors. The air in the shop is as good as in any shop. About 350 hands work there, about half a dozen of whom are what is called ten hour men. They all would be ten hour men if they could get as good pay.

The only witnesses whom the Committee examined, whose names were not on the petition, were Mr. Adams and Mr. Isaac Cooper, a member of the House from Lowell, and also has worked as an overseer in the Lawrence Cotton Mills for nine years. His evidence was very full. He gave it as his opinion that the girls in the mills enjoy the best health, for the reason that they rise early, go to bed early, and have three meals regular. In his room there are 60 girls, and since 1837, has known of only one girl who went home from Lowell and died. He does not find that those who stay the longest in the mill grow sickly and weak. The rooms are heated by steampipes, and the temperature of the rooms is regulated by a thermometer. It is so he believes in all the mills. The heat of the room varies from 62 to 68 degrees.

The above testimony embraces all the important facts which were elicited from the persons who appeared before the Committee. . . .

HOURS OF LABOR

From Mr. Clark, the agent of the Merrimack Corporation, we obtained the following table of the time which the mills run during the year.

Begin work.—From 1st May to 31st August, at 5 o'clock.
    From 1st September to 30th April, as soon as they can see.
Breakfast.—From 1st November to 28th February, before going to work.
    From 1st March to 31st of March, at 7½ o'clock.
    From 1st April to 19th September, at 7 o'clock.
    From 20th Sept. to 31st October, at 7½ o'clock.
    Return in half an hour.
Dinner.—Through the year at 12½ o'clock.
    From 1st May to 31st Aug., return in 45 minutes.
    From 1st Sept. to 30th April, return in 30 minutes.
Quit work.—From 1st May to 31st August, at 7 o'clock.
    From 1st September to 19th Sept., at dark.
    From 20th Sept. to 19th March, at 7½ o'clock.
    From 20th March to 30th April, at dark.

Lamps are never lighted on Saturday evenings. The above is the time which is kept in all the mills in Lowell, with a slight difference in the machine shop; and it makes the average daily time throughout the year, of running the mills, to be 12 hours and ten minutes.

There are four days in the year which are observed as holidays, and on which the mills are never put in motion. These are Fast Day, Fourth of July, Thanksgiving Day, and Christmas Day. These make one day more than is usually devoted to pastime in any other place in New England. The following table shows the average hours of work per day, throughout the year, in the Lowell Mills:

	Hours	Min.		Hours	Min.
January	11	24	July	12	45
February	12		August	12	45
March*	11	52	September	12	23
April	13	31	October	12	10
May	12	45	November	11	56
June	12	45	December	11	24

* The hours of labor on the 1st of March are less than in February, even though the days are a little longer, because 30 minutes are allowed for breakfast from the 1st of March to the 1st of September.

. . .

THE GENERAL HEALTH OF THE OPERATIVES

In regard to the health of the operatives employed in the mills, your Committee believe it to be good. The testimony of the female petitioners does not controvert this position, in general, though it does in particular instances. The population of the city of Lowell is now rising 26,000, of which number, about 7,000 are females employed in the mills. It is the opinion of Dr. Kimball, an eminent physician of Lowell, with whom the Committee had an interview, that there is less sickness among the persons at work in the mills, than there is among those who do not work in the mills; and that there is less sickness now than there was several years ago, when the number was much less than at present. This we understood to be also the opinion of the city physician, Dr. Wells, from whose published report for the present year, we learn that the whole number of deaths in Lowell, during the year 1844, was 362, of which number, 200 were children under ten years of age. . . .

The petitioners thought that the statements made by our city physician, as to the number of deaths, were delusive, inasmuch as many of the females when taken sick in Lowell do not stay there, but return to their homes in the country and die. Dr. Kimball thought that the number who return home when seized with sickness was small. Mr. Cooper, whose testimony we have given, and who is a gentleman of great experience, says that he has known but one girl who, during the last eight years, went home from Lowell and died. We have no doubt, however, that many of the operatives do leave Lowell and return to their homes when their health is feeble, but the proportion is not large. Certainly it has created no alarm, for the sisters and acquaintances of those who have gone home return to Lowell to supply the vacancies which their absence had created.

In the year 1841, Mr. French, the agent of the Boott Mills, adopted a mode of ascertaining from the females employed in that mill the effect which factory labor had upon their health. The questions which he put were:

"What is your age?"
"How long have you worked in a cotton mill?"
"Is your health as good as before?"

These questions were addressed to every female in "No. 2, Boott Mill." The Committee have the names of the females interrogated, and the answers which they returned, and the result is as follows:

List of Girls in Boott Mill, No. 2—May 1st, 1841.

Where Employed.	Whole No. of Girls.	Average Age.		Average time employed in a Mill.		Effect upon Health.		
						Impr'd.	As good.	Not as gd.
		Y.	D.	Y.	D.			
Carding Room	20	23	30	5	25	3	12	5
Spinning "	47	28	38	4	10	14	29	4
Dressing "	25	26	60	7	25	2	16	7
Weaving "	111	22	98	3	84	10	62	39
Whole No.	203	22	85	4	29	29	119	55

. . .

Your Committee have not been able to give the petitions from the other towns in this State a hearing. We believed that the whole case was covered by the petition from Lowell, and to the consideration of that petition we have given our undivided attention, and we have come to the conclusion *unanimously*, that legislation is not necessary at the present time . . .

The Committee do not wish to be understood as conveying the impression, that there are no abuses in the present system of labor; we think there are abuses; we think that many improvements may be made, and we believe will be made, by which labor will not be so severely tasked as it now is. We think that it would be better if the hours for labor were less,—if more time was allowed for meals, if more attention was paid to ventilation and pure air in our manufactories, and workshops, and many other matters. We acknowledge all this, but we say, the remedy is not with us. We look for it in the progressive improvement in art and science, in a higher appreciation of man's destiny, in a less love for money, and a more ardent love for social happiness and intellectual superiority. . . .

"Sweethearts and Wives" by T. S. Arthur a Story from *Godey's Lady's Book**

Under the editorship of Sarah Josepha Hale, Godey's Lady's Book became an acknowledged arbiter of female responsibility and genteel conduct. It contained fiction, editorial comments, information on the latest fashions, and advice on domestic management. T. S. Arthur's didactic stories "Written for the Lady's Book" appeared frequently through the 1840s.

WRITTEN FOR THE LADY'S BOOK

SWEETHEARTS AND WIVES

"When you come to deal with the sober realities of a married life, Agnes, you will, I fear, find less of sunshine than you fondly hope for."

"Aunt Mildred, how can you talk so! Surely, you ought to have more regard for William Fairfield's true character, than to insinuate, as you evidently intend to do, that he will not be the same to me after we are married, than he now is."

"Sweethearts and wives, are, somehow or other, looked at with different eyes, Agnes."

"Aunt Mildred, you will offend me if you talk so!"

"You are willing to be offended, because I speak the truth. I had hoped more from the good sense of my niece"—Aunt Mildred said, in a tone of rather more seriousness than that in which she had, at first, spoken.

"But, Aunt Mildred," said her niece, looking into her face, while the moisture gathered in her eyes, "How can I bear to hear you talk so! Do I not know that William Fairfield loves me, as he loves his own life, and that he would sooner die than give me a moment's pain?"

"You must not be offended at me when I speak what I feel to be the truth, my dear child. I have lived longer, and have seen more of the world than you have. It is not, then, let me tell you, according to the nature of men to love any one as they love their own lives, nor to prefer

* *Godey's Lady's Book*, XXIII (December, 1841), pp. 264–269. Philadelphia: Louis A. Godey, 1841.

death to giving pain to those they do love. This is all romance, Agnes, and the sooner you get it out of your head, the better. It will take itself out, if you don't, mark my word for it!"

"But Aunt, William has said so to me himself," urged the blushing maiden, "and I am sure, by his very manner, and the tone of his voice, that he was in earnest. Surely, *he* would not deceive me!"

"I have no idea, Agnes, that William meant to deceive you; I believe him to be above wilful deception. But, in the warmth of a first, ardent affection, he is carried out of himself, and led to mistake his real feelings."

"O Aunt, you will kill me if you talk so! If I thought that William did not love me as deeply as he says that he does, I would never see him again. I never can and never will be satisfied with any thing but a love that will sacrifice all for me. *I* will give such a pure, fervent love—nothing less than a like return can make me happy."

"You do not know yourself my child. You offer more than you will be able to give, and ask more than you ever can receive. None of us are perfect; all of us are selfish. You are, in a certain degree, selfish, so is William. And in just so far as this selfish principle comes into activity, will both of you expect to receive more from the other, than you are willing to give. Then will come secret pains."

"Indeed, indeed, Aunt Mildred, you frighten me! I fear some sad experience of your own has made you doubt every one—doubt even the possibility of being happy here."

A shadow flitted across Aunt Mildred's benevolent face, but it was gone in an instant; "I have not lived thus long in the world," she said, "without having learned many of its painful secrets; and one of these is that young love's promise is never realized. I have known many as full of the romance of love as you, and yet, all have been disappointed."

"And I know a good many, too, aunt, whose marriage promise has utterly failed. But, then, how could it have been otherwise; where there was no character or principle in the husband? I have built my happiness on a safer foundation. No one, I am sure, can breathe ought against William Fairfield."

"He is, if I judge him rightly, Agnes, a young man of a good heart, and sound principles. Indeed, I know of no one to whom I had rather commit the happiness of my niece."

"Thank you, my dear aunt, for that admission! And do not trouble yourself; I shall be as happy as I expect."

"But not in the way you expect, my child."

"You deal in riddles, aunt," said the now laughing girl, kissing fondly the cheek of her who had been from early years to her, a mother and friend; and then danced lightly from the room, humming a pleasant ditty.

That evening her lover came as usual. It need not be denied that Aunt Mildred's warning had made some impression upon her mind, notwithstanding her effort to throw it off. And as this impression was of a somewhat sombre cast, a slight shadow was thrown upon her countenance.

"You do not seem as lively as usual," William said, half an hour, perhaps, after he had come in.

"Don't I? Well, the fact is, Aunt Mildred has been saying something to me, that, if I could believe there was any truth in it, would make me feel gloomy enough."

"Indeed! And what is that, Agnes?"

"Why, she says," replied the simple-hearted maiden looking him in the face, "that you will not love me after we are married, as you do now."

"She is right there, dear Agnes! for I will love you a thousand times more"; the lover responded fervently, kissing at the same time the glowing cheek of his affianced bride.

Agnes did not reply; but her heart seemed too large for her bosom.

"And you did not believe it?"

"O no, no, not for a moment!" said the warm-hearted girl.

Three weeks after saw them in a new relation, that of husband and wife.

"You do not love me less, I know," said the young wife a month after the happy day of their marriage, leaning her head back upon her husband's bosom, and looking up into his face with eyes beaming with love's own peculiar brightness.

"I love you more and more, every hour, my dear Agnes," replied the fond husband, touching his lips to her's, and smoothing with his fingers the dark hair that covered her brow of snowy whiteness.

"How happy we shall be, dear husband!"

"I shall be happy, I know. But I have sometimes feared, that I might not be able to make you always feel happy."

"Only love me, dear husband, and that is all I ask."

"If my love for you will make you happy, then, no shadow can ever fall upon your heart."

"Love me, as you now do, and no shadow, I know, will ever darken it."

Our fond lovers are now united; and, as the honey moon is over, it becomes necessary for them to come down from their romance, and enter upon the sober duties of a married life. Aunt Mildred, though a very sensible woman, had not acted with her usual good sense towards her niece. She had thoroughly accomplished her in every thing but what she most needed, to make her competent to fill the place of wife and mother. She had not failed to warn her of the coming sober realities of a married life, but had, alas! neglected to prepare her to encounter them aright.

It was not long, therefore, before her husband began to experience little annoyances, in consequence of her want of domestic knowledge; and what was worse, from her distaste for the practical duties required of every wife. She seemed to have looked forward to the married state, as one that was to elevate her to a higher degree of happiness, and yet bring with it no cares nor duties. When, therefore, repeated irregularities in household economy occurred, and were felt by the husband as annoyances, he could not help thinking, sometimes, that the wife he so dearly loved, was not as thoughtful of his comfort, as he was of her's. Such thoughts will always produce corresponding feelings, and these latter cannot exist without in some way showing themselves. In the case of William Fairfield, they were exhibited in the form of a reserve, sometimes, that, while it existed, was exceedingly painful to his young wife. Besides this cause, fruitful in domestic disquietude, there was another that too frequently intrudes itself upon the first few years of marriage, a desire to lead, rather than to be led by the husband, in little things,—a habit of expecting him to consult, in all things, the will and tastes of the wife even at the sacrifice, sometimes, of duty and judgment. In fact, the wife, unconscious that in the marriage relation the husband should be looked to as of some consequence and consideration, as possessing claims upon her will to be guided by his understanding,—still imagines that all the power and peculiar influence which she possessed over him in the sweetheart-state, must of right continue. From this false view, induced by the self-sacrificing devotion of the lover, much unhappiness flows when the sweetheart becomes the wife.

We will now look in upon our young couple, and see how they get along during their first and most trying year—most trying usually, to all new married pairs.

Fairfield installed his wife mistress of a neatly furnished house, and both settled themselves down in it, brimfull of present pleasure, and delightful anticipations. The two servants managed things pretty well for the first few weeks, but after that, many irregularities became apparent. The meals were often half an hour beyond the usual and set time, and were frequently very badly cooked. The sweeping and dusting were carelessly done, and the furniture, from want of attention, began to look a little dingy, much to the annoyance of Mrs. Fairfield. Still, it did not occur to her, that she was wrong in leaving every thing to her servants. It never came into her thoughts that her mind should be the governing one of her household, in *all things*, great and small, as much as was her husband's the governing mind in his business. The idea, that she was to take pleasure in exemption from domestic duties, and not in the performance of them, was fully entertained by her, and this her husband soon perceived, and it pained him much, for he saw that in this false idea was an active germ of future disquietude.

Punctual, almost, some would say, to a fault, he felt much the want of regularity, which was daily growing worse instead of better. Too frequently he was kept from his store in the morning, half an hour later than business required him to be there, in consequence of breakfast not being ready. Whenever this happened, he usually hurried away without the parting kiss which young wives most usually expect, for he did not feel like giving it. Sometimes Agnes would claim the token of love, but she felt that it was coldly given, and its price was a gush of tears, as soon as he had passed from her sight.

But the evening usually compensated for the disquietude of the day. Then, no duties unperformed vexed the feelings of either. Agnes sung, and played sweetly, and had, besides these accomplishments a mind well stored, and a taste highly cultivated. Home was to each a little paradise and they felt how happy they were in each other. Gradually, however, the shadows, too frequently cast over their feelings, passed not off entirely, even when all duties and cares were laid aside.

"Why does not Agnes think!" Fairfield would sometimes exclaim internally. "Surely, she cannot but perceive that these things annoy me very much. I spare no toil or pains to make her happy, and, surely, she ought to be willing to assume some cares and duties for my sake!"

"I fear he does not love me!" the young wife would often say, bursting into tears, as she closed her chamber door after her, and sat down to weep in abandonment of feelings after her husband had gone out to his business. "What would I not do to retain the love once given me so freely! But he is, I fear, disappointed in me. O I would rather die than lose the pure love he once lavished upon me!"

Notwithstanding William Fairfield would often suffer his feelings to be disturbed, in consequence of the irregularities which appertained to his household economy, he more frequently endeavoured to palliate the cause of these, and tried to feel willing to bear any thing unpleasant for the sake of his wife.

"If it is irksome to her to attend to domestic affairs," he would say to himself on these occasions, "why, it would be selfish in me to wish to confine her to them merely for my own comfort."

Such reasonings, however, did not long exercise an influence over him. They soon proved to be powerless. And he would again give way mentally to regrets and censure. One day, perhaps six months after their marriage, Fairfield, much pressed and perplexed with business, left his store at the usual hour for dinner. On his way home, his mind was still intent upon business affairs, and he walked faster than usual, anxious to get back as soon as possible, as his presence was needed. Much to his disappointment, he found the cloth not even laid for dinner.

"It isn't dinner time, surely?" Agnes said, as he came into the parlor, where she was practising a new piece on the piano.

"Indeed then, it is," he replied in a tone of disappointment.

"Why, I'm sure it can't be two o'clock," responded Agnes, getting up and examining a time-piece on the mantel, that struck the hour regularly. "It is, as I live! Why how swiftly the time has passed, I had no idea that it was so late." Then ringing the bell, she directed the cook to get dinner immediately.

"It won't be done for half an hour," the cook replied carelessly.

"Half an hour! that is too bad!" Fairfield said, impatiently.

"Indeed, Sally, you must be more punctual," said Mrs. Fairfield, her cheek colouring, for she always felt distressed when her husband was moved to displeasure.

"I've got it as quick as I could," Sally replied, tartly, gliding off to the kitchen.

An oppressive silence followed the withdrawal of the cook.

"Why don't she go down and hurry the dinner?" the husband could not help saying, after some fifteen minutes had elapsed, and there was no reappearance of Sally, for the purpose of arranging the table. "If I were to leave every thing in my store to clerks and porters, my business would soon run into disorder."

After awhile, Mrs. Fairfield rung the bell again, and on Sally's appearance said, "Why don't you set the table?"

Sally did not reply, but jerked out the table, threw on the cloth, and then made the dishes rattle upon it, grumbling all the while in an under tone. Fairfield was irritated, and his wife much annoyed. He dared not trust himself to speak, and she was distressed at his moody silence.

It was near three o'clock when the meal was ready, but neither had any appetite for it. After swallowing a few mouthfuls, Fairfield hurried away to his store, and got there just too late to meet an important customer, who he knew was in town, and had been expecting all the morning. Mrs. Fairfield, who had been left sitting at the table, got up instantly and retired to her chamber, to spend the afternoon in weeping. She knew that her husband blamed her, but this she could not help feeling to be unreasonable.

"How could I help it?" she asked herself, as a fresh gush of tears streamed down her cheeks, "am I not dependent upon worthless servants? Surely, he don't expect me to go into the kitchen! If he does, he is much mistaken!" This last sentence was uttered in a calm, and somewhat indignant tone.

That evening, the supper passed off in moody silence. Fairfield, though disposed, when he came in, to lay aside, if possible, his vexed and unpleasant feelings, found a cloud upon his wife's face, and this created a positive indisposition on his part, to say even the first kind word that was to bring about a reaction. She felt that he blamed her, and she thought unjustly, and this prevented her from speaking in her usual kind and affectionate tone.

Evening passed away, and they retired for the night, still oppressed and gloomy, and each still disposed to blame the other. The morning found them in a much calmer frame of mind, and the husband's affectionate tones restored the light to Agnes' countenance. After conversing freely at the breakfast table, Fairfield said, just before rising, "I wish, Agnes, you would try to have dinner on the table punctually at two; my business requires all my attention just now, and a little delay is often a serious disadvantage to me."

The face of Agnes coloured deeply, and for a few moments she was too much disturbed to speak. At last she said, "I know you blame me,

William. But how can I help it? Sally will have her own way. I can't go into the kitchen myself and do the cooking."

"But, then, Agnes, you know you could keep an eye over Sally, and when you see she is likely to be behindhand, hurry her on a little."

"Yes, and I might be at it everlastingly," Agnes responded, rather warmly. "If I have got to be at the heels of servants all the while, I might as well give up at once."

"But, Agnes, how do other ladies get along with their domestics?"

"I don't know any that get along better than I do. They have to put up with them, and we will have to do the same."

William Fairfield felt that it would be useless to urge the matter further on his young wife, and so did not reply. But he felt a good deal discouraged as he left the house, and hurried along to his store. Agnes saw that his manner towards her was altered after what she had said, and she was equally troubled with himself. Dinner happened to be in good time this day, and, as William Fairfield ignorantly supposed it was in consequence of more attention having been given to the operations of the cook, by his wife, he felt relieved, and pleased. His kind manner— so kind, when it was genuine—made the heart of Agnes leap again. She was once more happy.

But this pleasant sunshine was not of long continuance. Causes of unpleasant feeling, other than those relating to the domestic arrangements of the family, were in existence. For the first few months, the tastes and preferences of Agnes were consulted by her husband, in every thing. But now he began to feel that she exacted too much, and considered him too little. She evidently preferred, in all things, her own will, to his; and expected him, as a matter of course, always to yield to her inclinations. This began to annoy him, and its impropriety to force itself upon his thoughts. He also began to yield to her with less apparent willingness. This was, of course, perceived, and thought to be an evidence of declining affection, and its discovery was a new source of pain to the heart of Agnes. Visions of estrangement, and entire loss of affection, began to flit before her mental vision, and many hours were passed in tears, when no eye but that of the Invisible was upon her. Still, she never seemed to imagine the true cause. No more attention was given to domestic affairs, and when the kind manner of her husband would return, after a temporary reserve, she would be as wilful, and as exacting as ever. If he proposed a call on some friend, during the evening, it was almost sure that she not only preferred going somewhere else, but expressed her wish to go there. In this wish, her husband generally acquiesced, thus denying himself to gratify her. Instead of trying to become assimilated to his tastes, or at least, of endeavouring to tolerate them, she generally expressed a difference, where any existed; and not content with this, looked for him to enter into her gratifications. Even in walking along the street, instead of leaving him to choose the right way, she would object as he turned into this street, wishing to go by another—or to crossing here or there; thus, constantly checking him, and annoying him. So uniformly was this the case, that they never walked out, without his having to yield to her will in such unimportant matters, some half dozen times. It was so little a thing to feel annoyed at, that he would chide himself for his foolishness; but it was no use, upon every recurrence of the same thing, the same feelings would return. At last, he got so, that when she checked him, he would slightly resist. But she was so thoughtless and wilful, as to, as uniformly, pull against him, saying, "No, this is the best way, I want to go this way."

Then, as she seemed so much determined on having her own will, he would not resist. But he condemned in his mind her conduct, distinctly. With all this she would be full of expressions and tokens of love, would tell him how dear he was to her, and how she could not live without him. Sometimes, while thus lavishing upon him acts of affection, and words of love, he would ask almost involuntarily, "If she so really loved me, would it not lead her to do more for my comfort, to consult my wishes more. Love, it is said, speaks plainer in actions than words. I fear she is too selfish, too much disposed to seek for happiness away from, instead of in, her duties."

It was impossible for such thoughts to be passing in the mind of a husband, without the wife perceiving in some way, that all within was not as her fond heart could wish it. And Agnes always saw something in the manner of her husband that pained her; something that sent the blood coldly about her heart; yet, she seemed utterly ignorant of the true cause.

This evident unconsciousness, was also a source of trouble to William Fairfield. He saw that she was pained, even at times distressed, by his manner, and yet, he felt that he could not tell her the cause of that manner. She would not, he feared, understand him. Indeed, when he came to think of one source of disquietude, her consultation of her own, instead of his wishes, it seemed to him so selfish, that he should want her to look to, and be guided by him, that he could not entertain the idea of breathing it to her, for a moment. Notwithstanding this, however, he was none the less annoyed by it; nor did his judgment condemn it the less as a wrong in his wife.

Fortunately for them, one source of trouble was for a time removed. Agnes obtained a much better cook, and things under her arrangement, went on like clock work. But she remained only a few months. The next obtained by Mrs. Fairfield, was one of those creatures that seem made to try the patience of even the best and most attentive housekeepers. Under her administration, all the irregularities which characterised the culinary department of the family, while Sally was cook, were not only renewed, but increased tenfold.

Fairfield lost all command over his patience, and now and then exhibited traits of no very amiable character. This added to his wife's distress of mind, but did not cause her to reflect as she should have done. The reader must not suppose that the discord which reigned too frequently in this family, or its effects, were at all perceptible to the friends and casual visitors of the young couple. All upon the surface presented to the world, was smooth and beautiful. Often the remark was made, in speaking of them.—"What a happy union! How well they have both done!" And they did, really love one another, but had not yet learned to accommodate themselves to each other's peculiarities. Fairfield was to blame, as well as Agnes. He should have been open and candid towards her, and have explained to her rationally, calmly, and affectionately, her duty; but he shrunk from this for fear of wounding her, thus wounding her a thousand times more acutely, in permitting her to go on in actions and omissions the natural results of which, were exceedingly painful to the heart of a young and loving wife.

One evening they started out to take a walk, neither of them feeling as happy as once they did, when, as lover and maiden, they had strolled along under the soft light of a quiet moon. Fairfield was silent, and Agnes but little inclined to talk, and each was too much occupied in mind with the other's peculiarities and faults. It so happened that, as the husband made a movement to turn down a certain street, as they were going home, that the wife objected and held back. The husband persevered, and the wife continued to resist; when, finding that he was not at all disposed to yield, she let go, saying, "Well, I am going this way, you can go that, if you would rather."

Surprised, yet irritated, and too much under the influence of the latter feeling to pause a moment for reflection, Fairfield, without replying, kept on, and Agnes, repenting her wilfulness, but too proud to pause, went another direction. Both arrived at home nearly at the same moment; and both had experienced in the five minutes since they parted, an age of misery. Neither of them spoke as they entered the house together. Agnes went up to her chamber, and her husband seated himself in the parlour below. In about half an hour, the excitement of the young wife's feelings began to subside, and with this calmer mood, came a distinct perception that she had done wrong; and with this consciousness, arose the determination to tell the husband so, as soon as he came up stairs. But the time continued to wear away, and yet he came not. Wearied and anxious, she laid herself across the bed and fell asleep.

In the mean time, Fairfield sat in the parlour, an agitated and miserable man. An open rupture had at last occurred, and he was reasoning himself into the determination not to suffer it to be healed until there was a full explanation and understanding between them. He also felt much anger towards the affectionate, but thoughtless and wilful, girl who had cast her lot in life with his, who had, in the confidence of a trusting maiden, committed her happiness to his keeping. Thus he sat, hour after hour, brooding over the incidents of the past year, and extracting accusation after accusation against her.

Startled by a painful dream, Agnes awoke about midnight, and rousing herself up, looked around in alarm for her husband. When she recovered her bewildered senses, the scene of the evening previous came up vividly before her mind.

"Where is he?" she asked herself, in a husky whisper.

Then catching up the light she hurried down stairs. The sound of her hastening feet startled her husband, who instantly thought, truly, that she had fallen asleep, and had just awakened; and now, in surprise and fear at his absence, had come to seek him. This thought at once modified and tendered his feelings towards her.

"O William! William!" she exclaimed, springing forward towards him, "can you, will you forgive me!"

Then sinking into his arms, she buried her head in his bosom, and lay trembling and sobbing like a frightened child.

After this excitement had, in a degree, subsided, Fairfield bent down, and kissing her cheek, whispered—"All is forgiven, dear Agnes! But let us now try so to understand each other, that no further cause for unhappiness may exist. We have not been happy during the past year, the first of our marriage—and yet, we love each other, and desire to make each other happy. Something must, then, be wrong in both of us. Now, let us lay aside all reserves, and be open, honest, and candid with each other. Do you tell me wherein I pain you, and I will tell you the same in frankness, but yet in affection. Will you do this, Agnes?"

"O I have nothing to complain of, dear husband! You have always been good and kind to me!"

"My own conscience does not acquit me in this, Agnes; neither, I am sure, can your heart. Speak out plainly, then, I will love you the better for it."

But Agnes could not speak; she only continued to hide her face in his bosom, and weep.

Gradually, however, she grew calm, and by degrees, her husband, who felt the necessity for a perfect understanding at that particular time, got her into a state of mind to converse. He then, as she would not bring a word against him, reluctantly entered upon his complaints against her, in regard to her want of due attention to the concerns of her household. This roused her up a little.

"Surely," she said "William, you do not wish to see your wife a drudge?"

"Not by any means, Agnes. But, then, I wish to see her engaged in the steady performance of every duty required by her station; because I know that only by doing so, can she render herself and family truly happy. No station, my dear wife, is exempt from its cares and its duties; if these are faithfully and willingly assumed, peace of mind will follow; if neglected, pain. As the mistress of a family, the comfort of others is placed in your hands, and, particularly, that of your husband. If you put aside your care and responsibility, and refer them to hired servants, you are in the neglect of plain and important duties; and one of the consequences which follows is, that your domestic arrangements are disturbed, and your family subjected to many annoyances. Suppose, for instance, during the past year, instead of trusting every thing to your cook, you had yourself had a careful eye, every day, over her department—had superintended the cooking so far as to know that dinner went on in time, and was properly served up at the exact hour, do you not perceive that the care which this would have subjected you to, would have been happiness compared with the feelings you have experienced in seeing me, almost daily, annoyed by irregularities which I saw you could correct, and blamed you for not correcting?"

Agnes heaved a long, deep sigh, but made no answer.

"I speak thus plain," continued the husband, "because I think it best for our happiness that I should do so. Your error lies in a false idea which you have entertained, that your happiness was to come somewhere from out of your domestic duties, instead of in the performance of them—that they were not part of a wife's obligations, but something that she could put aside if she were able to hire enough servants. I cannot, thus, delegate my business duties to any one; without my governing mind and constant attention, every thing would soon be in disorder, and an utter failure, instead of prosperity, be the result of my efforts. By my carefulness and constant devotion to business, I am enabled to provide you with every comfort; surely, then, you should be willing also to give careful attention to your department, that I may feel home to be a pleasant place. Under this view, my dear Agnes, do you conceive that I am ungenerous or unkind in wishing to see you take upon yourself more cares, and to perform more domestic duties?"

"Oh, no—no—no, dear husband!" said his wife, twining her arms around his neck, and kissing his cheek fondly. "I see very plainly how wrong I have been, and how false the views were that I have entertained. Hereafter I will strive to find my delight in what I now perceive, plainly, to be my duties. And if, at any time, I grow weary or think them irksome, I will say to myself—'I am but trying to make my husband happy, and his home a home indeed.' Only keep an unclouded brow, William—only love me, and I ask nothing more."

"I have always loved you tenderly, Agnes, although you sometimes tried me sorely."

"I know I have, my dear husband. And now, if there is any thing else, speak out plainly; I would know my faults, that I may correct them. It will be true charity for you to do so now."

"I believe it will, Agnes," he said, touching his lips to hers; "and if I pain you, remember it is only that you may be freed from a greater and lasting pain. Do not think me selfish in what I am about to say, or that I desire to rule over you tyrannically. In the wise order of Providence, there is a distinct and important difference in the relation of the sexes; and, particularly, in that which a man and his wife bear to each other. He is stronger, and his mind is a form receptive of more wisdom; she is weaker, and her mind is a form receptive of more affection. Thus they are radically different. As husband and wife, his wisdom becomes, as it were, joined to her affection, and her affection to his wisdom; thus they mutually act and react upon each other, and in just so far as each acts in a true position, do they become one, and happy in the marriage union. But if the wife attempt to guide or to force his understanding, then discord will occur, in the very nature of things; for only in just so far as her will is united with his understanding, can they, or will they act in harmony. Now one fault which you have, Agnes, is a disposition to have little things your own way, even in opposition to my expressed or implied preference. Whenever you do this, I feel as if you were unwilling to be influenced at all by me—as if you wished to be understanding and will both; thus making me a mere cypher. No man can or ought to bear this, without feeling that it is wrong. Do you understand me, Agnes?"

"I think I understand you perfectly, William. And what is better, you will say I see my fault distinctly, and will try my best to correct it. I did not think, before, that I was so selfish and wilful as I now perceive myself to be. You will forgive me the past, dear husband, will you not?"

"All—all is forgiven," he said, earnestly, again kissing her tear-moistened cheek. "And now let us begin life anew, each trying to make the other happy."

It was near morning when they retired to rest, but the few hours given to slumber were sweet and refreshing. Every thing wore a different aspect. The shadow that had begun to settle upon the brow of Mrs. Fairfield, quickly disappeared; for her husband, always meeting with order and an affectionate and constant consideration of his wishes, repaid, a hundred fold, her kind care, in increasing and manifested love. Fatigue often followed her now constant attention to her household duties; but when thus fatigued, she remembered that he, too, devoted himself day by day to business and care for her sake; and, also, that though wearied, it was from a devotion to her husband and family.

It was, perhaps, a year after, that, in a conversation with Aunt Mildred, she ventured an allusion to her first year of painful trial, and to contrast it with her present happiness. After she had done speaking, her Aunt said, smiling—"You will now acknowledge, I suppose, Agnes, that there is a very great difference between a sweetheart and a wife."

"And yet I would sooner be a wife than a sweetheart, a thousand times," responded Agnes, the tears of delight starting to her eyes.

"No doubt," Aunt Mildred said, with her usual gentle tone and quiet smile.

ON The Peculiar Responsibilities of American Women by Catharine Beecher*

Daughter of the famous preacher Lyman Beecher, and sister to Harriet Beecher Stowe and Henry Ward Beecher, Catharine Beecher made a name for herself through her books, lectures, and actions advancing education and self-improvement for women. While a firm believer that woman's sphere was the home, Beecher advocated education for females to prepare them for efficient domestic management, and to afford them a better sense of their responsibilities to themselves and to their families.

THE PECULIAR RESPONSIBILITIES OF AMERICAN WOMEN

There are some reasons, why American women should feel an interest in the support of the democratic institutions of their Country, which it is important that they should consider. The great maxim, which is the basis of all our civil and political institutions, is, that "all men are created equal," and that they are equally entitled to "life, liberty, and the pursuit of happiness."

But it can readily be seen, that this is only another mode of expressing the fundamental principle which the Great Ruler of the Universe has established, as the law of His eternal government. "Thou shalt love thy neighbor as thyself"; and "Whatsoever ye would that men should do to you, do ye even so to them," are the Scripture forms, by which the Supreme Lawgiver requires that each individual of our race shall regard the happiness of others, as of the same value as his own; and which forbid any institution, in private or civil life, which secures advantages to one class, by sacrificing the interests of another.

The principles of democracy, then, are identical with the principles of Christianity.

But, in order that each individual may pursue and secure the highest degree of happiness within his reach, unimpeded by the selfish interests of others, a system of laws must be established, which sustain certain

* From Catharine E. Beecher, *Treatise on Domestic Economy* (rev. 3d ed.; New York: Harper and Brothers, 1847), pp. 25–27, 33–34, 36–43.

relations and dependencies in social and civil life. What these relations and their attending obligations shall be, are to be determined, not with reference to the wishes and interests of a few, but solely with reference to the general good of all; so that each individual shall have his own interest, as well as the public benefit, secured by them.

For this purpose, it is needful that certain relations be sustained, which involve the duties of subordination. There must be the magistrate and the subject, one of whom is the superior, and the other the inferior. There must be the relations of husband and wife, parent and child, teacher and pupil, employer and employed, each involving the relative duties of subordination. The superior, in certain particulars, is to direct, and the inferior is to yield obedience. Society could never go forward, harmoniously, nor could any craft or profession be successfully pursued, unless these superior and subordinate relations be instituted and sustained.

But who shall take the higher, and who the subordinate, stations in social and civil life? This matter, in the case of parents and children, is decided by the Creator. He has given children to the control of parents, as their superiors, and to them they remain subordinate, to a certain age, or so long as they are members of their household. And parents can delegate such a portion of their authority to teachers and employers, as the interests of their children require.

In most other cases, in a truly democratic state, each individual is allowed to choose for himself, who shall take the position of his superior. No woman is forced to obey any husband but the one she chooses for herself; nor is she obliged to take a husband, if she prefers to remain single. So every domestic, and every artisan or laborer, after passing from parental control, can choose the employer to whom he is to accord obedience, or, if he prefers to relinquish certain advantages, he can remain without taking a subordinate place to any employer.

Each subject, also, has equal power with every other, to decide who shall be his superior as a ruler. The weakest, the poorest, the most illiterate, has the same opportunity to determine this question, as the richest, the most learned, and the most exalted.

And the various privileges that wealth secures, are equally open to all classes. Every man may aim at riches, unimpeded by any law or institution which secures peculiar privileges to a favored class, at the expense of another. Every law, and every institution, is tested by examining whether it secures equal advantages to all; and, if the people become convinced that any regulation sacrifices the good of the majority to the interests of the smaller number, they have power to abolish it. . . .

The tendencies of democratic institutions, in reference to the rights and interests of the female sex, have been fully developed in the United States; and it is in this aspect, that the subject is one of peculiar interest to American women. In this Country, it is established, both by opinion and by practice, that woman has an equal interest in all social and civil concerns; and that no domestic, civil, or political, institution, is right, which sacrifices her interest to promote that of the other sex. But in order to secure her the more firmly in all these privileges, it is decided, that, in the domestic relation, she take a subordinate station, and that, in civil and political concerns, her interests be intrusted to the other sex, without her taking any part in voting, or in making and administering laws. . . .

It appears, then, that it is in America, alone, that women are raised to an equality with the other sex; and that, both in theory and practice, their interests are regarded as of equal value. They are made subordinate in station, only where a regard to their best interests demands it, while, as if in compensation for this, by custom and courtesy, they are always treated as superiors. Universally, in this Country, through every class of society, precedence is given to woman, in all the comforts, conveniences, and courtesies, of life.

In civil and political affairs, American women take no interest or concern, except so far as they sympathize with their family and personal friends; but in all cases, in which they do feel a concern, their opinions and feelings have a consideration, equal, or even superior, to that of the other sex.

In matters pertaining to the education of their children, in the selection and support of a clergyman, in all benevolent enterprises, and in all questions relating to morals or manners, they have a superior influence. In such concerns, it would be impossible to carry a point, contrary to their judgement and feelings; while an enterprise, sustained by them, will seldom fail of success.

If those who are bewailing themselves over the fancied wrongs and injuries of women in this Nation, could only see things as they are, they would know, that, whatever remnants of a barbarous or aristocratic age may remain in our civil institutions, in reference to the interests of women, it is only because they are ignorant of them, or do not use their influence to have them rectified; for it is very certain that there is nothing reasonable, which American women would unite in asking, that would not readily be bestowed.

The preceding remarks, then, illustrate the position, that the democratic institutions of this Country are in reality no other than the principles of Christianity carried into operation, and that they tend to place woman in her true position in society, as having equal rights with the other sex; and that, in fact, they have secured to American women a lofty and fortunate position, which, as yet, has been attained by the women of no other nation. . . .

The success of democratic institutions, as is conceded by all, depends upon the intellectual and moral character of the mass of the people. If they are intelligent and virtuous, democracy is a blessing; but if they are ignorant and wicked, it is only a curse, and as much more dreadful than any other form of civil government, as a thousand tyrants are more to be dreaded than one. It is equally conceded, that the formation of the moral and intellectual character of the young is committed mainly to the female hand. The mother forms the character of the future man; the sister bends the fibres that are hereafter to be the forest tree; the wife sways the heart, whose energies may turn for good or for evil the destinies of a nation. Let the women of a country be made virtuous and intelligent, and the men will certainly be the same. The proper education of a man decides the welfare of an individual; but educate a woman, and the interests of a whole family are secured.

If this be so, as none will deny, then to American women, more than to any others on earth, is committed the exalted privilege of extending over the world those blessed influences, which are to renovate degraded man, and "clothe all climes with beauty."

No American woman, then, has any occasion for feeling that hers is an humble or insignificant lot. The value of what an individual accomplishes, is to be estimated by the importance of the enterprise achieved, and not by the particular position of the laborer. The drops of heaven which freshen the earth, are each of equal value, whether they fall in the lowland meadow, or the princely parterre. The builders of a temple are of equal importance, whether they labor on the foundations, or toil upon the dome.

Thus, also, with those labors which are to be made effectual in the regeneration of the Earth. And it is by forming a habit of regarding the apparently insignificant efforts of each isolated laborer, in a comprehensive manner, as indispensable portions of a grand result, that the minds of all, however humble their sphere of service, can be invigorated and cheered. The woman, who is rearing a family of children; the woman, who labors in the schoolroom; the woman, who, in her retired chamber, earns, with her needle, the mite, which contributes to the intellectual and moral elevation of her Country; even the humble domestic, whose example and influence may be moulding and forming young minds, while her faithful services sustain a prosperous domestic state;—each and all may be animated by the consciousness, that they are agents in accomplishing the greatest work that ever was committed to human responsibility. It is the building of a glorious temple, whose base shall be coextensive with the bounds of the earth, whose summit shall pierce the skies, whose splendor shall beam on all lands; and those who hew the lowliest stone, as much as those who carve the highest capital, will be equally honored, when its top-stone shall be laid, with new rejoicings of the morning stars, and shoutings of the sons of God.

DIFFICULTIES PECULIAR TO AMERICAN WOMEN

And as it has been shown, that American women have a loftier position, and a more elevated object of enterprise, than the females of any other nation, so it will appear, that they have greater trials and difficulties to overcome, than any other women are called to encounter. . . .

Now, the larger portion of American women are the descendants of English progenitors, who, as a nation, are distinguished by systematic housekeeping, and for a great love of order, cleanliness, and comfort. And American women, to a greater or less extent, have inherited similar tastes and habits. But the prosperity and democratic tendencies of this Country produce results, materially affecting the comfort of housekeepers, which the females of monarchical and aristocratic lands are not called to meet. In such countries, all ranks and classes are fixed in a given position, and each person is educated for a particular sphere and style of living. And the dwellings, conveniences, and customs of life, remain very nearly the same, from generation to generation. This secures the preparation of all classes for their particular station, and makes the lower orders more dependent, and more subservient to employers.

But how different is the state of things in this Country. Every thing is moving and changing. Persons in poverty, are rising to opulence, and persons of wealth, are sinking to poverty. The children of common laborers, by their talents and enterprise, are becoming nobles in intellect, or wealth, or office; while the children of the wealthy, enervated by indulgence, are sinking to humbler stations. The sons of the wealthy are leaving the rich mansions of their fathers, to dwell in the log cabins of the forest, where very soon they bear away the daughters of ease and refinement, to share the privations of a new settlement. Meantime, even in the more stationary portions of the community, there is a mingling of all grades of wealth, intellect, and education. There are no distinct classes, as in aristocratic lands, whose bounds are protected by distinct and impassable lines, but all are thrown into promiscuous masses. Thus, persons of humble means are brought into contact with those of vast wealth, while all intervening grades are placed side by side. Thus, too, there is a constant comparison of conditions, among equals, and a constant temptation presented to imitate the customs, and to strive for the enjoyments, of those who possess larger means.

In addition to this, the flow of wealth, among all classes, is constantly increasing the number of those who live in a style demanding much hired service, while the number of those, who are compelled to go to service, is constantly diminishing. Our manufactories, also, are making increased demands for female labor, and offering larger compensation. In consequence of these things, there is such a disproportion between those who wish to hire, and those who are willing to go to domestic service, that, in the non-slaveholding States were it not for the supply of poverty-stricken foreigners, there would not be a domestic for each family who demands one. And this resort to foreigners, poor as it is, scarcely meets the demand; while the disproportion must every year increase, especially if our prosperity increases. For, just in proportion as wealth rolls in upon us, the number of those, who will give up their own independent homes to serve strangers, will be diminished.

The difficulties and sufferings, which have accrued to American women, from this cause, are almost incalculable. There is nothing, which so much demands system and regularity, as the affairs of a housekeeper, made up, as they are, of ten thousand desultory and minute items; and yet, this perpetually fluctuating state of society seems forever to bar any such system and regularity. The anxieties, vexations, perplexities, and even hard labor, which come upon American women, from this state of domestic service, are endless; and many a woman has, in consequence, been disheartened, discouraged, and ruined in health. The only wonder is, that, amid so many real difficulties, American women are still able to maintain such a character for energy, fortitude, and amiableness, as is universally allowed to be their due.

But the second, and still greater difficulty, peculiar to American women, is, a delicacy of constitution, which renders them early victims to disease and decay. . . .

It would seem as if the primeval curse, which has written the doom of pain and sorrow on one period of a young mother's life, in this Country had been extended over all; so that the hour seldom arrives, when "she forgetteth her sorrow for joy that a man is born into the world." Many a mother will testify, with shuddering, that the most exquisite sufferings she ever endured, were not those appointed by Nature, but those, which, for week after week, have worn down health and spirits, when nourishing her child. And medical men teach us, that this, in most cases, results from a debility of constitution, consequent on the mismanagement of early life. And so frequent and so mournful are these, and the other distresses that result from the delicacy of the female constitution, that the writer has repeatedly heard mothers say, that they had wept tears of bitterness over their infant daughters, at the thought of the sufferings which they were destined to undergo; while they cherished the decided wish, that these daughters should never marry. At the same time, many a reflecting young woman is looking to her future prospects, with very different feelings and hopes from those which Providence designed.

IV

Slavery and Sex

FROM *Letters on the Equality of the Sexes* by Sarah Grimké*

With her *Letters on the Equality of the Sexes and the Condition of Women,* which first appeared in serial form, but which were collected in one volume in 1838, Sarah M. Grimké became the first American woman to publish a cross-cultural examination of the condition of women and a reasoned feminist argument against the injustice of that condition. She had been born into a wealthy slaveholding family in South Carolina, but in revulsion against slavery she left the South when she was a young woman, adopted the Quaker faith, and found friends among Quaker antislavery sympathizers in Philadelphia. Her sensitivity to the abuses of female slaves was always a part of her feminist thought, as the following selection from her *Letters* indicates.

LETTER VIII

ON THE CONDITION OF WOMEN IN THE UNITED STATES

Brookline, 1837

My Dear Sister,—I have now taken a brief survey of the condition of woman in various parts of the world. I regret that my time has been so much occupied by other things, that I have been unable to bestow that attention upon the subject which it merits, and that my constant change of place has prevented me from having access to books, which might probably have assisted me in this part of my work. I hope that the principles I have asserted will claim the attention of some of my sex, who may be able to bring into view, more thoroughly than I have done, the situation and degradation of woman. I shall now proceed to make a few remarks on the condition of women in my own country.

During the early part of my life, my lot was cast among the butterflies of the *fashionable* world; and of this class of women, I am constrained to say, both from experience and observation, that their education is miserably deficient; that they are taught to regard marriage as the one thing needful, the only avenue to distinction; hence to attract the notice

* Sarah M. Grimké, *Letters on the Equality of the Sexes and the Condition of Women* (Boston: Isaac Knapp, 1838), pp. 46–54.

and win the attentions of men, by their external charms, is the chief business of fashionable girls. They seldom think that men will be allured by intellectual acquirements, because they find, that where any mental superiority exists, a woman is generally shunned and regarded as stepping out of her "appropriate sphere," which, in their view, is to dress, to dance, and to set out to the best possible advantage her person, to read the novels which inundate the press, and which do more to destroy her character as a rational creature, than any thing else. Fashionable women regard themselves, and are regarded by men, as pretty toys or as mere instruments of pleasure; and the vacuity of mind, the heartlessness, the frivolity which is the necessary result of this false and debasing estimate of women, can only be fully understood by those who have mingled in the folly and wickedness of fashionable life; and who have been called from such pursuits by the voice of the Lord Jesus, inviting their weary and heavy laden souls to come unto Him and learn of Him, that they may find something worthy of their immortal spirit, and their intellectual powers; that they may learn the high and holy purposes of their creation, and consecrate themselves unto the service of God; and not, as is now the case, to the pleasure of man.

There is another and much more numerous class in this country, who are withdrawn by education or circumstances from the circle of fashionable amusements, but who are brought up with the dangerous and absurd idea, that *marriage* is a kind of preferment; and that to be able to keep their husband's house, and render his situation comfortable, is the end of her being. Much that she does and says and thinks is done in reference to this situation; and to be married is too often held up to the view of girls as the sine qua non of human happiness and human existence. For this purpose more than for any other, I verily believe the majority of girls are trained. This is demonstrated by the imperfect education which is bestowed upon them, and the little pains taken to cultivate their minds, after they leave school, by the little time allowed them for reading, and by the idea being constantly inculcated, that although all household concerns should be attended to with scrupulous punctuality at particular seasons, the improvement of their intellectual capacities is only a secondary consideration, and may serve as an occupation to fill up the odds and ends of time. In most families, it is considered a matter of far more consequence to call a girl off from making a pie, or a pudding, than to interrupt her whilst engaged in her studies. This mode of training necessarily exalts, in their view, the animal above

the intellectual and spiritual nature, and teaches women to regard themselves as a kind of machinery, necessary to keep the domestic engine in
order, but of little value as the *intelligent* companions of men.

Let no one think, from these remarks, that I regard a knowledge of
housewifery as beneath the acquisition of women. Far from it: I believe
that a complete knowledge of household affairs is an indispensable requisite in a woman's education,—that by the mistress of a family, whether
married or single, doing her duty thoroughly and *understandingly*, the
happiness of the family is increased to an incalculable degree, as well as
a vast amount of time and money saved. All I complain of is, that our
education consists so almost exclusively in culinary and other manual
operations. I do long to see the time, when it will no longer be necessary for women to expend so many precious hours in furnishing "a well
spread table," but that their husbands will forgo some of their accustomed indulgences in this way, and encourage their wives to devote
some portion of their time to mental cultivation, even at the expense of
having to dine sometimes on baked potatoes, or bread and butter. . . .

There is another way in which the general opinion, that women are
inferior to men, is manifested, that bears with tremendous effect on the
laboring class, and indeed on almost all who are obliged to earn a subsistence, whether it be by mental or physical exertion—I allude to the
disproportionate value set on the time and labor of men and of women.
A man who is engaged in teaching, can always, I believe, command a
higher price for tuition than a woman—even when he teaches the same
branches, and is not in any respect superior to the woman. This I know
is the case in boarding and other schools with which I have been acquainted, and it is so in every occupation in which the sexes engage in-
discriminately. As for example, in tailoring, a man has twice, or three
times as much for making a waistcoat or pantaloons as a woman, although the work done by each may be equally good. In those employments which are peculiar to women, their time is estimated at only half
the value of that of men. A woman who goes out to wash, works as hard
in proportion as a wood sawyer, or a coal heaver, but she is not
generally able to make more than half as much by a day's work. The
low remuneration which women receive for their work, has claimed the
attention of a few philanthropists, and I hope it will continue to do so
until some remedy is applied for this enormous evil. I have known a
widow, left with four or five children, to provide for, unable to leave
home because her helpless babes demand her attention, compelled to

earn a scanty subsistence, by making coarse shirts at 12½ cents a piece, or by taking in washing, for which she was paid by some wealthy persons 12½ cents per dozen. All these things evince the low estimation in which woman is held. There is yet another and more disastrous consequence arising from this unscriptural notion—women being educated, from earliest childhood, to regard themselves as inferior creatures, have not that self-respect which conscious equality would engender, and hence when their virtue is assailed, they yield to temptation with facility, under the idea that it rather exalts than debases them, to be connected with a superior being.

There is another class of women in this country, to whom I cannot refer, without feelings of the deepest shame and sorrow. I allude to our female slaves. Our southern cities are whelmed beneath a tide of pollution; the virtue of female slaves is wholly at the mercy of irresponsible tyrants, and women are bought and sold in our slave markets, to gratify the brutal lust of those who bear the name of Christians. In our slave States, if amid all her degradation, and ignorance, a woman desires to preserve her virtue unsullied, she is either bribed or whipped into compliance, or if she dares resist her seducer, her life by the laws of some of the slave States may be, and has actually been sacrificed to the fury of disappointed passion. Where such laws do not exist, the power which is necessarily vested in the master over his property, leaves the defenceless slave entirely at his mercy, and the sufferings of some females on this account, both physical and mental, are intense. Mr. Gholson, in the House of Delegates of Virginia, in 1832, said, "He really had been under the impression that he owned his slaves. He had lately purchased four women and ten children, in whom he thought he had obtained a great bargain; for he supposed they were his own property, *as were his brood mares*." But even if any laws existed in the United States, as in Athens formerly, for the protection of female slaves, they would be null and void, because the evidence of a colored person is not admitted against a white, in any of our Courts of Justice in the slave States. . . .

S. A. Forrall, speaking of the state of morals at the South, says, "Negresses when young and likely, are often employed by the planter, or his friends, to administer to their sensual desires. This frequently is a matter of speculation, for if the offspring, a mulatto, be a handsome female, 800 or 1000 dollars may be obtained for her in the New Orleans market. It is an occurrence of no uncommon nature to see a Christian father sell his own daughter, and the brother his own sister." The following is copied by the N. Y. Evening Star from the Picayune, a paper published in New Orleans. "A very beautiful girl, belonging to the estate of John French, a deceased gambler at New Orleans, was sold a few days since for the round sum of $7,000. An ugly-looking bachelor named Gouch, a member of the Council of one of the Principalities, was the purchaser. The girl is a brunette; remarkable for her beauty and intelligence, and there was considerable contention, who should be the purchaser. She was, however, persuaded to accept Gouch, he having made her princely promises.". . .

Nor does the colored woman suffer alone: the moral purity of the white woman is deeply contaminated. In the daily habit of seeing the virtue of her enslaved sister sacrificed without hesitancy or remorse, she looks upon the crimes of seduction and illicit intercourse without horror, and although not personally involved in the guilt, she loses that value for innocence in her own, as well as the other sex, which is one of the strongest safeguards to virtue. She lives in habitual intercourse with men, whom she knows to be polluted by licentiousness, and often is she compelled to witness in her own domestic circle, those disgusting and heart-sickening jealousies and strifes which disgraced and distracted the family of Abraham. In addition to all this, the female slaves suffer every species of degradation and cruelty, which the most wanton barbarity can inflict; they are indecently divested of their clothing, sometimes tied up and severely whipped, sometimes prostrated on the earth, while their naked bodies are torn by the scorpion lash.

> "The whip on WOMAN's shrinking flesh!
> Our soil yet reddening with the stains
> Caught from her scourging warm and fresh."

Can any American woman look at these scenes of shocking licentiousness and cruelty, and fold her hands in apathy, and say, "I have nothing to do with slavery"? *She cannot and be guiltless.*

Narratives from Escaped Slaves*

The following narratives of life under slavery were recorded by Benjamin Drew as told to him by black residents of Canada, fugitives from slavery in the American South. Drew, a Bostonian, traveled to Canada in 1855 to collect the true stories of black refugees.

NARRATIVES FROM ESCAPED SLAVES

MRS. ——— ———

[The lady who gave the following narrative wished to withhold her name, for private reasons. She is well known at St. Catharines as a very intelligent and respectable person.]

I was held as a slave in ———, without even legal right according to the slave laws. When I was ten years old, a young man was punishing me—I resisted: I was in consequence called "a rebellious wretch," and put out of the family. At the place where I was hired, it happened on communion Sunday in March, that the dogs got hold of a pig, and bit a piece off its ear. In consequence of this misfortune to the pig, a boy of sixteen years, or thereabouts, was whipped in the barn; and a man-slave was tied up to a tree, with his arms extended, and whipped. I was peeping and saw the man whipped. The blood ran as they whipped him. His wife had to take care of him and dress his wounds. It affected me so that I cried and said I wouldn't stay at the place,—then the same man—the man of the house—whipped me. At twelve o'clock that night, I ran away to my owners. He came to the folks where I was, and requested them to send me back, lest the others should follow my example. I went back and stayed two weeks,—when I had got within a mile of home, my master got on his horse, and trotted along behind me, to let folks see that he had got the runaway.

After my escape from slavery, I married a free colored man. We

* From Benjamin Drew (ed.), *A Northside View of Slavery: The Refugee, or the Narratives of Fugitive Slaves in Canada, Related by Themselves* (Boston: John P. Jowett, 1856), pp. 31–32, 41–43, 44, 50–51, 138, 140–141, 224–227.

were comfortably settled in the States, and were broken up by the fugitive slave law,—compelled to leave our home and friends, and to go at later than middle life into a foreign country among strangers.

I look upon slavery as the worst evil that ever was. My life has been taken from me in a measure by it. If any are disposed to apologize for slavery, it would be well for them to try it awhile.

MRS. JAMES SEWARD

The slaves want to get away bad enough. They are not contented with their situation.

I am from the eastern shore of Maryland. I never belonged but to one master; he was very bad indeed. I was never sent to school, nor allowed to go to church. They were afraid we would have more sense than they. I have a father there, three sisters, and a brother. My father is quite an old man, and he is used very badly. Many a time he has been kept at work a whole long summer day without sufficient food. A sister of mine has been punished by his taking away her clothes and locking them up, because she used to run when master whipped her. He kept her at work with only what she could pick up to tie on her for decency. He took away her child which had just begun to walk, and gave it to another woman,—but she went and got it afterward. He had a large farm eight miles from home. Four servants were kept at the house. My master could not manage to whip my sister when she was strong. He waited until she was confined, and the second week after her confinement he said, "Now I can handle you, now you are weak." She ran from him, however, and had to go through water, and was sick in consequence.

I was beaten at one time over the head by my master, until the blood ran from my mouth and nose: then he tied me up in the garret, with my hands over my head,—then he brought me down and put me in a little cupboard, where I had to sit cramped up, part of the evening, all night, and until between four and five o'clock, next day, without any food. The cupboard was near a fire, and I thought I should suffocate.

My brother was whipped on one occasion until his back was as raw as a piece of beef, and before it got well, master whipped him again. His back was an awful sight.

We were all afraid of master: when I saw him coming, my heart would jump up into my mouth, as if I had seen a serpent.

I have been wanting to come away for eight years back. I waited for

Jim Seward to get ready. Jim had promised to take me away and marry me. Our master would allow no marriages on the farm. When Jim had got ready, he let me know,—he brought to me two suits of clothes—men's clothes—which he had bought on purpose for me. I put on both suits to keep me warm. We eluded pursuit and reached Canada in safety.

MRS. ELLIS

It is more than a year ago, that I left slavery in Delaware, having been thirty-two years a slave. I was treated tolerably well, compared with others. I was brought up in ignorance. I felt put down—oppressed in spirit. I did a great deal of heavy out-door work,—such as driving team, hauling manure, etc. I have been whipped with a wagon whip and with hickories,—have been kicked and hit with fists. I have a bunch on my head from a blow my master gave me, and I shall carry it to my grave. I have had four children—two died there, and two I brought with me.

I thought I had paid my master for raising me, and I wanted some time of my own: and when he threatened to sell me, and keep my children, I left him. I got off without much trouble. I suffered a great deal from wet and cold, on the first part of the way—afterwards, I was helped on by kind white men.

Rents and provisions are dear here, and it takes all I can earn to support myself and children. I could have one of my children well brought up and taken care of, by some friends in Massachusetts, which would much relieve me,—but I cannot have my child go there on account of the laws, which would not protect her. This is a hardship: but had I to struggle much harder than at present, I would prefer it to being a slave. Now, I can lie down at night in peace,—there I had no peace even at night, on account of my master's conduct.

Slavery is a wicked institution. I think if the whites were to free the slaves, they would incur no danger. I think the colored people would go to work without any trouble.

MRS. NANCY HOWARD

I was born in Anne Arundel county, Maryland,—was brought up in Baltimore. After my escape, I lived in Lynn, Mass., seven years, but I left there through fear of being carried back, owing to the fugitive slave law. I have lived in St. Catharines less than a year.

The way I got away was,—my mistress was sick, and went into the country for her health. I went to stay with her cousin. After a month, my mistress was sent back to the city to her cousin's, and I waited on her. My daughter had been off three years. A friend said to me,—"Now is your chance to get off." At last I concluded to go,—the friend supplying me with money. I was asked no questions on the way north.

My idea of slavery is, that it is one of the blackest, the wickedest things that ever were in the world. When you tell them the truth, they whip you to make you lie. I have taken more lashes for this, than for any other thing, because I would not lie.

One day I set the table, and forgot to put on the carving-fork—the knife was there. I went to the table to put on a plate. My master said,— "Where is the fork?" I told him "I forgot it." He says,—"You d——d black b——, I'll forget you!"—at the same time hitting me on the head with the carving-knife. The blood spurted out,—you can see. [Here the woman removed her turban and showed a circular cicatrice denuded of hair, about an inch in diameter, on the top of her head.] My mistress took me into the kitchen and put on camphor, but she could not stop the bleeding. A doctor was sent for. He came, but asked no questions. I was frequently punished with raw hides,—was hit with tongs and poker and any thing. I used when I went out, to look up at the sky, and say, "Blessed Lord, oh, do take me out of this!" It seemed to me I could not bear another lick. I can't forget it. I sometimes dream that I am pursued, and when I wake, I am scared almost to death.

HENRY GOWENS

I have had a wide experience of the evils of slavery, in my own person, and have an extensive knowledge of the horrors of slavery, in all their length and breadth, having witnessed them in Old Virginia, North Carolina, New Virginia, Tennessee, Alabama, and Mississippi. I belonged in the State of Virginia, and am, I suppose, about forty years old. . . .

About the first of Gen. Jackson's Presidency, my master employed an overseer, named Kimball, over one hundred and thirty slaves, in Lauderdale Co., Alabama. This Kimball was one of the most cruel men I ever saw. . . .

In the picking cotton season, Mr. K. would punish the women in the severest manner, because they did not pick cotton fast enough. He would thrust their heads into a cotton basket. What I say now would scarcely be believed only among those who are in that neighborhood, because it looks too cruel for any one to do or to believe, if they had no experience of such things or had not seen the like,—they would not dare lift up their heads, as perhaps he would punish them twice as much. Then he would throw their clothes up over their heads and the basket, and flog them as hard as he could with a rugged lash, cutting their flesh terribly, till the blood ran to their heels. Sometimes they would from the torment lift their heads, when he would perhaps give them a third more than he otherwise would; and this without reference to any particular condition they might be in at the time. The men he would generally place across a log, tie their hands together, and their feet together, and put a rail through under the log with the ends between their feet and hands; and in this condition, which is itself painful, he would apply the lash. Sometimes, to cramp down the mind of the husband, he would compel him to assist in the punishment of his wife. Who will tell of the good of slavery? I would rather be a brute in the field, than to endure what my people have to endure, what they have endured in many parts of the slave-holding States.

There was one religious old woman, Aunt Dinah,—very pious: all believed she was, even my master. She used to take care of the infants at the quarters while the mothers were out at work. At noon, the mothers would come home to nurse their children, unless they were too far off— then the infants were carried to them. Aunt Dinah, knowing how cruelly the women were treated, at last, when the master was absent, picked up courage to go to the mistress and complain of the dealings of the overseer. My mistress belonged to the Presbyterian Church; Aunt Dinah to the Baptist. The mistress then began to my master about the cruelty on the place, without disclosing how she got her information. I do not think the master would have interfered, were it not that the mistress also told him of the overseer's intimacy with some of the female slaves. She being a well-bred lady, the master had to take some notice of the management. He told the overseer to change his mode of punishing the women; to slip their clothes down from their shoulders, and punish them on their backs. No interference was ever made except in this one instance.

The overseer had one child by a slave woman. I left the child there a slave. At the expiration of a year Kimball left. Three months after, or thereabouts, he was hanged in Raleigh, N. C., for the murder of his step-father. The slaves were rejoiced at his being hung, and thought he ought to have been hung before he came there to be overseer.

MRS. JOHN LITTLE

I was born in Petersburg, Va. When very young, I was taken to Montgomery county. My old master died there, and I remember that all the people were sold. My father and mother were sold together about one mile from me. After a year, they were sold a great distance, and I saw them no more. My mother came to me before she went away, and said, "Good by, be a good girl; I never expect to see you any more."

Then I belonged to Mr. T— N—, the son of my old master. He was pretty good, but his wife, my mistress, beat me like sixty. Here are three scars on my right hand and arm, and one on my forehead, all from wounds inflicted with a broken china plate. My cousin, a man, broke the plate in two pieces, and she said, "Let me see that plate." I handed up the pieces to her, and she threw them down on me: they cut four gashes, and I bled like a butcher. One piece cut into the sinew of the thumb, and made a great knot permanently. The wound had to be sewed up. This long scar over my right eye, was from a blow with a stick of wood. One day she knocked me lifeless with a pair of tongs,— when I came to, she was holding me up, through fright. Some of the neighbors said to her, "Why don't you learn Eliza to sew?" She answered, "I only want to learn her to do my housework, that's all." I can tell figures when I see them, but cannot read or write.

I belonged to them until I got married at the age of sixteen, to Mr. John Little, of Jackson. My master sold me for debt,—he was a man that would drink, and he had to sell me. I was sold to F— T—, a planter and slave-trader, who soon after, at my persuasion, bought Mr. Little.

I was employed in hoeing cotton, a new employment: my hands were badly blistered. "Oh, you must be a great lady," said the overseer, "can't handle the hoe without blistering your hands!" I told him I could not help it. My hands got hard, but I could not stand the sun. The hot sun made me so sick I could not work, and, John says if I had not come away, they would surely have sold me again. There was one weakly woman named Susan, who could not stand the work, and she was sold to Mississippi, away from her husband and son. That's one way of taking care of the sick and weak. That's the way the planters do with a weakly, sickly "nigger."—they say "he's a dead expense to 'em," and put him off as soon as they can. After Susan was carried off, her husband went to see her: when he came back he received two hundred blows with the paddle.

I staid with T—— more than a year. A little before I came away, I heard that master was going to give my husband three hundred blows with the paddle. He came home one night with an axe on his shoulder, tired with chopping timber. I had his clothes all packed up, for I knew he would have to go. He came hungry, calculating on his supper,—I told him what was going. I never heard him curse before—he cursed then. Said he, "If any man, white or black, lays his hand on me to-night, I'll put this axe clear through him—clear through him": and he would have done it, and I would not have tried to hinder him. But there was a visitor at the house, and no one came: he ran away. Next morning, the overseer came for him. The master asked where he was; I could have told him, but would not. My husband came back no more.

When we had made arrangements for leaving, a slave told of us. Not long after, master called to me, "Come here, my girl, come here." I went to him: he tied me by the wrist with a rope. He said, "Oh, my girl, I don't blame you,—you are young, and don't know; it's that d——d infernal son of a ——; if I had him here, I'd blow a ball through him this minute." But he was deceived about it: I had put John up to hurrying off.

Then master stood at the great house door, at a loss what to do. There he had Willis, who was to have run away with us, and the man who betrayed us. At last he took us all off about half a mile to a swamp, where old A—— need not hear us as he was going to meeting, it being Sunday. He whipped Willis to make him tell where we were going. Willis said, "Ohio State." "What do you want to be free for? G—— d—— you, what do you know about freedom? Who was going with you?" "Only Jack." "G—— d—— Jack to h——, and you too." While they were whipping Willis, he said, "Oh, master, I'll never run away." "I didn't ask you about that, you d——d son of a ——, you." Then they tried to make him tell about a slave girl who had put her child aside: but he knew nothing about that. As soon as they had done whipping him, they put a plough clavis about his ankle to which they attached a chain which was secured about his neck with a horse-lock.

Then they took a rheumatic boy, who had stopped with us, whom I had charged not to tell. They whipped him with the paddle, but he said he was ignorant of it: he bore the whipping, and never betrayed us.

Then they questioned him about the girl and the child, as if that boy could know anything about it! Then came my turn; they whipped me in the same way they did the men. Oh, those slaveholders are a brutish set of people,—the master made a remark to the overseer about my shape. Before striking me, master questioned me about the girl. I denied all knowledge of the affair. I only knew that she had been with child, and that now she was not, but I did not tell them even that. I was ashamed of my situation, they remarking upon me. I had been brought up in the house, and was not used to such coarseness. Then he (master) asked, "Where is Jack?" "I don't know." Said he, "Give her h——, R——." That was his common word. Then they struck me several blows with the paddle. I kept on telling them it was of no use to whip me, as I knew nothing to tell them. No irons were ready for me, and I was put under a guard,—but I was too cunning for him, and joined my husband.

FROM *An Appeal to the Women of the Nominally Free States* by Angelina Grimké*

Thirteen years younger than her sister Sarah, Angelina Grimké took the same path away from her native South, to the North, to Quakerism, abolitionism, and feminism. Angelina became the more sought after of the two as an anti-slavery lecturer, because of her eloquence. Her background as a native southerner and feminist injected a certain dynamism into her abolitionist views, which she was able to express in such documents as her letter to William Lloyd Garrison's journal the *Liberator*, in her *Appeal to the Christian Women of the South*, and her *Appeal to the Women of the Nominally Free States*.

From AN APPEAL TO THE WOMEN OF THE NOMINALLY FREE STATES

. . . [In] a country where women are degraded and brutalized, and where their exposed persons bleed under the lash—where they are sold in the shambles of "negro brokers"—robbed of their hard earnings—torn from their husbands, and forcibly plundered of their virtue and their offspring; surely in *such* a country, it is very natural that *women* should wish to know "the reason *why*"—especially when these outrages of blood and nameless horror are practiced in violation of the principles of our national Bill of Rights and the Preamble of our Constitution. We do not, then, and cannot concede the position, that because this is a *political subject* women ought to fold their hands in idleness, and close their eyes and ears to the "horrible things" that are practiced in our land. The denial of our duty to act, is a bold denial of our right to act; and if we have no right to act, then may *we* well be termed "the white slaves of the North"—for, like our brethren in bonds, we must seal our lips in silence and despair. . . .

Slavery exerts a most deadly influence over the morals of our country,

* Angelina Grimké, *An Appeal to the Women of the Nominally Free States*, Issued by an Anti-slavery Convention of American Women (2d ed.; Boston: Isaac Knapp, 1838), pp. 13–16, 19–23, 49–53, 60–61.

not only over that portion of it where it actually exists as "a domestic institution," but like the miasma of some pestilential pool, it spreads its desolating influence far beyond its own boundaries. Who does not know that licentiousness is a crying sin at the North as well as at the South? and who does not admit that the manners of the South in this respect have had a wide and destructive influence on Northern character? Can crime be fashionable and common in one part of the Union and unrebuked by the other without corrupting the very heart's blood of the nation, and lowering the standard of morality everywhere? Can Northern men go down to the well-watered plains of the South to make their fortunes, without bowing themselves in the house of Rimmon and drinking the waters of that river of pollution which rolls over the plain of Sodom and Gomorrah? Do they return uncontaminated to their homes, or does not many and many a Northerner dig the grave of his virtue in the Admahs and Zeboims of our Southern States. And can our theological and academic institutions be opened to the sons of the planter without endangering the purity of the morals of our own sons, by associations with men who regard the robbery of the poor as no crime, and oppression as no wrong? Impossible! . . .

But this is not all; our people have erected a false standard by which to judge men's character. Because in the slaveholding States colored men are plundered and kept in abject ignorance, are treated with disdain and scorn, so here, too, in profound deference to the South, we refuse to eat, or ride, or walk, or associate, or open our institutions of learning, or even our zoological institutions to people of color, unless they visit them in the capacity of *servants*, of menials in humble attendance upon the Anglo-American. Who ever heard of a more wicked absurdity in a Republican country?

Have Northern women, then, nothing to do with slavery, when its demoralizing influence is polluting their domestic circles and blasting the fair character of *their* sons and brothers? Nothing to do with slavery when *their* domestics are often dragged by the merciless kidnapper from the hearth of their nurseries and the arms of their little ones? Nothing to do with slavery when Northern women are chained and driven like criminals, and incarcerated in the great prison-house of the South? Nothing to do with slavery? . . .

We have hitherto addressed you more as moral and responsible beings, than in the distinctive character of women; we have appealed to you on the broad ground of *human rights* and human responsibilities, rather than on that of your peculiar duties as women. We have pursued this course of argument designedly, because, in order to prove that you have any duties to perform, it is necessary first to establish the principle of moral being—for all our rights and all our duties grow out of this principle. *All moral beings have essentially the same rights and the same duties*, whether they be male or female. . . .

WOMEN THE VICTIMS OF SLAVERY

Out of the millions of slaves who have been stolen from Africa, a very great number must have been women who were torn from the arms of their fathers and husbands, brothers and children, and subjected to all the horrors of the middle passage and the still greater sufferings of slavery in a foreign land. Multitudes of these were cast upon our inhospitable shores; some of them now toil out a life of bondage, "one hour of which is fraught with more misery than ages of that" which our fathers rose in rebellion to oppose. But the great mass of female slaves in the southern States are the descendants of these hapless strangers; 1,000,000 of them now wear the iron yoke of slavery in this land of boasted liberty and law. They are our country women—*they are our sisters;* and to us, as women, they have a right to look for sympathy with their sorrows, and effort and prayer for their rescue. Upon those of us especially who have named the name of Christ, they have peculiar claims, and claims which *we must answer, or we shall incur a heavy load of guilt.* . . .

WOMEN ARE SLAVEHOLDERS

Multitudes of the Southern women hold men, women and children as *property. They* are pampered in luxury, and nursed in the school of tyranny; *they* sway the iron rod of power, and *they* rob the laborer of his hire. Immortal beings tremble at *their* nod, and bow in abject submission at *their* word, and under the cowskin too often wielded by *their* own delicate hands. Women at the South hold *their own sisters* and brothers in bondage. Start not at this dreadful assertion—we speak that which some of us do know—we testify that which some of us have seen. Such facts ought to be known, that the women of the North may understand *their* duties, and be incited to perform *them.*

Southern families often present the most disgusting scenes of dissen-

sion, in which the mistress acts a part derogatory to her own character
as a woman. . . .

[T]here are *female tyrants* too, who are prompt to lay their complaints of misconduct before their husbands, brothers and sons, and to
urge them to commit acts of violence against their helpless slaves. Others
still more cruel, place the lash in the hands of some trusty domestic, and
stand by whilst he lays the heavy strokes upon the unresisting victim,
deaf to the cries for mercy which rend the air, or rather the more
enraged at such appeals, which are only answered by the Southern
lady with the prompt command of "give her more for that." This work
of chastisement is often performed by a brother, or other relative of the
poor sufferer, which circumstance stings like an adder the very heart of
the slave while her body writhes under the lash. Other mistresses who
cannot bear that their delicate ears should be pained by the screams of
the poor sufferers, write an order to the master of the Charleston work-
house, or the New Orleans calaboose, where they are most cruelly
stretched in order to render the stroke of the whip or the blow of the
paddle more certain to produce cuts and wounds which cause the
blood to flow at every stroke. And let it be remembered that these poor
creatures are often *women* who are most indecently divested of their
clothing and exposed to the gaze of the executioner of a *woman's*
command.

What then, our beloved sisters, must be the effects of such a system
upon the domestic character of the white females? Can a corrupt tree
bring forth good fruit? Can such despotism mould the character of the
Southern woman to gentleness and love? or may we not fairly conclude
that all that suavity, for which slaveholding ladies are so conspicuous,
is in many instances the paint and the varnish of hypocrisy, the fashionable polish of a heartless superficiality?

But it is not the character alone of the mistress that is deeply injured
by the possession and exercise of such despotic power, nor is it the
degradation and suffering to which the slave is continually subject; but
another important consideration is, that in consequence of the dreadful
state of morals at the South, the wife and the daughter sometimes find
their homes a scene of the most mortifying, heart-rending preference of
the degraded domestic, or the colored daughter of the head of the
family. There are, alas, too many families, of which the contentions of
Abraham's household is a fair example. But we forbear to lift the veil of
private life any higher; let these few hints suffice to give you some idea

of what is daily passing *behind* that curtain which has been so carefully drawn before the scenes of domestic life in Christian America.

THE COLORED WOMEN OF THE NORTH ARE OPPRESSED

[Another] reason we would urge for the interference of northern women with the system of slavery is, that in consequence of the odium which the degradation of slavery has attached to *color* even in the free States, our *colored sisters* are dreadfully oppressed here. Our seminaries of learning are closed to them, they are almost entirely banished from our lecture rooms, and even in the house of God they are separated from their white brethren and sisters as though we were afraid to come in contact with a colored skin. . . .

Here, then, are some of the bitter fruits of that inveterate prejudice which the vast proportion of northern women are cherishing towards their colored sisters; and let us remember that every one of us who denies the sinfulness of this prejudice, . . . is awfully guilty in the sight of Him who is no respecter of persons. . . .

But our colored sisters are oppressed in other ways. As they walk the streets of our cities, they are continually liable to be insulted with the vulgar epithet of "nigger"; no matter how respectable or wealthy, they cannot visit the Zoological Institute of New-York except in the capacity of nurses or servants—no matter how worthy, they cannot gain admittance into or receive assistance from any of the charities of this city. In Philadelphia, they are cast out of our Widow's Asylum, and their children are refused admittance to the House of Refuge, the Orphan's House and the Infant School connected with the Alms-House, though into these are gathered the very offscouring of our population. These are only specimens of that soul-crushing influence from which the colored women of the north are daily suffering. Then, again, some of them have been robbed of their husbands and children by the heartless kidnapper, and others have themselves been dragged into slavery. If they attempt to travel, they are exposed to great indignities and great inconveniences. Instances have been known of their actually dying in consequence of the exposure to which they were subjected on board of our steamboats. No money could purchase the use of a berth for a delicate female because she had a colored skin. Prejudice, then, degrades and fetters the minds, persecutes and murders the bodies of our free colored sisters. Shall *we* be silent at such a time as this? . . .

Much may be done, too, by sympathizing with our oppressed colored sisters, who are suffering in our very midst. Extend to them the right hand of fellowship on the broad principles of humanity and Christianity, treat them as *equals*, visit them as *equals*, invite them to co-operate with you in Anti-Slavery and Temperance and Moral Reform Societies —in Maternal Associations and Prayer Meetings and Reading Companies. . . .

Multitudes of instances will continually occur in which you will have the opportunity of *identifying yourselves with this injured class* of our fellow-beings: embrace these opportunities at all times and in all places, in the true nobility of our great Exemplar, who was ever found among the *poor and the despised,* elevating and blessing them with his counsels and presence. In this way, and this alone, will you be enabled to subdue that deep-rooted prejudice which is doing the work of oppression in the free States to a most dreadful extent.

When this demon has been cast out of your own hearts, when *you* can recognize the colored woman as a WOMAN—*then* will you be prepared to send out an appeal to our Southern sisters, entreating them to "go and do likewise."

The Trials of Girlhood by Linda Brent*

The true names and places are concealed in this autobiography, written as an antislavery document by a black woman who had been born and reared as a slave, and lived under slavery for twenty-seven years until her successful escape. At the time her story was published, she had lived and worked in New York for seventeen years, active in antislavery circles.

THE TRIALS OF GIRLHOOD

During the first years of my service in Dr. Flint's family, I was accustomed to share some indulgences with the children of my mistress. Though this seemed to me no more than right, I was grateful for it, and tried to merit the kindness by the faithful discharge of my duties. But I now entered on my fifteenth year—a sad epoch in the life of a slave girl. My master began to whisper foul words in my ear. Young as I was, I could not remain ignorant of their import. I tried to treat them with indifference or contempt. The master's age, my extreme youth, and the fear that his conduct would be reported to my grandmother, made him bear this treatment for many months. He was a crafty man, and resorted to many means to accomplish his purposes. Sometimes he had stormy, terrific ways, that made his victims tremble; sometimes he assumed a gentleness that he thought must surely subdue. Of the two, I preferred his stormy moods, although they left me trembling. He tried his utmost to corrupt the pure principles my grandmother had instilled. He peopled my young mind with unclean images, such as only a vile monster could think of. I turned from him with disgust and hatred. But he was my master. I was compelled to live under the same roof with him—where I saw a man forty years my senior daily violating the most sacred commandments of nature. He told me I was his property; that I must be subject to his will in all things. My soul revolted against the mean tyranny. But where could I turn for protection? No matter

* From Linda Brent, *Incidents in the Life of a Slave Girl* (ed.), Lydia Maria Child (Boston, published for the author, 1861), pp. 44–46, 49, 51–55, 82–86, 77–81. According to Cushing's *Initials and Pseudonyms*, Linda Brent's real name was Mrs. Harriet Jacobs.

whether the slave girl be as black as ebony or as fair as her mistress. In either case, there is no shadow of law to protect her from insult, from violence, or even from death; all these are inflicted by fiends who bear the shape of men. The mistress, who ought to protect the helpless victim, has no other feelings towards her but those of jealousy and rage. The degradation, the wrongs, the vices, that grow out of slavery, are more than I can describe. . . .

Every where the years bring to all enough of sin and sorrow; but in slavery the very dawn of life is darkened by these shadows. Even the little child, who is accustomed to wait on her mistress and her children, will learn, before she is twelve years old, why it is that her mistress hates such and such a one among the slaves. Perhaps the child's own mother is among those hated ones. She listens to violent outbreaks of jealous passion, and cannot help understanding what is the cause. She will become prematurely knowing in evil things. Soon she will learn to tremble when she hears her master's footfall. She will be compelled to realize that she is no longer a child. If God has bestowed beauty upon her, it will prove her greatest curse. That which commands admiration in the white woman only hastens the degradation of the female slave. I know that some are too much brutalized by slavery to feel the humiliation of their position; but many slaves feel it most acutely, and shrink from the memory of it. I cannot tell how much I suffered in the presence of these wrongs, nor how I am still pained by the retrospect. My master met me at every turn, reminding me that I belonged to him, and swearing by heaven and earth that he would compel me to submit to him. If I went out for a breath of fresh air, after a day of unwearied toil, his footsteps dogged me. If I knelt by my mother's grave, his dark shadow fell on me even there. . . .

Mrs. Flint possessed the key to her husband's character before I was born. She might have used this knowledge to counsel and to screen the young and the innocent among her slaves; but for them she had no sympathy. They were the objects of her constant suspicion and malevolence. She watched her husband with unceasing vigilance; but he was well practised in means to evade it. . . .

I had entered my sixteenth year, and every day it became more apparent that my presence was intolerable to Mrs. Flint. Angry words frequently passed between her and her husband. He had never punished me himself, and he would not allow any body else to punish me. In that respect, she was never satisfied; but, in her angry moods, no terms were too vile for her to bestow upon me. Yet I, whom she detested so bitterly, had far more pity for her than he had, whose duty it was to make her life happy. I never wronged her, or wished to wrong her; and one word of kindness from her would have brought me to her feet.

After repeated quarrels between the doctor and his wife, he announced his intention to take his youngest daughter, then four years old, to sleep in his apartment. It was necessary that a servant should sleep in the same room, to be on hand if the child stirred. I was selected for that office, and informed for what purpose that arrangement had been made. By managing to keep within sight of people, as much as possible, during the day time, I had hitherto succeeded in eluding my master, . . . But he resolved to remove the obstacle in the way of his scheme; and he thought he had planned it so that he should evade suspicion.

. . . A kind Providence interposed in my favor. During the day Mrs. Flint heard of this new arrangement, and a storm followed. I rejoiced to hear it rage.

After a while my mistress sent for me to come to her room. Her first question was, "Did you know you were to sleep in the doctor's room?"

"Yes, ma'am."

"Who told you?"

"My master."

"Will you answer truly all the questions I ask?"

"Yes, ma'am."

"Tell me, then, as you hope to be forgiven, are you innocent of what I have accused you?"

"I am."

She handed me a Bible, and said, "Lay your hand on your heart, kiss this holy book, and swear before God that you tell me the truth."

I took the oath she required, and I did it with a clear conscience.

"You have taken God's holy word to testify your innocence," said she. "If you have deceived me, beware! Now take this stool, sit down, look me directly in the face, and tell me all that has passed between your master and you."

I did as she ordered. As I went on with my account her color changed frequently, she wept, and sometimes groaned. She spoke in tones so sad, that I was touched by her grief. The tears came to my eyes; but I was soon convinced that her emotions arose from anger and wounded pride. She felt that her marriage vows were desecrated, her dignity insulted; but she had no compassion for the poor victim of her husband's perfidy. She pitied herself as a martyr; but she was incapable of feeling for the condition of shame and misery in which her unfortunate, helpless slave was placed.

. . . I pitied Mrs. Flint. She was a second wife, many years the junior of her husband; and the hoary-headed miscreant was enough to try the patience of a wiser and better woman. She was completely foiled, and knew not how to proceed. She would gladly have had me flogged for my supposed false oath; but, as I have already stated, the doctor never allowed any one to whip me. The old sinner was politic. The application of the lash might have led to remarks that would have exposed him in the eyes of his children and grandchildren. How often did I rejoice that I lived in a town where all the inhabitants knew each other! If I had been on a remote plantation, or lost among the multitude of a crowded city, I should not be a living woman at this day. . . .

[Then] Dr. Flint contrived a new plan. He seemed to have an idea that my fear of my mistress was his greatest obstacle. In the blandest tones, he told me that he was going to build a small house for me, in a secluded place, four miles away from the town. I shuddered; but I was constrained to listen, while he talked of his intention to give me a home of my own, and to make a lady of me. Hitherto, I had escaped my dreaded fate, by being in the midst of people. . . .

And now, reader, I come to a period in my unhappy life, which I would gladly forget if I could. The remembrance fills me with sorrow and shame. It pains me to tell you of it; but I have promised to tell you the truth, and I will do it honestly, let it cost me what it may. I will not try to screen myself behind the plea of compulsion from a master; for it was not so. Neither can I plead ignorance or thoughtlessness. For years, my master had done his utmost to pollute my mind with foul images, and to destroy the pure principles inculcated by my grandmother, and the good mistress of my childhood. The influences of slavery had had the same effect on me that they had on other young girls; they had made me prematurely knowing, concerning the evil ways of the world. I knew what I did, and I did it with deliberate calculation.

But, O, ye happy women, whose purity has been sheltered from childhood, who have been free to choose the objects of your affection, whose homes are protected by law, do not judge the poor desolate slave girl too severely! If slavery had been abolished, I, also, could have married the man of my choice; I could have had a home shielded by the laws; and I should have been spared the painful task of confessing what I am now about to relate; but all my prospects had been blighted by slavery. I wanted to keep myself pure; and, under the most adverse circumstances, I tried hard to preserve my self-respect; but I was struggling alone in the powerful grasp of the demon Slavery; and the monster proved too strong for me. I felt as if I was forsaken by God and man; as if all my efforts must be frustrated; and I became reckless in my despair.

I have told you that Dr. Flint's persecutions and his wife's jealousy had given rise to some gossip in the neighborhood. Among others, it chanced that a white unmarried gentleman had obtained some knowledge of the circumstances in which I was placed. . . .

He constantly sought opportunities to see me, and wrote to me frequently. I was a poor slave girl, only fifteen years old.

So much attention from a superior person was, of course, flattering; for human nature is the same in all. I also felt grateful for his sympathy, and encouraged by his kind words. It seemed to me a great thing to have such a friend. By degrees, a more tender feeling crept into my heart. He was an educated and eloquent gentleman; too eloquent, alas, for the poor slave girl who trusted in him. Of course I saw whither all this was tending. I knew the impassable gulf between us; but to be an object of interest to a man who is not married, and who is not her master, is agreeable to the pride and feelings of a slave, if her miserable situation has left her any pride or sentiment. It seems less degrading to give one's self, than to submit to compulsion. There is something akin to freedom in having a lover who has no control over you, except that which he gains by kindness and attachment. A master may treat you as rudely as he pleases, and you dare not speak; moreover, the wrong does not seem so great with an unmarried man, as with one who has a wife to be made unhappy. There may be sophistry in all this; but the condition of a slave confuses all principles of morality, and, in fact, renders the practice of them impossible.

When I found that my master had actually begun to build the lonely cottage, other feelings mixed with those I have described. Revenge, and calculations of interest, were added to flattered vanity and sincere gratitude for kindness. I knew nothing would enrage Dr. Flint so much as to know that I favored another; and it was something to triumph over my tyrant even in that small way. I thought he would revenge himself by selling me, and I was sure my friend, Mr. Sands, would buy me. . . . Pity me, and pardon me, O virtuous reader! You never knew what it is to be a slave; to be entirely unprotected by law or custom; to have the laws reduce you to the condition of a chattel, entirely subject to the will of another. You never exhausted your ingenuity in avoiding the snares, and eluding the power of a hated tyrant; you never shuddered at the sound of his footsteps, and trembled within hearing of his voice. I know I did wrong. No one can feel it more sensibly than I do. The painful and humiliating memory will haunt me to my dying day. Still, in looking back, calmly, on the events of my life, I feel that the slave woman ought not to be judged by the same standard as others.

SKETCHES OF NEIGHBORING SLAVEHOLDERS

I could tell of more slaveholders as cruel as those I have described. They are not exceptions to the general rule. I do not say there are no humane slaveholders. Such characters do exist, notwithstanding the hardening influences around them. But they are "like angels' visits—few and far between."

I knew a young lady who was one of these rare specimens. She was an orphan, and inherited as slaves a woman and her six children. Their father was a free man. They had a comfortable home of their own, parents and children living together. The mother and eldest daughter served their mistress during the day, and at night returned to their dwelling, which was on the premises. The young lady was very pious, and there was some reality in her religion. She taught her slaves to lead pure lives, and wished them to enjoy the fruit of their own industry. *Her* religion was not a garb put on for Sunday, and laid aside till Sunday returned again. The eldest daughter of the slave mother was promised in marriage to a free man; and the day before the wedding this good mistress emancipated her, in order that her marriage might have the sanction of *law*.

Report said that this young lady cherished an unrequited affection for a man who had resolved to marry for wealth. In the course of time a rich uncle of hers died. He left six thousand dollars to his two sons by a colored woman, and the remainder of his property to this orphan niece. The metal soon attracted the magnet. The lady and her weighty purse became his. She offered to manumit her slaves—telling them that her marriage might make unexpected changes in their destiny, and she wished to insure their happiness. They refused to take their freedom, saying that she had always been their best friend, and they could not be so happy any where as with her. I was not surprised. I had often seen them in their comfortable home, and thought that the whole town did not contain a happier family. They had never felt slavery; and, when it was too late, they were convinced of its reality.

When the new master claimed this family as his property, the father became furious, and went to his mistress for protection. "I can do nothing for you now, Harry," said she. "I no longer have the power I had a week ago. I have succeeded in obtaining the freedom of your wife; but I cannot obtain it for your children." The unhappy father swore that nobody should take his children from him. He concealed them in the woods for some days; but they were discovered and taken. The father was put in jail, and the two oldest boys sold to Georgia. One little girl, too young to be of service to her master, was left with the wretched mother. The other three were carried to their master's plantation. The eldest soon became a mother; and, when the slave-holder's wife looked at the babe, she wept bitterly. She knew that her own husband had violated the purity she had so carefully inculcated. She had a second child by her master, and then he sold her and his offspring to his brother. She bore two children to the brother, and was sold again. The next sister went crazy. The life she was compelled to lead drove her mad. The third one became the mother of five daughters. Before the birth of the fourth the pious mistress died. To the last, she rendered every kindness to the slaves that her unfortunate circumstances permitted. She passed away peacefully, glad to close her eyes on a life which had been made so wretched by the man she loved.

This man squandered the fortune he had received, and sought to retrieve his affairs by a second marriage; but, having retired after a night of drunken debauch, he was found dead in the morning. He was called a good master; for he fed and clothed his slaves better than most masters, and the lash was not heard on his plantation so frequently as on many others. Had it not been for slavery, he would have been a better man, and his wife a happier woman.

No pen can give an adequate description of the all-pervading corruption produced by slavery. The slave girl is reared in an atmosphere of licentiousness and fear. The lash and the foul talk of her master and his sons are her teachers. When she is fourteen or fifteen, her owner, or his sons, or the overseer, or perhaps all of them, begin to bribe her with presents. If these fail to accomplish their purpose, she is whipped or starved into submission to their will. She may have had religious principles inculcated by some pious mother or grandmother, or some good mistress; she may have a lover, whose good opinion and peace of mind are dear to her heart; or the profligate men who have power over her may be exceedingly odious to her. But resistance is hopeless. . . .

The slaveholder's sons are, of course, vitiated, even while boys, by the unclean influences every where around them. Nor do the master's daughters always escape. Severe retributions sometimes come upon him for the wrongs he does to the daughters of the slaves. The white daughters early hear their parents quarrelling about some female slave. Their curiosity is excited, and they soon learn the cause. They are attended by the young slave girls whom their father has corrupted; and they hear such talk as should never meet youthful ears, or any other ears. They know that the women slaves are subject to their father's authority in all things; and in some cases they exercise the same authority over the men slaves. I have myself seen the master of such a household whose head was bowed down in shame; for it was known in the neighborhood that his daughter had selected one of the meanest slaves on his plantation to be the father of his first grandchild. She did not make her advances to her equals, nor even to her father's more intelligent servants. She selected the most brutalized, over whom her authority could be exercised with less fear of exposure. Her father, half frantic with rage, sought to revenge himself on the offending black man; but his daughter, foreseeing the storm that would arise, had given him free papers, and sent him out of the state.

In such cases the infant is smothered, or sent where it is never seen by any who know its history. But if the white parent is the *father*, instead of the mother, the offspring are unblushingly reared for the market. If they are girls, I have indicated plainly enough what will be their inevitable destiny.

You may believe what I say; for I write only that whereof I know. I was twenty-one years in that cage of obscene birds. I can testify, from my own experience and observation, that slavery is a curse to the whites as well as to the blacks. It makes the white fathers cruel and sensual; the sons violent and licentious; it contaminates the daughters, and makes the wives wretched. And as for the colored race, it needs an abler pen than mine to describe the extremity of their sufferings, the depth of their degradation.

Yet few slaveholders seem to be aware of the widespread moral ruin occasioned by this wicked system. Their talk is of blighted cotton crops —not of the blight on their children's souls.

If you want to be fully convinced of the abominations of slavery, go on a southern plantation, and call yourself a negro trader. Then there will be no concealment; and you will see and hear things that will seem to you impossible among human beings with immortal souls.

A Confederate Lady's Diary
by Mary Boykin Chesnut*

These excerpts are from the remarkable diary of Mary Boykin Chesnut. Wife of a Confederate general, she was not only well-read and articulate, but a keen observer of Confederate society.

A CONFEDERATE LADY'S DIARY

March, 1861

I wonder if it be a sin to think slavery a curse to any land. Men and women are punished when their masters and mistresses are brutes, not when they do wrong. Under slavery, we live surrounded by prostitutes, yet an abandoned woman is sent out of any decent house. Who thinks any worse of a Negro or mulatto woman for being a thing we can't name? God forgive us, but ours is a monstrous system, a wrong and an iniquity! Like the patriarchs of old, our men live all in one house with their wives and their concubines; and the mulattoes one sees in every family partly resemble the white children. Any lady is ready to tell you who is the father of all the mulatto children in everybody's household but her own. Those, she seems to think, drop from the clouds. My disgust sometimes is boiling over. Thank God for my country women, but alas for the men! They are probably no worse than men everywhere, but the lower their mistresses, the more degraded they must be.

I think this journal will be disadvantageous for me, for I spend my time now like a spider spinning my own entrails, instead of reading as my habit was in all spare moments. . . .

August, 1861

Today our assemblage of women, Confederate, talked pretty freely. Let us record some samples. "You people who have been stationed all

* From Mary Boykin Chesnut, *A Diary from Dixie* (ed.), Ben Ames Williams (Boston: Houghton Mifflin Co., 1949), pp. 21–22, 121–123, 126, 139–140, 148–149, 163–164, 199–200. Reprinted by permission of Houghton Mifflin Co. Copyright 1949 by Houghton Mifflin Co.

over the United States and have been to Europe and all that; tell us home-biding ones. Are our men worse than the others? Does Mrs. Stowe know? You know what I mean?" "No, our men are no worse. Lady Mary Montagu found we were all only men and women, everywhere. But Mrs. Stowe's exceptional cases may be true. You can pick out horrors from any criminal court record or newspaper in any country." "You see, irresponsible men do pretty much as they please."

Russell now, to whom London and Paris and India were everyday sights—and every night too, streets and all: for him to go on in indignation because there were women in Negro plantations who were not vestal virgins! Negro women are married, and after marriage behave as well as other people. Marrying is the amusement of their life. They take life easily. So do their class everywhere. Bad men are hated here as elsewhere.

I hate slavery. You say there are no more fallen women on a plantation than in London, in proportion to numbers; but what do you say to this? A magnate who runs a hideous black harem with its consequences under the same roof with his lovely white wife, and his beautiful and accomplished daughters? He holds his head as high and poses as the model of all human virtues to these poor women whom God and the laws have given him. From the height of his awful majesty, he scolds and thunders at them, as if he never did wrong in his life. Fancy such a man finding his daughter reading "Don Juan." "You with that immoral book!" And he orders her out of his sight. You see, Mrs. Stowe did not hit the sorest spot. She makes Legree a bachelor.

Someone said: "Oh, I know half a Legree, a man said to be as cruel as Legree. But the other half of him did not correspond. He was a man of polished manners, and the best husband and father and church-member in the world." "Can that be so?" "Yes, I know it. And I knew the dissolute half of Legree. He was high and mighty, but the kindest creature to his slaves; and the unfortunate results of his bad ways were not sold. They had not to jump over ice blocks. They were kept in full view, and were provided for, handsomely, in his will. His wife and daughters, in their purity and innocence, are supposed never to dream of what is as plain before their eyes as the sunlight. And they play their parts of unsuspecting angels to the letter. They profess to adore their father as the model of all earthly goodness."

"Well, yes. If he is rich, he is the fountain from whence all blessings flow."

"The one I have in my eye, my half of Legree, the dissolute half, was so furious in his temper, and so thundered his wrath at the poor women that they were glad to let him do as he pleased if they could only escape his everlasting fault-finding and noisy bluster."

"Now, now, do you know any woman of this generation who would stand that sort of thing?"

"No, never, not for one moment. The make-believe angels were of the last century. We know, and we won't have it. These are Old World stories. Women were brought up not to judge their fathers or their husbands. They took them as the Lord provided, and were thankful."

"How about the wives of drunkards? I heard a woman say once, to a friend, of her husband, as a cruel matter of fact without bitterness and without comment: 'Oh, you have not seen him. He is changed. He has not gone to bed sober in thirty years.' She has had her purgatory, if not what Mrs. —— calls 'the other thing,' here in this world. We all know what a drunken man is. To think that for no crime a person may be condemned to live with one thirty years."

"You wander from the question" I asked. "Are Southern men worse because of the slave system, and the facile black women?"

"Not a bit! They see too much of them. The barroom people don't drink, the confectionary people loathe candy. Our men are sick of the black sight of them!"

"You think a nice man from the South is the nicest thing in the world?" "I know it. Put him by any other man and see!" "And you say there are no saints and martyrs now; those good women who stand by bad husbands? Eh?" "No use to mince matters. Everybody knows the life of a woman whose husband drinks."

"Some men have a hard time, too. I know women who are—well, the very devil and all his imps." "Ah, but men are dreadful animals." "Seems to me those of you who are hardest on men here are soft enough with them when they are present. Now everybody knows I am 'the friend of man' and I defend them behind their backs as I take pleasure in their society, well, before their faces." . . .

My experience does not coincide with the general idea of public life; I mean the life of a politician or statesman. Peace, comfort, quiet, happiness, I have found away from home. Only your own family, those nearest and dearest, can hurt you. Wrangling, rows, heart-burnings, bitterness, envy, hatred, malice, unbrotherly love, family snarls, neighborhood strife, and ill blood—a lovely brood I have conjured up. But they were all there, and for these many years I have almost forgotten them. I find them always alive and rampant when I go back to semi-village life. For after all, though we live miles apart, everybody flying round on horses or in carriages, it amounts to a village community. Everybody knows exactly where to put the knife. . . .

September, 1861

September 21st.—Last night when the mail came in, I was seated near the lamp. Mr. Chesnut, lying on a sofa at a little distance, called out to me: "Look at my letters and tell me whom they are from?" I began to read one of them aloud. It was from Mary Witherspoon, and I broke down; horror and amazement was too much for me. Poor cousin Betsey Witherspoon was murdered! She did not die peacefully in her bed, as we supposed, but was murdered by her own people, her Negroes. I remember when Dr. Keith was murdered by his Negroes, Mr. Miles met me and told me the dreadful story. "Very awkward indeed, this sort of thing. There goes Keith in the House always declaiming about the 'Benificent Institution'—How now?" Horrible beyond words! Her household Negroes were so insolent, so pampered, and insubordinate. She lived alone. She knew, she said, that none of her children would have the patience she had with these people who had been indulged and spoiled by her until they were like spoiled children, simply intolerable. Mr. Chesnut and David Williams have gone over at once. . . .

September 24th.—The men who went to Society Hill (the Wither-spoon home) have come home again with nothing very definite. William and Cousin Betsey's old maid, Rhody, are in jail; strong suspicion but as yet no proof of their guilt. The neighborhood is in a ferment. Evans and Wallace say these Negroes ought to be burnt. Lynching proposed! But it is all idle talk. They will be tried as the law directs, and not otherwise. John Witherspoon will not allow anything wrong or violent to be done. He has a detective there from Charleston.

Hitherto I have never thought of being afraid of Negroes. I had never injured any of them; why should they want to hurt me? Two thirds of my religion consists in trying to be good to Negroes, because they are so in our power, and it would be so easy to be the other thing. Somehow today I feel that the ground is cut away from under my feet. Why should they treat me any better than they have done Cousin Betsey Witherspoon?

Kate and I sat up late and talked it all over. Mrs. Witherspoon was a saint on this earth, and this is her reward. Kate's maid Betsey came in—a strong-built, mulatto woman—dragging in a mattress. "Missis, I have brought my bed to sleep in your room while Mars' David is at Society Hill. You ought not to stay in a room by yourself these times." She went off for more bed gear. "For the life of me," said Kate gravely, "I cannot make up my mind. Does she mean to take care of me, or to murder me?" I do not think Betsey heard, but when she came back she said: "Missis, as I have a soul to be saved, I will keep you safe. I will guard you." We know Betsey well, but has she soul enough to swear by? She is a great stout, jolly, irresponsible, unreliable, pleasant-tempered, bad-behaved woman, with ever so many good points. Among others, she is so clever she can do anything and she never loses her temper; but she has no moral sense whatever.

That night, Kate came into my room. She could not sleep. The thought of those black hands strangling and smothering Mrs. Witherspoon's grey head under the counterpane haunted her; we sat up and talked the long night through. . . .

October, 1861

October 13th.—Mulberry. We went in the afternoon to the Negro church on the plantation. Manning Brown, a Methodist minister, preached to a very large black congregation. Though glossy black, they were well dressed and were very stylishly gotten up. They were stout, comfortable looking Christians. The house women, in white aprons and white turbans, were the nicest looking. How snow white the turbans on their heads appeared! But the youthful sisters flaunted in pink and sky blue bonnets which tried their complexions. For the family, they had a cushioned seat near the pulpit, neatly covered with calico. Manning Brown preached Hell fire so hot, I felt singed, if not parboiled. I could not remember any of my many sins that were worthy of an eternity in torment; but, if all the world's misery, sin, and suffering came from so small a sin as eating that apple, what mighty proportions mine take!

Jim Nelson, the driver, the stateliest darky I ever saw, tall and straight as a pine tree, with a fine face, and not so very black but a full-blooded African, was asked to lead in prayer. He became wildly excited, on his knees, facing us with his eyes shut. He clapped his hands at the end of every sentence, and his voice rose to the pitch of a shrill shriek, yet was strangely clear and musical, occasionally in a plaintive minor key that went to your heart. Sometimes it rang out like a trumpet. I wept bitterly. It was all sound, however, and emotional pathos. There was literally nothing in what he said. The words had no meaning at all. It was the devotional passion of voice and manner which was so magnetic. The Negroes sobbed and shouted and swayed backward and forward, some with aprons to their eyes, most of them clapping their hands and responding in shrill tones: "Yes, God!" "Jesus!" "Savior!" "Bless de Lord, amen," etc. It was a little too exciting for me. I would very much have liked to shout, too. . . .

November, 1861

On one side Mrs. Stowe, Greeley, Thoreau, Emerson, Sumner. They live in nice New England homes, clean, sweet-smelling, shut up in libraries, writing books which ease their hearts of their bitterness against us. What self-denial they do practice is to tell John Brown to come down here and cut our throats in Christ's name. Now consider what I have seen of my mother's life, my grandmother's, my mother-in-law's. These people were educated at Northern schools, they read the same books as their Northern contemporaries, the same daily papers, the same Bible. They have the same ideas of right and wrong, are high-bred, lovely, good, pious, doing their duty as they conceive it. They live in Negro villages. They do not preach and teach hate as a gospel, and the sacred duty of murder and insurrection; but they strive to ameliorate the condition of these Africans in every particular. They set them the example of a perfect life, a life of utter self-abnegation. Think of these holy New Englanders forced to have a Negro village walk through their houses whenever they see fit, dirty, slatternly, idle, ill-smelling by nature. These women I love have less chance to live their own lives in peace than if they were African missionaries. They have a swarm of blacks about them like children under their care, not as Mrs. Stowe's fancy painted them, and they hate slavery worse than Mrs. Stowe does. . . .

The Mrs. Stowes have the plaudits of crowned heads; we take our chances, doing our duty as best we may among the woolly heads. My husband supported his plantation by his law practice. Now it is running him in debt. Our people have never earned their own bread. . . . I say we are no better than our judges in the North, and no worse. We are human beings of the nineteenth century and slavery has to go, of course.

All that has been gained by it goes to the North and to Negroes. The slave owners, when they are good men and women, are the martyrs. I hate slavery. I even hate the harsh authority I see parents think it their duty to exercise toward their children. . . .

January, 1862

Surely women have a right to a maintenance, even when they are penniless girls before the wedding and bring no dowry. We had our share of my father's estate. It came into our possession not long after we were married, and it was spent for debts already contracted. A man with a rich father is offered every facility for plunging in debt head foremost. That being the case, why feel like a beggar, utterly humiliated and degraded, when I am forced to say I need money? I cannot tell, but I do; and the worst of it is, this thing grows worse as one grows older. Money ought not to be asked for, or given to a man's wife as a gift. Something must be due her, and that she should have, and with no growling and grumbling nor warnings against waste and extravagance, nor hints as to the need of economy, nor amazement that the last supply has given out already. What a proud woman suffers under all this, who can tell? One thing is sure. Nothing but the direst necessity drives her to speak of an empty purse. What a world of heart-burning some regular arrangement of pin money must save.

March, 1862

Read "Uncle Tom's Cabin" again. These Negro women have a chance here that women have nowhere else. They can redeem themselves—the "impropers" can. They can marry decently, and nothing is remembered against these colored ladies. It is not a nice topic, but Mrs. Stowe revels in it. How delightfully Pharisaic a feeling it must be to rise superior, and fancy we are so degraded as to defend and like to live with such degraded creatures around us—such men as Legree and his women.

The best way to take Negroes to your heart is to get as far away from them as possible. As far as I can see, Southern women do all that missionaries could do to prevent and alleviate evils. The social evil has not been suppressed in old England or in New England, in London or in Boston. People in those places expect more virtue from a plantation

African than they can insure in practice among themselves, with all their own high moral surroundings—light, education, training, and support. . . . The Northern men and women who came here were always hardest, for they expected an African to work and behave as a white man. We do not.

V
Nineteenth-Century Alternatives:
Pioneers and Utopians

ON "Free Enquiry" by Frances Wright*

Frances Wright gained notoriety as the first female in America to lecture publicly before audiences of men and women. Born in Scotland, she came to America as a sympathizer in the Owenite movement of utopian socialists in the 1820s. Her contribution to the list of failed experimental communities was Nashoba, in Tennessee, a biracial cooperative community that she conceived of as a way to educate slaves and provide congenial people with a place in which to pursue truth and happiness. Though Nashoba fell apart within two years, Frances Wright used the written and spoken word to propagate her ideas on the rational search for truth, the condition of women, the abuses of slavery, and the benefits of organization for the worker. She wrote for the newspaper of Owen's New Harmony community, edited her own paper *Free Enquiry*, and undertook a whirlwind speaking tour of American cities in 1828/29.

On FREE ENQUIRY

It is my object to show, that, before we can engage successfully in the work of enquiry, we must engage in a body; we must engage collectively; as human beings desirous of attaining the highest excellence of which our nature is capable; as children of one family, anxious to discover the true and the useful for the common advantage of all. It is my farther object to show that no co-operation in this matter can be effective which does not embrace the two sexes on a footing of equality; and, again, that no co-operation in this matter can be effective, which does not embrace human beings on a footing of equality. . . .

Who, then, shall say, enquiry is good for him and not good for his children? Who shall cast error from himself, and allow it to be grafted on the minds he has called into being? Who shall break the chains of his own ignorance, and fix them, through his descendants, on his race? But, there are some who, as parents, make one step in duty, and halt at the second. We see men who will aid the instruction of their sons, and

* From Lecture II, "Of Free Enquiry, Considered as a Means of Obtaining Just Knowledge," in Frances Wright, *Course of Popular Lectures* (New York: Office of the Free Enquirer, 1829), pp. 45-46, 52-55.

condemn only their daughters to ignorance. "Our sons," they say, "will have to exercise political rights, may aspire to public offices, may fill some learned profession, may struggle for wealth and acquire it. It is well that we give them a helping hand; that we assist them to such knowledge as is going, and make them as sharp witted as their neighbors. But for our daughters," they say—if indeed respecting them they say any thing—"for our daughters, little trouble or expense is necessary. They can never *be any thing;* in fact, they *are nothing.* We had best give them up to their mothers, who may take them to Sunday's preaching; and, with the aid of a little music, a little dancing, and a few fine gowns, fit them out for the market of marriage."

Am I severe? It is not my intention. I know that I am honest, and I fear that I am correct. Should I offend, however, I may regret, I shall not repent it; satisfied to incur displeasure, so that I render service.

But to such parents I would observe, that with regard to their sons, as to their daughters, they are about equally mistaken. If it be their duty, as we have seen, to respect in their children the same natural liberties which they cherish for themselves—if it be their duty to aid as guides, not to dictate as teachers—to lend assistance to the reason, not to command its prostration,—then have they nothing to do with the blanks or the prizes in store for them, in the wheel of worldly fortune. Let possibilities be what they may in favor of their sons, they have no calculations to make on them. It is not for them to ordain their sons magistrates nor statesmen; nor yet even lawyers, physicians, or merchants. They have only to improve the one character which they receive at the birth. They have only to consider them as *human beings,* and to ensure them the fair and thorough developement of all the faculties, physical, mental, and moral, which distinguish their nature. In like manner, as respects their daughters, they have nothing to do with the injustice of laws, nor the absurdities of society. Their duty is plain, evident, decided. In a daughter they have in charge a human being; in a son, the same. Let them train up these *human beings,* under the expanded wings of liberty. Let them seek *for* them and *with* them just knowledge; encouraging, from the cradle upwards, that useful curiosity which will lead them unbidden in the paths of free enquiry; and place them, safe and superior to the storms of life, in the security of well regulated, self-possessed minds, well grounded, well reasoned, conscientious opinions, and self-approved, consistent practice.

I have as yet, in this important matter, addressed myself only to the reason and moral feelings of my audience; I could speak also to their interests. Easy were it to show, that in proportion as your children are enlightened, will they prove blessings to society and ornaments to their race. But if this be true of all, it is more especially true of the now more neglected half of the species. Were it only in our power to enlighten part of the rising generation, and should the interests of the whole decide our choice of the portion, it were the females, and not the males, we should select.

. . . It has already been observed, that women, wherever placed, however high or low in the scale of cultivation, hold the destinies of humankind. Men will ever rise or fall to the level of the other sex; and from some causes in their conformation, we find them, however armed with power or enlightened with knowledge, still held in leading strings even by the least cultivated female. Surely, then, if they knew their interests, they would desire the improvement of those who, if they do not advantage, will injure them; who, if they elevate not their minds and meliorate not their hearts, will debase the one and harden the other; and who, if they endear not existence, most assuredly will dash it with poison. How many, how omnipotent are the interests which engage men to break the mental chains of women! How many, how dear are the interests which engage them to exalt rather than lower their condition, to multiply their solid acquirements, to respect their liberties, to make them their equals, to wish them even their superiors! Let them enquire into these things. Let them examine the relation in which the two sexes stand, and ever must stand, to each other. Let them perceive, that, mutually dependent, they must ever be giving and receiving, or they must be losing;—receiving or losing in knowledge, in virtue, in enjoyment. Let them perceive how immense the loss, or how immense the gain. Let them not imagine that they know aught of the delights which intercourse with the other sex can give, until they have felt the sympathy of mind with mind, and heart with heart; until they bring into that intercourse every affection, every talent, every confidence, every refinement, every respect. Until power is annihilated on one side, fear and obedience on the other, and both restored to their birthright—equality. Let none think that affection can reign without it; or friendship, or esteem. Jealousies, envyings, suspicions, reserves, deceptions—these are the fruits of inequality. Go, then! and remove the evil first from the minds of women, then from their condition, and then from your laws. Think it no longer indifferent whether the mothers of the rising generation are wise or foolish. Think it not indifferent whether your own companions are ignorant or enlightened. Think it not indifferent whether those who are to form the opinions, sway the habits, decide the destinies, of the species—and that not through their children only, but through their lovers and husbands—are enlightened friends or capricious mistresses, efficient coadjutors or careless servants, reasoning beings or blind followers of superstition.

Emigration from New York to Michigan
by Harriet Noble*

Harriet Noble told her story of moving west in the 1820s to Elizabeth Ellet, who compiled the histories of pioneer women up to the mid-nineteenth century.

EMIGRATION FROM NEW YORK TO MICHIGAN

"My husband was seized with the mania, and accordingly made preparation to start in January with his brother. They took the Ohio route, and were nearly a month in getting through; coming by way of Monroe, and thence to Ypsilanti and Ann Arbor. Mr. John Allen and Walter Rumsey with his wife and two men had been there some four or five weeks, had built a small house, moved into it the day my husband and his brother arrived, and were just preparing their first meal, which the newcomers had the pleasure of partaking. They spent a few days here, located a farm a little above the town on the river Huron, and returned through Canada. They had been so much pleased with the country, that they immediately commenced preparing to emigrate; and as near as I can recollect, we started about the 20th of September, 1824, for Michigan. We travelled from our house in Geneva to Buffalo in wagons. The roads were bad, and we were obliged to wait in Buffalo four days for a boat, as the steamboat 'Michigan' was the only one on the lake. After waiting so long we found she had put into Erie for repairs, and had no prospect of being able to run again for some time. The next step was to take passage in a schooner, which was considered a terrible undertaking for so dangerous a voyage as it was then thought to be. At length we went on board 'the Prudence,' of Cleveland, Capt. Johnson. A more inconvenient little bark could not well be imagined. We were seven days on Lake Erie, and so entirely prostrated with seasickness, as scarcely to be able to attend to the wants of our little ones. I had a little girl of three years, and a babe some months old, and Sister Noble had six children, one an infant. It was a tedious voyage; the lake was very rough most of

* From Elizabeth F. Ellet, *Pioneer Women of the West* (New York: Charles Scribner's Sons, 1856), pp. 388–395.

the time, and I thought if we were only on land again, I should be satisfied, if it was a wilderness. I could not then realize what it would be to live without a comfortable house through the winter, but sad experience afterwards taught me a lesson not to be forgotten.

"We came into the Detroit river; it was beautiful then as now; on the Canada side, in particular, you will scarce perceive any change. As we approached Detroit, the 'Cantonment' with the American flag floating on its walls, was decidedly the most interesting of any part of the town; for a city it was certainly the most filthy, irregular place I had ever seen; the streets were filled with Indians and low French, and at that time I could not tell the difference between them. We spent two days in making preparations for going out to Ann Arbor, and during that time I never saw a genteelly-dressed person in the streets. There were no carriages; the most wealthy families rode in French carts, sitting on the bottom upon some kind of mat; and the streets were so muddy these were the only vehicles convenient for getting about. I said to myself, 'if this be a Western city, give me a home in the woods.' I think it was in the 3d of October we started from Detroit, with a pair of oxen and a wagon, a few articles for cooking, and such necessaries as we could not do without. It was necessary that they should be few as possible, for our families were a full load for this mode of travelling. After travelling all day we found ourselves but ten miles from Detroit (at what is now Dearborn); here we spent the night at a kind of tavern, the only one west of the city. Our lodging was the floor, and the other entertainment was to match. The next day we set out as early as possible, in hopes to get through the woods before dark, but night found us about half way through, and there remained no other resource but to camp out, and make ourselves contented. The men built a large fire and prepared our supper. My sister and myself could assist but little, so fatigued were we with walking and carrying our infants. There were fifteen in our company. Two gentlemen going to Ypsilanti had travelled with us from Buffalo; the rest were our own families. We were all pretty cheerful, until we began to think of lying down for the night. The men did not seem to dread it, however, and were soon fast asleep, but sleep was not for me in such a wilderness. I could think of nothing but wild beasts, or something as bad; so that I had the pleasure of watching while the others slept. It seemed a long, long night, and never in my life did I feel more grateful for the blessing of returning day. We started again as early as possible, all who could walk moving on a little in advance of the wagon;

the small children were the only ones who thought of riding. Every few rods it would take two or three men to pry the wagon out of the mud, while those who walked were obliged to force their way over fallen timber, brush, &c. Thus passed the day; at night we found ourselves on the plains, three miles from Ypsilanti. My feet were so swollen I could walk no further. We got into the wagon and rode as far as Woodruff's grove, a little below Ypsilanti. There were some four or five families at this place. The next day we left for Ann Arbor. We were delighted with the country before us, it was beautiful in its natural state; and I have sometimes thought that cultivation has marred its loveliness. Where Ypsilanti now stands, there was but one building—an old trading-house on the west side of the river; the situation was fine—there were scattering oaks and no brushwood. Here we met a large number of Indians: and one old squaw followed us some distance with her papoose, determined to swap babies. At last she gave it up, and for one I felt relieved.

"We passed two log houses between this and Ann Arbor. About the middle of the afternoon we found ourselves at our journey's end—but what a prospect? There were some six or seven log huts occupied by as many inmates as could be crowded into them. It was too much to think of asking strangers to give us a place to stay in even for one night under such circumstances. Mr. John Allen himself made us the offer of sharing with him the comfort of a shelter from storm, if not from cold. His house was large for a log one, but quite unfinished; there was a ground floor and a small piece above. When we got our things stored in this place, we found the number sheltered to be twenty-one women and children, and fourteen men. There were but two bedsteads in the house, and those who could not occupy these, slept on feather beds upon the floor. When the children were put in bed you could not set a foot down without stepping on a foot or hand; the consequence was we had music most of the time.

"We cooked our meals in the open air, there being no fire in the house but a small box-stove. The fall winds were not very favorable to such business; we would frequently find our clothes on fire, but fortunately we did not often get burned. When one meal was over, however, we dreaded preparing the next. We lived in this way until our husbands got a log house raised and the roof on; this took them about six weeks, at the end of which time we went into it, without door, floor, chimney, or anything but logs and roof. There were no means of getting boards for a floor, as everything must be brought from Detroit, and we could not think of drawing lumber over such a road. The only alternative was to split slabs of oak with an axe. My husband was not a mechanic, but he managed to make a floor in this way that kept us from the ground. I was most anxious for a door, as the wolves would come about in the evening, and sometimes stay all night and keep up a serenade that would almost chill the blood in my veins. Of all noises I think the howling of wolves and the yell of Indians the most fearful; at least it appeared so to me then, when I was not able to close the door against them. I had the greatest terror of Indians; for I had never seen any before I came to Michigan but Oneidas, and they were very different, being partially civilized.

"We had our house comfortable as such a rude building could be, by the first of February. It was a mild winter; there was snow enough to cover the ground only four days, a fortunate circumstance for us. We enjoyed uninterrupted health, but in the spring the ague with its accompaniments gave us a call, and by the middle of August there were but four out of fourteen who could call themselves well. We then fancied we were too near the river for health. We sold out and bought again ten miles west of Ann Arbor, a place which suited us better; and just a year from the day we came to Ann Arbor, moved out of it to Dexter. There was one house here, Judge Dexter's; he was building a sawmill, and had a number of men at work at the time; besides these there was not a white family west of Ann Arbor in Michigan territory. Our log house was just raised, forming only the square log pen. Of course it did not look very inviting, but it was our home, and we must make the best of it. I helped to raise the rafters and put on the roof, but it was the last of November before our roof was completed. We were obliged to wait for the mill to run in order to get boards for making it. The doorway I had no means of closing except by hanging up a blanket, and frequently when I would raise it to step out, there would be two or three of our dusky neighbors peeping in to see what was there. It would always give me such a start, I could not suppress a scream, to which they would reply with 'Ugh!' and a hearty laugh. They knew I was afraid, and liked to torment me. Sometimes they would throng the house and stay two or three hours. If I was alone they would help themselves to what they liked. The only way in which I could restrain them at all, was to threaten that I would tell Cass; he was governor of the territory, and they stood in great fear of him. At last we got a door.

The next thing wanted was a chimney; winter was close at hand and the stone was not drawn. I said to my husband, 'I think I can drive the oxen and draw the stones, while you dig them from the ground and load them.' He thought I could not, but consented to let my try. He loaded them on a kind of sled; I drove to the house, rolled them off, and drove back for another load. I succeeded so well that we got enough in this way to build our chimney. My husband and myself were four days building it. I suppose most of my lady friends would think a woman quite out of 'her legitimate sphere' in turning mason, but I was not at all particular what kind of labor I performed, so we were only comfortable and provided with the necessaries of life. Many times I had been obliged to take my children, put on their cloaks, and sit on the south side of the house in the sun to keep them warm; anything was preferable to smoke. When we had a chimney and floor, and a door to close up our little log cabin, I have often thought it the most comfortable little place that could possibly be built in so new a country; and but for the want of provisions of almost every kind, we should have enjoyed it much. The roads had been so bad all the fall that we had waited until this time, and I think it was December when my husband went to Detroit for supplies. Fifteen days were consumed in going and coming. We had been without flour for three weeks or more, and it was hard to manage with young children thus. After being without bread three or four days, my little boy, two years old, looked me in the face and said, 'Ma, why don't you make bread; don't you like it? I do.' His innocent complaint brought forth the first tears I had shed in Michigan on account of any privations I had to suffer, and they were about the last. I am not of a desponding disposition, nor often low-spirited, and having left New York to make Michigan my home, I had no idea of going back, or being very unhappy. Yet the want of society, of church privileges, and in fact almost every thing that makes life desirable, would often make me sad in spite of all effort to the contrary. I had no ladies' society for one year after coming to Dexter, except that of sister Noble and a Mrs. Taylor, and was more lonely than either of them, my family being so small.

"The winter passed rather gloomily, but when spring came, everything looked delightful. We thought our hardships nearly at an end, when early in the summer my husband was taken with the ague. He had not been sick at all the first year; of course he must be acclimated. He had never suffered from ague or fever of any kind before, and it was a severe trial for him, with so much to do and no help to be had. He would break the ague and work for a few days, when it would return. In this way he made his garden, planted his corn, and thought he was quite well. About August he harvested his wheat and cut his hay, but could get no help to draw it, and was again taken with ague. I had it myself, and both my children. Sometimes we would all be ill at a time. Mr. Noble and I had it every other day. He was almost discouraged, and said he should have to sell his cattle or let them starve. I said to him, 'to-morrow we shall neither of us have the ague, and I believe I can load and stack the hay, if my strength permits.' As soon as breakfast was over, I prepared to go into the meadow, where I loaded and stacked seven loads that day. The next day my husband had the ague more severely than common, but not so with me; the exercise broke the chills, and I was able to assist him whenever he was well enough, until our hay was all secured. In the fall we had several added to our circle. We were more healthy then, and began to flatter ourselves that we could live very comfortably through the winter of 1826; but we were not destined to enjoy that blessing, for in November my husband had his left hand blown to pieces by the accidental discharge of a gun, which confined him to the house until April. The hay I had stacked during the summer I had to feed out to the cattle with my own hands in the winter, and often cut the wood for three days at a time. The logs which I alone rolled in, would surprise any one who has never been put to the test of necessity, which compels people to do what under other circumstances they would not have thought possible. This third winter in Michigan was decidedly the hardest I had yet encountered. In the spring, Mr. Noble could go out by carrying his hand in a sling. He commenced ploughing to prepare for planting his corn. Being weak from his wound, the ague returned again, but he worked every other day until his corn was planted. He then went to New York, came back in July, and brought a nephew with him, who relieved me from helping him in the work out of doors. Although I was obliged to stack the hay this third fall. I believe it was the last labor of the kind I ever performed. At this time we began to have quite a little society; we were fortunate in having good neighbors, and for some years were almost like one family, our interests being the same, and envy, jealousy, and all bitter feelings unknown among us. We cannot speak so favorably of the present time.

"When I look back upon my life, and see the ups and downs, the hardships and privations I have been called upon to endure, I feel no wish to be young again. I was in the prime of life when I came to

Michigan—only twenty-one, and my husband was thirty-three. Neither of us knew the reality of hardship. Could we have known what it was to be pioneers in a new country, we should never have had the courage to come; but I am satisfied that with all the disadvantages of raising a family in a new country, there is a consolation in knowing that our children are prepared to brave the ills of life, I believe, far better than they would have been had we never left New York."

Letters of Narcissa Whitman*

Narcissa Prentiss Whitman joined the Presbyterian Church in a fervor of conversion during the 1818–19 revival in upstate New York, when she was ten years old. She was eager to do "home-missionary" work in the 1830s when the American Board of Commissioners for Foreign Missions was seeking recruits, and immediately after marrying Dr. Marcus Whitman, a physician and Presbyterian elder, in 1836, she set off with him to the Oregon Territory. They set up their mission among the Cayuse Indians at Waiilatpu, near Fort Walla Walla on the Columbia River, making Narcissa Whitman one of the first white women to take up residence there.

LETTERS OF NARCISSA WHITMAN

April 11, 1839, to her family in New York
. . . The books, etc., sent by the Board last summer, were injured very considerably by the salt water. The only piece of flannel sent was nearly destroyed. They should not exceed 100 pounds weight, for the convenience of the portages, and besides we shall find a few barrels very convenient in housekeeping. Clothing well packed, even with crockery in the center, would come safe. Besides the portages, we are obliged to convey our supplies on horses to our stations, and to be able to do this without unpacking will save much time, expense, and trouble. I thank Sister Jane very much for those numbers of the *Mothers' Magazine.* I should have done so before. Nothing can be more acceptable than regular numbers of such valuable publications. I am much pleased with W. A. Alcott's publications, what few numbers I have seen, and think them very useful, especially for mothers. If mothers need help in training up their children in Christian lands, surely we do here, in the midst of heathen, without one savory example before our eyes.

Were it not for the indelible impressions made upon my own heart, the influence of dear mother's precepts, prayer, and example, which

* "Letters of Mrs. Marcus Whitman," *Transactions* of the 19th Annual Reunion of the Oregon Pioneer Association, for 1891, pp. 104, 133–135, 146–147; and *Transactions* of the 21st Annual Reunion of the Oregon Pioneer Association, for 1893, pp. 154–155.

still retain their force, I should often be lost in my treatment of our dear daughter. I never can be sufficiently thankful for my education, and may it continually stimulate me to unwearied diligence for the good of others. . . .

Wieletpoo, May 2, 1840

My Dear Mother:—I cannot describe how much I have longed to see you of late. I have felt the want of your sympathy, your presence and counsel more than ever. One reason doubtless is it has been so long since I have received a single letter from any one of the dear friends at home. Could they know how I feel and how much good their letters do me, they would all of them write a great deal and write often, too, at least every month or two. . . .

A tide of immigration appears to be moving this way rapidly. What a few years will bring forth we know not. A great change has taken place even since we first entered the country, and we have no reason to believe it will stop here. Instead of two lonely American females we now number fourteen, and soon may twenty or forty more, if reports are true. We are emphatically situated on the highway between the states and the Columbia river, and are a resting place for the weary travelers, consequently a greater burden rests upon us than upon any of our associates—to be always ready. And doubtless many of those who are coming to this mission their resting place will be with us until they seek and find homes of their own among the solitary wilds of Oregon.

Could dear mother know how I have been situated the two winters past, especially winter before last, I know she would pity me. I often think how disagreeable it used to be to her feelings to do her cooking in the presence of men—sitting about the room. This I have had to bear ever since I have been here—at times it has seemed as if I could not endure it any longer. It has been the more trying because our house has been so miserable and cold—small and inconvenient for us—many people as have lived in it. But the greatest trial to a woman's feelings is to have her cooking and eating room always filled with four or five or more Indians—men—especially at meal time—but we hope this trial is nearly done, for when we get into our other house we have a room there we devote to them especially, and shall not permit them to go into the other part of the house at all. They are so filthy they make a great deal of cleaning wherever they go, and this wears out a woman very fast. We must clean after them, for we have come to elevate them and not to suffer ourselves to sink down to their standard. I hardly know how to describe my feelings at the prospect of a clean, comfortable house, and one large enough so that I can find a closet to pray in.

. . . Dear father, I will relate one more anecdote and then must close. Te-lou-ki-ke said to my husband this morning: "Why do you take your wife with you to Mr. Walker's? Why do you not go alone? You see I am here without my wife; why do you always want to take your wife with you when you go from home? What do you make so much of her for?" He told him it was good for me to go with him; that we were one, and that wives were given as companions. He replied "that it was so with Adam because a rib was taken from him to make his wife, but it was not so now; it was different with us." This has often been brought up by them; the way I am treated, and contrasted with themselves; they do not like to have it so; their consciences are troubled about it. May they be more and more so until a reformation is made among them.

October 6, 1841

. . . Mother also expresses [in her last letter] a "hope that I do not regret the step I have taken and the sacrifice made for Christ in behalf of the perishing heathen." I have no occasion to repent, or the least cause to regret, that I am here; but I wonder and am astonished, when I consider the qualifications necessary for the place I occupy, that I was permitted to come. I feel every day I live more and more that my strength is perfect weakness, and that I am entirely unfitted for the work, and have many gloomy, desponding hours, but that I wish myself back again, or that I had not come, I can safely say I have no such feeling; or that I would be in any other field than this, notwithstanding all our perplexities, trials, and hardships. Yet I sometimes doubt my motive in this feeling, whether it is purely with a single eye for the glory of God or from some selfish principle. I find one of my most difficult studies is to know my own heart, the motive by which I am actuated from day to day, and feel more than ever to cling closely to the word of God as our *only guide* in this dark and dreary wilderness world.

November 19th—I began this sheet some time ago, but was not able to finish it at that time. I have not enjoyed such a season as I have now for a few weeks past and as we expect to this winter since we have been here. So free from care and none in our house but my own family, which consists of self, husband, and our two little girls. Mrs. Gray has the care of all the laborers, etc., of the station, as my health would not admit of my doing it—being entirely without help.

It is useful and necessary for us, for we greatly need time for reflection and study, having not had any scarcely from the time we left home till the present, except what was filled, with perplexing cares and trials. I feel that we have gained much in experience, but lost in mental culture, or, as it were, have been living on what we had stored up in our childhood and youth; and here I would speak of my feelings of gratitude to God for this unspeakable mercy of giving me such a mother to guide my youthful mind, directing my reading, and instead of allowing it to be filled with the light and vain trash of novel reading, I was directed to that which was more substantial and which feasted the immortal mind and laid up in store a rich inheritance for this time of need.

Mother's desire that we should have been blessed with a precious revival among us and enjoying the privilege of seeing the natives beginning to speak forth the praises of dying and redeeming love has not yet been realized in all its parts. Last winter we had a breaking down in our own hearts and the blessing seemed ready to break upon the people, as it has seemed many times before, but was stayed and has been stayed for reasons known best to Him "Who ruleth all thing well." The obstacles in the way of the conversion of this people are many and great with them as well as with their missionaries.

Waskopum, March 11th, 1843

My Dear [sister] Harriet:—I have just been reading your letter, written more than two years ago. I have been thinking all day of writing you, but can scarcely find courage enough; even now, I feel more like taking my bed rather than writing, much as I long to commune with you.

From a letter I received last fall from Mr. Dixon, I learn that my dear Harriet is now both a wife and a mother. Tender and endearing relations! May you ever prove worthy of the confidence and affection of your husband, and a tender, wise, and judicious mother, and never forget that you are training immortal spirits for an eternal world. If you have never read "Alcott's Young Wife and Young Mother," I beg you will procure and read them. You will derive great benefit from them. You cannot begin too soon to study your duty as a mother. It is a responsible station, and doubtless you feel it to be so. Be sure and make it your business to train them for the Lord, and hold them not as yours, but His, to be called away at His bidding. This is an interesting theme to me.

When you write, please tell me about your maternal association. I want to know all about them, and how the cause prospers. We have an association here consisting of the missionary mothers and two native mothers, who are the wives of the gentlemen of this country. We find it a great comfort to meet together, to pray and sympathise with and for each other in this desert land where we have so few privileges. Please remember me to your association, and solicit an interest in the prayers of those praying mothers for the missionary mothers of Oregon. . . .

Conversation with a Newly-wed Westerner by Eliza Farnham*

Eliza Farnham, a Hudson Valley native, lived in frontier Illinois during the first few years of her first marriage, in the late 1830s. Her travel book, *Life in Prairie Land* (1846), initiated her writing career, which culminated in *Woman and Her Era* (1864), her masterwork, which claimed to prove the biological superiority of the female sex. The following incident from *Life in Prairie Land* took place on an Illinois riverboat, where Farnham had been observing a western man and his new bride.

CONVERSATION WITH A NEWLY-WED WESTERNER

The strange character of the feeling manifested by [the] husband, made me very desirous of drawing him into an expression of it in words before he left us, and as their landing-place would probably be reached on the third morning, I availed myself of a chance meeting on the shady guard in the afternoon, to engage him in conversation. A few words about the height of the water, the timber, and the prairies, served the purpose.

"You are going to become a prairie farmer?" I said.

"No, I've been one afore, I've got a farm up the river *hyur* that I've *crapped* twice a'ready; there's a good cabin on it, and it's about as good a place, I reckon, as can be found in these diggins."

"Then you built a cage," I said, "and went back for your bird to put in it?"

He looked at me, and his face underwent a contortion, of which words will convey but a faint idea. It was a mingled expression of pride and contempt, faintly disguised by a smile that was intended to hide them.

"Why, I don't know what you Yankees call a bird," he replied, "but I call her a woman. I shouldn't make much account of havin a bird in

---

* From Eliza W. Farnham, *Life in Prairie Land* (New York: Harper & Brothers, 1846), pp. 36–43.

my cabin, but a good, stout woman I should calculate was worth somethin. She can pay her way, and do a handsome thing besides, helpin me on the farm."

Think of that, ye belles and fair-handed maidens! How was my sentiment rebuked!

"Well, we'll call her a woman, which is, in truth, much the more rational appellation. You intend to make her useful as well as ornamental to your home?"

"Why, yes; I calculate 'tain't of much account to have a woman if she ain't of no use. I lived up *hyur* two year, and had to have another man's woman do all my washin and mendin and so on, and at last I got tired o' *totin* my plunder back and forth, and thought I might as well get a woman of my own. There's a heap of things beside these, that she'll do better than I can, I reckon; every man ought to have a woman to do his cookin and such like, 'kase it's easier for them than it is for us. They take to it kind o' naturally."

I could scarcely believe that there was no more human vein in the animal, and determined to sound him a little deeper.

"And this bride of yours is the one, I suppose, that you thought of all the while you were making your farm and building your cabin? You have, I dare say, made a little garden, or set out a tree, or done something of the kind to please her alone?"

"No, I never allowed to get a woman till I found my neighbors went ahead of me with 'em, and then I should a got one right thar, but there wasn't any stout ones in our settlement, and it takes so long to make up to a *stranger,* that I allowed I mought as well go back and see the old folks, and git somebody that I know'd thar to come with me."

"And had you no choice made among your acquaintances? was there no one person of whom you thought more than another?" said I.

"Yas, there was a gal I used to know that was stouter and bigger than this one. I should a got her if I could, but she'd got married and gone off over the *Massissippi,* somewhar."

The cold-hearted fellow! it was a perfectly business matter with him.

"Did you select this one solely on account of her size?" said I.

"Why, pretty much," he replied; "I reckon women are some like horses and oxen, the biggest can do the most work, and that's what I want one for."

"And is that all?" I asked, more disgusted at every word. "Do you care nothing about a pleasant face to meet you when you go home from the field, or a soft voice to speak kind words when you are sick, or a gentle friend to converse with you in your leisure hours?"

"Why, as to that," he said. "I reckon a woman ain't none the worse for talk because she's stout and able to work. I calculate she'll mind her own business pretty much, and if she does she won't talk a great deal to me; that ain't what I got her for."

"But suppose when you get home she should be unhappy, and want to see her parents and other friends?"

"Why I don't allow she will; I didn't get her for that. . . . I shall give her enough to eat and wear, and I don't calculate she'll be very *daunsey* if she gets that; if she is she'll git *shet* of it after a while."

My indignation increased at every word.

"But you brought her away from her home to be treated as a human being, not as an animal or machine. Marriage is a moral contract, not a mere bargain of business. The parties promise to study each other's happiness, and endeavor to promote it. You could not marry a woman as you could buy a washing machine, though you might want her for the same purpose. If you take the machine there is no moral obligation incurred, except to pay for it. If you take the woman, there is. Before you entered into this contract I could have shown you a machine that would have answered your purpose admirably. It would have washed and ironed all your clothes, and when done, stood in some out-of-the-way corner till it was wanted again. You would have been under no obligation, not even to feed and clothe it, as you now are. It would have been the better bargain, would it not?"

"Why that would be according to what it cost in the fust place; but it wouldn't be justly the same thing as havin a wife, I reckon, even if it was give to you."

"No, certainly not; it would free you from many obligations that you are under to a wife" (it was the first time, by the way, he had used the word), "and leave you to pursue your own pleasure without seeing any sorrowful or sour faces about you."

"Oh, I calculate sour faces won't be of much account to me. If a woman 'll mind her business, she may look as thunderin as a live airthquake, I shan't mind it. . . . I reckon the Yankees may do as they like about them things, and I shall do jist the same. I don't think a woman's of much account anyhow, if she can't help herself a little and me too.

If the Yankee women was *raised up like the women* here *aar*, they'd cost a heap less and be worth more."

. . . I turned away, saying that I trusted his wife would agree with him in these opinions, or they might lead to some unpleasant differences.

"Oh, as to that," said he, "I reckon her pinions won't go fur anyhow; she'll think pretty much as I do, or not at all."

Letter from the
Union of Women for Association,
and Replies*

A Union of Women for Association, meeting in Boston in May, 1847, after an Associationists Convention, wrote the following open letter. Published in the newspaper that served as an organ of the socialist-communitarian movement, *The Harbinger*, it received several replies, two of which follow—one from a single woman, the other from the female members of the Fourierist Trumbull Phalanx.

TO THE WOMEN INTERESTED IN ASSOCIATION

"What shall I do? is a question asked with none the less trembling eagerness, by earnest souls at the present day, when the practical embodiment of Christianity seems dawning upon us, than at the first coming of Christ. Fully convinced of the doctrines of Association, our souls inspired by its great truths, our hearts warmed by the visions of beauty and harmony which it unfolds to us, are we doing (we at least who are not privileged to devote our whole lives to this cause) all that we might and should to co-operate with our brothers, in awakening our fellow beings to a knowledge of the high destiny which we believe a loving Father has designed for the human race? We cannot be satisfied with a fruitless expression of sympathy, or the trifling acts which opportunity offers to us; we must be up and doing (and the utmost limit of our capacity will alone suffice us), both for our own sakes, that we may come into possession of all our powers; and for the sake of the cause, which demands all that is holiest and best, the untiring zeal, the ever growing energy, of all who have been baptized into this new revelation.

"Certainly, there are many things which we can do. Funds must be raised, to send out lecturers, to publish papers and tracts, and so forth. How shall we aid in this important work? One friend suggests, that though alone we can do but little, some unitary effort might result in good, and proposes that each should offer her services to the Union

* From *The Harbinger*, V: 1 (June 12, 1847), and V: 9 (August 7, 1847). Reprinted by permission of the Harvard College Library.

with which she is connected, or to Associationists generally, in the department which nature, or acquired skill points out to her; promising if she cannot afford to give all her time, a certain per centage of the proceeds to the Union, for all work which they shall procure; and as a beginning, offering to the Boston Union the first ten dollars accruing from any orders they may send her for painting lampshades, fans, screens, books of flowers, birds, and so forth; and fifteen per cent. of all future profits.

"Might not something grow from this? Would it not be useful as well as pleasing to employ each other's skill and taste, in those little offices which strangers are constantly called upon to perform for us; and should we not thus at the same time be testing each others' talents and capacities, preparing the way for industrial groups, when in the fulness of time the grand experiment shall be made? And might not this be one opening, small though it seem, to a system of guarantees which should not be confined to the members of one Union, but embrace the whole body of Associationists throughout the country or the world?

"Again, we need to be united in one strong, living body, and as a preparatory step, a free and friendly correspondence is proposed among the various Unions. Surely, we are not strangers to each other. Devotion to a cause like this is a bond of union such as the trivial intercourse of society can never give. We wish to know each and all, to know your plans, and hopes, and wishes, and fears; we would gladly be known by you, and by a friendly interchange of thoughts and feelings, of words and deeds, become 'a body fitly joined together, and compacted'; strong and active to hasten the coming of the kingdom of Heaven.

"Another friend writes, and do we not all heartily respond to the sentiment? 'I feel as if we wanted some sacred, holy union. I long for something which shall wholly rouse up my own soul and that of other men and women devoted to the cause, and wind them up to the highest pitch of devotion and self-sacrifice. I would concentrate all energies upon some higher, nobler, more solemn organization. Some Association we must have, which shall be a kind and watchful Providence, over all its members. We should unite ourselves most solemnly as a band of brothers and sisters, doing for each other in cases of sickness or misfortune, all that brothers and sisters should do, and feeling for each other that interest and affection which belong to members of one family. The religious element must be at the foundation of such an organization. There must be a moral and religious consecration of ourselves and of each other, to the work, by fitting ceremonies and symbols, as well as in our own hearts. Next, an appropriate sphere of action must be sought for every member. There should be ascending ranks, according to knowledge, virtue, and devotion; and there should be a fund given generously, according to the ability of each, for the dissemination of our views, or helping the suffering of our own members.'

"Joyfully should we welcome such an organization; for this work of Universal Unity, based on a recognition of God's laws of order, by which we come into unity with Him, with man and with nature, is the most truly and deeply religious one, in which mankind have ever been called to engage, or it is nothing. May not this very act of communing with you, be a preliminary step to such a result?

"Sisters, will you not let us hear from you? Will you not tell us of the measures for promulgating our views, the prospects of our cause in your respective homes? Will you not tell us what you think of these propositions? Will you not aid us by your suggestions, and unite with us, to devise and adopt some method of collective action (each doing, meanwhile, as much as possible in her individual sphere) by which we can most effectively co-operate with our brothers, whose privilege it is to devote themselves to such a cause?

"And remember, friends, though at present we seem a small and feeble band, we are not alone. God and all good spirits work with us for the redemption of the race. Hosts of noble men and women are pressing forward to the same goal, though they may know it not. Let us stretch out to them in all charity and Christian fellowship the friendly hand; speak the cheering word of sympathy; and aid whenever we can by worthy deeds. Believing as we do in the solidarity of the race, we are doubly urged on in our holy work. We know that the good, both on earth and in the world of spirits, are aiding us. We feel the evils, suffering, sin, of humanity as our own, for are we not one? and thank Heaven, there can be no well being for us, until our brothers are also redeemed. But, alas, all do not know this; all cannot recognize how truly we are devoted to them, and we must not be embittered or impatient if they do not understand us. If none more keenly, deeply, feel the evils of society, none more clearly see the cause and the remedy; and pity and sorrow and hope should so fill our hearts as to leave no room for indignation and despair. Baptised anew in a spirit of love, let us go forth on our mission, prepared 'to die daily' if need be; content to be poor, outcast, and despised, to cheerfully meet contumely and reproach; and to pour back on those who condemn us floods of all-subduing love, of generous, hearty forgiveness; to tenderly shelter and cherish them; for indeed 'they know not what they do,' and God in His own good time and way will give the victory.

[Signed by the Committee.]

"Boston, May 28th, 1847."

REPLIES

Tupperford, near Marietta, O., June 23, 1847

I have read, in "The Harbinger" of the 12th of July, the Circular letter of our sister Associationists. Allow me to answer them through your means.

Dear Sisters:—Your letter through the Harbinger has conferred on me a deep, an intense blessing! How long have I not prayed with the most earnest fervor of the heart, to the Almighty Power who rules us all, to inspire my sisters who were so situated, to *unite together* in their own behalf and that of the human family! At last, my ardent wish is accomplished. Dear sisters, you come out with broad and noble views, in search of undisguised truth! in search of the means to redeem our unfortunate Race from the chaotic discordance and misery into which it has fallen for so long! Then, Dear Sisters, behold a new era opening before us, as never was one before! Women (made by the laws of Nature the ministering angels for their Race) no longer shy or cringing, confined in obscurity, where they do isolatedly, the little good they can, in impotence, ignorance, and feebleness; but coming forward with the noble determination to unite their energies with those of their brothers in the work of restoring human society to harmony and happiness! Oh Sisters, persevere and it will be done, for you will possess among you all the necessary materials to accomplish it. From the moment that hideous, brutal War grasped unfortunate females, and made them slaves and victims wherever it reigned, the responsibility of social order devolved entirely on men. What have we had since? War! war! war! discord, confusion, wranglings, all sorts of miseries, and sufferings. Not because men are naturally bad; but because they are only one half of the social body, and they can act but that half. The *moral* and intellectual powers of the Mothers of our Race are as necessary to create social harmony, as their physical powers for the creation and suckling of their offspring.

Whatever power I have, pecuniary or mental, whatever exertion I am capable of, I will cheerfully lend it to assist you in your movements; only let me know them and what I can do. We should command a Press. No doubt there are some among you, who could undertake the management of it. I would wish to see some females among your lecturers. Does the sincerity of moral persuasion lose all its power in coming from a woman's lips, that I see so very few of them undertake the task? By all means establish a reciprocal guarantee among you. Ask some of our kind brothers who sympathize with us to put you in the way of it. But act for yourselves. It is high time that the *Mother of Mankind* should cease to play the *child!*

May the Almighty bless your efforts in the most holy cause that woman ever undertook!

Your devoted sister.

Trumbull Phalanx, Braceville, Ohio, July 15, 1847

It was with great pleasure that we received your letter. It was read in a meeting called upon the occasion. To the reflections and sentiments therein we heartily respond. It is joyful to feel and to know that the women of the Capital Region of the enlightened state of Massachusetts are engaged in the same work that we are: Immediately do we sympathize with you. Immediately do we recognize you as Sisters. Then, sisters dear, may God give us feeling, and strength to support that feeling, so that we shall be urged forward in the work.

It is plain that our efforts must be different from yours. Yours is the part to arouse the idle and indifferent by your conversation, and by contributing funds to sustain and aid publications. Ours is the part to organize ourselves in all the affairs of life, in the best manner that our imperfect institution will permit; and, not least, to have faith in our own efforts. In this last particular we are sometimes deficient, for it is impossible for us with our imperfect and limited capacities, clearly and fully to foresee what faith and confidence in God's providence can accomplish. We have been brought hither through doubts and dangers, and through the shadows of the Future we have no guide save when duty points the way.

Our trials lie in the commonest walks. To forego conveniences, to live poorly, dress homely, to listen calmly, reply mildly, and wait patiently, are what we must become familiar with. True, these are requirements by no means uncommon; but imperfect beings like ourselves are apt to imagine that they alone are called upon to endure. Yet, perhaps, we enjoy no less than the most of our sex; nay, we are in truth, sisters the world round—if one suffers, all suffer, no matter whether she tends her husband's dogs amidst the Polar snows, or mounts her consort's funeral pile upon the banks of the Ganges. Together we weep, together we rejoice. We rise, we fall together.

It would afford us much pleasure could we be associated together. Could all the women fitted to engage in Social Reform be located on one domain, one cannot imagine the immense changes that would there ensue. We pray that we, or at least our children, may live to see the day when kindred souls shall be permitted to co-operate in a sphere sufficiently extensive to call forth all our powers.

We number about three hundred—with forty-five families. Let us hear from you soon, and often.

Domestic Relations in a Utopian Community*

This letter, full of utopian ideals, was addressed by a male resident of an Association to a skeptical friend; it also appeared in the newspaper of the Fourierist movement.

DOMESTIC RELATIONS IN A UTOPIAN COMMUNITY

My Dear W.—I have just finished reading your last two letters, which, by chance, I received together, and hasten to reply to them.

I confess my surprise at the step they inform me of. From the tenor of your recent communications, I had supposed that you were completely converted to the doctrines of Association, and from the dislike to mercantile transactions which you used to express so freely, I should hardly have supposed it possible for you to engage in business. I had, too, looked forward to a renewal of our former intimacy, with the new bond of common devotion to a great cause, and had often pleased myself with imagining the ardor with which you would engage both in spreading the doctrine and in practical experiment.

I fear that I have erred in not making to you more distinct and complete statements of the principles on which the Associative movement is founded, and urging them directly upon your mind. . . .

Do not expect me to make a complete statement of the grounds upon which we stand—for that is impossible. A universal philosophy cannot be expressed in a single sheet. I say a universal philosophy. I should rather say, the true doctrine of Society; for it is of its social aspects that I wish to speak. If, then, what I shall say seem inconclusive to you, do not imagine that I have said all. . . .

And now for the particular things in your letters, which are the domestic relations, the position of women, and the education of children. Upon these points you have, I think, failed to grasp the theory of Association, both because it has not been sufficiently explained to you,

* From *The Phalanx*, I: 21 (February 8, 1844), pp. 317–319. Reprinted by permission of the Harvard College Library.

and because you have taken a partial view of what has been said. It is generally necessary in public lectures and in conversation upon the subject, to select some single aspect of the doctrine and make it prominent otherwise we should not be understood. If we endeavored to state universal principles in their universality, but few minds could receive them. But the misfortune is that in thus dwelling upon a particular view of the great Truth, it is often supposed that we cannot take any other, so much are people accustomed to one-sided teaching. Thus, when we say, that the isolated household is a source of innumerable evils, which Association alone can remedy, the mind of the hearer sometimes rushes to the conclusion that we mean to destroy the home relations entirely, and that we leave out of our account all those delicate and beautiful affections which form so much of the best life of man, but which, in the present unfortunate situation of the world, are *possible* only to a minority, so small, that in a general view of Humanity, they cannot be so much as reckoned. When, too, we say, that the existing system of Education is wholly wrong, it is feared that we design some violence to the parental sentiment, or that, in your own words, we would give children "wholly up to the care of others, when only a mother can bear and forbear with a child, and yet love it." Now, my dear W., these are not our doctrines but your misconceptions of them. You say that we "war against Nature." We hold to the most implicit obedience to her, but it must be to the whole of Nature and every one of her promptings, and not to any one or two or more of them, to the exclusion of all the others, or any one of them. . . .

Although I have not had a home of my own for these many years, still I am not ignorant of what home is; I have seen the most beautiful homes that the world has, and that not casually and transiently, but intimately. But even if I had known nothing of this, I should have learned from the very theory which seems to you to militate against the domestic ties, how absolutely necessary they are to man. Association does not propose to weaken them, but to give them new strength, and to free them from what does really tend to destroy them and mar their beauty. The privacy of domestic life, association aims to render more sacred as well as to extend it to all men. It does this also in accomplishing what benevolence must always wish for, the conciliation of the family interest, with all the other interests of society, so that a man in working for his family, "in caring for his home and loved ones," works for the general good also. Association is not a mere conglomeration of heterogeneous masses, but an orderly arrangement of society. It acts upon families as upon individuals, preserving the freedom and natural affinities, and guaranteeing the rights of all with jealous care. You seem to have confounded the pecuniary independence of individual members of families, with a kind of entire independence or rather a sundering of all the bonds that unite them. We believe that pecuniary independence will tend to unite them closer. Will the father love the child less because he owes him love and not money? Will the husband have less affection for his wife because she does not make a perpetual demand upon his purse? Is love strongest in those families where the father is driven almost to despair by perpetual costs for the support of the wife and children? Is the beautiful attachment which exists between his brother and himself at all indebted to pecuniary dependence for its strength? Ah no! Love, my dear friend, grows in its own atmosphere and needs not to be nurtured, save only by love, free as itself. But I am sure you cannot mean what you seem to say; a little reflection cannot fail to show you that the pecuniary independence of all persons which association promises, is precisely what all desire and thus is the desire of *Nature*, and necessary to the dignity and happiness of life.

The isolated household is wasteful in economy, is untrue to the human heart, and is not the design of God, and therefore it must disappear, but the domestic relations are not so, however they may have been falsified and tarnished by what man has mixed with them. Of these relations the present position of woman is an essential part, and she can be raised out of that position only by purging them of what is alien to their essential character. Now, as we think, the pecuniary dependence which society establishes for woman, is one of the most hurtful of these foreign elements, and we do not doubt that with its removal we shall see social relations generally rise to a degree of truth and beauty, to which they cannot at present attain. In the progress of society we see that the position of woman is a hinge on which all other things seem more or less to turn. In the savage state she is the drudge and menial of man; in the barbarous state she is his slave and plaything, and in the civilized state she is as you confess, his "upper servant." Society rises with the degree of freedom it bestows on woman, and it is only by raising her to "integral independence," and making her as she should be, and as God made her, the equal of Man, though not by making her precisely the same as Man as some mistaken reformers have wished, the world can be saved. You must not judge in matters of such importance from the few facts that your own personal knowledge may give you; your comparatively fortunate education, has shown you but little of the worst side of the world. A few days after I received your letter of September, I was driving through one of the richest parts of the State of New-York, where Nature seemed to have expended her utmost wealth for the benefit of man. I happened to turn my head and saw a middle aged woman bare-foot carrying around the hovel in which she lived, the food for some half dozen swine. "That," said I, "is the position of Woman in civilization." The few women who seem to fill their appropriate spheres are as nothing to the great majority, that toil in poverty, in degradation and in unhappiness, or even to those that drag out a short but wretched life, lost to all that renders life anything but a curse. Of all the foul spots on the face of civilization, the lot of woman in it is the worst. I speak from a knowledge of facts, and not from vague impressions. I could tell you of things that would fill your soul with a horror it has never dreamed of, and almost make you despair of the world. If there be anything which is to me a perpetual incitement to more devoted exertion, and a more generous sacrifice of all things, so that Man may reap some advantages, it is the lot of woman. . . .

But it is not possible, as you seem to suppose, for woman by individual virtue and endeavors to rescue the sex from this frightful condition. Individual exertion may in favorable cases rescue individuals, but like alms-giving, private or public, it cannot prevent a recurrence of the very evil it attempts to remedy. What is an essential element in any order of things, can never be altered except by alteration of the whole order. Thus the social position of woman can be generally and surely changed only by carrying society out of civilization into a higher phasis. I might maintain this by very many proofs, but cannot think that it will not already be plain to you. Woman is not an "upper servant," because she "cares too much for earthly things," or because she is not sufficiently educated, but because the whole structure of society makes her an "upper servant." . . .

As to Education let me first remind you that the theory of association, is the theory of attraction, and not at all of compulsion, as your remarks seem strangely to imply. All are made free in association to follow the bent of their own tastes, and to develope their faculties in the methods which God points out in the nature of every individual, and not according to the arbitrary notions of this or that philosopher, or pedagogue. The mother does not consign her child to the care of others because she *must*, nor does the child engage in industry because it *must*. Association delivers us from these miserable necessities, and leaves the whole and not a part of man's nature free to act. In civilization it is not free, but hampered and choked at almost every point. The mother *must* consign her child to the care, not of beautiful and loving persons in apartments furnished with conveniences and elegancies which a prince's palace is without, but to servants who oftenest are fitted neither by character nor education for the momentous office of influencing an immortal being at an age when it most needs the kindliest cares. But, in association, the word *must* is not known. The mother may keep her children entirely under her own care, if she wishes, even more than in ordinary society. The Association, which is bound as far as possible to satisfy the tastes of every one, would furnish her with the means of doing so at much less expense than they could possibly be procured elsewhere. But let us look a little more into the plan of Nature in this respect. To ascertain what this is, however, we must be careful to divest our minds of prejudices, and not to substitute them for Nature, whose views are formed by a higher wisdom than ours. Now, you will find that every mother has not the constant and tender devotion to her children which is necessary to them, especially in their infancy.

Very many women find other employments more attractive than the care of their children, and consequently the children receive comparatively little attention from them. Now, this seems to me to show the plan of Nature, who does not form every woman to take care of children, but only a certain proportion of women. You will, perhaps, say that these are not good mothers, and that they *ought* to discharge so interesting an office. But is not this to substitute for the method of Nature certain notions which you have formed for yourself, and which Nature does not at all recognize? I think it is, but granting that every mother *ought* to take charge of her children, the fact remains that many do not, and will not, to say nothing of the majority who absolutely cannot. Should the children therefore, suffer? The associationist says no! Let them be cared for, not by menials whom accident furnishes, and who may be the most corrupt persons in the world. Let them be given to the charge of persons of high character and education, in whom the maternal instinct is so largely developed that they discharge with delight the duty which the mother of the child does not, and which Nature may, perhaps, have unfitted her for, in bestowing upon her the most brilliant talents in other spheres. . . .

The education of association has but one *tone* in all its spheres. The family, the school, and society, all breathe kindred influences. In civilization, it is entirely the opposite. The training of home, of school, and of society or the world, are all discordant with each other, and it is impossible that one who has passed through them can, except in rare instances, have anything like unity or consistency of character, to say nothing of being really educated.

Diary and Letter of
Mrs. Elizabeth Dixon Smith Geer*

On the westward journey to Oregon, Mrs. Geer (then Mrs. Smith) wrote in her diary at the close of each day, after her eight children were asleep. Soon after her arrival in Oregon, she sent it in letter form to her friends back in La Porte, Indiana.

DIARY AND LETTER OF MRS. ELIZABETH DIXON SMITH GEER

Dear Friends—By your request I have endeavored to keep a record of our journey from "the States" to Oregon, though it is poorly done, owing to my having a young babe and besides a large family to do for; and, worst of all, my education is very limited.

April 21, 1847—Commenced our journey from La Porte, Indiana, to Oregon; made fourteen miles. . . .

[After six months of overland travel the party has reached the Columbia River.]

November 9—Finds us still in trouble. Waves dashing over our raft and we already stinting ourselves in provisions. My husband started this morning to hunt provisions. Left no man with us except our oldest boy. It is very cold. The icicles are hanging from our wagon beds to the water. Tonight about dusk Adam Polk expired. No one with him but his wife and myself. We sat up all night with him while the waves was dashing below.

November 10—Finds us still waiting for calm weather. My husband returned at 2 o'clock. Brought 50 pounds of beef on his back 12 miles, which he had bought from another company. By this time the water became calm and we started once more, but the wind soon began to blow and we were forced to land. My husband and boy were an hour and a half after dark getting the raft landed and made fast while the water ran knee deep over our raft, the wind blew, and was freezing cold. We women and children did not attempt to get out of our wagons tonight.

* From 35th *Transactions* of the Oregon Pioneer Association (1907), 153, 171–178.

November 11—Laid by most all day. Started this evening. Ran about three miles and landed after dark. Here we found Welch and our boys with our cattle, for they could be driven no farther on this side for mountains. Here was a ferry for the purpose of ferrying immigrants' cattle.

November 12—Ferried our cattle over the river and buried Mr. Polk. Rain all day. We are living entirely on beef.

November 18—My husband is sick. It rains and snows. We start this morning around the falls with our wagons. We have 5 miles to go. I carry my babe and lead, or rather carry, another through snow, mud and water, almost to my knees. It is the worst road that a team could possibly travel. I went ahead with my children and I was afraid to look behind me for fear of seeing the wagons turn over into the mud and water with everything in them. My children gave out with cold and fatigue and could not travel, and the boys had to unhitch the oxen and bring them and carry the children on to camp. I was so cold and numb that I could not tell by the feeling that I had any feet at all. We started this morning at sunrise and did not get to camp until after dark, and there was not one dry thread on one of us—not even my babe. I had carried my babe and I was so fatigued that I could scarcely speak or step. When I got here I found my husband lying in Welch's wagon, very sick. He had brought Mrs. Polk down the day before and was taken sick here. We had to stay up all night tonight for our wagons are left half-way back. I have not told half we suffered. I am not adequate to the task. Here was some hundreds camped, waiting for boats to come and take them down the Columbia to Vancouver or Portland or Oregon City.

November 19—My husband is sick and can have but little care. Rain all day.

November 20—Rain all day. It is almost an impossibility to cook, and quite so to keep warm or dry. I froze or chilled my feet so that I cannot wear a shoe, so I have to go around in the cold water barefooted.

November 21—Rain all day. The whole care of everything falls upon my shoulders. I cannot write any more at present.

November 27—Embarked once more on the Columbia on a flatboat. Ran all day, though the waves threatened hard to sink us. Passed Fort Vancouver in the night. Landed a mile below. My husband never has left his bed since he was taken sick.

November 28—Still moving on the water.

November 29—Landed at Portland on the Willamette, 12 miles above the mouth, at 11 o'clock at night.

November 30—Raining. This morning I ran about trying to get a house to get into with my sick husband. At last I found a small, leaky concern, with two families already in it. Mrs. Polk had got down before us. She and another widow was in this house. My family and Welch's went in with them, and you could have stirred us with a stick. Welch and my oldest boy was driving the cattle around. My children and I carried up a bed. The distance was nearly a quarter of a mile. Made it down on the floor in the mud. I got some men to carry my husband up through the rain and lay him on it, and he never was out of that shed until he was carried out in his coffin. Here lay five of us bedfast at one time . . . and we had no money, and what few things we had left that would bring money, I had to sell. I had to give 10 cents a pound for fresh pork, 75 cents per bushel for potatoes, 4 cents a pound for fish. There are so many of us sick that I cannot write any more at present. I have not time to write much, but I thought it would be interesting to know what kind of weather we have in the winter.

1848—January 14—Rain this morning. Warm weather. We suppose it has rained half of the time that I have neglected writing.

January 15—My husband is still alive, but very sick. There is no medicine here except at Fort Vancouver, and the people there will not sell one bit—not even a bottle of wine.

January 16—Warm and dry. We are still living in the old, leaky shed in Portland. It is six miles below Vancouver, down the Columbia and 12 miles up the Willamette. Portland has two white houses and one brick and three wood-colored frame houses and a few cabins. . . .

January 20—Cool and dry. Soldiers are collecting here from every part of Oregon to go and fight the Indians in middle Oregon in consequence of the massacre at Whitman's mission. I think there were 17 men killed at the massacre, but no women or children, except Whitman's wife.[1] They killed every white man there except one, and he was an Englishman. They took all the young women for wives. Robbed them of their clothing and everything. The Oregon government bought the prisoners at a dear rate, and then gave the Indians fight; but one white man, I believe, was killed in the war, and not many Indians. The murderers escaped. . . .

[1] Narcissa Whitman was killed by Indians in 1847. —Ed.

January 31—Rain all day. If I could tell you how we suffer you would not believe it. Our house, or rather a shed joined to a house, leaks all over. The roof descends in such a manner as to make the rain run right down into the fire. I have dipped as much as six pails of water off of our dirt hearth in one night. Here I sit up, night after night, with my poor sick husband, all alone, and expecting him every day to die. I neglected to tell you that Welch's and all the rest moved off and left us. Mr. Smith has not been moved off his bed for six weeks only by lifting him by each corner of the sheet, and I had hard work to get help enough for that, let alone getting watchers. I have not undressed to lie down for six weeks. Besides all our sickness, I had a cross little babe to take care of. Indeed, I cannot tell you half.

February 1—Rain all day. This day my dear husband, my last remaining friend, died.

February 2—Today we buried my earthly companion. Now I know what none but widows know; that is, how comfortless is that of a widow's life, especially when left in a strange land, without money or friends, and the care of seven children. Cloudy. . . .

Butteville, Oregon Territory, Yamhill County, September 2, 1850
Dear and Estimable Friends, Mrs. Paulina Foster and Mrs. Cynthia Ames:

I promised when I saw you last to write to you when I got to Oregon, and I done it faithfully, but as I never have received an answer, I do not know whether you got my letter and diary or not, consequently I do not know what to write now. I wrote four sheets full and sent it to you, but now I have not time to write. I write now to know whether you got my letter; and I will try to state a few things again. My husband was taken sick before we got to any settlement, and never was able to walk afterwards. He died at Portland, on the Willamette River, after an illness of two months. I will not attempt to describe my troubles since I saw you. Suffice it to say that I was left a widow with the care of seven children in a foreign land, without one solitary friend, as one might say, in the land of the living; but this time I will only endeavor to hold up the bright side of the picture. I lived a widow one year and four months. My three boys started for the gold mines, and it was doubtful to me whether I ever saw them again. Perhaps you will think it strange that I let such young boys go; but I was willing and helped them off in as good style as I could. They packed through by land. Russell Welch went by water. The boys never saw Russell in the mines. Well, after the boys were gone, it is true I had plenty of cows and hogs and plenty of wheat to feed them on and to make my bread. Indeed, I was well off if I had only known it; but I lived in a remote place where my strength was of little use to me. I could get nothing to do, and you know I could not live without work. I employed myself in teaching my children: yet that did not fully occupy my mind. I became as poor as a snake, yet I was in good health, and never was so nimble since I was a child. I could run a half a mile without stopping to breathe. Well, I thought perhaps I had better try my fortune again; so on the 24th of June, 1849, I was married to a Mr. Joseph Geer, a man 14 years older than myself, though young enough for me. He is the father of ten children. They are all married, but two boys and two girls. He is a Yankee from Connecticut and he is a Yankee in every sense of the word, as I told you he would be if it ever proved my lot to marry again. I did not marry rich, but my husband is very industrious, and is as kind to me as I can ask. Indeed, he sometimes provokes me for trying to humor me so much. He is a stout, healthy man for one of his age.

. . . At this time we are all well but Perley. I cannot answer for him; he has gone to the Umpqua for some money due him. The other two are working for four dollars a day. The two oldest boys have got three town lots in quite a stirring place called Lafayette in Yamhill County. Perley has four horses. A good Indian horse is worth one hundred dollars. A good American cow is worth sixty dollars. My boys live about 25 miles from me, so that I cannot act in the capacity of a mother to them; so you will guess it is not all sunshine with me, for you know my boys are not old enough to do without a mother. Russell Welch done very well in the mines. He made about twenty hundred dollars. He lives 30 miles below me in a little town called Portland on the Willamette River. Sarah has got her third son. It has been one year since I saw her. Adam Polk's two youngest boys live about wherever they see fit. The oldest, if he is alive, is in California. There is some ague in this country this season, but neither I nor my children, except those that went to California, have had a day's sickness since we came to Oregon.

I believe I will say no more until I hear from you. Write as soon as possible and tell me everything. My husband will close this epistle.

Elizabeth Geer

Vindication of the Beecher-Tilton Scandal by Victoria Woodhull*

Victoria Woodhull pioneered on the frontier of personal and sexual freedom. In her brief career in the United States press limelight, she was known as a New York stock broker, a champion of female suffrage, an editor of a newspaper weekly (with her sister), and a candidate for President of the United States in 1872. She gained credibility with the women's rights movement by testifying on behalf of female suffrage before a Congressional committee, but lost respectability by her open advocacy of "free love" and "spiritualism." One of her more sensational actions was the revelation of a love affair between the eminently respectable liberal minister Henry Ward Beecher and a member of his church, Elizabeth Tilton. She printed the following explanation of her action in her *Weekly*.

VINDICATION OF THE BEECHER-TILTON SCANDAL

The following is the re-statement from notes, aided by my recollection, of the interviewing upon this subject by the press reporter already alluded to:

Reporter:—"Mrs. Woodhull, I have called to ask if you are prepared and willing to furnish a full statement of the Beecher-Tilton scandal for publication in the city papers?"

Mrs. Woodhull:—"I do not know that I ought to object to repeating whatever I know in relation to it. You understand, of course, that I take a different view of such matters from those usually avowed by other people. Still I have good reason to think that far more people entertain views corresponding to mine than dare to assert them or openly live up to them."

Reporter:—"How, Mrs. Woodhull, would you state in the most condensed way your opinions on this subject, as they differ from those avowed and ostensibly lived by the public at large?"

* "The Beecher-Tilton Scandal Case: The Detailed Statement of the Whole Matter by Mrs. Woodhull," *Woodhull and Claflin's Weekly* (New York), November 2, 1872, pp. 9–13. Reprinted by permission of The Schlesinger Library at Radcliffe College, from the Olympia Brown Collection, A–69, folder 101.

Mrs. Woodhull:—"I believe that the marriage institution, like slavery and monarchy, and many other things which have been good or necessary in their day, is now *effete,* and in a general sense injurious, instead of being beneficial to the community, although of course it must continue to linger until better institutions can be formed. I mean by marriage, in this connection, any *forced* or *obligatory tie* between the sexes, *any legal intervention* or *constraint* to prevent people from adjusting their love relations precisely as they do their religious affairs in this country, in complete personal freedom; changing and improving them from time to time, and according to circumstances."

Reporter:—"I confess, then, I cannot understand why you of all persons should have any fault to find with Mr. Beecher, even assuming everything to be true of him which I have hitherto heard only vaguely hinted at."

Mrs. Woodhull:—"*I* have no fault to find with him in any such sense as you mean, nor in any such sense as that in which the world will condemn him. I have no doubt that he has done the very best which he could do under all the circumstances—with his demanding physical nature, and with the terrible restrictions upon a clergyman's life, imposed by that ignorant public opinion about physiological laws, which they, nevertheless, more, perhaps, than any other class, do their best to perpetuate. The fault I find with Mr. Beecher is of a wholly different character, as I have told him repeatedly and frankly, and as he knows very well. It is, indeed, the exact opposite to that for which the world will condemn him. I condemn him because I know, and have had every opportunity to know, that he entertains, on conviction, substantially the same views which I entertain on the social question; that, under the influence of these convictions, he has lived for many years, perhaps for his whole adult life, in a manner which the religious and moralistic public ostensibly, and to some extent really, condemn; that he has permitted himself, nevertheless, to be over-awed by public opinion, to profess to believe otherwise than as he does believe, to have helped to maintain for these many years that very social slavery under which he was chafing, and against which he was secretly revolting both in thought and practice; and that he has, in a word, consented, and still consents to be a hypocrite. The fault with which I, therefore, charge him, is not infidelity to the old ideas, but unfaithfulness to the new. He is in heart, in conviction and in life, an ultra socialist reformer; while in seeming and pretension he is the upholder of the old social slavery, and, therefore, does what he can to crush out and oppose me and those who act and believe with me in forwarding the great social revolution. I know, myself, so little of the sentiment of fear, I have so little respect for an ignorant and prejudiced public opinion, I am so accustomed to say the thing that I think and do the thing that I believe to be right, that I doubt not I am in danger of having far too little sympathy with the real difficulties of a man situated as Mr. Beecher has been, and is, when he contemplates the idea of facing social opprobrium. Speaking from my feelings, I am prone to denounce him as a poltroon, a coward and a sneak; not, as I tell you, for anything that he has done, and for which the world would condemn him, but for failing to do what it seems to me so clear he ought to do; for failing, in a word, to stand shoulder to shoulder with me and others who are endeavoring to hasten a social regeneration which he believes in. . . . Let it be once understood *that whosoever is true to himself or herself is thereby, and necessarily, true to all others,* and the whole social question will be solved. *The barter and sale of wives stands on the same moral footing as the barter and sale of slaves.* The god-implanted human affections cannot, and will not, be any longer subordinated to these external, legal restrictions and conventional engagements. *Every human being belongs to himself or herself by a higher title than any which, by surrenders or arrangements or promises, he or she can confer upon any other human being. Self-ownership is inalienable.* These truths are the latest and greatest discoveries in true science. . . ."

So much for the interviewing which was to have been published some months ago; but when it failed or was suppressed, I was still so far undecided that I took no steps in the matter, and had no definite plan for the future in respect to it, until the events as I have recited then, which occurred at Boston. Since then I have not doubted that I must make up my mind definitely to act aggressarily in this matter, and to use the facts in my knowledge to compel a more wide-spread discussion of the social question. I take the step deliberately, as an agitator and social revolutionist, which is my profession. . . .

I believe, as the law of peace, *in the right of privacy*, in the sanctity of individual relations. It is nobody's business but their own, in the absolute view, what Mr. Beecher and Mrs. Tilton have done, or may choose at any time to do, as between themselves. And the world needs, too, to be taught just that lesson. . . . It is not, therefore, Mr. Beecher as the individual that I pursue, but Mr. Beecher as the representative man: Mr. Beecher as a power in the world; and Mr. Beecher as my auxiliary in a great war for freedom, or Mr. Beecher as a violent enemy and a powerful hindrance to all that I am bent on accomplishing.

To Mr. Beecher, as the individual citizen, I tender, therefore, my humble apology, meaning and deeply feeling what I say, for this or any interference on my part, with his private conduct. I hold that Mr. Tilton himself, that Mrs. Beecher herself, have no more right to inquire, or to know or to spy over, with a view to knowing, what has transpired between Mr. Beecher and Mrs. Tilton than they have to know what I ate for breakfast, or where I shall spend my next evening; and that Mr. Beecher's congregation and the public at large have just as little right to know or to inquire. I hold that the so-called morality of society is a complicated mass of sheer impertinence and a scandal on the civilization of this advanced century, that the system of social espionage under which we live is damnable, and that the very first axiom of a true morality is for the people *to mind their own business,* and learn to respect, religiously, the social freedom and the sacred social privacy of all others; but it was the paradox of Christ, that as the Prince of Peace, he still brought on earth, *not peace* but *a sword.* It is the paradox of life that, in order to have peace, we must first have war; and it is the paradox of my position that, believing in the right of privacy and in the perfect right of Mr. Beecher socially, morally and divinely to have sought the embraces of Mrs. Tilton, or of any other woman or women whom he loved and who loved him, and being a promulgator and a public champion of those very rights, I still invade the most secret and sacred affairs of his life, and drag them to the light and expose him to the opprobrium and vilification of the public. I do again, and with deep sincerity, ask his forgiveness. But the case is exceptional, and what I do I do for a great purpose. The social world is in the very agony of its new birth, or, to resume the warlike simile, the leaders of progress are in the very act of storming the last fortress of bigotry and error. Somebody must be hurled forward into the gap. I have the power, I think, to compel Mr. Beecher to go forward and to do the duty for humanity from which he shrinks; and I should, myself, be false to the truth if I were to shrink from compelling him. . . . I believe I see clearly and prophetically for him in the future a work a hundred times greater than all he has accomplished in the past. I believe, as I have said, a wise Providence, or, as I term it, and believe it to be, the conscious and well calculated interference of the spirit world, has forecast and prepared these very events as a part of the drama of this great social revolution. . . .

So again, it was not the coming together of these two loving natures in the most intimate embrace, nor was it that nature blessed that embrace with the natural fruits of love which was the bad element in this whole transaction. They, on the contrary, were good elements, beautiful and divine elements, and among God's best things for man.

The evil and the whole evil in this whole matter, then, lies elsewhere. It lies in a false and artificial or manufactured opinion, in respect to this very question of what is good or what is evil in such matters. It lies in the belief that society has the right to prohibit, to prescribe and regulate, or in any manner to interfere with the private love manifestations of its members, any more than it has to prescribe their food and their drink. It lies in the belief consequent upon this, that lovers own their lovers, husbands their wives and wives their husbands, and that they have the right to complain of, to spy over, and to interfere, even to the extent of murder, with every other or outside manifestation of love. It lies in the *compulsory hypocrisy and systematic falsehood* which is thus enforced and inwrought into the very structure of society, and in the consequent and wide-spread injury to the whole community.

VI
Sexuality and Gynecology
in the Nineteenth Century

ON Female Health in America
by Catharine Beecher*

Catharine Beecher's attention to the circumstances of American women, and the need to restructure their education and attitudes to fit their responsibilities, included a great concern over the lack of female healthiness and vigor. For girls' schools she recommended physical education as well as domestic education. The following excerpt comes from her *Letters to the People on Health and Happiness*.

On FEMALE HEALTH IN AMERICA

STATISTICS OF FEMALE HEALTH

During my extensive tours in all portions of the Free States, I was brought into most intimate communion, not only with my widely-diffused circle of relatives, but with very many of my former pupils who had become wives and mothers. From such, I learned the secret domestic history both of those I visited and of many of their intimate friends. And oh! what heartaches were the result of these years of quiet observation of the experience of my sex in domestic life. How many young hearts have revealed the fact, that what they had been trained to imagine the highest earthly felicity, was but the beginning of care, disappointment, and sorrow, and often led to the extremity of mental and physical suffering. Why was it that I was so often told that "young girls little imagined what was before them when they entered married life"? Why did I so often find those united to the most congenial and most devoted husbands expressing the hope that their daughters would never marry? For years these were my quiet, painful conjectures.

But the more I traveled, and the more I resided in health establishments, the more the conviction was pressed on my attention that there was a terrible decay of female health all over the land, and that this evil was bringing with it an incredible extent of individual, domestic, and social suffering, that was increasing in a most alarming ratio. At last, certain developments led me to take decided measures to obtain some

* From Catharine Beecher, *Letters to the People on Health and Happiness* (New York: Harper & Bros., 1855), pp. 121–123, 129–130, 132–138.

263

reliable statistics on the subject. During my travels the last year I have sought all practicable methods of obtaining information, and finally adopted this course with most of the married ladies whom I met, either on my journeys or at the various health establishments at which I stopped.

I requested each lady first to write the *initials* of *ten* of the married ladies with whom she was best acquainted in her place of residence. Then she was requested to write at each name, her impressions as to the health of each lady. In this way, during the past year, I obtained statistics from about two hundred different places in almost all the Free States.

Before giving any of these, I will state some facts to show how far they are reliable: In the first place, the *standard of health* among American women is so low that few have a correct idea of *what a healthy woman is*. I have again and again been told by ladies that they were "perfectly healthy," who yet, on close inquiry, would allow that they were subject to frequent attacks of neuralgia, or to periodic nervous headaches, or to local ailments, to which they had become so accustomed, that they were counted as "nothing at all." A woman who has tolerable health finds herself so much above the great mass of her friends in this respect, that she feels herself a prodigy of good health.

In the next place, I have found that women who enjoy universal health are seldom well informed as to the infirmities of their friends. Repeatedly I have taken accounts from such persons, that seemed singularly favorable, when, on more particular inquiry, it was found that the greater part, who were set down as perfectly healthy women, were habitual sufferers from serious ailments. The delicate and infirm go for sympathy, not to the well and buoyant, but to those who have suffered like themselves. . . .

It must be remembered, that in regard to those marked as "sickly," "delicate," or "feeble," there can be no mistake, the knowledge being in all cases *positive*, while those marked as "well" may have ailments that are not known. For multitudes of American women, with their strict notions of propriety, and their patient and energetic spirit, often are performing every duty entirely silent as to any suffering or infirmities they may be enduring. . . .

[Here the statistics are entered, showing the large majority to be either delicate or sickly.]

I will now add my own personal observation. First, in my own family connection: I have nine married sisters and sisters-in-law, all of them either delicate or invalids, except two. I have fourteen married female cousins, and not one of them but is either delicate, often ailing, or an invalid. In my wide circle of friends and acquaintance all over the land out of my family circle, the same impression is made. In Boston I can not remember but one married female friend who is perfectly healthy. In Hartford, Conn., I can think of only one. In New Haven, but one. In Brooklyn, N. Y., but one. In New York city, but one. In Cincinnati, but one. In Buffalo, Cleveland, Chicago, Milwaukee, Detroit, those whom I have visited are either delicate or invalids. I am not able to recall, in my immense circle of friends and acquaintance all over the Union, so many as *ten* married ladies born in this century and country, who are perfectly sound, healthy, and vigorous. Not that I believe there are not more than this among the friends with whom I have associated, but among all whom I can bring to mind of whose health I have any accurate knowledge, I can not find this number of entirely sound and healthy women.

Another thing has greatly added to the impression of my own observations, and that is the manner in which my inquiries have been met. In a majority of cases, when I have asked for the number of perfectly healthy women in a given place, the first impulsive answer has been "not one." In other cases, when the reply has been more favorable, and I have asked for specifics, the result has always been such as to diminish the number calculated, rather than to increase it. With a few exceptions the persons I have asked, who had not directed their thoughts to the subject, and took a favorable view of it, have expressed surprise at the painful result obtained in their own immediate circle.

But the thing which has pained and surprised me the most is the result of inquiries among the country-towns and industrial classes in our country. I had supposed that there would be a great contrast between the statements gained from persons from such places, and those furnished from the wealthy circles, and especially from cities. But such has not been the case. It will be seen that the larger portion of the accounts inserted in the preceding pages are from country-towns, while a large portion of the worst accounts were taken from the industrial classes.

As another index of the state of health among the industrial classes may be mentioned these facts: During the past year I made my usual inquiry of the wife of a Methodist clergyman, who resided in a small country-town in New York. Her reply was, "There are no healthy women where I live, and my husband says he would travel a great many miles for the pleasure of finding one."

In another case I conversed with a Baptist clergyman and his wife, in Ohio, and their united testimony gave this result in three places where his parishioners were chiefly of the industrial class. They selected at random ten families best known in each place:

Worcester, Ohio: Women in perfect health, two. In medium health, one. *Invalids, seven.*

Norwalk, Ohio: Women perfectly healthy, one, but doubtfully so. Medium, none. *Invalids, nine.*

Cleveland, Ohio: Women in perfect health, one. Medium health, two. *Invalids, seven.*

In traveling at the West the past winter, I repeatedly conversed with drivers and others among the laboring class on this subject, and always heard such remarks as these: "Well! it is strange how sickly the women are getting!" "Our women-folks don't have such health as they used to do!" . . .

Let these considerations now be taken into account. The generation represented in these statistics, by universal consent, is a feebler one than that which immediately preceded. Knowing the changes in habits of living, in habits of activity, and in respect to *pure air*, we properly infer that it must be so, while universal testimony corroborates the inference.

The present generation of parents, then, have given their children, so far as the mother has hereditary influence, feebler constitutions than the former generation received, so that most of our young girls have started in life with a more delicate organization than their mothers. Add to this the sad picture given in a former letter of all the abuses of health suffered by the young during their early education, and what are the present prospects of the young women who are now entering married life?

This view of the case, in connection with some dreadful developments which will soon be indicated, proved so oppressive and exciting that it has been too painful and exhausting to attempt any investigation as to the state of health among young girls. But every where I go, mothers are constantly saying, "What shall I do? As soon as my little girl begins school she has the headache." Or this—"I sent my daughter to such a boarding-school, but had to take her away on account of her health."

The public schools of our towns and cities, where the great mass of the people are to be educated, are the special subject of remark and complaint in this respect.

Consider also that "man that is born of a woman" depends on her not only for the constitutional stamina with which he starts in life, but for all he receives during the developments of infancy and the training of childhood, and what are we to infer of the condition and prospects of the other sex now in the period of education?

ABUSES OF MEDICAL TREATMENT

Some of the results of experience and observation to be set forth in this letter, are of a description the most difficult of all possible to be brought before the public; and yet, when they are fully comprehended, it is certain that every benevolent and intelligent person must say, that nothing but the most selfish timidity would prompt to any other course.

A few preliminary words on the subject of delicacy and propriety will not be inappropriate. In regard to this, all persons agree that there are such qualities as genuine, pure, and proper modesty and delicacy, and that above almost any other virtues, these are desirable in a woman. There is no less unanimity as to the existence of a mawkish, false, and ridiculous excess, which goes by the name of prudery, false delicacy, mock modesty, and the like. Now, is there any reliable rule for our guidance in discriminating between the true and the false?

No doubt there is, and it is this: There are certain objects which are to be excluded from sight and from pictures, and there are certain topics which are to be entirely shut out from ordinary conversation. All persons, in all ages, agree as to what these objects and subjects are. And the progress of nations, both in civilization and moral worth, are distinctly shown by their less or greater strictness in these respects.

But there is a second rule not less stringent, and that is: when is it necessary in order to save from sickness, suffering, and death, or from moral contamination, to speak on these subjects, it should not only be done as fully as the case demands, but done with such an unembarrassed and full conviction of purity and rectitude, as makes it as easy and natural as it is to speak on ordinary topics.

With these rules for our guidance, the American people deserve to be placed higher than any other nation, as it regards obedience to the laws of true delicacy and refinement. Some of those topics referred to, are, even in the highest circles in England, introduced at times when there is not the least necessity for such freedoms. In France the latitude allowed is still greater, and it will be found that just in proportion as a country rises in civilization, in general culture, and *in respect for, and obedience to the Bible,* do these rules become more and more respected. The reverse is equally true, till in our downward progress we come to savages, who have almost no rules of delicacy or refinement.

But still, the American people have erred in not fully applying the second rule of propriety on these subjects. Their strictness in regard to the first has not been excessive, but their *want of discrimination in applying the second,* has led to much suffering, sickness, and death, and what is worse, to moral contamination. It is under the guidance of these rules that this letter has been written and should be read.

During the later periods of my investigations in regard to health, I became aware, not only of the general decay of the health of my own sex, but of the terrible suffering, both physical and mental, produced by internal organic displacements, resulting chiefly from a general debility of constitution, and various abuses already indicated. And what seemed the more shocking, was the fact that so many patients of this class were young girls.

But when the fact was ascertained that, in multitudes of cases, there was no possible remedy for this appalling evil but such *daily mechanical operations, both external and internal,* as are indicated in an article from a medical writer on another page, and that this was in most cases performed with bolted doors and curtained windows, and with no one present but patient and operator, there was a painful apprehension of evils which foreshadowed future revelations. Finally, by a most remarkable combination of circumstances, developments were made and, without any prosecuting of the matter by me, facts were presented from various quarters of a most astounding nature. But before indicating these facts, some farther incidental experience should be detailed that would render what will be stated less improbable.

In my travels I have met persons of both sexes, of the highest cultivation and refinement, whose conduct was every way reputable, and whose morals were never in any way impeached, who freely advocated the doctrine that there was no true marriage but the union of persons who were in love; that such union needed not legal or religious rites, and that it was those only who were held together by such restraints, who, having ceased to love each other, were guilty of adultery in the only proper sense of the word. I have seen books and papers freely circulated that advocate the same view by the most plausible arguments.

Then, again, there are articles on physiology circulated freely, that maintain that the exercise of all the functions of body and mind is *necessary to health,* and that no perfectly-developed man or woman is possible, so long as any of the functions and propensities are held in habitual constraint. With these creeds is usually combined an entire want of reverence for the Bible as *authoritative* in teaching truth or regulating morals.

Let us now suppose the case of a physician, neither better nor worse than the majority of that honorable profession. He has read the writings of the semi-infidel school, till he has lost all reverence for the Bible as *authoritative* in faith or practice. Of course he has no guide left but his own feelings and notions. Then he gradually adopts the above views in physiology and social life, and really believes them to be founded on the *nature of things,* and the intuitive teachings of his own mind. Next he has patients of interesting person and character put under his care, and he very naturally takes the means, which these books and papers in his reach afford, to lead them to adopt *his views of truth and right* on these subjects. Then he daily has all the opportunities indicated. Does any one need more than to hear these facts to know what the not un-frequent results must be? . . .

These things being premised, I would state that, *during the last two years,* facts have been brought to my knowledge of a most shocking nature, and from the most unimpeachable sources. The information relied on was not received at second hand, but from ladies of the highest character and position, and involved narratives of their own hazards and escapes.

In other cases, most mournful histories were given from direct and reliable quarters of the most terrible wrongs perpetrated without any possibility of redress, except by a publicity that would inflict heavier penalties on the victims than on the wrong-doers. . . .

A terrific feature of these developments has been the *entire helpless-ness* of my sex, amidst present customs and feelings, as to any *redress* for such wrongs, and the reckless and conscious impunity felt by the wrong-doers on this account. What can a refined, delicate, sensitive woman do when thus insulted? The dreadful fear of *publicity* shuts her lips and restrains every friend. And it would seem, from some of the cases here indicated, as if it was the certainty of this that withdrew restraint, so that the very highest, not only in character but in position, have not escaped. When *such as these* have been thus assailed, who can hope to be safe?

Another alarming circumstance has been the character of several of the physicians implicated. After intimate acquaintance with some of them, I was impressed with the belief that they were, at least, men of benevolence and professional honor, while in some cases their conversation and deportment led to the hope that they were persons of consistent piety. Of course the painful inquiry has arisen, how can a woman *ever know* to whom she may safely intrust herself or her child in such painful and peculiar circumstances? No doubt the medical profession embraces multitudes of persons of the highest delicacy, honor, and principle, and those who are in long and close proximity can be sure of their rectitude. But how can *the public* discriminate? Some of these guilty men were receiving patients sent to their care by the *regular* physicians, while the great body of their patients, who had escaped all knowledge of their guilt, were earnest in their representations of their high character.

Another painful consideration is the number of cases, the short space of time in which these developments have been made, the fact that they came, as it were, by accident, and that they were met in so many different quarters; these things of course produce a strong apprehension that the extent of the evil is not by any means confined to the cases thus disclosed.

Communication from Mrs. R. B. Gleason
of the Elmira Water Cure*

The following information was communicated to Catharine Beecher at her request by Mrs. R. B. Gleason, who had practiced medicine for ten years at the Elmira Water-Cure establishment, devoting herself mainly to problems of females. Mrs. Gleason had first studied medicine with her physician husband, but managed to gain attendance at two courses of medical lectures, and received a medical diploma. The "Water-Cure," which achieved some popularity in the mid-nineteenth century, was a method employing hot and cold water packs that were applied to and wrapped around the body to remedy a variety of ills.

COMMUNICATION FROM MRS. R. B. GLEASON

SYMPTOMS OF PELVIC DISPLACEMENT, AND THEIR TREATMENT

The fact that the development of this particular form of disease among women, until lately, has been rare, and that there has been but little popular published information on the subject, has led to other incidental evils which need to be noticed.

The pelvic organs are subject to a great variety of displacements, and of functional and organic diseases. And yet they all have so many symptoms in common, that it requires not only good anatomical, pathological, and physiological knowledge, but close and well-cultivated diagnostic powers to decide *which* organ is diseased, and *how* it is diseased. For example, sometimes a displacement of the uterus will cause a sense of weight, dragging, and throbbing, accompanied by pain in the back and in front of the hips. But inflammation, ulceration, and induration of this organ will produce precisely the same results; and sometimes *mere nervous debility* in these parts will induce these symptoms, especially when the imagination is excited in reference to the subject. It also is often the case that extreme prolapsus occurs *in which there is no pain at all.*

* Communication from Mrs. Gleason, Note 1, pp. 7–13, in *Letters to the People on Health and Happiness* by Catharine Beecher (New York: Harper & Bros., 1855).

So also diseases of the urinary eyst are indicated by symptoms precisely similar to those which mark the disease of the adjacent organ. These organs lying in close proximity, and supplied with nerves from the same source, would necessarily sympathize, and show disease by similar symptoms. Just as in the toothache, many a one has been unable to point out the diseased tooth. How much more difficulty exists in a case where most women are profoundly ignorant on the subject!

It has become a very common notion, that when any local displacement of the pelvic organs occur, a woman must cease to use her arms, cease to exercise vigorously, and keep herself on the bed much of her time. All which, in most cases, is exactly the three things which she ought not to do. And thus it is that, when from want of fresh air and exercise, and from the many pernicious practices that debilitate the female constitution, the pelvic organs indicate debility, and these nerves begin to ache, immediately a harness is put on for local support, and the bed becomes the constant resort. And thus the muscular debility and nervous irritability are increased. And yet, all that is needed is fresh air, exercise, simple diet, and *proper* mental occupation.

In this condition, perhaps, resort is had to some ignorant or inexperienced practitioner, who has some patent supporter to sell, or who has some secret and wonderful method of curing such diseases. Then commences, in many cases, a kind of local treatment most trying to the feelings, *which is but seldom required,* and which, in a majority of cases, results in no benefit.

Many a one has recited to me the mental and physical suffering she has endured for months, in such a course of treatment, and all to no purpose. A touching case of this kind recently occurred, in the case of a beautiful young lady, who was a listener to a course of lectures on the pelvis and its diseases, given by me to the graduating class of a female seminary. At the close, she came to me, and with tearful eyes and a quivering lip, she said, "I see now why all I have suffered in body and mind from my physician is worse than useless. I see now that I have never had the disease for which I have been treated. Is it not shocking that I should have suffered what was so needless, when my physician did or ought to have known better?"

Woman's trusting confiding nature is beautiful; but oh! how much it needs to be protected by an intelligence on such subjects, that will enable her properly to exercise her own judgment! And surely in such cases, above all others, a woman should be sure that her medical adviser has had a proper education, and possesses a well-established moral character.

EFFECTS OF IMAGINATION IN REFERENCE TO THESE DISEASES

Besides the evils of misunderstanding and mistreating these affections, we have a host of evils from the effects of imagination. Multitudes of women, who hear terrific accounts of the nature of these complaints, and of the treatment that is inevitable, have their imagination so excited that aches and pains that are really trifling become magnified into all the symptoms of the dreaded evil. They betake themselves to bed, become more and more nervous as they give up air, exercise, and occupation; and thus drag out a useless life, a burden to themselves and to their families. Again and again, I have had such cases brought to me, where for years they could not leave their beds or walk at all, when I had nothing to do but make them understand their own organism, and convince them that they needed little else except to get up and go to work in order to be healthy women. It is such cases that furnish a large portion of the "wonderful cures" that attract patients into the hands of some poorly-qualified practitioners.

It is probable that thousands of women who are suffering from pain in the back and pelvic evils, and who either will soon be invalids or imagine themselves so, could be relieved entirely by obeying these directions:

1. Wash the whole person on rising in cool water. Dress loosely, and let *all* the weight of clothing rest on the shoulders.

2. Sleep in a well-ventilated room; exercise the muscles a great deal, especially those of the arms and trunk, taking care to lie down and rest as soon as fatigue is felt.

3. Take a sitting-bath ten minutes at a time, in the middle of the forenoon and afternoon, with water at 85, reducing it gradually each day till at 60. Let the water reach above the hip, and while bathing rub and press the abdomen *upward*.

Wear a wet double girdle by night around the lower part of the body. Make it one-third of a yard wide; wring it well, and when on, cover it with double cotton flannel. If pain and weakness are felt, wear it by day also, adding clothing enough to prevent chilliness.

EFFECTS OF THESE COMPLAINTS ON CHARACTER
AND DOMESTIC HAPPINESS

My heart aches when I see how the mass of women, by ignorance and by blind bondage to custom and fashion, bring on themselves pangs innumerable and premature old age. Many a blooming bride at twenty, finds herself, at thirty, wrinkled and care-worn; unhappy as a wife, unreasonable as a mother, and almost useless as a citizen. While some have inherited too much physical depravity to be preserved by any methods in good health, the majority have been most miserably spendthrift in using up their vital powers, thus rendering the joy of their married life as evanescent as the morning cloud. Many a wife who, but for her physical condition, would have been happy in her social relation, says to me, with a sigh, "I ought never to have been married, for my life is one prolonged agony. I could endure it myself alone, but the thought that I am, from year to year, becoming the mother of those who are to partake of and perpetuate the misery that I endure, makes me so wretched that I am well-nigh distracted."

A wife of more than ordinary intelligence and attainments, who had, during the ten years of her married life, been suffering from these evils, asked me, after I had examined her case, if I thought it curable. I told her she could be made more comfortable, but such organic changes *could never be cured.* She burst into tears, and said, "Oh, that I might die then!" I asked if she was weary of life? She said, "No, it is not on my own account, but my condition is such a trial to my husband; I wish I could give him freedom by taking rest to myself in the grave."

The young miss who wickedly wastes her health, and receives with an indifferent toss of the head all cautions in regard to health, little dreams of the bitter tears she will shed when it is too late for repentance to avail. The prospective husband may take great care to protect the fair but frail one of his choice; he may in after years fondly cherish the wife of his youth when she aches constantly and fades prematurely; still he has no helpmate—no one to double life's joys or lighten life's labors for him. Some sick women grow selfish and forget that, in a partnership such as theirs, others suffer when they suffer. Every true husband has but half a life who has a sick wife.

A few days since a gentleman living with his third wife, whom he had just placed under my care, said, "There is nothing that I have so much desired as a companion *in good health;* but it is what I have seldom enjoyed in all my married life." Then, with a sigh, he rose, and walked quickly to and fro in his spacious parlors, saying, "my home is again shaded by sickness and sorrow, and my last hope of domestic joy is blighted." His elegant residence and political honors could give him no enjoyment while his wife was an invalid.

A young husband, in thriving business, of naturally a hopeful heart, presents the case of his wife, and asks, "Can she ever be well? Will she ever have her former hopeful, loving, patient spirit?" Then the tears gathered as he said, "We used to be happy, but now, when I come from business, she can only tell of her suffering, and reproach me because I do not try more to relieve her." Then he added, by way of self-defense, "I do try to nurse her, and tend baby when I can be spared from business; I get the best help I can, but nothing satisfies—*she is so nervous!*" The wife, I found, had been brought up elegantly but indolently, and so neither body nor spirit were developed sufficiently to bear healthfully the changes which maternity induces.

There are no class of infirmities more likely to induce irritability of temper and depression of spirit than those that affect the pelvic organs. A husband, whose wife had spent some months with us as a patient, said afterward that he should consider her stay there the best investment he ever made, even if there had been no other improvement in his wife than the change in her temper.

PECULIAR INSTRUCTION NEEDED BY YOUNG CHILDREN

Through information gained from my husband, from other physicians, from teachers, from medical writers, and from the reports of insane hospitals, it has become clear to my mind that there are secret and terrific causes preying extensively upon the health and nervous energy of childhood and youth of both sexes, such as did not formerly exist, and such as demand new efforts to eradicate and prevent.

Parents and teachers all over the land need to be made aware that a secret vice is becoming frequent among children of both sexes, that is taught by servants and communicated by children at school. Indeed, it may result from accident or disease, with an innocent unconsciousness of the evil done, on the part of the child, while the practice may thus ignorantly be perpetuated to maturity. This practice leads to diseases of the most horrible description, to mania, and to fatuity. Death and the mad-house are the last resort of these most miserable victims.

To protect childhood and youth from this, it is not only needful to cultivate purity of mind and personal modesty, but to teach them, while quite young, that any fingering of the parts referred to involves terrible penalties. No such explicit information should be given as would tempt the incautious curiosity of childhood, but the child should be impressed with a sense of guilt and awful punishment as connected with *any thing* of this kind, that would instantly recur to mind if led by accident or instruction to this vice.

In regard to those who have already become victims, to a greater or less degree, to this vice, one caution is very important. Medical writers and others who have attempted to guard the young in this direction, have painted not only the danger but the wickedness of this practice, in such strong colors that, when a young person first discovers the nature of a practice that has been indulged with little conception of the danger or wrong, overaction on the fears and the conscience is not unfrequently the result. Such horror and despair sometimes ensue as almost paralyze any effort on the part of medical advisers to remedy the evil.

In all such cases, it is safest and best to assume that the sin is one of ignorance, and that the cure is almost certain if the directions given are strictly obeyed. Unstimulating diet, a great deal of exercise in the open air, daily ablution of the whole person, control of the imagination, and occupation of the mind in useful pursuits, will usually remedy the evil after its nature is understood.

In reference to *social*, as well as secret vices of this description, it seems to me the protection of ignorance should be preserved as long as possible, and yet, so that when such knowledge dawns, there shall immediately recur the needful impression of danger and sin. These duties belong especially to parents and teachers; and the circulation of books and papers, with the gross and pernicious information that many have recommended and practiced, involves, as it seems to me, most hazardous results.

FROM *The Young Woman's Book of Health* by William Alcott*

William Alcott (a cousin to Bronson Alcott) contributed to the health reform movement of the mid-nineteenth century, which included the Graham diet and hydropathy, or water cure. Advocates of this movement emphasized daily bathing, proper diet, and hygiene as the requisites for good health, and as the means to avoid doctors' methods such as "bleeding" and drugs. The recommended diet stressed whole grains, fruits, and vegetables, and frowned on animal foods and caffeinated beverages. Aside from numerous guides for young women,[1] Alcott published health-etiquette books for young men, and a "Physiology of Marriage."

From THE YOUNG WOMAN'S BOOK OF HEALTH

Were every thing as it should be in regard to the female; did she inherit a sound constitution; and were her whole education, physical, intellectual, and moral, such as is desirable,—the following would be among the natural and healthy developments of character.

The changes which, in our climate, and where there is no precocity, take place at about the age of fourteen, are numerous and striking. They are physical, intellectual, and moral. Let me speak, first, of those which are more purely physical.

Till the approach of the age above mentioned, it would not be very easy to distinguish the two sexes, by external form and appearance, unless it were by their dress. At this time, however, the following remarkable changes begin to be visible.

First, a sudden expansion of the cranium and the pelvis, owing to the fact that those portions of the human machinery which are contained within those cavities, have been suddenly enlarged. Especially is there an expansion of the lower part of the brain, and the upper part of the chest. Doubtless there is a determination of the blood, in greater quantity than before, to these parts.

* William A. Alcott, *The Young Woman's Book of Health* (New York: Miller, Orton, and Mulligan, 1855), pp. 119–127, 215–219, 243–249.

[1] Note Narcissa Whitman's recommendation of Alcott's books, *The Young Wife* and *The Young Mother*, in her letter to her sister.—Ed.

As a consequence of this change in the system, the female head becomes larger in proportion to the body than that of the male, and is much more elongated backward. The chest also becomes larger, though it must not be forgotten, that by the arrangement of the ribs with respect to it, it becomes, at the same time, rather shorter.

But, although the head is larger, the nerves are smaller and more delicate than those of the male. The sensibility and the imagination, however, become of a sudden greatly developed and increased. As a necessary result, there is an increased susceptibility to impressions.

In the second place, the muscular or moving powers of the body also differ. The muscles and bones are, relatively, smaller. Their activity is, at the same time, increased. What makes the muscles appear smaller than they really are, however, is the fact that the spaces between them are better filled with cellular substance, and sometimes, also, with fat, giving to the parts a more rounded appearance.

Thirdly, the skin undergoes changes. It was delicate before; but now it suddenly becomes much more so. It is not only finer, but more polished and transparent. It is at once exquisitely sensitive and beautiful. Its sympathies are equally remarkable, as well as equally rapid in their development.

Finally, there is even a change in the form of the limbs. The hips appear not only broader, but larger; and what, in our own sex, would be a deformity, becomes in woman a beauty. In man, the shoulders are much broader than the hips. In adult woman, the reverse is true.

The shoulders, in woman, may indeed sometimes appear enlarged, but it is in consequence of an expansion of the fore part of the chest, externally, or as a consequence of fashion in dress.

On the whole, the organization, especially that of the nervous and muscular systems, is such as to impart a tendency to nervous and spasmodic diseases, and to render them peculiarly liable to be excited and moved by extra stimulants, external and internal, and both moral and physical.

In summing up these changes, allow me to quote from Dr. Morrill, in his work on the Physiology of Woman, and her Diseases, at p. 41.

"The young girl who, till now, was an equivocal, non-sexual creature, becomes a woman, in her countenance, and in all the parts of her body, in the elegance of her stature, and beauty of her form, the delicacy of her features, in her constitution, in the sonorous and melodious tones of her voice, in her sensibility and affections, in her character, her inclinations, her tastes, her habits, and even her maladies. Very soon, all the traits of resemblance between the two sexes are found to be effaced.

"The physiognomy of the young woman has now acquired a new expression; her gestures bear the stamp of her feelings; her language has become more touching and pathetic; her eyes, full of life, but languishing, announce a mixture of desires and fears, of modesty and love.

"Her tastes, her enjoyments, and her inclinations, are modified, like the rest; her most pressing want is to experience frivolous emotions; she is passionately given to the dance, shows, and company; the curiosity so natural to her sex, acquires new force and activity. She devours books of romance, or more than ever fervent in devotion, is excited by the expansive passions, and particularly by religious piety, which is to her a sort of love.

"At this brilliant period of her life, her moral, which depends upon her physical condition, undergoes great mutation. The young girl becomes more tender-hearted, more sensitive, more compassionate, and appears to attach herself to every thing about her. The new sensations of her soul make her timid in approaching the companions of her childhood; a strange trouble, a sort of restlessness, an agitation, before unknown, are the heralds of a power, whose existence she does not even suspect."

Let this, then, be regarded as the standard of healthy development and healthy womanhood—the beau ideal of healthy female existence, beyond the age of fourteen or fifteen. Instead, however, of the regular developments above mentioned, we have numerous irregularities. . . .

Young females who are precocious, though naturally reserved and pure, sometimes, under abnormal circumstances and the influence of bad associates, become the very reverse.

The erratic conduct to which they are thus led, by the combined influence of bodily and mental disease and miseducation appears in two different forms—solitary vice and social. I do not mean that these are not the result of a great variety of causes; but precocity will *often* account for them.

Instances occur, no doubt, in which there is both action and reaction. What I have spoken of as a mere effect, becomes, also, a cause. And this cause exists, *as* a cause, much earlier, I say again, as well as much more frequently, than is usually supposed.

Dr. Morrill speaks of solitary vice as existing among youth of both sexes to an alarming extent, and apologizes for mentioning it. But his apology is by no means necessary, if his broad statement is true,—and what medical man of large experience doubts it?—that thousands of our youth are being sacrificed to its shrine.

The consequences of this vice, whether we regard it in the light of cause or effect, are dreadful, both to the individual herself, and to society generally. For, if woman deteriorates, *all* deteriorate.

In reference, moreover, to its deteriorating effects, Boerhaave thus remarks: "It causes convulsions, emaciation, and pain in the membranes of the brain; it deadens the senses, particularly the sight; gives rise to dorsal consumption, and various other mental and bodily disorders."

He might have added much more. It makes the young unsocial, timid, shamefaced, unhappy. Conscious of guilt, they seem to imagine every one they meet with ready to suspect them. Imagining themselves unable to resist the impulses which they know are urging them downward, they gradually and insensibly become helpless in reality, and suffer themselves to be swept along in the downward current.

The result is, that, if healthy,—that is, by inheritance,—most persons go on in their mad career, for some time, without much fear; till of a sudden, unless something from without changes the current, they begin to verge towards insanity. Soon, if the cause continues in full operation, they pass, with rapidity, to absolute and remediless idiocy.

Nor is it easy to arrest their progress, even if we remove the cause, when once they have begun to approach the region of insanity. Few, indeed, are the cases found to be within the reach of the healing art. Or if, perchance, a few are recovered, it is, for the most part, with a shattered constitution. But the far greater part of our young men and young women, who fall into this destructive vice, terminate their usefulness and their days in a very different manner.

UTERINE MADNESS, OR NYMPHOMANIA

This disease, most happily, is rare. I have not seen half a dozen cases of it in twenty-five years. Indeed, I am not without hope that it is less frequent than formerly. And yet, as long as a single case of so dreadful a disease can be found, the young should be apprised of its existence and character. . . .

The best account I have seen of the causes of this disease is as follows.

The writer, having made the usual division into predisposing and exciting causes, thus goes on:—

"In the former should be included all circumstances capable of producing an exaltation of excitement in the brain and nervous system, such as the reading of lascivious and impassioned works, viewing voluptuous paintings, romantic conversations, associating with corrupt companions, frequent visits to balls or theatres, disappointed love, the too assiduous cultivation of the fine arts, the influence of imitation on beholding it in others, the abuse of aphrodisiac remedies, or of spirituous liquors, or of aromatics and perfumes, which excite too much the brain and general sensibility.

"The causes which act directly upon the genital organs (the exciting causes), and which may afterwards act sympathetically upon the brain, are masturbation, the abuse of coition, pruritus of the vulva, inflammation of the nymphae, clitoris, neck of the uterus and ovaries; to which we may add the irritation of ascarides in the rectum; and, finally, the use of drastic purgatives, and the internal or extensive external employment of cantharides."

One thing should be mentioned, in passing, concerning its resemblance to *pruritus*—mentioned above, as one of its causes. They are sometimes mistaken for each other. But they need not be. Nymphomania is accompanied by venereal desire; but in pruritus, though there is a most intolerable itching, there is seldom any sexual impulse or desire; indeed, it is usually the very reverse of all this.

Warm baths have been recommended in this disease; but, as it seems to me, without due consideration. I do not believe that any sensible practitioner would be willing to risk them. The cold bath—I mean the use of cold water on the whole surface of the body—is far preferable.

Indeed, the whole treatment, both external and internal, should be cooling. None but cooling drinks are at all admissible, and none but the most bland food. Farinaceous food,—bread of various kinds, arrowroot, sage, tapioca, rice, and potatoes,—with mild sub-acid fruits, and milk, is the best. Animal food, especially salted animal food, and old salted butter, should be avoided as carefully as if they were rank poison.

Opposed as I am to the use of medicine in most female diseases, my views of its application in nymphomania will be easily guessed. I regard it as not only useless in this disease, but positively and greatly hurtful. I never knew the least benefit derived from it.

There is one surgical operation which has occasionally been resorted to; but in a book for young women, it is entirely unnecessary to describe it. What they need is, to know the causes, that they may know how to prevent it. For here, if nowhere else in the wide world, prevention is better than cure—immensely better.

The Scriptures speak of a period in the early history of our world when the thoughts of mankind were only evil, and that continually. The thoughts and imagination of every female afflicted with this species of madness are in the same predicament.

It often happens, moreover, that these unhallowed thoughts and feelings are fed and nurtured by reading doubtful romances, if not even those books which are printed with a special design to excite lascivious feelings. This suggests an important item in the treatment of these persons. It consists in watching over and endeavoring to control and direct about their mental food, no less than their physical.

If the mind cannot be rightly directed in any other way, it may be advisable to travel, but not without a judicious companion, as a protector. But even in this there will be some danger of too great excitement. The country is preferable to the city, to travel in; and a private carriage better than the tumult and whirl of railroads and steamboats.

My views of feather beds are already fully known; but if there be a case in which, more than any other, they are inadmissible, it is that of nymphomania. The coarsest, most porous, and coolest beds are to be secured; and if a companion is admissible at all, a judicious selection should be made. Better sleep entirely alone than with those whose imprudence will tend to perpetuate the disease.

Nor should there be the least indulgence in late hours in the morning. The patient should leave the bed the instant she wakes. One evil connected with comfortables and feather beds is, that, by their unnatural warmth and stimulus, they tempt to late hours in the morning.

Artificial heat in sleeping-rooms for young women who are afflicted with this disease is also to be shunned with the greatest care and solicitude. They are of doubtful utility to any body; but here there is no apology for them.

The frequent recommendation to marry, as a means of removing the tendency to this disease, must not be received and acted upon without a good deal of qualification. It may be useful; but it is also true that it may be utterly inadmissible. On this point, consult the proper authorities.

PROLAPSUS UTERI

. . . Were it even true that young women were always to *remain* young women, it would still be necessary they should be informed of the nature, causes, and management of prolapsus. If only one in ten, or even one in twenty, is to suffer, the causes of suffering and means of prevention should be fully pointed out to them. But much more than this is true; for most young women expect one day to be old women; and, as Dr. Hamilton has well said, of all the chronic diseases arising from a local cause, to which women in civilized society are liable, prolapsus uteri, or displacement of the womb, is perhaps the most frequent.

I have said that the whole tendency of modern education is, directly or indirectly, to induce female disease, especially prolapsus. But perhaps it may be well to show, more particularly, *why* this is so.

Although the structure, position, and circumstances of the uterus are most admirably adapted to the free, and proper, and perfect discharge of all its offices when healthy, yet, in order to render it most efficient, it has been so arranged as to be somewhat exposed to disease whenever the usual causes of ill health, whether general or local, come to be applied. . . .

Under these circumstances, what is to be expected by those who know any thing of the habits of civic life, and especially of female life? What, indeed, but just what is seen and experienced—a world of female woe and suffering, and, of consequence, a world of physical deterioration? For when females, as a race, are suffering, all are so, and must be so, inevitably. . . .

But what *is* prolapsus uteri—that is, physiologically? For I find that very few, even of those who suffer from it, and who have been subjected to medical treatment, and have thus had opportunities to ask for information, are able to form any thing like a correct notion of its character.

By prolapsus, then, we mean the falling or sliding down of the uterus, so that its mouth—the os tincae—is too near the outside of the body. Sometimes, indeed, it slides down so far as actually to protrude as large as a child's head. In such cases, the vagina, or passage to the uterus, is turned inside out.

This, however, is not all. The internal organs that lie in the vicinity of the uterus, being thrown out of their respective places, also suffer much; especially the bladder and the ovaria. For the bladder is drawn down along with the uterus, and sometimes so situated, that the patient is compelled to make use of a catheter. The Fallopian tubes and ovaria also will be dragged down in a similar manner.

From what has been said of the weakness of the reproductive system in females, and of the causes which operate to produce it, may be readily inferred what might otherwise be repeated here, concerning the immediate or direct causes of prolapsus. The parts not only become weakened, but, by the pressure upon them, actually more thin and delicate than is natural. . . .

There are women who conceal this painful disease for many years, and even reach a very considerable old age in spite of it. And there can be little doubt that if, from the first of its appearance, such a course were pursued as a wise physician might prescribe, the number of this class might be greatly increased.

Owing, however, to ignorance, pride, fastidiousness, morbid delicacy, carelessness, and recklessness, very few ever pursue this wise course. Or, if they pursue it a little way, they soon tire. . . . But I have one more method of preventive treatment. . . .

It has been found that young women, whether in wedlock or out of it, when afflicted with prolapsus which seemed to be incurable, have, by becoming mothers, been entirely restored to health. In truth, it is even affirmed that some severe cases have been restored in this way.

The Murders of Marriage
by Mary Gove Nichols*

Restive in the bonds of a deplorable first marriage, which brought her one child and several miscarriages, Mary Gove Nichols embarked on a career of health reform. She began giving classes and public lectures on female physiology to women in Lynn and Boston in the late 1830s. Then, taking the definitive step of leaving her husband Hiram Gove, she continued counseling women through the 1840s, compounding her diagnoses and remedies from the Graham diet, the water cure, and phrenology. After she met and married T. L. Nichols in 1847–48, they set up a water-cure establishment in New York City. At the time they coauthored *Marriage* . . . , they were planning to set up an Institute of Desarrollo, or School of Life, where students would find the material and spiritual bases of life and free themselves from all "arbitrary despotisms" and "hypocritical virtues."

THE MURDERS OF MARRIAGE

People are constantly asking the question, What would become of children if married persons were allowed to separate? *Let me tell conservatism that nine-tenths of the children that now burden the world would never be born.* Couples are held together by their own prejudices and the pressure of public opinion till a child is born. This child belongs to the father, and he wants a housekeeper and a nurse for it; he wants some one to reputably supply the amative want; perhaps the woman may be attractive to him—besides, the whole social mechanism holds this couple as in a vice together. The wife may have an utter indifference to the husband, or a loathing and abhorrence of him; but she must bear more children as a condition of support, and for the privilege of keeping the babe of her love in her bosom—of having something to fill her poor, desolate heart, and compensate her for a life of impurity which her spirit revolts against, till its oft violated instincts are unable to distinguish good from evil. . . .

* T. L. Nichols, M.D., and Mrs. Mary S. Gove Nichols, *Marriage: Its History, Character and Results; Its Sanctities, and Its Profanities; Its Science and Its Facts* (New York: T. L. Nichols, 1854), pp. 200–202, 215–216, 223–224, 228–230, 240–242, 244–245.

The general idea and feeling, whether we know it or not, is that woman is property. She has no right to herself if she is married. Nine-tenths of the children born in marriage are not desired by the mother, often not by the father, though it is a great blessing that great love is born with them. Women have not, as a universal fact, the passion that asks the sexual indulgence. Vast numbers of the women of civilization have neither the sexual nor maternal passion. All women want love and support. They do not want to bear children, or to be harlots for this love or this support. In marriage as it at present exists, the instinct against bearing children and against submitting to the amative embrace, is almost as general as the love for infants after they are born. The obliteration of the maternal and sexual instincts in woman is a terrible pathological fact. It has not been defined by theologians, physicians, or political economists. People know no more its meaning than they know the meaning of purity in woman.

A healthy and loving woman is impelled to material union as surely, often as strongly, as man. Would it not be great injustice in our Heavenly Father to so constitute woman as to suffer the pangs of childbirth with no enjoyment of the union that gives her a babe. The truth is that healthy nerves give pleasure in the ultimates of love with no respect to sex; and the same exhausted and diseased nerves, that deny to woman the pleasures of love, give her the dreadful pangs of childbirth.

The apathy of the sexual instinct in woman is caused by the enslaved and unhealthy condition in which she lives. Many inherit from mothers, who are victims in unloving marriage, the diseased amativeness that makes them early subject to masturbation; and this habit destroys the health of the nervous system. Others inherit an apathetic state that does not impel them to any material union. Healthy and loving women are destroyed by being made bond-women, having no spontaneity, and bearing children more rapidly than they ought, and in unhealthy condition. . . .

People talk of the sanctity of marriage. Is there any sanctity where there is force on the one side, and fear on the other? And yet men have no faith in themselves, and less than none in women. They say, "We must keep to such a state as this for fear we should fall into something worse." The perpetuation of hate, discord, and impurity in children, is the lowest and worst that I can conceive for our human race. . . .

Because I speak of the false and evil, I am by no means unconscious of the good and true. There is much love and consequent sanctity in our marriages; but there are sad mistakes, and horrible, adulterous unions. When marriage becomes what it must be in a true freedom, *union in love*, it will be divinely beautiful. When it is a bargain, a sacrifice, made from other motives than affection, and, besides, is indissoluble, it is shocking to all true moral sense. When we consider love as alone sanctifying the union of the sexes, then we see the necessity of divorce, to prevent people living in adultery, who have married without love, or who have ceased to love after marriage. . . .

The hereditary evils to children born in a sensual and unloving marriage are everywhere visible. They are written in every lineament of the Present,—sensuality, sickness, suffering, weakness, imbecility, or outrageous crime. I speak what I know, and testify what I have seen in a long and varied medical practice, when I assert that masturbation in children, and every evil of sensuality, spring from the polluted hot-bed of a sensual and unloving marriage, where woman is subjected to a destroying sensualism during pregnancy and lactation. I have been consulted by mothers for children born without love, where the mother was subjected to intercourse during pregnancy. The children seemed incurable masturbators, and though with good intellect and much clear perception, and delicacy, and modesty, it was often a work of time, and much labor and care to cure them. I have also known cases where subsequent children, born in a second marriage which was loving and healthful, had no such tendency. They were pure from birth, as the first were impure. . . .

Another instance of this kind, though not so aggravated in its character, nor attended with like results, is revived in my memory. A lady of the finest intellect, most devoted piety, great fascination and charm of manner and qualities, but delicate and weak in health, was loved and sought in marriage by a truly great man; one of the best our present age has had the good fortune to produce. This lady was from an early age a victim of diseased amativeness in the form of solitary vice. Her standard of purity was that unconsciously adopted by the Church and the world, that a woman should be "chaste as ice";* that there should

* I remember a distinguished Physiologist once boasted to me that his wife was "chaste as ice." The poor creature was so destroyed by amative disease, that the

be no attraction felt by her, or, at least, manifested for the masculine principle; that all such attraction derogates from feminine purity and propriety. This lady, as hundreds of others have done, brought her disease and false virtue to me. She told me that she felt herself pure, that God had delivered her from all temptation to a sensual life. That though she loved her husband most tenderly, she had never the slightest sensual attraction toward him. He was a man of great strength, and delicacy, and beauty of character; she said though not delivered by God from the temptation to amative indulgence, he still respected her slightest wish, and was as separate from her, as if not her husband, and yet perfectly faithful to the bond of marriage.

She gave him great credit for his forbearance toward her, and his self government, but lamented very sincerely his temptations to a sensual life. In the early years of her marriage she had several times miscarried, proving that she had no right to be a mother, for she was placed in the best conditions for bearing her children, and yet was not able to nourish the foetus above three or four months. She told me the story with self righteous complacency, and yet she was full of sorrow for her husband. Whilst she talked, I silently took the measure of my auditor and patient. Could she understand me? Would she confess that she was a victim to masturbation? Could she know how false, diseased, and impure she was, and could she be made to see that her noble and self sacrificing husband was a true, pure and natural human being. I mentally answered my own questions in the affirmative.

"My dear," said I, "you are very sick and weak. Your nervous system is drained of its life. It is not natural, or true, for woman to be without the amative passion. It is a great wrong in her nature when she is deprived of the wish and power for amative pleasure. She is diseased, and this disease has a cause." "What is the cause?" said she, thoughtfully. "Atony of the nervous system from birth, or a diseased amativeness that causes solitary vice, and thus results in the same atonic condition which is termed virtue and purity in woman." I talked on in this way—she bowed her beautiful head in tears and deep humiliation. So sudden and

uterus was nearly or quite cancerous, and the marital union was of course a terror and a curse to her, in such a situation. The comfort the husband found in such condition was, that his wife was "chaste as ice"—that she would never be tainted by the breath of scandal—that she was a woman of undoubted piety and purity. Purity!! Pah!

woman-like was her perception, that she saw her life of falseness, her whole inheritance of evil, and all the injustice she had done her husband at a glance. . . .

The slavery, and consequent unsanctified sensuality of the present and past, have debased and degraded the world's idea of material union, until their thought is as impure as their deed. The human mind must be redeemed from this impurity and disgust, and love is the only redemption. The law of life and of growth, of all good, is—We must be free to act, so long as we do not unjustly interfere with the well-being of others. . . .

When a conservator of public morals, such as Horace Greeley, regards with horror the assertion that woman has the right to choose the father of her child, the fact proves much—alas! how much. It proves the low estate from which woman has just begun to emerge. She is degraded by law and custom even lower than the beasts which perish; and if one asserts her right to any ownership of herself, so-called moralists, and philosophers reject the thought with horror. Is there no sacredness left in this man's heart? Does he wish to be the father of babes when the mother has no choice, when she would come loathing to his arms, feeling that the union scarred her soul for eternity, and with the thought of murder in her mind rather than bear the babe thus forced upon her? Is this Mr. Greeley's morality when he says, "I utterly abhor what you term the right of a woman to choose the father of her child"? Alas for woman if men are not better than this creed! They are, and they are not. The best are enslaved by law, custom and organization, and go on murdering frail wives, not daring to think of any escape from the necessity, not even when their material wants are healthful and legitimate, and a wife utterly unfit to be a wife or a mother. I have no doubt that Mr. Greeley has at times the conception of what love and purity are, and what they would do for the world in pure births; but the bondage of public opinion, and his own nature is upon him. He has not leisure or ability to comprehend a world's want, and he only asks that mankind be saved from a worse estate than their miserable present; and the only means of salvation he sees is law, binding people to an outward decency, if possible, whilst their internal life is a foul, rotting ulcer—and if their children live they perpetuate the sad state of their parents. Thus the world is filled with disease, misery, crime and premature death. . . .

I clip an illustration from yesterday's paper:

"CHILD SUPPOSED TO BE MURDERED BY ITS MOTHER.—On Thursday a servant girl living at the house of S. T. Wright, Esq., West Morrissiania, who was pregnant, was suspected by some of the family of intending to use foul means to dispose of her infant when born. They followed her; finding she was likely to be detected, she drew a knife she had in her hand across the child's throat, but in her hurry she did not strike the throat, but nearly cut off its jaw, then throwing it down the sink, left it. The alarm was immediately spread, and the neighbors, throwing off the building, discovered the child already dead. An investigation was held by Coroner Johnson, which resulted in the arrest of the inhuman mother."—*Tribune*.

"If a black mother or slave at the south had committed such a crime, we should have been told that it was to save the child from the horrors of slavery, and another 'Uncle Tom's Cabin' would be written. But black mothers do not commit such follies, and the crime is too common among our white servants to meet more than a passing notice."—*Day Book*.

Here is a crime, committed under one oppressive institution, made a sort of indirect apology for another institution which is nearly parallel in its evils. This servant girl, who is the horror of almost all who read of her crime, may have a more natural and loving heart than many who shudder at her sin. She may have been utterly maddened by her terrible conditions, and therefore irresponsible. . . . And who caused the crime and the punishment? Who but a society steeped in murder and adultery? for at this same time I had a lady patient, the wife of a man worth half a million, who confessed to me that she had six times had abortion procured, and by her family physician, too. "I could not bear children to such a brute," were her words of excuse.

Again the question occurs, What is to become of children if married people are allowed to separate? The answer again is what becomes of them now?

I believe that the number of children murdered in marriage before birth, is as much greater than by unmarried women, as the proportion of children born in marriage, is greater than the number of illegitimate offspring. Society asks, What is to become of children that women are forced to bear? Society provides prisons for them, and the death penalty now. Might it not be well to leave women the liberty to choose whether they will bear children to be hung, or not?

by Dr. George Austin,
with Mary Livermore's Recommendatory Letter*

Dr. Austin's book, written in the last quarter of the nineteenth century, followed the mode of earlier medical advice books addressed to women, but
incorporated Dr. Austin's Darwinian insights. Mary Livermore, veteran of the
Sanitary Commission, and active W.C.T.U. and women's-suffrage worker, was
willing to recommend it, as her letter shows. Perhaps anything was preferable to Dr. E. A. Clarke's infamous *Sex in Education* (1875), which maintained
that intense mental effort by women damaged their reproductive capacities,
and that higher education for women thus endangered the human species.

From *PERILS OF AMERICAN WOMEN*

RECOMMENDATORY LETTER

Melrose, July 19, 1882

Dear Mr. Fairchild,

I have read Dr. Austin's book *thoroughly*. Have re-read some portions. It is an improvement on any of the books for women that I have
read—and I am familiar with all that have been published in my day.
And this seems to me its characteristic excellence: while it speaks plainly
and warningly of the perils which encompass the path of woman, both
physically and mentally, when she violates the laws of her being, it does
not start out with the monstrous assumption that woman is a natural
invalid. Nor does it give directions, that followed, would tend to make
and keep her so.

It was from this false standpoint that the impertinent book of Dr.
E. A. Clarke was written as also the sentimental one of Michelet, and
others of the same sort. They have done no end of mischief—whistling
down the brakes on the wheels of progress for woman.

Dr. Austin's book is full of hope, and will prove as powerful a tonic

* George L. Austin, M.D., *Perils of American Women, or, a Doctor's Talk with
Maiden, Wife, and Mother*, with a recommendatory letter from Mrs. Mary A.
Livermore (Boston: Lee and Shepard, 1883), pp. 28–40, 183–189, 223–225.

to young women of ambition and promise, as those of Clarke, Michelet
& Co., have proved discouraging and enfeebling. Before them lies health
and vigor, and the enjoyment and usefulness coming from both—*if they
will acquaint themselves with the laws of their being, and will obey
them.*

I am especially thankful for Dr. Austin's disparaging words concerning the unclean army of "gynecologists," who seem desirous to
convince women that they possess but one set of organs—and that these
are always diseased. I regard these specialists as a pestiferous set. And
the bare mention of them is the same in its effect upon me, as a red rag
is to a bull.

I do not see how the most prurient can be moved to salacious
thoughts by this book or its plates. Not knowing its author, I rise from
the reading of his book with the conviction that he is a clean man. It is
a profanation for some to discuss these topics—but I have not experienced one emotion of revolt against Dr. Austin's treatment of them.
I will bring you the sheets of the book when I next go to Boston.

Yrs. truly,
Mary A. Livermore

THE RELATIONS BETWEEN LOVE AND MARRIAGE

With the first manifestation of the female sexual instincts, as we have
seen, there ensues an indescribable change in feeling for the opposite
sex. It is then that love begins to dawn,—that form of love which consti-
tutes the foundation of human nature, which is the motor power of all
action and the principal of all the passions. As it exists between the boy
and the girl, it is an attraction towards the beautiful, the good, and the
true; but between man and woman it is that secret affinity which draws
one to the other, enchains them by the sweet sympathies of the soul and
the irresistible attraction of the senses, and confounds them in a voluptuous union, indeed, for the perpetuation of the species. How potent is
the instinct! The Creator has lodged it within us in order that we may
continue his work, charging us to repair the ravages of death by a
continual transmission of life.

Love seems to respond to two inseparable necessities of human nature,
—the desire of living in another, and the desire of renewed life in another.

Man loves because he abhors isolation, because he has need of immortality even on this earth; has the desire of surviving himself, of prolonging his existence, in being born again in his children. . . . In love man is more adventurous, more audacious: he gives to it only a part of his heart and spirit, reserving himself for other passions. On the other hand, more impressionable, more tender, than man, woman is more sensible to love: she is more sincere in her passion, gives herself up to it entirely, sacrifices herself without reserve.

We have already noticed some of the wonderful phenomena which manifest themselves in the organism at the epoch of puberty, the dawn of love. They concur in preparing both sexes with physical and moral attributes which render them worthy of the reproduction of the species. . . .

At length the young man and the young woman have discovered each the other. He has sought physical beauty, she moral beauty. He exhibits a love more sensual, more jealous, more transitory; she a love more tender, more trusting, more faithful. Who concedes the most, loves the most. Before sexual union, man loves the more earnestly, because he sacrifices more,—pains, marches, contests: he spares nothing. But, when the act is consummated, she, in turn, loves more, and for a longer time. Her love then becomes labor and suffering. She must nourish with her blood the being to which man has communicated life; she must bring it into the world in the midst of cruel pains; she must continue for it incessant cares.

Thus we are enabled to understand, with Madame de Staël, how that "love, which is only an episode in the life of men, is the entire history of the life of women." Nature, as it were, has given to woman only one desire,—love; only one duty,—love; only one recompense,—love. . . .

When love is pure and true, it finds its complete satisfaction only in the indissoluble bond of marriage. Marriage is its natural consummation, because it gives to it union, peace, stability, and all the advantages which it cannot possess of itself. . . . Marriage, which enfranchises man from the tyranny of the senses, leaves to love all of its buoyancy: it is even its emancipation, the only true, the only real one. In marriage passion is less vivacious; but that which it loses in freshness, it gains in maturity. The flower withers; but the roots penetrate deeper, and the fruits are multiplied.

Marriage, then, is the only means to regulate love, and to direct it to its proper object. It equally prevents dissipation, and cold and unnatural indifference; it prolongs life, promotes *domestic* joy, which is the purest, the most uniform, and the least wasting of all happiness. It tends to moderate over-strained hope and enthusiastic speculation as well as excessive care. . . .

Marriage is accomplished. In this new life the husband and the wife stand in the relation of preceptors to each other. The woman, more of a stranger to practical life, less serious, less strong, becomes the pupil of the husband, who, by his tender relations, initiates her, little by little, into the intellectual and moral world in which he dwells. The husband learns as much as he teaches: he discovers, in the depths of the soul of her whom he loves, treasures of affection, of goodness, of delicacy, before unknown to him.

If they are wise, the young married couple will retire from the noise and distractions of the world, living together in the greatest possible intimacy; for it is in silence and solitude that their metamorphosis will take place, and they will form themselves most quickly for this life of two.

Finally, woman must regard marriage as a serious condition. In the most humble acts of family life it is possible to have an art for pleasing the taste, the imagination. At the domestic fireside, grace, elegance, poetry even, should reign; for all animate, vivify, and become colored with the breath of sentiment. Let the wife still be the intellectual companion of man, raising herself to his level, sharing in the interest of his thoughts and his career, refreshing his moments of leisure by the accomplishments and charms of a cultivated mind.

RELATIONS OF SEXUAL DISORDERS TO THE BRAIN AND NERVOUS SYSTEM

Few women appear to realize what important influences are exerted by the sexual organs upon the brain and nervous system in health and disease; much less, that one organ, or indeed one part of an organ, exercises a higher and better defined influence upon the rest of the organization than another. . . .

We have, in a previous chapter, studied briefly the physiological relations of the ovaries to the other sexual organs, and have seen that their function is primary in the process of reproduction; that their activity precedes the uterine functions, and continues, as a rule, until the cessation of menstruation. It would seem, then, that the functions of the other sexual organs are responsive to the influence of the ovaries;

in other words, that the ovaries are the prime movers and controlling spirits in the sexual system.

Dr. Henry Maudsley of London has written a book, entitled "Body and Mind,"—a very thoughtful production, and one, too, which we wish all of our readers would peruse. In it he states that "the organic system has most certainly an essential part in the constitution and the functions of the mind. In the great mental revolution caused by the development of the sexual system at puberty, we have the most striking example of the intimate and essential sympathy between the brain as a mental organ and other parts of the body. . . . It has been affirmed by some philosophers that there is no essential difference between the mind of a woman and that of a man; and that, if a girl were subjected to the same education as a boy, she would resemble him in tastes, feelings, pursuits, and powers. To my mind it would not be one whit more absurd to affirm that the antlers of the stag, the human beard, and the cock's comb are the effects of education; or that, by putting a girl to the same education as a boy, the female generative organs might be transformed into male organs. The physical and mental differences between the sexes intimate themselves very early in life, and declare themselves most distinctly at puberty. They are connected with the influence of the organs of generation."

We have cited these words because they emanate from a high authority, and because we wish them to serve as a prelude to what follows. To return to the ovaries, about which we were speaking: they it is which give to woman all her characteristics of body and mind,—we need not explain how or why. Were the ovaries absent, woman would tend towards the masculine type of the race. . . .

It follows, then, that, if the ovaries are so essential to the well-being of the individual in health, these organs, when diseased, must exercise a potent influence in deranging the brain and nervous system. . . . Recall to mind how speedily any derangement of menstruation will cause a disturbance, or even disease, of the nervous system. . . .

But it is not our purpose to describe all the diseases to which the ovaries are subject, or to estimate the effect exerted by them upon the nervous system. Suffice it to say, briefly, that any inflammatory affection of the ovaries, any displacement, produces most marked effects upon the brain and nervous system. Thus we see indigestion, spinal irritation, many forms of neuralgia, headaches, mental irritability, and insanity, all largely attributable to some disease of the ovaries.

We find many of these signs in the affection termed "hysteria,"—a disease which has long been but poorly understood even by the medical profession. That hysteria may exist independently of sexual causes, we do not deny: some cases amply prove this. But that it is, as a rule, due to a derangement of the female sexual organs, especially of the ovaries, is equally certain.

Some types of hysteria are undoubtedly inherited: of these we shall have nothing to say. The hysteria which concerns us is that which we so often encounter, and of which the essential factor, as we know, is some ovarian derangement. Any thing that weakens a woman generally may revert to the ovaries, and thus, by altering the relation of the several nervous functions, bring about the condition of nervous disturbance known as hysteria. . . . The patient, when the hysterical feelings come over her, does not show any disposition to resist them, but willingly yields to her emotions whatever they may be. She will laugh or cry on the slightest provocation, and is very nervous and irritable; she cares nothing for her duties, and seemingly takes pleasure in exaggerating all her slight discomforts and annoyances, and, by her suspicious, exacting, and unreasonable behavior, makes life generally uncomfortable to those about her. The more one undertakes to do for such a person by way of giving advice, comfort, or the means of cure, so much the more will he be resented: on the contrary, every word of sympathy, pity, or condolence will be heartily appreciated. . . .

CONCLUSION

. . . At the start our purpose and aim were distinctly stated, and we leave it to our fair readers to decide whether we have succeeded in fulfilling them.

Our subject is far from being a pleasant one. It is not one which you would wish to discuss around the fireside, nor is it one either which many women care to have frequently brought to their attention. Nevertheless, that it must be discussed is beyond any question or doubt. False modesty seems well enough; but it covers up a vast amount of ignorance, and too often adjudges suffering to be a sin. Were we not impressed with the belief that more than half of woman's ills are due wholly to herself, partly in ignorance and partly in sin, we should have refrained wholly from writing as plainly as we hope we have done in these pages. When women shall begin to see and to know themselves as the Creator intended that they should, then shall we hear of fewer invalids, and the papers will record fewer stories of public crime.

This beginning should be made in youth at the time when the girl approaches the period of pubescence. It is a duty for mothers to perform, and not one for physicians or moralists. One of the greatest practical results of the discovery by Mr. Darwin of the descent of man from the animals which have gone before him is, that by it the sexual instincts, or, as they are generally and most unfortunately termed, the sexual passions, are shown to be the most necessary as well as the most prevalent of all the instincts which have been evolved by the necessities of animal existence. The female organism has always been merely the vehicle for the maturation of the ovum, and for the reception of the fertilizing influence of the male; being, in fact, what we may call the passive factor in the reproductive act. For her part of the process, then, only enough of sexual passion or instinct is required to indicate to the male the stage at which his share may be effectually performed.

For the male, on the contrary, a constant tendency to aggression is necessary that he may be in readiness at the time required. Further, the struggle for the survival of the fittest has constantly been carried out in its chiefest severity amongst the males of all animals, and only partially amongst the females, so that it has come to be that the physically fittest has necessarily been also the sexually most powerful. It ought to be, therefore, no matter of surprise that in the human race the sexual instinct is very powerful in man, and comparatively weak in woman.

ON Sexual Passion in Men and Women
by Dr. Elizabeth Blackwell*

When Elizabeth Blackwell wanted to attend an American medical college in the 1840s, she applied to twenty-nine institutions without avail until Geneva College admitted her (by accident more than by principle). Her experience at medical school was studded with attempts at humiliation—but this was little compared to the difficulty she faced after graduating at the top of her class, and furthering her studies in Europe, when she returned to New York to attempt to practice medicine. She was avoided by other doctors, without access to hospitals or means of attracting private patients. Again relying on her own initiative, she set up her own dispensary in a New York slum, and gave a course of lectures. This became the core of her New York Infirmary, which opened in 1857, staffed entirely by women. In the 1860s the Infirmary added a nurses' training school and then became accredited as a medical college, to make available to women a good course of medical education. Dr. Elizabeth Blackwell's contributions to community hygiene and medical education were significant, as well as the new light she shed on women's capacities, both in her life and in her work. The following excerpt from her later writing touches on themes that interested her through her career.

On SEXUAL PASSION IN MEN AND WOMEN

One of the first subjects to be investigated by the Christian physiologist is the truth or error of the assertion so widely made, that sexual passion is a much stronger force in men than in women. Very remarkable results have flowed from the attempts to mould society upon this assertion. A simple Christian might reply, our religion makes no such distinction; male and female are as one under guidance and judgment of the divine law. . . .

It is necessary, therefore, to determine what is meant by strength, and what is meant by passion. . . .

In determining the strength of races and the strength of individuals, the various elements which constitute vital power must be considered.

* From Elizabeth B. Blackwell, *The Human Element in Sex: Being a Medical Inquiry into the Relation of Sexual Physiology to Christian Morality* (new ed.; London: J. A. Churchill, 1894), pp. 44–54.

Endurance, longevity, special aptitudes with the proportionate amount of vital force given to their fulfilment,—these are all elements of relative strength.

In any attempt to settle the comparative strength of man and woman, therefore, all these elements must be weighed. Thus the powers of endurance which are demanded by each kind of life must be accurately measured; the care of a sick child must be balanced against the anxiety of business, the ceaseless cares of indoor life against the changes of out-door life, &c. The impossibility of so weighing the burden which each sex bears in the various trials and difficulties of practical life shows the futility of attempting to measure the amount of vital power possessed by men or by women separately.

Any attempt at a comparison of absolute sexual power between men and women will be found to be equally futile. The varying manifestations of the sexual faculties, as exhibited in their male and female phases, make the relative measurement of this vital force in men and women quite impossible. Considering, however, the enormous practical edifice of law and custom, which has been built up on the very sandy foundation of the supposed stronger character of male sexual passion, it is necessary to examine closely the facts of human nature, and challenge many erroneous conclusions. Any theory which proposes two methods of judgment, or two measures of law, in consequence of a supposed difference of vital power, is emphatically uncertain, and lays itself open to just suspicion of dangerous error.

The equal numbers of men and women, their equal longevity, and consequently equal power of enduring the wear and tear of life, prove the equal general vital power of the sexes.

In considering further the special sexual manifestations of the two sexes, we observe that the power of reproduction commences at an earlier age in women than in men. . . .

At a later age, when physical sex is fully developed in the young adult, we are still struck by the greater proportion of vital force demanded from or given by women to all that is involved in sexual life. The physical functions of sex weigh more imperiously upon the woman than the man, compel more thought and care, and necessitate more enlightened intelligence in the general arrangements of life. Physical sex is a larger factor in the life of the woman, unmarried or married, than in the life of the man; and this is the case at every period of the full vigour of life. In order to secure the perfect health and independent freedom which is the birthright of every rational human being, larger wisdom is required for the maintenance of perfect physical health in the woman than in the man, this function being a more important element in the one than in the other.

If this be true of the physical element of sex, it is equally true of the mental element. No careful observer can fail to remark the larger proportionate amount of thought and feeling, as compared with the total vital force of the individual, which we find given by women to all that concerns the subject of sex. Words spoken, slight courtesies rendered, excite a more permanent interest in women. . . . All that concerns the mental aspect of sex, the special attraction which draws one sex towards the other, is exhibited in greater proportionate force by women, is more steady and enduring, and occupies a larger amount of their thought and interest.

The frivolity and ephemeral character of the seducer's impulses, as compared with the earnestness of the seduced, illustrates the profounder character of sexual passion in woman.

Wide-spread unhappiness, social disturbance, and degradation continually arise from the vital force of human sex in woman, unguarded, unguided, and unemployed.

Passion and appetite are not identical. The term passion, it should always be remembered, necessarily implies a mental element. For this reason it is employed exclusively in relation to the powers of the human being, not to those of the brute. Passion rises into a higher rank than instinct or physical impulse, because it involves the soul of man. In sexual passion this mental, moral, or emotional principle is as emphatically sex as any physical instinct, and it grows with the proportional development of the nervous system.

This mental element of human sex exists in major proportion in the vital force of women, and justifies the statement that the compound faculty of sex is as strong in woman as in man. Those who deny sexual feeling to women, or consider it so light a thing as hardly to be taken into account in social arrangements, confound appetite and passion; they quite lose sight of this immense spiritual force of attraction, which is distinctly human sexual power, and which exists in so very large a proportion in the womanly nature. The impulse towards maternity is an inexorable but beneficent law of woman's nature, and it is a law of sex.

The different form which physical sensation necessarily takes in the two sexes, and its intimate connection with and development through

the mind (love) in women's nature, serve often to blind even thoughtful and painstaking persons, as to the immense power of sexual attraction felt by women. Such one-sided views show a misconception of the
meaning of human sex in its entirety.

The affectionate husbands of refined women often remark that their
wives do not regard the distinctively sexual act with the same intoxi-
cating physical enjoyment that they themselves feel, and they draw the
conclusion that the wife possesses no sexual passion. A delicate wife will
often confide to her medical adviser (who may be treating her for
some special suffering) that at the very time when marriage love seems
to unite them most closely, when her husband's welcome kisses and
caresses seem to bring them into profound union, comes an act which
mentally separates them, and which may be either indifferent or repug-
nant to her. But it must be understood that it is not the special act
necessary for parentage which is the measure of the compound moral
and physical power of sexual passion. It is the profound attraction of
one nature to the other which marks passion; and delight in kiss and
caress—the love touch—is physical sexual expression as much as the
special act of the male.

It is well known that terror or pain in either sex will temporarily
destroy all physical pleasure. In married life, injury from childbirth, or
brutal or awkward conjugal approaches, may cause unavoidable shrink-
ing from sexual congress, often wrongly attributed to absence of sexual
passion. But the severe and compound suffering experienced by many
widows who were strongly attached to their lost partners is also well
known to the physician; and this is not simply a mental loss that they
feel, but an immense physical deprivation. It is a loss which all the senses
suffer, by the physical as well as moral void which death has created.

Although physical sexual pleasure is not attached exclusively, or in
woman chiefly, to the act of coition, it is also a well-established fact
that in healthy loving women, uninjured by the too frequent lesions
which result from childbirth, increasing physical satisfaction attaches
to the ultimate physical expression of love. A repose and general well-
being results from this natural occasional intercourse, whilst the total
deprivation of it produces irritability. . . . The prevalent fallacy that
sexual passion is the almost exclusive attribute of men, and attached exclusively to the act of coition—a fallacy which exercises so disastrous an
effect upon our social arrangements, arises from ignorance of the distinctive character of human sex, viz. its powerful mental element. . . .

The comparison so often drawn between the physical development of the comparatively small class of refined and guarded women, and the men of worldly experience whom they marry, is a false comparison. These women have been taught to regard sexual passion as lust and as sin—a sin which it would be a shame for a pure woman to feel, and which she would die rather than confess. She has not been taught that sexual passion is love, even more than lust, and that its ennobling work in humanity is to educate and transfigure the lower by the higher element. The growth and indications of her own nature she is taught to condemn, instead of to respect them as foreshadowing that mighty impulse towards maternity which will place her nearest to the Creator if reverently accepted.

But if the comparison be made between men and women of loose lives—not women who are allowed and encouraged by money to carry on a trade in vice, but men and women of similar unrestrained and loose life, the unbridled impulse of physical lust is as remarkable in the latter as in the former. The astounding lust and cruelty of women, uncontrolled by spiritual principle, is an historical fact. . . .

This is not the place to speak of the moral danger inseparable from a corrupt bargain which debases the highest function, the creative, to the low status of trade competition; but the Christian physician is bound to consider this.

Some medical writers have considered that women are more tyrannically governed than men by the impulses of physical sex. They have dwelt upon the greater proportion of work laid upon women in the reproduction of the race, the prolonged changes and burden of maternity, and the fixed and marked periodical action needed to maintain the aptitude of the physical frame for maternity. They have drawn the conclusion that sex dominates the life of women, and limits them in the power of perfect human growth. This would undoubtedly be the case were sex simply a physical function.

The fact in human nature which explains, guides, and should elevate the sexual nature of woman, and mark the beneficence of Creative Force, is this very mental element which distinguishes human from brute sex. This element, gradually expanding under religious teaching, and the development of true religious sentiment, becomes the ennobling power of love. Love between the sexes is the highest and mightiest form of human sexual passion. . . .

ON Female Invalidism
by Dr. Mary Putnam Jacobi*

Dr. Jacobi's opinions here give some insight into the attitude toward "female invalidism" held by a progressive female physician at the end of the nineteenth century. An outstanding doctor and a pioneer in women's medical education, Dr. Jacobi shows her animus against the school of thought proceeding from Edward Clarke's *Sex in Education.*

On FEMALE INVALIDISM

In the first place, it seems to me that this entire question [of female invalidism] needs to be dealt with on a much larger scale, and from a more anthropologic standpoint than is usually the case. Impairment of reproductive function through disease, or imperfect development of the reproductive organs, is a race fact of the greatest importance; and much evidently depends on quite a combination of conditions. To assume, as good old Miss Beecher did, that all the troubles connected with reproductive organs can be explained by the habit of wearing many petticoats, is to rely upon a most superficial and inadequate explanation. Miss Beecher suggested, as a remedy for the evil, a hoop skirt, which actually and by independent agency came into fashion a few years later; but I doubt, if it greatly changed the conditions Miss Beecher was considering.

In the most general sense, and apart from specific infections and mechanical injury, utero-ovarian disease is evidently traceable to imperfect development; and it cannot be denied that this is alarmingly prevalent among American, and especially among New England girls. But I think it is putting the cart before the horse to assert that this imperfect development of the reproductive organs and corresponding

* From letter to Dr. Edes on Female Invalidism (1895), in *Mary Putnam Jacobi, M.D.: Pathfinder in Medicine,* ed. the Women's Medical·Association of New York City (New York and London: G. P. Putnam's Sons, 1925), pp. 478, 480–482. Reprinted by permission of the Women's Medical Association. Copyright 1925 by the Women's Medical Association.

nerve centres, is due to over-stimulus, over-education of the intellectual centres. . . .

I believe it is also true that the imperfect development of reproductive organs, nerve centres, and correlatively of sexual instincts, is one reason that the intellectual life of women, and the cerebral cortex, has in the present generation become more active. To suppose that cerebral activity could dwarf sexual activity (which is often alleged) is absurd, or rather, though theoretically conceivable, is in contradiction with known facts. The one fact, now noted by ethnologists, that sexual passion is far more highly developed among highly civilized peoples than among savages, shows that normally the two poles of existence develop *pari passu* and not in antagonism to each other. Detailed proof could easily be furnished were it necessary.

But until now, women have not held a normal position as complete human beings; their mental activity, though often considerable has been spontaneous, untrained, unsubjected to systematic educational drill. I think the flagging of reproductive activities, due to temporary impairment of race vitality, has facilitated this extraordinary new departure in the *régime* of the race, whereby the sex whose brain has been hitherto neglected, is to-day educated, stimulated, often unfortunately forced.

But because this new departure is a race innovation, it undoubtedly involves difficulties and dangers, risks a certain dislocation of organic adjustment, which can only be gradually triumphed over. It requires the most careful study of individual cases, and recollection of three facts. First, that the girls already in possession of the most active, responsive and readily educatable brains, may be essentially deficient in general organic force, and especially as manifested in the reproductive organs, hence unprovided with the undercurrent of sexual strength which is needed to healthfully support cerebral activities. Second, that the other girls—and there are to-day not a few of this class—who are not only mentally active but seem physically sound and strong, may not have the final reproductive strength; their menstrual life is healthy, but they may either break down in child-bearing or have delicate children. Third, that the reproductive imperfection in question may show itself at first by no more tangible symptoms than moral incapacity for love or marriage, or fantastic perversity of sentiment in regard to these fundamental interests, this incapacity frequently involving or determining social situations that react most disastrously upon the health of the "highly strung" individual.

With all these race and constitutional complications, when educational systems are adopted which not only ignore such general considerations but violate the most elementary principles of ordinary hygiene; when brains which are not only immature but female, and whose stock of inherited capacity for trained work has all been derived from the parent of the opposite sex; when such brains are submitted to an often illogical cramming; when food is inadequate and exercise absolutely neglected; when hours of work are imposed which no adult woman would bear, and few men; when all this work is carried on under the stimulus of high-pressure competition, emulation, vanity, sometimes fear; when hundreds of girls are shut up together in the exciting atmosphere of a college life, so that their nerves are mutually reacting on each other,—under all these circumstances it is not at all wonderful that towards the close of adolescence so many girls exhibit constitutional debility and uterine disease.

It must, however, be noted, and contrary to what might theoretically be expected, that the influence of superior education, although occasionally seeming to be detrimental, is far less so than any other observed agency. Where there is to be trouble, this is always distinctly foreshadowed at or before the ages of sixteen, seventeen, eighteen, when the college education begins. My own statistics, as collected in the essay on "Rest in Menstruation," and also those which have since been collected by college alumnae, all show that the least ill-health is found among the women who have been most highly educated. Of course, the fact partly shows that only healthy girls complete their course and graduate; others fall away earlier. At all events, the college-bred women are still so much in the minority that the general statistics are hardly affected by them; yet physicians often write as if these constituted the mass of nervous invalids.

But the list of causes of the special invalidism of the century is not yet ended. Every city physician who has also seen country people must have noticed that while mechanical injuries from childbirth are rather more common among country people, their influence is apt to remain limited to mechanical discomfort. But a much less degree of injury in city women excites, or is liable to excite, a protean swarm of nervous disorders. The French comment emphatically on this contrast between the Parisian and peasant women. Evidently this implies more delicately strung nervous organization, in more unstable equilibrium, as more developed among the inhabitants of cities, or specifically among the women who have been freed from manual labor. I think Tolstoi is quite right in asserting that such freedom is a curse to the "upper classes."

If the excessive drudgery of New England ancestors under unfavorable conditions weakened the constitution of their descendants, the excessive luxury of these descendants is certainly a second cause of weakness. I am not speaking now of coarse and unreasonable luxury, but of the refined and delicate ease of life and sensibility in which so many thousands now contrive to live—up to a certain point an advantage and a grace, beyond this a dangerous effeminacy. In manual drudgery, or in Puritan asceticism, there are dangers from exhaustion, depression, or gloom; but there is at least a discipline, an enforced stoicism, which is of immense value in bearing toil, trouble or shock. To-day stoicism has vanished from education, as asceticism from creeds; it is considered natural and almost laudable to break down under all conceivable varieties of strain—a winter dissipation, a houseful of servants, a quarrel with a female friend, not to speak of more legitimate reasons.

Women who expect to go to bed every menstrual period expect to collapse if by chance they find themselves on their feet for a few hours during such a crisis. Constantly considering their nerves, urged to consider them by well-intentioned but short-sighted advisers, they pretty soon become nothing but bundles of nerves. They suffer from lack of the wholesome neglect to which their grandmothers were habitually consigned; too much attention is paid to women as objects, while yet they remain in too many cases insufficiently prepared to act as independent subjects. A healthy objectivity is one of the greatest desiderata for modern women. To knock the nonsense out of them, to direct attention from self, to substitute a cosmic horizon for that of their own feelings, who does not know the importance of this for thousands of hysterical women? and equally the impossibility of attaining it?

I think, finally, it is in the increased attention paid to women, and especially in their new function as lucrative patients, scarcely imagined a hundred years ago, that we find explanation of much ill-health among women, freshly discovered to-day, but which always excited, and which is often due to conditions arising among men, and not therefore new. Shattered nervous systems are inherited by girls from the alcoholism of the fathers; gonorrhea contracted by wives from husbands; sterility due to licentiousness in which the innocent woman may have no share; enforced celibacy due to bad social arrangements; occasionally, though less and less frequently, childbirths too close together; certainly all these causes of ill-health to women have existed for centuries. I think the peculiarity of the present time is that now attention is being drawn to the special effects produced upon women by these general causes.

VII
Industrialization and Women's Work

The Working Girls of Boston*

This report was published in 1884, the result of an investigation by the Massachusetts Bureau of Statistics of Labor.

THE WORKING GIRLS OF BOSTON

The population of the city of Boston, according to the Tenth United States Census, in 1880, was 362,839; of this number 172,368 were males and 190,571 were females. The whole number of persons engaged in that year in all occupations was 149,194, the males numbering 110,313 and the females 38,881; out of this latter number of females employed in all occupations, there were, in round numbers, 20,000 employed in occupations other than domestic service, and these constitute the body of the working girls of Boston.

. . . The bureau undertook to ascertain the moral, sanitary, physical, and economical conditions of the working girls of Boston. Of course it was not possible to get a complete personal history of every one of the 20,000 involved, nor was it necessary. . . .

We secured the personal history of these 1,032 of the whole 20,000 working girls of Boston, a number amply sufficient for the scientific purposes of the investigation; what these personal histories teach, the information to be drawn from them, the conclusions resulting from such information, constitute the points or the bases for the analysis of the tables herewith presented. . . .

* The Working Girls of Boston, from the 15th Annual Report of the Massachusetts Bureau of Statistics of Labor, for 1884, by Carroll Wright (reprint ed.; Boston, 1889), pp. 3, 5, 16–17, 64–66, 69–75, 92–93, 110–113, 116–120.

TABLE II. Occupations of Working Girls in Boston

[Comprehending the 1,032 included in the investigation.]

Occupations.	Number.	
	Detail.	Aggregates.
PERSONAL SERVICE	–	83
Carpet sewers	12	–
Copyists	3	–
Dye house employés	6	–
Laundry employés	8	–
Matrons and nurses	7	–
Restaurant employés	18	–
Sewing machine teachers	3	–
Telegraph operators	3	–
Other personal service	23	–
TRADE	–	123
Bookkeepers	11	–
Clerks	15	–
Cashiers	5	–
Cash dial tenders	7	–
Errand girls	5	–
Writers	3	–
Saleswomen	77	–
MANUFACTURES	–	826
Bookbinderies	29	–
Boots and shoes	26	–
Brooms and brushes	9	–
Buttons and dress trimmings	17	–
Carpetings	17	–
Clocks and watches	7	–
Clothing, men's—		
Tailoresses	72	–
Coats	87	–
Pantaloons	26	–
Vests	9	–
Hats and caps	11	–
Neckties and furnishing goods	7	–
Oiled clothing	3	–
Overalls, jumpers, and colored shirts	5	–
Shirts	27	–
Suspenders	10	–

TABLE II. *continued*

Occupations.	Number.	
	Detail.	Aggregates.
Clothing, women's—		
Dressmakers: in business for themselves	38	–
Dressmakers: at work for others	62	–
Milliners	15	–
Seamstresses	36	–
Bonnets and hats	7	–
Cloaks, sacks, and suits	26	–
Corsets	7	–
Hoopskirts and bustles	8	–
Cotton, woollen, and worsted goods	12	–
Drugs and medicines	5	–
Food preparations	33	–
Furniture	18	–
Hair	4	–
Leather	3	–
Metals and metallic goods	15	–
Musical instruments and strings	3	–
Nets, seines, etc.	4	–
Paper	14	–
Paper boxes	32	–
Photographs	3	–
Polishes and dressings	4	–
Printing and publishing	28	–
Rubber and elastic goods	55	–
Scientific instruments and appliances	7	–
Silk	3	–
Straw goods	11	–
Tobacco	11	–

SANITARY SURROUNDINGS AT HOME

. . . In numerous cases . . . girls were found living for the sake of economy in very limited quarters, which could not be conducive to good sanitary conditions. In some instances, girls were found living in small attic rooms, lighted and ventilated by the skylight only; the furnishings generally consisted of a small single bed, bureau and chair, with no wardrobe, except one curtained in the corner. In other cases, girls were forced to content themselves with small side rooms without a chance for a fire, which in some cases was sadly needed. One girl had a small side room in the third story of a respectable house, but said she could not expect much more at the present cost of living; still others were reported as living together with other members of the family in a tenement of one back room and side bedroom; another, as one of 18 families in a single building with hardly the necessary articles of furniture; another, occupying the third story of a house which seemed the poorest on the street. On the other hand, girls were found living in large rooms, quite well and sometimes handsomely furnished, in some instances with side rooms adjoining, not perhaps because they could really afford such quarters, but because they preferred to economize in other ways, in order to have some of the comforts, in looks at least, of home.

In a few cases where girls reported their health as being poor, or not good, they also complained of the poor board provided, as well as of the unpleasant surroundings at home; one girl made the statement that her home was pleasant and healthy, but to the agent of the bureau the reverse seemed to be the case, for the hall was dirty, the floor covered with a worn-out rag carpet while the air was filled with disagreeable odors; the girl appeared to be in poor health, untidily dressed, and dirty. Another was found living in the upper story of a cheap tenement house, directly in the rear of a kerosene factory having a tall chimney that constantly puffed out thick black smoke, which together with the offensive smell of the kerosene, forced the occupants always to keep the kitchen windows closed. In another case, one of the girls said that she spent all her spare time and Sundays with her sister in another part of the city, as her home was very unpleasant and uncomfortable; she also said the Board of Health had visited the house last year and recommended many alterations, but she did not know whether they were attended to or not. Another girl was found living in four small rooms as one of a family of 12, in a house located very near a stable and having bad drainage. One other girl complained of the odor from the water-closets in the halls, and said it was anything but agreeable.

In a house where a considerable number of girls are cared for, it was found that there was no elevator in the building, and some of the girls were obliged to go up five flights of stairs to reach their rooms, two or three girls being placed in each room; the upper story of the building was without heat, and in winter was said to be like an ice house; radiators are placed at the ends of halls, and transoms open into the rooms, but these have no particular effect on the temperature of the rooms and there are no other ways of heating; extra charge is made for rooms heated directly by the register and even then such rooms are not always to be obtained, they being generally occupied, and there being but a few of them. . . .

EFFECT OF WORK ON HEALTH

Long hours, and being obliged to stand all day, are very generally advanced as the principal reasons for any lack or loss of health occasioned by the work of the girls. The nature of the work is mentioned as a cause for decline, which together with the other causes described will be found to be prevalent in all the various branches of their work.

Feather sorters, cotton sorters, and workers on any material which in its nature is apt to give off a "dust," complain of the disagreeable if not actually injurious effect on the health of persons so employed.

Taking the question by industries and occupations in detail, we find in "Personal Service," that the restaurant employés generally complain of long hours, no dinner hour to speak of, and the great strain upon them from being busy all day on their feet. They all complain of a low state of health, and are pretty much tired out on reaching home. . . .

In "Trade," a bookkeeper was found who had ruined her eyes, by bringing her books home nights and working until twelve and one o'clock. Among the saleswomen, "standing all day" is generally reported as being very trying on their health and strength. In one store, no stools are provided, the girls being obliged to go to one end of the store to sit down.

. . . A good many saleswomen consider their work very hard, and that it has a bad effect on their health; in one instance, a girl says she has paid out over $500 in doctor's bills during the past few years. In one store, it is very unsatisfactory in this respect; no talking is allowed, only half enough time is given for dinner, and being obliged to walk home at night, the girl is completely exhausted; on Saturday she brings dinner and supper. . . .

In bakeries the strain of long hours and standing is especially felt by the salesgirls, while in other branches of business the health of many girls is so poor as to necessitate long rests, one girl being out a year on this account. Another girl in poor health was obliged to leave her work, while one other reports that it is not possible for her to work the year round, as she could not stand the strain, not being at all strong. A girl, who had worked in one place for three years, was obliged to leave on account of poor health, being completely run down from badly venti-lated workrooms, and obliged to take an eight months' rest; she worked a week when not able, but left to save her life. She says she has to work almost to death to make fair compensation (now $12 per week).

Under "Manufactures," in *Bookbinderies* and in the manufacture of *Brushes,* girls complain of their health being run down on account of work, or from over-work. In *Boots and shoes,* the work is very hard, the girls being obliged to be on their feet all day, and in cases where they have to walk any great distance to their homes they become very tired at night.

In the manufacture of *Buttons,* the girls say the work is rather dangerous, as they are liable to get their fingers jammed under the punch, or caught in the die when it comes down to press the parts of the button together. A man (although not a surgeon) is provided to dress wounds three times for each individual without charge; after-wards, the person injured must pay all expenses. There are 35 machines in use, and accidents are of very frequent occurrence. . . .

In making *Paper boxes,* the girls are obliged to stand, a practice they think is very injurious. The coloring matter in materials used in the construction and covering of boxes is considered dangerous to health by some, one girl being at home sick three months from blood poisoning caused by work. . . .

In the *Clothing* business, the general testimony is that the work is very hard, and is the cause of a great deal of sickness among the working girls so employed. The tax on the strength is very great, and it would seem that unless a girl is strong and robust, the work soon proves too severe for her, and if followed thereafter results disastrously. The running of heavy sewing machines by foot power soon breaks down a girl's health, as several girls have testified. One girl says that steam was introduced six month's ago to her great satisfaction, as she thinks foot power machines too severe for female operators. The girls think all the ma-chines should be run by steam.

Other girls object to standing so much, and say that being on their feet all day and then walking to their homes makes them very tired at night.

The effect of the work on the health of the working girls engaged in tailoring is very apparent from their testimony. A girl who used to bring her work home, says she overtaxed her strength and is now sick. Others tell the same story, and say that overwork, and the desire to do more than strength would allow, has very seriously affected their health, in one case, the overstraining of the nerves causing deafness, while another girl says, "overwork, cold dinners, and constant application, has brought on chronic rheumatism." . . .

In one or two cases, the girls report that the sewing has affected the eyes, compelling the use of glasses at all times and blue glasses on the street.

Under *Food preparations*, a girl engaged in salt packing is troubled with asthma and bronchitis; she was told at the hospital that the salt would eat into her lungs, as they are diseased; she would leave, if she could find other work.

In the manufacture of confectionery, on account of hot temperatures of rooms, etc., the work is not considered healthy. Some of the girls say work is very severe, they being on their feet all day, while others are out sick, being run down from work.

In the cleaning and packing of fish, the girls say that the fishermen put cayenne pepper and saltpetre on the fish, and girls in handling get their hands and fingers blistered, and often the outside skin taken off; the effect being the same as though they were obliged to keep their hands in a strong caustic solution. One girl says she has tried rubber gloves, but without success. Another girl (a fish packer) says in consequence of the steam necessary to be used the atmosphere is very damp. She says other girls are obliged to stand in cold water all day, having their hands exposed to cold water, and when one was questioned as to what shop she worked in, she answered, "they're not shops, they're working stalls where we are." The same complaint as to standing all day is noticed in this branch of business.

In *Type foundries*, the workroom is always filled with a fine lead dust, caused by "rubbing"; in some shops, this is quite perceptible when standing at one end of the room. . . .

In *Straw goods*, the girls very generally speak of the unhealthy nature of their business. In working on dyed braids, especially green, there is, according to the testimony of one girl, a very fine dust which produces a hacking which is almost constant, and to persons of consumptive tendencies, very injurious. Girls are advised by physicians in such cases to abandon the work. . . . Some throat or lung trouble is very prevalent among the girls working on straw, and the hacking cough peculiar to the business is well-nigh universal. A great many girls are said to die of consumption, while many are often subject to severe cases of sickness, the direct result of work. . . .

The individual testimony regarding shops and their surroundings, and the effect of work upon health, has been given, as nearly as possible, in the language of the person interviewed. This testimony is that of the few, the great majority being in good health and in good surroundings.

It is in evidence from other sources that in a few stores, and in some of considerable size, the water-closet accommodations are very deficient, in one instance 60 women being obliged to use one closet. The evil effect of waiting for the use of a closet common to so large a number is apparent. Many of these women are constantly under the care of physicians for some disease growing out of the condition or things described. . . .

INCOME

Brought into specific averages, we find that the average weekly income for the year was in personal service $5.25, in trade $4.81, in manufactures $5.22, or the general average for all involved for the whole year was $5.17 per week. This latter figure must stand as the total average weekly income from all sources, earnings, assistance, and other work, of the working girls of Boston. . . .

A good deal of complaint is made in regard to the low wages quite generally paid to working girls in all the various occupations in which they were found employed. The cause of complaint, especially under "Trade," is ascribed to the fact that girls living "at home," with little or no board to pay, work for very low wages. This is considered a great hardship to the lone working girl who is entirely dependent upon her own resources. . . .

In the manufacture of men's clothing, considerable complaint is made by the girls as to the very small wages now made in the business. Almost invariably, when anything was said by them concerning wages, the cry was "pay is too small": in these cases, the pay ranges from $3 to $6 generally, a baster on canvas (13½ years old) reporting only $1.25. It is said that many of the girls get discouraged, as they hardly earn enough to pay running expenses, and are obliged to practise the most rigid economy. . . .

In paper box making, one girl receiving $8 a week says girls work harder than the men, and are paid much less—unjustly, she thinks. The wages in this occupation are reported as falling off. Another girl, who formerly worked as saleswoman at $4.50 a week, says it was not sufficient to pay for room and board, provide suitable clothing to make a decent appearance in the store, and meet other ordinary expenses.

In some cases girls testify that their work is worth more than they receive for it, and think they ought to have better wages. But as others always stand ready to take their places at even less pay, they have to be satisfied with what they get.

HOME LIFE

The information furnished by the working girls shows that the wages earned by them constitute in many cases the chief, and sometimes the entire support of the family, the parents looking to the earnings of one, two, three, and four daughters to pay the household bills; the father often being reported not able to work much or always, on account of disability, from lack of steady work, or possibly, from disinclination to work while there is revenue from any other source. In large families, the earnings of the girls, together with the wages of the father, when all are working, do not more than cover living expenses. . . . In cases where the father is dead, or not living with the family, the mother is often wholly dependent upon the girls and boys working for her support, and where there are younger children, for their education and support as well; the mother working also at times, or keeping the house only. . . .

Girls who have no parents living either provide support for other members of the family, or divide the expense with other brothers or sisters, usually finding it hard work to get along. Others have been obliged to leave their homes on account of bad treatment or conduct of dissipated father, or because they felt the need of work, and not finding it at home, have come to Boston, and are dependent upon themselves for maintenance; these girls also generally contribute something to the support of parents and family at home. . . .

Married women living with their husbands are at work, and very often report their earnings as being the major part of joint income. The husbands are reported as either being out of health and not able to work, or only working at times or about half the time, and contributing but little towards the support of the family.

In quite a number of cases, the girls report, that living at home or with some members of the family, they are not obliged to work, but do so from choice, or because they do not care to become a burden to their parents, in some cases, paying no board and in dull times staying at home idle; if any board is required, it is always stopped when out of work. Others prefer to work in Boston rather than remain at home, but go home a part of each year on a visit; still others live with friends, are very easily circumstanced and are very well satisfied. In a few instances, married women at work say there is no necessity for working, as their husbands with whom they live are well able to support them; they work from choice only. . . .

It is interesting to note the "life" experiences of a few who have been at work for a number of years and have a history, and from them learn what the future of working girls entirely dependent upon their own labor may be, if the conditions developed in regard to small pay, etc., should continue.

A carpet sewer, 34 years of age, and now earning six dollars a week, says she was married at 29 and lived with her husband until, on account of his dissipated habits and neglect of her, she finally left him and went to work, earning $2 a week and running up a board and lodging bill of $35. She has received since a little money from her husband's lodge and makes a little extra by crocheting tops on woollen mittens at ten cents per dozen pairs. She gets her own meals on a little parlor stove and is compelled to live in a small way in order to keep herself and boy alive; she spends scarcely anything for clothing. . . .

In a garret, four stories up, was found a machine operator on men's clothing who said she was married at the age of 20; her husband was consumptive but lived 16 years after her marriage. During her married life she worked more or less, at home and in stores. She has two children, a boy of 11 and a girl of 5, but they do not now live with her; up to a short time since, the boy lived with her and went to school; her work failing, she could not pay his board in advance, and he was sent to live with relatives. At night, after working through the day, she makes clothes for her children and does her own sewing and washing; she has not had a new dress for three years, and she says it sometimes costs a good deal more than she earns to provide for herself and children, and that she has often had to go without her supper.

In another instance, a very bright, smart and most intelligent woman was found living in a small attic room lighted and ventilated by the skylight only. In her younger years, she said she taught school in summer and went to school in winter, studying music and preparing herself to enter the Normal school to become a teacher. Disappointed in this respect, she has had a rather hard life since, and now has a little child to support. While at work, she leaves her little girl at the Day Nursery and pays five cents for the privilege. In the dull season, she has lived on less than a dollar a week for food for herself and child. When seen she was doing quite well as compared with her experience for some years; she had paid her rent to date and had the first five dollars in her pocket over and above living expenses for many a day, with a prospect of earning sufficient to fully meet running expenses. She felt quite elated over what seemed good fortune to her, it being something new in her experience as a working woman.

MORAL CONDITION

. . . It has often been said that the shop girls are an immoral class, that it is largely from their ranks that prostitution is recruited, and the vile charge has often been made that in great stores where many girls are employed, an engagement often depends upon the willingness of the saleswoman or shop girl to become the intimate friend of either the proprietor or head of a department. . . .

Only five girls were found of the whole number interviewed who gave any specific reasons why their surroundings in the shops and places of employment were not of a moral character. In almost every case, the answer was that, so far as known, there were no immoral influences exerted over the girls at their work, but rather that the moral atmosphere of the places where employed was very good and as pleasant as could be wished. In fact, it is reasonable to suppose that employers are as anxious to have good moral conditions exist in their places as any other class of men.

Speak-out on Domestic Service*

To wealthy observers who bemoaned the "servant problem" in the latter part of the nineteenth century, it was always a question why working women seemed to prefer the factory, grim though it was, over the security of domestic service. Helen Campbell, who investigated the circumstances of working women as a journalist in the 1880s, and wrote moving stories of "prisoners of poverty" who were unable to support themselves in industrial employments, asked this question about domestic service to working women of her acquaintance.

SPEAK-OUT ON DOMESTIC SERVICE

Our interest lies in discovering what is at the bottom of the objection to domestic service; how far these objections are rational and to be treated with respect, and how they may be obviated. The mistress's point of view we all know. We know, too, her presentation of objections as she fancies she has discovered them. What we do not know is the ground taken by sensible, self-respecting girls, who have chosen trades in preference, and from whom full detail has been obtained as to the reasons for such choice. . . .

In the present case it seems well to take the individual testimony, each girl whose verdict is chosen representing a class, and being really its mouthpiece.

First on the list stands Margaret M——, an American, twenty-three years old, and for five years in a paper-box factory. Seven others nodded their assent, or added a word here and there as she gave her view, two of them Irish-Americans who had had some years in the public schools.

"It's freedom that we want when the day's work is done. I know some nice girls, Bridget's cousins, that make more money and dress better and everything for being in service. They're waitresses, and have Thursday afternoon out and part of every other Sunday. But they're never sure of one minute that's their own when they're in the house. Our day is ten hours long, but when it's done it's done, and we can do

* From Helen Campbell, *Prisoners of Poverty* (Boston: Little Brown and Co., 1900), pp. 222–231.

what we like with the evenings. That's what I've heard from every nice girl that ever tried service. You're never sure that your soul's your own except when you are out of the house, and I couldn't stand that a day. Women care just as much for freedom as men do. Of course they don't get so much, but I know I'd fight for mine."

"Women are always harder on women than men are," said a fur-sewer, an intelligent American about thirty. "I got tired of always sitting, and took a place as chambermaid. The work was all right and the wages good, but I'll tell you what I couldn't stand. The cook and the waitress were just common, uneducated Irish, and I had to room with one and stand the personal habits of both, and the way they did at table took all my appetite. I couldn't eat, and began to run down; and at last I gave notice, and told the truth when I was asked why. The lady just looked at me astonished: 'If you take a servant's place, you can't expect to be one of the family,' she said. 'I never asked it,' I said; 'all I ask is a chance at common decency.' 'It will be difficult to find an easier place than this,' she said, and I knew it; but ease one way was hardness another, and she couldn't see that I had any right to complain. That's one trouble in the way. It's the mixing up of things, and mistresses don't think how they would feel in the same place."

Third came an Irish-American whose mother had been cook for years in one family, but who had, after a few months of service, gone into a jute-mill, followed gradually by five sisters.

"I hate the very words 'service' and 'servant,'" she said. "We came to this country to better ourselves, and it's not bettering to have anybody ordering you round."

"But you are ordered in the mill."

"That's different. A man knows what he wants, and doesn't go beyond it; but a woman never knows what she wants, and sort of bosses you everlastingly. If there was such a thing as fixed hours it might be different, but I tell every girl I know, 'Whatever you do, don't go into service. You'll always be prisoners and always looked down on.' You can do things at home for them as belongs to you that somehow it seems different to do for strangers. Anyway, I hate it, and there's plenty like me."

"What I minded," said a gentle, quiet girl, who worked at a stationer's, and who had tried household service for a year,—"what I minded was the awful lonesomeness. I went for general housework, because I knew all about it, and there were only three in the family. I never minded being alone evenings in my own room, for I'm always reading or something, and I don't go out hardly at all, but then I always know I can, and that there is somebody to talk to if I like. But there, except to give orders, they had nothing to do with me. It got to feel sort of crushing at last. I cried myself sick, and at last I gave it up, though I don't mind the work at all. I know there are good places, but the two I tried happened to be about alike, and I shan't try again. There are a good many would feel just the same."

"Oh, nobody need to tell me about poor servants," said an energetic woman of forty, Irish-American, and for years in a shirt factory. "Don't I know the way the hussies'll do, comin' out of a bog maybe, an' not knowing the names even, let alone the use, of half the things in the kitchen, and asking their twelve and fourteen dollars a month? Don't I know it well, an' the shame it is to 'em! but I know plenty o' decent, hard-workin' girls too, that give good satisfaction, an' this is what they say. They say the main trouble is, the mistresses don't know, no more than babies, what a day's work really is. A smart girl keeps on her feet all the time to prove she isn't lazy, for if the mistress finds her sitting down, she thinks there can't be much to do and that she doesn't earn her wages. Then if a girl tries to save herself or is deliberate, they call her slow. They want girls on tap from six in the morning till ten and eleven at night. 'Tisn't fair. And then, if there's a let-up in the work, maybe they give you the baby to see to. I like a nice baby, but I don't like having one turned over to me when I'm fit to drop scrabbling to get through and sit down a bit. I've naught to say for the girls that's breaking things and half doing the work. They're a shameful set, and ought to be put down somehow; but it's a fact that the most I've known in service have been another sort that stayed long in places and hated change. There's many a good place too, but the bad ones outnumber 'em. Women make hard mistresses, and I say again, I'd rather be under a man, that knows what he wants. That's the way with most."

"I don't see why people are surprised that we don't rush into places," said a shop-girl. "Our world may be a very narrow world, and I know it is; but for all that, it's the only one we've got, and right or wrong, we're out of it if we go into service. A teacher or cashier or anybody in a store, no matter if they have got common-sense, doesn't want to associate with servants. Somehow you get a sort of smooch. Young men think and say, for I have heard lots of them, 'Oh, she can't amount to

much if she hasn't brains enough to make a living outside of a kitchen!'
You're just down once for all if you go into one."

"I don't agree with you at all," said a young teacher who had come
with her. "The people that hire you go into kitchens and are not disgraced. What I felt was, for you see I tried it, that they oughtn't to
make me go into livery. I was worn out with teaching, and so I concluded to try being a nurse for a while. I found two hard things: one,
that I was never free for an hour from the children, for I took meals
and all with them, and any mother knows what a rest it is to go quite
away from them, even for an hour; and the other was that she wanted
me to wear the nurse's cap and apron. She was real good and kind; but
when I said, 'Would you like your sister, Miss Louise, to put on cap
and apron when she goes out with them?' she got very red, and
straightened up. 'It's a very different matter,' she said; 'you must not
forget that in accepting a servant's place you accept a servant's limitations.' That finished me. I loved the children, but I said, 'If you have no
other thought of what I am to the children than that, I had better go.'
I went, and she put a common, uneducated Irish girl in my place. I
know a good many who would take nurse's places, and who are sensible
enough not to want to push into the family life. But the trouble is that
almost every one wants to make a show, and it is more stylish to have
the nurse in a cap and apron and so she is ordered into them."

"I've tried it," said one who had been a dressmaker and found her
health going from long sitting. "My trouble was, no conscience as to
hours; and I believe you'll find that is, at the bottom, one of the chief
objections. My first employer was a smart, energetic woman, who had
done her own work when she was first married and knew what it
meant, or you'd think she might have known. But she had no more
thought for me than if I had been a machine. She'd sit in her sitting-
room on the second floor and ring for me twenty times a day to do
little things, and she wanted me up till eleven to answer the bell, for she
had a great deal of company. I had a good room and everything nice,
and she gave me a great many things, but I'd have spared them all if
only I could have had a little time to myself. I was all worn out, and at
last I had to go. There was another reason. I had no place but the
kitchen to see my friends. I was thirty years old and as well born and
well educated as she, and it didn't seem right. The mistresses think it's
all the girls' fault, but I've seen enough to know that women haven't

found out what justice means, and that a girl knows it, many a time, better than her employer. Anyway, you couldn't make me try it again."

"My trouble was," said another, who had been in a cotton-mill and gone into the home of one of the mill-owners as chambermaid, "I hadn't any place that I could be alone a minute. We were poor at home, and four of us worked in the mill, but I had a little room all my own, even if it didn't hold much. In that splendid big house the servants' room was over the kitchen,—hot and close in summer, and cold in winter, and four beds in it. We five had to live there together, with only two bureaus and a bit of a closet, and one washstand for all. There was no chance to keep clean or your things in nice order, or anything by yourself, and I gave up. Then I went into a little family and tried general housework, and the mistress taught me a great deal, and was good and kind, only there the kitchen was a dark little place and my room like it, and I hadn't an hour in anything that was pleasant and warm. A mistress might see, you'd think, when a girl was quiet and fond of her home, and treat her different from the kind that destroy everything; but I suppose the truth is, they're worn out with that kind and don't make any difference. It's hard to give up your whole life to somebody else's orders, and always feel as if you was looked at over a wall like; but so it is, and you won't get girls to try it, till somehow or other things are different."

The Sweating System, Charity, and Organization by Ida Van Etten*

Ida M. Van Etten's experience of the lack of organization among working women formed the background for this address that she delivered at the national convention of the American Federation of Labor in 1890. At the AF of L convention the following year, she acted as secretary of a committee chaired by Eva MacDonald Valesh, which recommended that the convention create a salaried office for a national women's organizer, and amend the AF of L constitution to make the woman organizer a member of the Executive Board. The former recommendation was acted upon (with the appointment of Mary Kenney); the latter was not.

THE SWEATING SYSTEM, CHARITY, AND ORGANIZATION

THE SWEATING SYSTEM

Any review of the condition of women workers, however brief, would be incomplete without an exposition of the "sweating" system—a system which thrives upon the ignorance of the newly-arrived immigrants, the miseries and misfortunes of the very poor and upon the helplessness of women and little children, which pays no regular rate of wages and has no prescribed hours of work.

The "sweater" is only possible under a competitive system of industry. He is the natural outcome of cupidity and the intense desire for large profits and quick returns on the one side and the want, misery, degradation and ignorance of the workers on the other.

Neither capital nor skill are requisite for a sweater, only the heartlessness and cunning of a slave-driver. He is usually one of the workmen who saves enough money to hire a room in a tenement house, buys or rents a few machines, for which he charges his employees three dollars a month, obtains a supply of work for some large manufacturer of cloaks or ready-made clothing, secures his "hands" and begins business.

* From Ida M. Van Etten, "The Condition of Women Workers Under the Present Industrial System," an address at the National Convention of the American Federation of Labor, Detroit, December 8, 1890. Published by the American Federation of Labor, 7–10, 12–14.

These "sweater's" dens are always located in the most wretched, overcrowded tenement house districts. He has no scale of wages, but pays the lowest that he can possibly induce his miserable victims to work for. He trades upon the unhappiness and misfortunes of the dwellers in the neighborhood.

If a woman has a sick husband or children, she becomes a choice bit of speculation to this human shark. He says to her, "I will give you so much." She must take it or see her children starve.

Bad as is the condition of women-workers in factories, that of tenement-house workers is infinitely worse. In the factory, from the mere presence of a number of people, a sort of public opinion is formed which is often powerful enough to deter in some measure the employer from many acts of extreme oppression and injustice. Then, too, they are under the active operations of the factory law, which, however incomplete and badly executed, affords some protection to the workers.

With the present force of factory inspectors it is impossible to reach and properly inspect these dens, hidden away as they are in the cellars and garrets and rear buildings of tenement houses. And even were the force ten times greater than it now is, it would be necessary to have a law compelling the registration of all factories employing three or more persons.

One of the most frightful features of the "sweating" system is the unchecked employment of very young children. In these districts it is no unusual sight to see children of five, six, or even four years, employed all day sewing on buttons, pulling out bastings, or carrying huge piles of work to and from the "sweater's" shop.

A teacher in one of the primary schools on the East Side told me not long since of a little girl in her class who was constantly falling asleep. When she asked her at what time she usually went to bed, to her astonishment the child answered, "One o'clock," and explained that she had to "pull out bastings" until that time. The family were Russians and employed by a "sweater" in the cloak trade.

About three months ago I was able to get together thirty-five coat makers, all of whom worked under the "sweating" system, for the purpose of forming an organization.

Familiar as I was with many of the hardships of the working-women of New York, still what these girls told me, and which I afterwards verified by investigation, was a revelation to me. I found that the *usual* work-day of girls in this trade was from five or six o'clock in the morning until seven, eight, and often in the busy season until ten, o'clock at night; that in the clothing trade there exists an iniquitous system of "task" work which surpasses in cold-blooded cruelty anything I had ever before heard or read of.

The "sweater" in this trade pays so much a day, usually from 50 cents to $1.00, but in order to receive this sum the worker must perform a certain task—so many pieces of work. This task is beyond the ability of any girl to perform in any decent work-day, or at any reasonable degree of swiftness. To do even a portion of it, it is necessary that the girls should begin at five or six o'clock in the morning and work until late at night.

Even with these hours, the girls told me it was the exception when a worker finished her task in a day; but she is not paid for a day until the allotted task is fully completed. So that, even with these inhuman hours and the frightful rate of speed with which these girls worked, one day's work always lapped over upon the next day, and although doing six, and often even seven, days' work of from sixteen to eighteen hours' duration, they rarely received but four days' pay.

And mark the subtle cruelty and cunning of this! There are no hours prescribed. If you ask the "sweater," he will say: "Oh, my girls can come to work if they like at eight o'clock." But the "task" is made so herculean that it is impossible to accomplish it in less than a work-day of from sixteen to eighteen hours. And with the cruel necessity of want driving these young girls on, the "sweater" needs no other slave-driver, no superintendent, no foreman.

The thirty-five girls, many of whom were mere children, resembled in no respect other young girls. They were pale, spiritless, bent, and weary. So young, and yet with all youthful joy and buoyancy crushed out of them by the workings of a social system which systematically allows the weaker to go to the wall!

And, remember, it is not hundreds, but thousands, of women and girls who work under these conditions.

One day last August I visited a tenement-house in Ludlow street, entirely given up to the "sweaters." In every room were crowded together from six to ten men and women, four or five machines, with a cooking-stove at white heat, for the use of the pressers. Women, with white, pinched faces, unkempt hair, dressed in ragged, dirty, "unwomanly rags," were working from sixteen to eighteen hours a day for a pittance of from 50 to 75 cents. No words of mine can picture to you the horror of it—the dirt, the squalor, the food these people eat, the clothes they wear, the beds they sleep in, the air they breathe, and, more pitiful than all, their weary faces, out of which all hope and joy had long since been banished. All make up a scene that would linger in the mind, like Doré's pictures of Dante's "Inferno."

The overcrowding on the East Side must be seen to be appreciated.

In Essex street is a boarding-house frequented by cloak and knee-pants makers. It is on the first floor of an old tumbledown rookery, and comprises a front room, perhaps 16 x 14 feet, two dark bedrooms, one a mere passage-way, and a rear room with one window opening upon a tall brick wall. The family consisted of a man and his wife and six children. They kept eleven boarders in these quarters.

And this is the system we are living under—for let it be borne in mind that the "sweating" system is but the logical carrying out of the principles of the competitive system of industry, the natural result of the control of the means of production for private profit. You see in the "sweating" system the future condition of the working class foreshadowed, unless a radical change is brought about by you in the laws regulating the production and distribution of wealth. . . .

CHARITABLE INSTITUTIONS

So awful has become the condition of working-women in large cities that it has become the shame and disgrace of our times, and so gigantic has the evil become that even the bravest shrink back from undertaking its amelioration. Workingmen, engaged in the work of building up their own trade unions, and with, in many cases, a fancied antagonism of interests existing between the men and women workers in a trade—although I am convinced that men are opposed to women as co-workers only when they become a factor in reducing wages—still, all has contributed to cause the working-man, whose duty it naturally was to teach and train these women in the principles and methods of organized labor, to become passive lookers-on in their struggle for existence.

The result of this inaction on the part of working-men, and the increasing horrors of women's condition, has caused a multitude of palliative and charitable schemes for their relief to spring up in all large cities which still further increases the evils of working-women's condition.

Working-men, by their sturdy independence, achieved chiefly

through the power of organization, have placed themselves beyond the ordinary workings of charity. In times of sickness and out of work, the workman turns for relief and help to his trade union, and without loss of self-respect accepts aid from its fund, which he has himself helped to accumulate by his dues and assessments.

But working-women, without the moral and financial support of organization and with the more wretched conditions prevailing, as a result of this lack, have truly become the *victims of charity and philan-thropy*. So great has this evil become that I hold that charity should be classed as *one* of the direct causes of the wretched industrial condition of working-women.

Charity has for a long time tried its hand at alleviating the evils of their condition. It has built lodging-houses, Christian Homes, refuges, reformatories, etc., and still the evils go on increasing—nay, these very methods have added a fearful impetus to the causes of the evils.

The evils of charity are both moral and economic. It robs the char-acter of the working-woman of its qualities of self-respect, its moral and intellectual independence and in the place of these sterling virtues implants the seeds of distrust and a cringing, false respect for money and position.

From an economic standpoint the evils are still more serious and far-reaching. Although charity undoubtedly had its origin in the noblest and most unselfish motives of human conduct, it has, in later times, been warped and turned aside from its original and legitimate purpose and become a disturbing element in industrial affairs. In a simpler state of society, its only function was the care and relief of the sick and those disabled by age or accident: but in the nineteenth century it has become the most powerful ally of the competitive system of industry and forms one of the strongest bulwarks of its support and continuance. Accord-ing to the reports of the Commissioners of Charities the amount ex-pended in public and private charity during the last ten years has enormously increased.

We find charity everywhere supplementing the present industrial system, bolstering it up and making its operations possible; accepting its horrible results as a normal state of things; and instead of bitterly and relentlessly attacking the root of the evil, attempting to plaster up and palliate its *consequences*.

Charity has only succeeded in making it easier for the unscrupulous employers of women to exploit them safely and respectably. By the side of the huge factory, whose owner is growing enormously rich, upon the spoilation of his women workers, it builds the Lodging House or Christian Home, and this enables the manufacturer to pay wages below the living point.

The "sweating" system would in many cases be almost impossible, were it not for the thoughtless charity of innumerable Church Relief, St. Vincent de Paul Societies, etc., etc. . . .

ORGANIZATION

Thus it can readily be seen that women-workers either must become organized and receive not only equal pay for equal work, but also equal opportunities for working, or they will, by degrees, naturally form an inferior class in every trade in which they enter; a class more poorly paid, and who will, in consequence, work longer hours; who will receive less consideration from their employers, and who will be without means of redress, even in those grievances which are most degrading to their womanhood. In this condition they will be a constant menace to wages; they will be used, in case of strikes and lockouts, to supply the places of union men; and, in short, we shall witness the horrible spectacle of workers whose interests are identical being used against each other for the purpose of lowering the general condition of their class.

The bitterness with which employers oppose the organization of women furnishes the best evidence of their present value in supplying them with ignorant, unthinking and consequently cheap laborers.

Testimony on Compensation for
Educated Women at Work*

To assess the comparison of educated women's wages with men's wages in professional, technical, and other white-collar jobs, the Association of Collegiate Alumnae undertook a survey in the early 1890s. They solicited responses in various parts of the United States from female employees who had had college or other training relevant to their occupations. Some of the published responses returned by the educated working women appear here.

TESTIMONY ON COMPENSATION FOR
EDUCATED WOMEN AT WORK

Women, as a class, have not as much confidence in themselves as men. In my opinion if women would give sufficient time to necessary preparation, in their chosen line of work, fully to equip themselves for that work and, at the same time, cultivate confidence in themselves, their ability, and their profession, they would, like men, be able to meet the question of wages with the words:—"I ask no more than I am worth but I believe myself to be worth all that I ask. Kindly give me a trial." An employer would admire this spirit sufficiently to permit the test, which in nine cases out of ten would prove the words true.

Therefore, I would say, let there be on the part of women thorough preparation, steadfast purpose, unflinching confidence, determination to become of such value to their employers as to merit remuneration equal to that accorded any other person of like ability.

My position is an anomalous one. I do a great deal of responsible work for the President of a University. I keep the entire accounts of the University, as far as they pertain to receipts and expenditures, and next year shall also keep the Treasurer's books. I am also the President's delegate in relation to all that concerns the interests and life of our

* From "Compensation in Certain Occupations of Graduates of Colleges for Women," from the *25th Annual Report* of the Massachusetts Bureau of Statistics of Labor, for 1894, by Horace G. Wadlin (Boston, 1895), 32–41.

women students. I don't regard my pay as holding any proper proportion to either the character or amount of work I do.

Women are fearful of asserting their inherent rights, standing, as they now do, just on the verge of freedom. The time, however, is not far off when women will have a voice in making just laws for themselves and others, and this will no doubt have an effect in securing equal remuneration for equal services to both sexes.

I fear I am not a fair representative of office working-women, at least my sympathies are not all with them. I do not think they are, as a class, as good workers as men, and if I had an office under my charge, I would put in almost all men clerks even at higher salaries, for I verily believe that I could get more and better work from them, with less complaints, than from women. In the first place they are stronger physically, do not look for the same favors and attentions that women expect, and they are willing to work until their work is completed, even though it be until 12 o'clock at night, or on Sundays in case of necessity, and their feelings are not easily hurt.

As to the question of men receiving higher pay for their services, in my opinion typewriting is peculiarly woman's work; she can do the work more neatly and takes pains to make her work look well. I do not see why she should not receive as much as men.

Women would, in my opinion, give better satisfaction as employés if they attended more strictly to all details of their business than many now do.

Women are more conscientious, more prompt, and feel that their employers' interests are theirs.

Great harm is done woman by woman, for it is most imperfect evidence of business quality, success, or tenacity to exhibit petty strife, carry personalities into business, or to blend the social distinctions and caste with the affairs of the work-a-day world.

I deplore the narrow-mindedness, gossip, slander, jealousies, the caste spirit. Fellowship, charity, and humanity are needed in place of the spirit of caste.

Men as a rule want women to work for them and not with them; hence at present few women do anything except the *"dead work."* Few women have ambition enough, or are well trained enough, to overcome the odds against their sex; but matters are improving; and the younger men I think are more ready than their elders to give women a chance to live up to the highest that is in them. Many women exhaust their energies doing outside work,—that is, assuming domestic responsibility. As far as my observation goes college women do just as good work as men.

While I was employed at $7.50 per week I believe $10 to $12 would have been paid a man for doing my work: when I reached $12 per week (which was in a business office where I worked four years and four months) a man would have received about $20 per week. I have been in the Government service three years and five months. My experience was that a woman had no right to expect good salaries, simply because she was a woman: the theory was kept constantly before the women in the office in which I have been employed until recently, that the only place for a woman was in doing domestic work. I am happy to say this state of affairs does not exist where I work at present.

I think that my experience will be of little value, in your inquiry, for my work has been varied, and, in many instances, I have refused a higher salary, preferring congenial and less monotonous work, even at a lower salary. I preferred to build a home and keep it by trying varied employments, rather than to bind myself down to one steady position, even though lucrative.

Aside from the fact that custom places a lower estimate of value on the work of a woman, I see no reason why a thoroughly capable and earnest woman should not receive what she is worth: and I think that this custom must be changed by demonstration through women themselves that their work is equally as valuable as that of men. It is also very necessary that women should make a point of demanding what they have reason to consider themselves worth. Every increase of salary, except the first, that I have had has come through a demand for it. Doubtless had my assurance equalled my conviction, I might now be earning much more, as I consider my services, as compared with those of others (men) employed with me, as underpaid. Women need firmness and push, without undue pugnacity, to secure what they are worth.

It must be said, however, that the majority of employed women belittle the position of women in the working ranks by their lack of earnestness and business conscience. I do not know whether this fact can be greatly altered, as it is doubtless the first destiny of women to marry, and their thoughts will probably have a stronger bent in this direction than in that of becoming highly proficient in the different branches of work which they undertake.

A woman who is earnest, who is capable, and who has an enthusiasm for her occupation, has, I think, as many doors open to her as a man. If she is underpaid it is largely her own fault, and I believe that the condition of inequality in wages is disappearing, and will finally wholly disappear.

Women do not put the ardor into their work that men, knowing that their work is for life, exhibit. Again, women as a rule feel that they have no hope of advancement, and must remain as employés, when a man may hope for larger results, even if he never obtains them.

This is truer, of course, of the mechanical and active employments than of the professions, where conditions are more nearly equal.

My observation leads me to conclude that women as a rule are to blame for low wages, and for several reasons. When women enter the business world, they carry with them false notions of what is due them. Everything beyond courteous justice is a privilege accorded them, but many demand these privileges as rights. This destroys their desirability as employés. When they lay aside the fol-de-rol of being "ladies" and are *business women* the way will be clear for an advance in their wages.

Further, when women are educated up to the point of caring for each other and each other's interests then will a better state arrive, and not before. Girls working, who are not obliged to do so for support, but in order to decorate themselves beyond their need and station, copying those who have dollars to their dimes, accept an unjust compensation, and also occupy the place which another should have. I repeat, as a rule, women are to blame for women's low wages.

The same work exactly, which I am engaged in, is done by men in the New York Department at double the pay.

I find where women are employed and men are at the head, favoritism plays a very decided part in the matter of salaries.

One reason for the inequality in women's wages, as compared with those paid men, is that women are patient in their willingness to earn something, be it ever so little. They *earn* it. They are not situated in life to apply the nerve required to demand what should be theirs justly. . . .

When Mr. —— was offered a position at a certain salary, he declined the offer and set his own terms, which after an interval of time were complied with, just as he demanded. Now, all of his friends say, "A very fine thing. Mr. —— got just what he demanded: His own price!" What would a woman have done? Taken, and been glad to take, just what they had a mind to give her. She would lack nerve.

I have fulfilled all the duties of a citizen, just as man does (with the exception of voting), reared three fatherless children from tender years, kept them in school until they were twenty-one, partially supported an invalid sister, assisted the young boys of her family, and I am a woman, living on wages much less than those of men.

Unionization for Women:
The Typographical Union
by Belva Mary Herron*

Belva Mary Herron's description of women's circumstances in the printing trade and in the Typographical Union was part of a larger academic study of labor organization among women.

UNIONIZATION FOR WOMEN: THE TYPOGRAPHICAL UNION

In considering the division of labor between men and women in the printing trade, the most significant fact is one that does not appear in a description of the processes; it is the custom, or unwritten law, that women enter the trade as regular workers, receiving regular pay after six weeks' tuition in type-setting, while men serve an apprenticeship of four years; this means of course that women learn merely setting up plain matter, while men go through a curriculum made up of all the processes of the trade. This places the two classes upon fundamentally different bases. If the man fails to find work in one department, he has the chance of turning to another; as opportunity offers he can pass from the lower to higher grades of work with increasing remuneration. Moreover, as an all round workman, he is worth more to his employer, for he can be turned from one kind of work to another as occasion demands. Women's work is largely confined to setting up "straight matter" and "distributing," or returning type to the proper boxes. Both processes are light, but require some education and constant attention. Imposing, or dividing the galleys into pages, is ordinarily done by men, because it involves considerable heavy lifting. So, too, locking up the properly placed pages into forms—which simply means putting a sort of frame on the collected sticks which are to constitute the page—is done by men, for the same reason. The hand or foot press upon which the trial galley is printed involves heavy work and is managed by men.

* From Belva Mary Herron, "Labor Organization Among Women," *University of Illinois Bulletin*, II: 12 (Urbana, 1905), 16–24.

In proof reading, however, no distinction is made between men and women. . . .

Of course, expert proof reading is an art not to be learned in a day, and hence the majority of readers are printers of long experience; although in a very high class printing establishment young college men are taking up proof reading, having just learned the necessary type-setting. Subordinate to the proof reader is the copy holder, who reads the manuscript or copy; this work of course requires only ability to read the text. The copy holder is nearly always a young girl who looks to learning type-setting later. Feeding the press is wearisome work, because it involves standing for a considerable time, but otherwise it requires no great strength and little skill; it is largely done by women. On the other hand, managing the press, adjusting the machine, watching its movements, etc., involves some knowledge of machinery, some dexterity and judgment, and considerable strength. It is dirty work, too, and necessitates climbing about the machines in a way that would be impossible for a woman on account of her dress. Hence, the pressmen have no competition from their sisters in the trade. Upon the linotype machine both men and women are at work; the key board is managed in much the same way as a typewriter and the same sort of skill is required. At the bottom of the scale of workers young girls are found doing simple unskilled tasks; the smarter ones of these are given a chance to learn the trade. The preparing of frontispieces, pamphlets, advertisements, hand bills, etc., is more difficult than setting up plain matter, for it requires some skill in making an attractive page; so, too, is the making up of a page of newspaper or other periodical. Men usually do these things, although women occasionally learn the art by watching men at their tasks and asking to be allowed to help at some opportune moment.

It will be seen from our account that the chief field of competition between men and women in the printing trade is in setting up straight matter. The women compare well with the men in accuracy of work, but can not ordinarily do so much as their male competitors in the same time. The Secretary of the Typographical Union says that all employers are agreed that women can not compete with men where the same wages are paid. . . . In one fine book establishment a number of women were found at work upon the linotype machine and were said to be as efficient as the men and were paid the same wages. Women are employed as proof readers, moreover, in Union book and newspaper offices, on the same time scale with men, but in non-union offices they get less. . . .

In the three kinds of work mentioned above women hold their own in the more difficult tasks, proof reading and linotype operating. Many parts of the trade are not suited to women's strength, but the more complicated kinds of of type-setting, advertising, bill heads, etc., seem to be a field where women might prove efficient. Why does she not learn this more difficult work is a question answered in different ways. She doesn't care to work hard for a larger salary, declares a prominent Union official; an employer, a leading member of the Typothetae, when asked if a woman would be given a chance to learn the more difficult and better paid processes, answers frankly, no; for the employer does not wish to have his workmen hindered with helping along girls who stay only a short time in his service. This gentleman, a person apparently without any prejudice on this subject, insisted upon the importance of the temporary character of women's labor as an influence keeping them from rising to the best classes of work. He admitted that a few women stayed on ten or more years, but a large proportion of his men had been with him for over that period. None of the women left for work in other houses; most of them were getting married; some went home to take care of parents or orphaned brothers and sisters; but matrimony was regarded as the main cause of women's position in the trade. Another large Boston employer thought that women were no more transient than men, but admitted that the majority of type-setters, both men and women, were not likely to remain long in one place. He explained his preference for girls by saying that they were more contented and of much higher character than the men.

The place of women in the International Typographical Union is of particular interest, for there is a greater degree of competition between the sexes in the printing than in most other trades. The constitution directs locals to organize all women within their jurisdiction as soon as possible, and place them upon the same basis with men as to wages, dues, and benefits. In 1902 the general convention made provision for the establishment of separate locals for women, but at the present time no such Unions exist. The results of the policy of an identical scale are difficult to decide. Employers say that insistance upon a uniform time scale for men and women is simply a means of putting women out of the trade. The head of a large Boston printing house is responsible for the statement that the printed reports of conferences between the representatives of the Typothetae, on the one hand, and of the Union, on the other, contain the declaration of the Union officers that the Union policy was to force women out of the trade by insisting upon the same scale for them as for men compositors. . . .

Printing is one of the trades in which direct competition between the sexes has led to some hard feeling. On the one hand, the local officials complain that they can "do nothing with the women," that they have failed after repeated efforts to enlist their sympathy and interest; and they seem disgusted with the frivolity of the sex. On the other hand, capable and intelligent Union women insist that the organization does not want them, and favors men, wherever possible, by giving them places and advancing them at the expense of women competitors. This action is possible because the foreman in all Union offices has the right to discharge for incompetency and to select the best workmen according to the Union scale, and can of course discriminate against women employees, if the feeling in the shop is with him. Instances were cited of foremen's refusing to consider the claims of women who were of unquestionable ability; men would boast that when they got to be foremen they would turn out all the women, but when it came to carrying out this threat they were not always ready to deprive themselves of some of their best workpeople. . . .

Yet there is often good fellowship between the men and women members of the local, and the man most discontented with the progress of the women spoke with great respect of some who were capable and dignified. A much larger percentage of the men in the craft than of the women are enrolled in the Union, and all Union representatives agree that women are much harder to organize than men. An explanation for this lack of interest is given by the general secretary as follows: "A large percentage of women who work, are merely doing so until they find the man of their choice, and become the head of a household. They do not expect to work at it for a life time; consequently there is no use of their joining the Union. Again, proprietors, as above stated, claim that they can not pay men and women the same wages for the reason that women can not perform the same amount of work as do men. Women therefore decline to join the Union, fearing displacement by men in case they do so." . . .

Once within the Union women seem, for some reasons, to lack interest in its activities; in the small towns it sometimes happens that they are of considerable influence, and acts as officers, but in the cities they hold no official positions, and do not largely attend meetings. In the general organization they are not represented among the officers and organizers, and are only occasionally sent as delegates to conventions. . . . The failure of women Unionists to attend local meetings is worth noting here, because it brings up certain features of the mixed local that are of significance. The policy of organizing according to the department of work results, in many trades, in practically separating men from women; the Typographical Union thinks it best to have all printers in a city as members of a single local, and the provision for separate locals for women has never been taken advantage of; hence we have in the cities very large bodies which are overwhelmingly masculine. If women came to meetings in the same proportion as men, they would still form a little group in a large roomful of men; they would have little influence; and would find the atmosphere little to their taste, for it is likely to be black with tobacco smoke. Like other politicians, the men wrangle and draw out the discussions to unconscionable length, and the women, taking little part in the discussion, naturally become tired and depart in disgust. Another reason for non-attendance at meetings is the fact that these are often held on Sunday afternoons, the only time which working women have for visiting and recreation; for they can not go out as freely in the evening as men. These considerations may seem trivial, but, in reality, they are suggestive of fundamental difficulties in mixed organizations. It is certain that women are most unlikely to speak freely, and take an active and unembarrassed part in gatherings where men are in the majority, and that men do feel themselves abused and imposed upon, if obliged, out of respect to women, to give up the privilege of smoking at regular meetings.

ON The Black Woman as Breadwinner by Mary White Ovington*

Mary White Ovington, a white woman, was one of the group of Progressives and radical blacks led by W. E. B. Du Bois who broke away from Booker T. Washington's gradualist approach to civil rights, and founded the National Association for the Advancement of Colored People in 1909. A social worker with a particular sympathy for the condition of black people, she carried on an investigation of the status of the Negro in New York under the auspices of Greenwich House, and published the results in 1911. Her discussion of the black woman as breadwinner is from that study.

On THE BLACK WOMAN AS BREADWINNER

[T]he life of the average New York white woman of the laboring class . . . is not, however, the life of the average colored woman. With her, self-sustaining work usually begins at fifteen, and by no means ceases with her entrance upon marriage, which only entails new financial burdens. The wage of the husband, as we have seen, is usually insufficient to support a family, save in extreme penury, and the wife accepts the necessity of supplementing the husband's income. This she accomplishes by taking in washing or by entering a private family to do housework. Sometimes she is away from her tenement nearly every day in the week; again the bulk of her earnings comes from home industry. Her day holds more diversity than that of her white neighbor; she meets more people, becomes familiar with the ways of the well-to-do,—their household decorations, their dress, their refinements of manner; but she has but few hours to give to her children. With her husband she is ready to be friend and helpmate; but should he turn out a bad bargain, she has no fear of leaving him, since her marital relations are not welded by economic dependence. An industrious, competent woman, she works and spends, and in her scant hours of leisure takes pride in keeping her children well-dressed and clean.

* From Mary White Ovington, *Half a Man: The Status of the Negro in New York* (New York: Longmans, Green and Co., 1911), pp. 140–144, 146–158, 162–164.

. . . White boys and girls in New York enter work that makes it possible and advantageous for them to dwell at home; Negroes must go out to service, accept long and irregular hours in hotel or apartment, travel for days on boat or train. The family home is infrequently available to them, and money given in to it brings small return. Under these circumstances it is not strange if the mother must continue her round of washing and scrubbing.

The last years of life of the Negro woman, probably a little more than the last years of the white, are likely to bring happiness. With a mother at work a grandmother becomes an important factor, and elderly colored women are often seen bringing up little children or helping in the laundry—that great colored home industry. Accustomed all their lives to hard labor, it is easy for them to find work that shall repay their support, and in their children's households they are treated with respect and consideration.

The contrast in the lives of the colored and white married women is not more strongly marked than the contrast in the lives of their unmarried daughters and sisters. Unable to enter any pursuit except housework, the unskilled colored girl goes out to service or helps at home with the laundry or sewing. Factory and store are closed to her, and rarely can she take a place among other working girls. Her hours are the long, irregular hours of domestic service. She brings no pay envelope home to her mother, the two then carefully discussing how much belongs rightfully for board, and how much may go for the new coat or dress, but takes the eighteen or twenty dollars given her at the end of the month, and quite by herself determines all her expenditures. Far oftener than any class of white girls in the city she lives away from the parental home. . . .

Scattered among the volumes on Population, Occupations, and Women at Work are many facts concerning Negro women workers of New York, all of them confirmatory of the description just given. We may note the most important.

In 1900, whereas 4.2 per cent of the white married women in New York were engaged in gainful occupations, 31.4 per cent of the Negro married women were earning their living, over seven times as many in proportion as the whites. . . .

Family life can be studied in the census table. While 59 per cent of the unmarried white girls at work live at home, this is found to be true of but 25 per cent of the colored girls; that is, 75 per cent, three-quarters of all the colored unmarried working women, live with their employers or board.

The census volume on occupations reveals at once the narrow range of the New York colored woman's working life. Personal and domestic service absorbs 90 per cent of her numbers against 40 per cent among the white. . . . This includes a variety of positions. Some Negro girls work in stores, dusting stock, taking charge of cloak or toilet rooms, scrubbing floors. Their hours are regular, but the pay, five or six, or very occasionally eight dollars a week, means a scanty livelihood without hope of advancement. The position of maid in a theatre where perquisites are larger is prized, and a new and pleasant place is that of a maid on a limited train. But the bulk of the girls are servants in boarding-houses, or are with private families as nurses, waitresses, cooks, laundresses, maids-of-all-work, earning from sixteen and eighteen to twenty-five and even thirty dollars a month. Occasionally a very skilful cook can command as high a monthly wage as fifty dollars.

The colored girl is frequently found engaged at general housework in a small apartment. . . . Work begins early, seven at the latest, and lasts until the dinner is cleared away, at half-past eight or nine. Released then from further tasks, the young girl goes to her tiny inner tenement room, dons a fresh dress, and then, as chance or her training determines, walks the streets, goes to the theatre, or attends the class meeting at her church. Entertainments among the Negroes are rarely under way until ten o'clock, and short hours of sleep in ill-ventilated rooms soon weaken the vitality of the new-comer. Housework under these conditions does not create much ambition; the mistress moves, flitting, in New York fashion, from one flat to another, and the girl also flits among employers, changing with the whim of the moment. . . .

Untrained herself, bereft of home influence, with an ancestry that sometimes cries out her parent's weakness in the contour and color of her face, the Negro girl in New York, more even than the foreign immigrant, is subject to degrading temptation. The good people, who are often so exacting, want her for her willingness to work long hours at a lower wage than the white; and the bad people, who are often so carelessly kind, offer her light labor and generous pay. It is small wonder that she sometimes chooses the latter.

Not all the colored girls who work in questionable places and with questionable people take the jobs from choice; some are sent without knowing the character of the house they enter. . . . Those familiar with the subject assert that there is a proportionately larger black slave than white slave traffic.

. . . It is pleasant and encouraging to turn from colored women who have given up the struggle, to ambitious, successful workers. Some among these are in the domestic service group and enjoy with heartiness their tasks as nurse-maid or cook. . . . Among the domestic service workers, as classified by the census, is the trained nurse, filling an increasingly important position in New York. In 1909, Lincoln Hospital graduated twenty-one colored nurses, some of whom remain in New York to do excellent work.

In the professions, with the women as with the men, the first place numerically is occupied by performers upon the stage. . . .

No record is kept of the number of colored teachers in the city's public schools, but each year Negro graduates from the normal college secure positions. These are found from the kindergarten through the primary and up to the highest grammar grade. The colored girl with intellectual ability, particularly if she comes of an old New York family, is apt to turn to teaching. . . .

But despite her efforts and occasional successes, the colored girl in New York meets with severer race prejudice than the colored man, and is more persistently kept from attractive work. *She gets the job that the white girl does not want.* It may be that the white girls want the wrong thing, and that the jute mill and tobacco shop and flower factory are more dangerous to health and right living than the mistress's kitchen, but she knows her mind, and follows the business that brings her liberty of action when the six o'clock whistle blows. What she desires for herself, however, she refuses to her colored neighbor. Occasionally an employer objects to colored girls, but the Manhattan Trade School repeatedly, in trying to place its graduates, has found that opposition to the Negro has come largely from the working girls. Race prejudice has even gone so far as to prevent a colored woman from receiving home work when it entailed her waiting in the same sitting-room with white women. Of course, this is not the universal attitude. In friendly talks with hundreds of New York's white women workers, I have found the majority ready to accept the colored worker. Jewish girls are especially tolerant. . . .

The shirtwaist makers' strike of 1910 was so profoundly important in its breaking down of feeling between nationalities, its union of all working women in a common cause, that the colored girl, while very slightly concerned in the strike itself, may profit by the more generous feeling it engendered. Certainly an entrance into store and workshop would be to her immense advantage. She needs the discipline of regular hours, of steady training, of order and system. She needs also to become part of a strong labor group, to share its working class ideal, to feel the weight of its moral opinion; instead of looking into the mirror of her wealthy mistress, she needs to reflect the aspirations of the strong, earnest women who toil.

VIII
Legacy of Leisure: Discontent

ON Marriage and Work
by Antoinette Brown Blackwell*

Antoinette Brown's feminist leanings brought her to Oberlin College in the 1840s, soon after it became the first American college to offer men and women the same course of study. She was the first American woman to be ordained a minister, and remained an active women's rights advocate, speaker, and writer, during a long life in which she was the wife of one of Elizabeth Blackwell's brothers, and the mother of six children. The following paper was her contribution to the 3rd Women's Congress of the Association for the Advancement of Women in 1875.

On MARRIAGE AND WORK

At this third Congress of Women my heart turns yet once again to the home, as at both the former sessions; to the general work to be done by the wives and mothers of America. We have long conceded to exceptional women, to unmarried women, the right, if intellectually gifted, to engage in literature or, if practically inclined, to occupy themselves in works of active benevolence.

But married women have been taught to feel but little more responsibility for the engrossing active duties of the outside world than the queen bee has for the active endless work carried on by the busy little colony from which she is set apart by her absorbing maternal functions. . . .

We still hear of the little use there is in giving a higher education to girls, since most of them will be married; and marriage is still held to be the grave of the feminine intellect in all its loftier forms of exercise. Our English sisters seem even to concede this point. At the recent Science Convention they brought forth the growing lateness of marriage as a valid reason for granting certain claims to women. But that involves a doubtful if not a most mischievous concession. It is our claim that maternity is no bar to the highest and broadest life-work which lies within the ability of any woman to achieve! Motherhood carries with it its own widening and strengthening of the feminine character; it is a

* From *Papers* read at the 3rd Women's Congress of the Association for the Advancement of Women, Syracuse, New York, October 13–15, 1875, 27–35.

natural barrier to mental overwork during the earlier years of comparative inexperience—that prolonged seed time of every human soul, male or female; when the years of harvest come, the children of a good mother should uphold her hands and her heart while she achieves the final consummation of her lifelong duties as an intelligent, an active, and a responsible citizen of the world.

What! does the husband exact more service than he gives in return? Is he strengthened and ennobled by family ties, and does he confer no compensating aid and encouragement in return? So surely as marriage is an institution grounded in human nature, no woman, worthily and happily married, is less fitted to aid the general progress of the world than she who stands alone with none to hinder; yes, with none to hinder, but with none to help her either, in the exercise of her best gifts. It is time that we utterly repudiate the pernicious dogma that marriage and a practical life-work are incompatible. . . .

To-day, it is not simply exceptional women who feel impelled to put their woman's shoulders to some of the lagging wheels of social revolution. There are multitudes who can no longer comfortably shake off the burden of direct responsibility. What was the temperance crusade in its initial stages? The spontaneous fire kindled in a few hearts, but spreading to a hundred thousand woman souls, some of them laden with private sorrows, and all of them aroused to an agony of sympathetic protest against the brutalizing crime of intemperance. What is the same movement to-day, in its organizing efforts to effectually crush the dominion of alcohol? It is the irrepressible expression of a settled purpose to put down a gigantic evil. It is womanhood awakened to a sense of its own most solemn responsibilities; reaching out after the most practical and effective methods of compassing its ends, of checkmating the destroyer who is annually plucking and trampling in the dust thousands of the brightest and most generous young men in all the land. Women belong to humanity; they must work, then, for the human weal.

Why have the farmers' granges, the out-growth of modern civilization, found a practical working position on all boards for women? They saw and comprehended the fundamental fact that women of the country, and more especially farmers' wives and daughters, whose homes are comparatively isolated, needed and desired to be healthfully active and useful. They foresaw that this influence could be made effective. They have practically decided that it is no better for a great working organization to be conducted by wholly male methods of work than for men to *live* alone in the household.

What women did in the war, the whole country can remember. It was then that multitudes of them put on the spirit of real work for the Commonwealth, a spirit which never again can be suppressed. What have women done, and what are they doing, for the Centennial? Giving it effective aid and comfort at every stage of its progress. Their organization is another great co-operative manifestation of the growing imperative need in women to identify themselves with the honor and well-being of their country, and the men have recognized them as a practical force in the nation. Non-voting citizens, they are still citizens; the vote is waiting for them just ahead. It is a question of time, the time depending upon the rapidity of our growth as a people. . . .

The harvest fields to-day are many. The same work is not for all. Personal ability is the limit of personal responsibility. The highest work for each is that to which she is most drawn in heart; that to which she is most nearly connected by the circumstances of her position and by the fitness of her special talents. The millions of local, benevolent, and church associations have long been an outlet for the quickened energies of many women. Now these are associating themselves more and more widely. Women's benevolent enterprises are becoming national. Missionary boards have their auxiliary female societies reaching to the ends of the earth. Church associations every year admit their women to a wider and more active co-operation in almost every church enterprise. And the majority of all these eager workers are wives and mothers! Their homes are better kept, their children are more wisely guided, and their husbands are more honored among their townsmen, because this energy of the soul has found expression and toned the whole nature to a broader harmony. It is a general impulse, and one of those tidal waves in social life, which is impelling so many women into such varied fields of activity. What influence is powerful enough to arrest it?

For many years, as class after class of girl graduates completed courses of study broad enough and solid enough to fit them for some of the higher work of the world, many of the oldest advocates for a wider field of occupation for women waited anxiously to see what would be the result. Year after year went by; the women thought and felt and waited. And then, as if impelled by a common impulse, ten thousand women at once quietly took up some broader work, each in her own line, associating together, and by an almost unconscious widening of methods, all these and many other growing organizations are the result. . . .

The platform of our Congress here to-day is fairly representative of all the women's organizations in the country in this respect. Probably three-fourths of all the members, as well as most of the active workers, are wives and mothers. Who thinks of asking whether a woman is married or unmarried when she is solicited or appointed to undertake any duty? The simple question is as to her fitness for the work to be done. . . .

Why, then, appeal particularly to married women to enter the lists as workers for the age in which they live? For three reasons: First, because of the lingering prejudice that wifehood and maternity are all-sufficient, life-long occupations for women. Not at all. Varied interests would give better health. They should enable one to be bright, active, steadily gaining in ability during the whole of middle life, and leave at least a quarter of a century of vigorous health beyond; when there are no little children and, too often, alas! no husband.

Sheer waste of human energy it is to persuade women that they ought to become superannuated before seventy-five or eighty, or indeed at any age when, by reason of strength, life and health still remain.

Second—The temptation to absorb all of one's powers in home affairs is specially strong with mothers. It is they who most need warning against this influence. When they believe that duty calls them to this, they, their families, and the world will all suffer together in consequence. The best mothers are always something more than mothers. Women with their eager mercurial temperaments have no right to crystallize their whole versatile natures into any one set of functions, however central and important these may be. This would be destruction to men; it has been destruction and desolation to women.

The third reason for particularly calling on the matrons of this country, earnestly and in singleness of purpose to take upon themselves the world's highest work, is that in their ranks we shall find the only existing, considerable American leisure class. Other countries have their men of leisure, the nobility who inherit wealth, position, and time for any pursuit to which they may be impelled by circumstances or by inclination.

But in our civilization it is the rich married women, the childless wives, and the "old wives"—classes in the earlier days despised and set aside as droning retailers of senseless fables—who now, in the normal progress of human events, are ordained to become standard-bearers of a higher culture; disinterested pioneers in every needed enterprise; careful and conscientious investigators into many of the marvellous but open secrets of the universe.

Does this claim for our only considerable leisure class seem too arrogant? Let us see. Would a successful business man, whose time is too precious to allow him to take up any of the menial offices of life, even if he had the inclination otherwise, desire his wife to be either cook, housemaid, or seamstress? Certainly not. Yet the home has need of her. She must rule there as a steady presiding and guiding spirit; since the highest interests of the household can thus be better promoted than by any gain which might accrue from her engaging in outside business occupations. Doing her duty thus, there remains no respectable pretence that she is supported in any degrading sense of that often odious term. Yet any competent woman, not greatly stinted in means, and having health and few or no little children to cherish and educate, is, if she so wills it, an honorable member of the enviable leisure class. Thus, like the cloisters of old, the home sanctuary can be made to foster learning and to offer its own appropriate contributions toward the progress of the race. . . .

Our leisure wives no doubt can utilize their time in making pretty, elaborate embroideries, or beautiful patch-work quilts; in brilliant and even good natured gossip; in fitting themselves to be the most graceful, the brightest of polite society; and they can easily give a whole life to ten thousand other amiable things. The world, and their friends in particular, would still be the better for their having lived. But we are not now in the dark ages. . . .

And the women of to-day are fully abreast of the century in which they live. Many of them now have the basis of a broad and sensible education. Will the matrons who have leisure, or can make leisure for themselves, consent to go on aimlessly frittering away their best energies? We have seen that they are not content. The busiest of them are taking up these many new co-operative enterprises; and they who have leisure are fast learning how to utilize it in line with the inquiring spirit of the times. Then, if the sexes are intellectual peers, the time has come for women of leisure, for all they who need neither toil continuously for the bread they eat, nor spin a thread of raiment which they wear; it is time for these steadily and persistently to take up the highest intellectual work of which they are capable. It is time for all women to begin fairly to test themselves and their capacities. This has never yet been done. . . . A mother's child is but an incident in her life. Love it as she will, it will grow up; and in a few years it is gone. But a life-work remains for a life-time!

The Snare of Preparation by Jane Addams*

This excerpt from Jane Addams' autobiography, *Twenty Years at Hull House*, describes some of the feelings that led her to establish the social settlement that became the most renowned one in the United States. Her intentions took shape while she was on her second trip to Europe in the late 1880s, after her graduation from college and a period of illness, indecision, and depression. What had been her own "subjective" need to found the settlement house she later developed into a more general formulation in her 1892 essay, "The Subjective Necessity for Social Settlements." Part of that essay, which she included in *Twenty Years at Hull House* as her best contemporary evaluation of the problem, follows to complement her autobiographical reminiscence.

THE SNARE OF PREPARATION

For two years in the midst of my distress over the poverty which, thus suddenly driven into my consciousness, had become to me the "Weltschmerz," there was mingled a sense of futility, of misdirected energy, the belief that the pursuit of cultivation would not in the end bring either solace or relief. I gradually reached a conviction that the first generation of college women had taken their learning too quickly, had departed too suddenly from the active, emotional life led by their grandmothers and great-grandmothers; that the contemporary education of young women had developed too exclusively the power of acquiring knowledge and of merely receiving impressions; that somewhere in the process of "being educated" they had lost that simple and almost automatic response to the human appeal, that old healthful reaction resulting in activity from the mere presence of suffering or of helplessness; that they are so sheltered and pampered they have no chance even to make "the great refusal."

In the German and French *pensions*, which twenty-five years ago were crowded with American mothers and their daughters who had crossed the seas in search of culture, one often found the mother making real connection with the life about her, using her inadequate German

*From Jane Addams, *Twenty Years at Hull House* (New York: The Macmillan Co., 1911), pp. 71–75, 77, 85–88, 118–122.

with great fluency, gayly measuring the enormous sheets or exchanging recipes with the German Hausfrau, visiting impartially the nearest kindergarten and market, making an atmosphere of her own, hearty and genuine as far as it went, in the house and on the street. On the other hand, her daughter was critical and uncertain of her linguistic acquirements, and only at ease when in the familiar receptive attitude afforded by the art gallery and the opera house. In the latter she was swayed and moved, appreciative of the power and charm of the music, intelligent as to the legend and poetry of the plot, finding use for her trained and developed powers as she sat "being cultivated" in the familiar atmosphere of the classroom which had, as it were, become sublimated and romanticized.

I remember a happy busy mother who, complacent with the knowledge that her daughter daily devoted four hours to her music, looked up from her knitting to say, "If I had had your opportunities when I was young, my dear, I should have been a very happy girl. I always had musical talent, but such training as I had, foolish little songs and waltzes and not time for half an hour's practice a day."

The mother did not dream of the sting her words left and that the sensitive girl appreciated only too well that her opportunities were fine and unusual, but she also knew that in spite of some facility and much good teaching she had no genuine talent and never would fulfill the expectations of her friends. She looked back upon her mother's girlhood with positive envy because it was so full of happy industry and extenuating obstacles, with undisturbed opportunity to believe that her talents were unusual. The girl looked wistfully at her mother, but had not the courage to cry out what was in her heart: "I might believe I had unusual talent if I did not know what good music was; I might enjoy half an hour's practice a day if I were busy and happy the rest of the time. You do not know what life means when all the difficulties are removed! I am simply smothered and sickened with advantages. It is like eating a sweet dessert the first thing in the morning."

This, then, was the difficulty, this sweet dessert in the morning, and the assumption that the sheltered, educated girl has nothing to do with the bitter poverty and the social maladjustment which is all about her, and which, after all, cannot be concealed, for it breaks through poetry and literature in a burning tide which overwhelms her; it peers at her in the form of heavy-laden market women and underpaid street laborers, gibing her with a sense of her uselessness.

I recall one snowy morning in Saxe-Coburg, looking from the window of our little hotel upon the town square, that we saw crossing and recrossing it a single file of women with semicircular heavy wooden tanks fastened upon their backs. They were carrying in this primitive fashion to a remote cooling room these tanks filled with a hot brew incident to one stage of beer making. The women were bent forward, not only under the weight which they were bearing, but because the tanks were so high that it would have been impossible for them to have lifted their heads. Their faces and hands, reddened in the cold morning air, showed clearly the white scars where they had previously been scalded by the hot stuff which splashed if they stumbled ever so little on their way. Stung into action by one of those sudden indignations against cruel conditions which at times fill the young with unexpected energy, I found myself across the square, in company with mine host, interviewing the phlegmatic owner of the brewery who received us with exasperating indifference, or rather received me, for the innkeeper mysteriously slunk away as soon as the great magnate of the town began to speak. I went back to a breakfast for which I had lost my appetite, as I had for Gray's "Life of Prince Albert" and his wonderful tutor, Baron Stockmar, which I had been reading late the night before. The book had lost its fascination; how could a good man, feeling so keenly his obligation "to make princely the mind of his prince," ignore such conditions of life for the multitude of humble, hard-working folk. We were spending two months in Dresden that winter, given over to much reading of "The History of Art" and to much visiting of its art gallery and opera house, and after such an experience I would invariably suffer a moral revulsion against the feverish search after culture. . . .

The two years which elapsed before I again found myself in Europe brought their inevitable changes. Family arrangements had so come about that I had spent three or four months of each of the intervening winters in Baltimore, where I seemed to have reached the nadir of my nervous depression and sense of maladjustment, in spite of my interest in the fascinating lectures given there by Lanciani of Rome, and a definite course of reading under the guidance of a Johns Hopkins lecturer upon the United Italy movement. . . .

It is hard to tell just when the very simple plan which afterward developed into the Settlement began to form itself in my mind. It may have been even before I went to Europe for the second time, but I gradually became convinced that it would be a good thing to rent a house in a part of the city where many primitive and actual needs are found, in which young women who had been given over too exclusively to study, might restore a balance of activity along traditional lines and learn of life from life itself; where they might try out some of the things they had been taught and put truth to "the ultimate test of the conduct it dictates or inspires." I do not remember to have mentioned this plan to any one until we reached Madrid in April, 1888.

We had been to see a bull fight rendered in the most magnificent Spanish style, where greatly to my surprise and horror, I found that I had seen, with comparative indifference, five bulls and many more horses killed. The sense that this was the last survival of all the glories of the amphitheater, the illusion that the riders on the caparisoned horses might have been knights of a tournament, or the matadore a slightly armed gladiator facing his martyrdom, and all the rest of the obscure yet vivid associations of an historic survival, had carried me beyond the endurance of any of the rest of the party. I finally met them in the foyer, stern and pale with disapproval of my brutal endurance, and but partially recovered from the faintness and disgust which the spectacle itself had produced upon them. I had no defense to offer to their reproaches save that I had not thought much about the bloodshed; but in the evening the natural and inevitable reaction came, and in deep chagrin I felt myself tried and condemned, not only by this disgusting experience but by the entire moral situation which it revealed. It was suddenly made quite clear to me that I was lulling my conscience by a dreamer's scheme, that a mere paper reform had become a defense for continued idleness, and that I was making it a *raison d'être* for going on indefinitely with study and travel. It is easy to become the dupe of a deferred purpose, of the promise the future can never keep, and I had fallen into the meanest type of self-deception in making myself believe that all this was in preparation for great things to come. Nothing less than the moral reaction following the experience at a bull-fight had been able to reveal to me that so far from following in the wake of a chariot of philanthropic fire, I had been tied to the tail of the veriest ox-cart of self-seeking.

I had made up my mind that next day, whatever happened, I would begin to carry out the plan, if only by talking about it. I can well recall the stumbling and uncertainty with which I finally set it forth to Miss Starr, my old-time school friend, who was one of our party. I even dared to hope that she might join in carrying out the plan, but nevertheless I told it in the fear of that disheartening experience which is so apt to afflict our most cherished plans when they are at last divulged, when we suddenly feel that there is nothing there to talk about, and as the golden dream slips through our fingers we are left to wonder at our own fatuous belief. But gradually the comfort of Miss Starr's companionship, the vigor and enthusiasm which she brought to bear upon it, told both in the growth of the plan and upon the sense of its validity, so that by the time we had reached the enchantment of the Alhambra, the scheme had become convincing and tangible although still most hazy in detail.

A month later we parted in Paris, Miss Starr to go back to Italy, and I to journey on to London to secure as many suggestions as possible from those wonderful places of which we had heard, Toynbee Hall and the People's Palace. So that it finally came about that in June, 1888, five years after my first visit in East London, I found myself at Toynbee Hall equipped not only with a letter of introduction from Canon Fremantle, but with high expectations and a certain belief that whatever perplexities and discouragement concerning the life of the poor were in store for me, I should at least know something at first hand and have the solace of daily activity. I had confidence that although life itself might contain many difficulties, the period of mere passive receptivity had come to an end, and I had at last finished with the everlasting "preparation for life," however ill-prepared I might be.

It was not until years afterward that I came upon Tolstoy's phrase "the snare of preparation," which he insists we spread before the feet of young people, hopelessly entangling them in a curious inactivity at the very period of life when they are longing to construct the world anew and to conform it to their own ideals.

"THE SUBJECTIVE NECESSITY FOR SOCIAL SETTLEMENTS"

I have seen young girls suffer and grow sensibly lowered in vitality in the first years after they leave school. In our attempt then to give a girl pleasure and freedom from care we succeed, for the most part, in making her pitifully miserable. She finds "life" so different from what she expected it to be. She is besotted with innocent little ambitions, and does not understand this apparent waste of herself, this elaborate preparation, if no work is provided for her. There is a heritage of noble obligation which young people accept and long to perpetuate. The desire for action, the wish to right wrong and alleviate suffering haunts them daily. Society smiles at it indulgently instead of making it of value to itself. The wrong to them begins even farther back, when we restrain the first childish desires for "doing good" and tell them that they must wait until they are older and better fitted. . . . Parents are often inconsistent: they deliberately expose their daughters to knowledge of the distress in the world; they send them to hear missionary addresses on famines in India and China; they accompany them to lectures on the suffering in Siberia; they agitate together over the forgotten region of East London. In addition to this, from babyhood the altruistic tendencies of these daughters are persistently cultivated. They are taught to be self-forgetting and self-sacrificing, to consider the good of the whole before the good of the ego. But when all this information and culture show results, when the daughter comes back from college and begins to recognize her social claim to the "submerged tenth," and to evince a disposition to fulfill it, the family claim is strenuously asserted; she is told that she is unjustified, ill-advised in her efforts. If she persists, the family too often are injured and unhappy unless the efforts are called missionary and the religious zeal of the family carry them over their sense of abuse. When this zeal does not exist, the result is perplexing. It is a curious violation of what we would fain believe a fundamental law—that the final return of the deed is upon the head of the doer. The deed is that of exclusiveness and caution, but the return, instead of falling upon the head of the exclusive and cautious, falls upon a young head full of generous and unselfish plans. The girl loses something vital out of her life to which she is entitled. She is restricted and unhappy; her elders, meanwhile, are unconscious of the situation and we have all the elements of a tragedy.

We have in America a fast-growing number of cultivated young people who have no recognized outlet for their active faculties. They hear constantly of the great social maladjustment, but no way is provided for them to change it, and their uselessness hangs about them heavily. Huxley declares that the sense of uselessness is the severest shock which the human system can sustain, and that if persistently sustained, it results in atrophy of function. These young people have had advantages of college, of European travel, and of economic study, but they are sustaining this shock of inaction. They have pet phrases, and they tell you that the things that make us all alike are stronger than the things that make us different. They say that all men are united by needs and sympathies far more permanent and radical than anything that temporarily divides them and sets them in opposition to each other. If they affect art, they say that the decay in artistic expression is due to the decay in ethics, that art when shut away from the human interests and from the great mass of humanity is self-destructive. They tell their elders with all the bitterness of youth that if they expect success from them in business or politics or in whatever lines their ambition for them has run, they must let them consult all of humanity; that they must let them find out what the people want and how they want it. It is only the stronger young people, however, who formulate this. Many of them dissipate their energies in so-called enjoyment. Others not content with that, go on studying and go back to college for their second degrees; not that they are especially fond of study, but because they want something definite to do, and their powers have been trained in the direction of mental accumulation. Many are buried beneath this mental accumulation with lowered vitality and discontent. . . .

This young life, so sincere in its emotion and good phrases and yet so undirected, seems to me as pitiful as the other great mass of destitute lives. One is supplementary to the other, and some method of communication can surely be devised. Mr. Barnett, who urged the first Settlement,—Toynbee Hall, in East London,—recognized this need of outlet for the young men of Oxford and Cambridge, and hoped that the Settlement would supply the communication. . . . The necessity of it was greater there, but we are fast feeling the pressure of the need and meeting the necessity for Settlements in America. Our young people feel nervously the need for putting theory into action, and respond quickly to the Settlement form of activity.

"The Story of an Hour" by Kate Chopin*

Kate O'Flaherty, daughter of an Irish immigrant father and a French mother, born and schooled in St. Louis, moved into French-speaking Acadian society in Louisiana after her marriage at eighteen to the French Creole Oscar Chopin. When their marriage ended after twelve years (and the birth of six children) with Oscar's early death, Kate Chopin moved back to St. Louis and in 1889 began writing fiction. Her writing displays the "local color" of the Louisiana bayou country she had come to know, but at a deeper level probes women's consciousness and their relationships with men. As the daughter of a merchant, and the wife of a banker, she had observed "society" women all her life. She ended her writing career in 1899, after her novel *The Awakening* was damned by reviewers for its characterization of a married woman's discovery of her own sensuousness.

THE STORY OF AN HOUR

Knowing that Mrs. Mallard was afflicted with a heart trouble, great care was taken to break to her as gently as possible the news of her husband's death.

It was her sister Josephine who told her, in broken sentences; veiled hints that revealed in half concealing. Her husband's friend Richards was there, too, near her. It was he who had been in the newspaper office when intelligence of the railroad disaster was received, with Brently Mallard's name leading the list of "killed." He had only taken the time to assure himself of its truth by a second telegram, and had hastened to forestall any less careful, less tender friend in bearing the sad message.

She did not hear the story as many women have heard the same, with a paralyzed inability to accept its significance. She wept at once, with sudden, wild abandonment, in her sister's arms. When the storm of grief had spent itself she went away to her room alone. She would have no one follow her.

There stood, facing the open window, a comfortable, roomy arm-

* From *The Complete Works of Kate Chopin*, ed. with an introduction by Per Seyersted (Baton Rouge: Louisiana State University Press, 1969), pp. 352–354. Originally published as "The Dream of an Hour" in *Vogue*, December 6, 1894.

chair. Into this she sank, pressed down by a physical exhaustion that haunted her body and seemed to reach into her soul.

She could see in the open square before her house the tops of trees that were all aquiver with the new spring life. The delicious breath of rain was in the air. In the street below a peddler was crying his wares. The notes of a distant song which some one was singing reached her faintly, and countless sparrows were twittering in the eaves.

There were patches of blue sky showing here and there through the clouds that had met and piled one above the other in the west facing her window.

She sat with her head thrown back upon the cushion of the chair, quite motionless, except when a sob came up into her throat and shook her, as a child who has cried itself to sleep continues to sob in its dreams.

She was young, with a fair, calm face, whose lines bespoke repression and even a certain strength. But now there was a dull stare in her eyes, whose gaze was fixed away off yonder on one of those patches of blue sky. It was not a glance of reflection, but rather indicated a suspension of intelligent thought.

There was something coming to her and she was waiting for it, fearfully. What was it? She did not know; it was too subtle and elusive to name. But she felt it, creeping out of the sky, reaching toward her through the sounds, the scents, the color that filled the air.

Now her bosom rose and fell tumultuously. She was beginning to recognize this thing that was approaching to possess her, and she was striving to beat it back with her will—as powerless as her two white slender hands would have been.

When she abandoned herself a little whispered word escaped her slightly parted lips. She said it over and over under her breath: "free, free, free!" The vacant stare and the look of terror that had followed it went from her eyes. They stayed keen and bright. Her pulses beat fast, and the coursing blood warmed and relaxed every inch of her body.

She did not stop to ask if it were or were not a monstrous joy that held her: A clear and exalted perception enabled her to dismiss the suggestion as trivial.

She knew that she would weep again when she saw the kind, tender hands folded in death; the face that had never looked save with love upon her, fixed and gray and dead. But she saw beyond that bitter moment a long procession of years to come that would belong to her absolutely. And she opened and spread her arms out to them in welcome.

There would be no one to live for her during those coming years; she would live for herself. There would be no powerful will bending hers in that blind persistence with which men and women believe they have a right to impose a private will upon a fellow-creature. A kind intention or a cruel intention made the act seem no less a crime as she looked upon it in that brief moment of illumination.

And yet she had loved him—sometimes. Often she had not. What did it matter! What could love, the unsolved mystery, count for in face of this possession of self-assertion which she suddenly recognized as the strongest impulse of her being!

"Free! Body and soul free!" she kept whispering.

Josephine was kneeling before the closed door with her lips to the keyhole, imploring for admission. "Louise, open the door! I beg; open the door—you will make yourself ill. What are you doing, Louise? For heaven's sake open the door."

"Go away. I am not making myself ill." No; she was drinking in a very elixir of life through that open window.

Her fancy was running riot along those days ahead of her. Spring days, and summer days, and all sorts of days that would be her own. She breathed a quick prayer that life might be long. It was only yesterday she had thought with a shudder that life might be long.

She arose at length and opened the door to her sister's importunities. There was a feverish triumph in her eyes, and she carried herself unwittingly like a goddess of Victory. She clasped her sister's waist, and together they descended the stairs. Richards stood waiting for them at the bottom.

Some one was opening the front door with a latchkey. It was Brently Mallard who entered, a little travel-stained, composedly carrying his grip-sack and umbrella. He had been far from the scene of accident, and did not even know there had been one. He stood amazed at Josephine's piercing cry; at Richards' quick motion to screen him from the view of his wife.

But Richards was too late.

When the doctors came they said she had died of heart disease—of joy that kills.

on Women's Evolution from Economic Dependence by Charlotte Perkins Gilman*

Among women's rights advocates at the turn of the century Charlotte Perkins Gilman stood out; her thoroughgoing analysis of women's economic depen-dence on men took her beyond simple reliance on the vote as a remedy for women's inferior position. In numerous books, articles, stories, poems, and speeches, between 1895 and 1930, Gilman explicated her views of the "sexuo-economic" bonds in which women had been held, and the progressive evolution of society which demanded that they free themselves.

On WOMEN'S EVOLUTION FROM ECONOMIC DEPENDENCE

Fortunately, the laws of social evolution do not wait for our recogni-tion or acceptance: they go straight on. And this greater and more important change than the world has ever seen, this slow emergence of the long-subverted human female to full racial equality, has been going on about us full long enough to be observed. . . .

The change in education is in large part a cause of this, and progres-sively a consequence. Day by day the bars go down. More and more the field lies open for the mind of woman to glean all it can, and it has responded most eagerly. Not only our pupils, but our teachers, are mainly women. And the clearness and strength of the brain of the woman prove continually the injustice of the clamorous contempt long poured upon what was scornfully called "the female mind." There is no female mind. The brain is not an organ of sex. As well speak of a female liver.

Woman's progress in the arts and sciences, and trades and professions, is steady; but it is most unwise to claim from these relative advances the superiority of women to men, or even their equality, in these fields. What is more to the purpose and easily to be shown is the superiority of the

* From Charlotte Perkins Gilman, *Women and Economics:* A Study of the Eco-nomic Relations Between Men and Women as a Factor in Social Evolution (6th ed.; Boston: Small Maynard and Co., 1913, originally published 1898), pp. 146, 149, 151–156, 210–211, 213, 215–216, 220, 223.

women of to-day to those of earlier times, the immense new development of racial qualities in the sex. . . .

No sociological change equal in importance to this clearly marked improvement of an entire sex has ever taken place in one century. Under it all, the *crux* of the whole matter, goes on the one great change, that of the economic relation. This follows perfectly natural lines. Just as the development of machinery constantly lowers the importance of mere brute strength of body and raises that of mental power and skill, so the pressure of industrial conditions demands an ever-higher specialization, and tends to break up that relic of the patriarchal age,—the family as an economic unit.

Women have been led under pressure of necessity into a most reluctant entrance upon fields of economic activity. The sluggish and greedy disposition bred of long ages of dependence has by no means welcomed the change. Most women still work only as they "have to," until they can marry and "be supported." Men, too, liking the power that goes with money, and the poor quality of gratitude and affection bought with it, resent and oppose the change; but all this disturbs very little the course of social progress.

A truer spirit is the increasing desire of young girls to be independent, to have a career of their own, at least for a while, and the growing objection of countless wives to the pitiful asking for money, to the beggary of their position. . . .

For a while the introduction of machinery which took away from the home so many industries deprived woman of any importance as an economic factor; but presently she arose, and followed her lost wheel and loom to their new place, the mill. To-day there is hardly an industry in the land in which some women are not found. Everywhere throughout America are women workers outside the unpaid labor of the home, the last census giving three million of them. This is so patent a fact, and makes itself felt in so many ways by so many persons, that it is frequently and widely discussed. Without here going into its immediate advantages or disadvantages from an industrial point of view, it is merely instanced as an undeniable proof of the radical change in the economic position of women that is advancing upon us. She is assuming new relations from year to year before our eyes; but we, seeing all social facts from a personal point of view, have failed to appreciate the nature of the change.

Consider, too, the altered family relation which attends this movement. Entirely aside from the strained relation in marriage, the other branches of family life feel the strange new forces, and respond to them. "When I was a girl," sighs the gray-haired mother, "we sisters all sat and sewed while mother read to us. Now every one of my daughters has a different club!" She sighs, be it observed. We invariably object to changed conditions in those departments of life where we have established ethical values. For all the daughters to sew while the mother read aloud to them was esteemed right; and, therefore, the radiating diffusion of daughters among clubs is esteemed wrong,—a danger to home life. In the period of the common sewing and reading the women so assembled were closely allied in industrial and intellectual development as well as in family relationship. They all could do the same work, and liked to do it. They all could read the same book, and liked to read it. (And reading, half a century ago, was still considered half a virtue and the other half a fine art.) Hence the ease with which this group of women entered upon their common work and common pleasure.

The growing individualization of democratic life brings inevitable change to our daughters as well as to our sons. Girls do not all like to sew, many do not know how. Now to sit sewing together, instead of being a harmonizing process, would generate different degrees of restlessness, of distaste, and of nervous irritation. And, as to the reading aloud, it is not so easy now to choose a book that a well-educated family of modern girls and their mother would all enjoy together. As the race become more specialized, more differentiated, the simple lines of relation in family life draw with less force, and the more complex lines of relation in social life draw with more force; and this is a perfectly natural and desirable process for women as well as for men.

It may be suggested, in passing, that one of the causes of "Americanitis" is this increasing nervous strain in family relation, acting especially upon woman. As she becomes more individualized, she suffers more from the primitive and undifferentiated conditions of the family life of earlier times. What "a wife" and "a mother" was supposed to find perfectly suitable, this newly specialized wife and mother, who is also a personality, finds clumsy and ill-fitting,—a mitten where she wants a glove. The home cares and industries, still undeveloped, give no play for her increasing specialization. Where the embryonic combination of cook-nurse-laundress-chambermaid-housekeeper-waitress-governess was content to be "jack of all trades" and mistress of none, the woman who is able to be one of these things perfectly, and by so much less able to be all the others, suffers doubly from not being able to do what she wants to do, and from being forced to do what she does not want to do. To the delicately differentiated modern brain the jar and shock of changing from trade to trade a dozen times a day is a distinct injury, a waste of nervous force. With the larger socialization of the woman of to-day, the fitness for and accompanying desire for wider combinations, more general interest, more organized methods of work for larger ends, she feels more and more heavily the intensely personal limits of the more primitive home duties, interests, methods. And this pain and strain must increase with the advance of women until the new functional power makes to itself organic expression, and the belated home industries are elevated and organized, like the other necessary labors of modern life. . . .

Is our present method of home life, based on the economic dependence of woman in the sex-relation, the best calculated to maintain the individual in health and happiness, and develope in him the higher social faculties? The individual is not maintained in health and happiness,— that is visible to all; and how little he is developed in social relation is shown in the jarring irregularity and wastefulness of our present economic system.

Economic independence for women necessarily involves a change in the home and family relation. But, if that change is for the advantage of individual and race, we need not fear it. It does not involve a change in the marriage relation except in withdrawing the element of economic dependence, nor in the relation of mother to child save to improve it. But it does involve the exercise of human faculty in women, in social service and exchange rather than in domestic service solely. This will of course require the introduction of some other form of living than that which now obtains. It will render impossible the present method of feeding the world by means of millions of private servants, and bringing up children by the same hand.

It is a melancholy fact that the vast majority of our children are reared and trained by domestic servants,—generally their mothers, to be sure, but domestic servants by trade. To become a producer, a factor in the economic activities of the world, must perforce interfere with woman's present status as a private servant. House mistress she may still be, in the sense of owning and ordering her home, but housekeeper or house-servant she may not be—and be anything else. Her position as mother will alter, too. Mother in the sense of bearer and rearer of noble children she will be, as the closest and dearest, the one most honored and best loved; but mother in the sense of exclusive individual nursery-maid and nursery-governess she may not be—and be anything else. . . .

Marriage and "the family" are two institutions, not one, as is commonly supposed. We confuse the natural result of marriage in children, common to all forms of sex-union, with the family,—a purely social phenomenon. Marriage is a form of sex-union recognized and sanctioned by society. It is a relation between two or more persons, according to the custom of the country, and involves mutual obligations. Although made by us an economic relation, it is not essentially so, and will exist in much higher fulfilment after the economic phase is outgrown.

The family is a social group, an entity, a little state. It holds an important place in the evolution of society quite aside from its connection with marriage. There was a time when the family was the highest form of social relation,—when to the minds of pastoral, patriarchal tribes there was no conception so large as "my country," no State, no nation. . . .

The family is a decreasing survival of the earliest grouping known to man. Marriage is an increasing development of high social life, not fully evolved. So far from being identical with the family, it improves and strengthens in inverse ratio to the family. . . .

Marriage has risen and developed in social importance as the family has sunk and decreased. . . . Marriage is not perfect unless it is between class equals. There is no equality in class between those who do their share in the world's work in the largest, newest, highest ways and those who do theirs in the smallest, oldest, lowest ways.

Granting squarely that it is the business of women to make the home life of the world true, healthful, and beautiful, the economically dependent woman does not do this, and never can. The economically independent woman can and will. . . . A noble home life is the product of a noble social life. The home does not produce the virtues needed in society. But society does produce the virtues needed in such homes as we desire to-day. The members of the freest, most highly civilized and individualized nations, make the most delightful members of the home and family. The members of the closest and most highly venerated homes do not necessarily make the most delightful members of society.

Suggestions for Further Reading

Abbott, Edith. *Women in Industry: A Study in American Economic History*. New York and London: D. Appleton & Co., 1910.

Benson, Mary S. *Women in Eighteenth-Century America: A Study of Opinion and Social Usage*. Columbia University Studies in History, Economics and Public Law, no. 405. New York: Columbia University Press, 1935.

Buhle, Mari Jo, Gordon, Ann, and Schrom, Nancy. "Women in American Society: An Historical Contribution," *Radical America*, V:4 (July–August, 1971), 3–66.

Carson, Josephine. *Silent Voices: The Southern Negro Woman Today*. New York: Delacorte Press, 1969.

Clark, Alice. *The Working Life of Women in the Seventeenth Century*. London: G. Routledge & Sons, Ltd., 1919.

Commetti, Elizabeth. "Women in the American Revolution," *New England Quarterly*, XX (1947), 329–347.

Davis, Angela. "Reflections on the Black Woman's Role in the Community of Slaves," *Black Scholar*, III (December, 1971), 3–15.

Demos, John. *A Little Commonwealth: Family Life in Plymouth Colony*. New York: Oxford University Press, 1970.

———. "Notes on Life in Plymouth Colony," *William and Mary Quarterly*, 3rd ser., XXII (1965), 264–286.

Dexter, Elizabeth A. *Colonial Women of Affairs: Women in Business and the Professions in America before 1776*. 2d rev. ed. Boston and New York: Houghton Mifflin Co., 1931.

Ditzion, Sidney. *Marriage, Morals and Sex in America: A History of Ideas*. New York: Octagon Books, 1970.

Flexner, Eleanor. *Century of Struggle: The Woman's Rights Movement in the United States*. New ed. New York: Atheneum, 1968.

Hamamsy, Laila S. "The Role of Women in Changing Navajo Society," *American Anthropologist*, LIX, 101–111.

Henry, Alice. *Women and the Labor Movement*. New York: Arno Press, 1971.

Irwin, Inez Hayes. *The Story of the Woman's Party*. New York: Kraus Reprint, 1971.

James, Edward and Janet (eds.). *Notable American Women*. 3 vols. Cambridge, Mass.: Harvard University Press, 1971.

Josephson, Hannah. *The Golden Threads: New England Mill-Girls and Magnates*. New York: Russell & Russell, 1967.

Kennedy, David. *Birth Control in America*. New Haven, Conn.: Yale University Press, 1970.

Klein, Viola. *The Feminine Character: History of an Ideology*. New York: K. Paul, Trench, Trubner & Co., Ltd., 1946.

Kraditor, Aileen S. *The Ideas of the Woman Suffrage Movement 1890–1920*. New York: Columbia University Press, 1965.

———. *Up from the Pedestal*. Chicago: Quadrangle Books, 1968, pp. 3–24.

Kuhn, Ann L. *The Mother's Role in Childhood Education: New England Concepts 1830–1860*. Yale Studies in Religious Education XIX. New Haven, Conn.: Yale University Press, 1947.

Lerner, Gerda. *The Grimké Sisters from South Carolina*. Boston: Houghton Mifflin Co., 1967.

———. "The Lady and the Mill-Girl: Changes in the Status of Women in the Age of Jackson," *Mid-Continent American Studies Journal*, X (1969), 5–15.

———. *Black Women in White America*. New York: Pantheon Books, 1972.

Lutz, Alma. *Crusade for Freedom: Women in the Anti-Slavery Movement*. Boston: Beacon Press, 1968.

Melder, Keith. "The Beginnings of the Women's Rights Movement, 1800–1840." Unpublished Ph.D. dissertation, Yale University, 1963.

Morgan, Edmund S. *The Puritan Family: Religious and Domestic Relations in Seventeenth-Century New England*. rev. ed. New York: Harper Torchbooks, 1966.

Morris, Richard B. *Studies in the History of American Law*, chapter III, "Women's Rights in Early American Law." New York: Columbia University Press, 1930.

Newcomer, Mabel. *A Century of Higher Education for Women*. New York: Harper & Bros., 1959.

O'Neill, William L. *Everyone Was Brave: The Rise and Fall of Feminism in America*. Chicago: Quadrangle Books, 1969.

Rosenberg, Carroll Smith. "Beauty, the Beast, and the Militant Woman: A Case Study in Sex Roles and Social Stress in Jacksonian America," *American Quarterly*, XXIII (1971), 562.

Scott, Anne Firor. *The Southern Lady: from Pedestal to Politics, 1830–1920*. Chicago: University of Chicago Press, 1970.

Smuts, Robert W. *Women and Work in America*. New York: Columbia University Press, 1959.

Spruill, Julia C. *Woman's Life and Work in the Southern Colonies*. New York: Russell & Russell, 1969.

Staples, Robert (ed.). *The Black Family: Essays and Studies*. Belmont, California: Wadsworth Publishing Co., 1971.

Taylor, William R., and Lasch, Christopher. "Two 'Kindred Spirits':

Sorority and Family in New England, 1839–1846," *New England Quarterly*, XXXVI (1963), 23–41.

Welter, Barbara. "The Cult of True Womanhood, 1820–1860," *American Quarterly*, XVIII (1966), 151–174.

Woodward, Helen B. *The Bold Women.* New York: Farrar, Straus, & Young, 1953.

Woody, Thomas. *A History of Women's Education in the United States.* 2 vols. New York: Octagon Books, 1966.

Yellis, Kenneth. "Prosperity's Child: Some Thoughts on the Flapper," *American Quarterly*, XXI (1969).

More Suggestions for Further Reading (1986)

Buhle, Mari Jo. *Women and American Socialism, 1870–1920*. Urbana: University of Illinois Press, 1981.

Clinton, Catherine. *The Other Civil War; American Women in the 19th Century*. New York: Hill and Wang, 1984.

———. *The Plantation Mistress: Woman's World in the Old South*. New York: Pantheon Books, 1982.

Cott, Nancy F. *The Bonds of Womanhood: 'Woman's Sphere' in New England, 1780–1835*. New Haven, Conn.: Yale University Press, 1977.

Cowan, Ruth Schwartz. *More Work for Mother: The Ironies of Household Technology from the Open Hearth to the Microwave*. New York: Basic Books, 1983.

Degler, Carl N. *At Odds: Women and the Family in America from the Revolution to the Present*. New York: Oxford University Press, 1980.

Dublin, Thomas. *Women at Work: The Transformation of Work and Community in Lowell, Massachusetts, 1826–1860*. New York: Columbia University Press, 1979.

Dubois, Ellen Carol. *Feminism and Suffrage: The Emergence of an Independent Women's Movement in America, 1848–1869*. Ithaca, N.Y.: Cornell University Press, 1978.

Ewen, Elizabeth. *Immigrant Women in the Land of Dollars: Life and Culture on the Lower East Side, 1890–1925*. New York: Monthly Review Press, 1985.

Faragher, John Mack. *Women and Men on the Overland Trail*. New Haven, Conn.: Yale University Press, 1979.

Foner, Philip S. *Women and the American Labor Movement from Colonial Times to the Eve of World War I*, and *Women and the American Labor Movement from World War I to the Present*. New York: Free Press, 1979–1980.

Freedman, Estelle B. *Their Sisters' Keepers: Women's Prison Reform in America, 1830–1930*. Ann Arbor: University of Michigan Press, 1980.

Giddings, Paula. *When and Where I Enter: The Impact of Black Women on Race and Sex in America*. New York: Bantam Books, 1984.

Gordon, Linda. *Woman's Body, Woman's Right: A Social History of Birth Control in America*. New York: Grossman Publishers, 1976.

Gutman, Herbert G. *The Black Family in Slavery and Freedom, 1750–1925*. New York: Random House, 1976.

Hayden, Dolores. *The Grand Domestic Revolution: A History of Feminist Designs for American Homes, Neighborhoods, and Cities*. Cambridge, Mass.: M.I.T. Press, 1981.

Hewitt, Nancy A. *Women's Activism and Social Change: Rochester, N.Y., 1822–1872*. Ithaca, N.Y.: Cornell University Press, 1984.

Jeffrey, Julie Roy. *Frontier Women: The Trans-Mississippi West, 1840–1880*. New York: Hill and Wang, 1979.

Jensen, Joan M. *Loosening the Bonds: Mid-Atlantic Farm Women, 1750–1850*. New Haven, Conn.: Yale University Press, 1986.

Jones, Jacqueline. *Labor of Love, Labor of Sorrow: Black Women, Work and the Family from Slavery to the Present*. New York: Basic Books, 1985.

Kerber, Linda. *Women of the Republic: Intellect and Ideology in Revolutionary America*. Chapel Hill: University of North Carolina Press, 1980.

Kessler-Harris, Alice. *Out to Work: A History of Wage-Earning Women in the United States*. New York: Oxford University Press, 1982.

Leach, William. *True Love and Perfect Union: The Feminist Reform of Sex and Society*. New York: Basic Books, 1980.

Lebsock, Suzanne. *The Free Women of Petersburg: Status and Culture in a Southern Town, 1784–1860*. New York: W. W. Norton and Co., 1984.

Lerner, Gerda. *The Majority Finds Its Past*. New York: Oxford University Press, 1980.

Norton, Mary Beth. *Liberty's Daughters: The Revolutionary Experience of American Women*. Boston: Little, Brown and Co., 1980.

Rothman, Ellen. *Hands and Hearts: A History of Courtship in America*. New York: Basic Books, 1984.

Ryan, Mary P. *Cradle of the Middle Class: The Family in Oneida County, New York, 1790–1865*. New York: Cambridge University Press, 1981.

———. *Womanhood in America: From Colonial Times to the Present*. 3d edition. New York: Franklin Watts, 1983.

Sklar, Kathryn Kish. *Catharine Beecher: A Study in American Domesticity*. New Haven, Conn.: Yale University Press, 1973.

Smith-Rosenberg, Carroll. *Disorderly Conduct: Visions of Gender in Victorian America*. New York: Alfred A. Knopf, 1985.

Tax, Meredith. *The Rising of the Women: Feminist Solidarity and Class Conflict, 1880–1917*. New York: Monthly Review Press, 1980.

Ulrich, Laurel, *Good Wives: Image and Reality in the Lives of Women in Northern New England, 1650–1750*. New York: Alfred A. Knopf, 1982.

Weiner, Lynn Y. *From Working Girl to Working Mother: The Female Labor Force in the United States, 1820–1980*. Chapel Hill: University of North Carolina Press, 1985.